March of America Facsimile Series

Number 6

The Conquest of the Weast India

Francisco López de Gómara

The Conquest of the Weast India

by Francisco López de Gómara

ANN ARBOR

UNIVERSITY MICROFILMS, INC.

A Subsidiary of Xerox Corporation

XEROX

Foreword

The Pleasant Historie of the Conquest of the Weast India, now called new Spayne was written by Francisco López de Gómara and originally published in Spanish in 1552. It provided the first detailed history of Cortés' conquest of Mexico for Spain. The many editions of the history, both in Spanish and in translation, including this English translation of 1578, attest to the enormous popularity of Gómara's book in 16th-century Europe.

Cortés had sailed from Santiago, Cuba, in 1519 with a fleet of eleven ships bound for Mexico. Shortly after landing on the Yucatán Peninsula, he built the fortified port of Veracruz. First defeating, then allying with the Indians in the region who were hostile to the Aztecs, Cortés determined to push on to the Aztec capital. When his men seemed to hesitate, Cortés exhorted them to continue their advance. What they were about to do, he said, was all "for the service of God, and the augmenting of his holy faith, & also the service of our saveraigne Lord the King now Emperour: and next for our owne commodite." The men listened and then agreed to march.

In November, 1519, they entered the Aztec capital, where the Emperor Montezuma II welcomed them. Thinking Cortés to be a divinity, the Aztecs allowed the Spaniards to demolish the idols in the city and to replace them with images of the Virgin and of the Saints. However, Spanish relations with the Aztecs quickly soured. Cortés suspected Montezuma of treachery and compelled him to acknowledge the sovereignty of Charles V. Gómara went on to describe the many subsequent crises which confronted Cortés. He told how Montezuma lost his life while trying to halt an Indian riot against the Spaniards. He described how the Spaniards later burned the city. "The slaughter was great that day, but the burning, and spoyle of houses was greater." In some of the final chapters Gómara recounted the return of Cortés, the rebuilding of Mexico City, and the subjugation of the Aztecs to Spanish administration.

Gómara never visited Mexico. All of his information came second and third hand. However, as chaplain to Cortés after the conqueror's return to Spain in 1540, he was in an enviable position to write his history. Indeed, Gómara did not so much write a history as he did a biography in glorification of Cortés. The historian Bernal Díaz del Castillo, who actually participated in the Mexican expedition, later pointed out numerous errors in Gómara's book. Nevertheless, Gómara had reached the public first and his book retained its popularity, despite Spanish censorship.

The contemporary English translator of Gómara, Thomas Nicholas, was a man who had spent much time in Spain, some of it in confinement. Nevertheless, he greatly admired the exploits of Cortés. Just as Cortés had done great things for Spain, so Nicholas hoped "that within this happie Realme is now living a Gentleman, whose zeale of travayle and valiant beginnings dothe prognosticate greate, marvellous, and happie successe." Nicholas omitted 101 of the original 252 chapters in his translation, however, and passed over the later disgrace of Cortés. More information about the history of Gómara is given by Roger B. Merriman in his edition of Francisco López de Gómara, *Annals of the Emperor Charles V* (Oxford, 1912), pp. ix-lv, and in an introduction by Lesley B. Simpson to his edition of Francisco López de Gómara, *Cortés: The Life of the Conqueror by His Secretary* (Berkeley, 1964), pp. xv-xxvi.

The Conquest of the Weast India

THE

Pleasant Historie of the Conquest of the VVeast India, *now called new Spayne,*

Atchieued by the vvorthy Prince *Hernando Cortes Marques of the valley of Huaxacac,* most delectable to Reade:

Tranflated out of the Spa- *nifhe tongue, by T. N.*

Anno. 1578.

¶ Imprinted at London by *Henry Bynneman.*

¶ TO THE RIGHT HO

norable, Sir Francis VValsingham
Knight, principall Secretary to the
Queenes most excellent Maiestie,
and one of hir highnesse most Honorable
priuie Counsell.

Hilest I abode (right Honorable) in the Isle of Palma, in affaires of merchandize for the vvorshipfull *Thomas Locke* deceased, and his company, time then permitted me, to haue cóference vvith auncient gentlemen vvhiche had serued in the Conquest of the vvest India, novve called nevve Spaine, vnder the princely Captaine *Hernando Cortez.* By vvhom as present vvitnesses at many of the actes herein contayned, I vvas credibly informed, that this delectable and vvorthy Historie is a most true and iust reporte of matter paste in effect: vvherefore I did the more vvillingly turne ouer and peruse the same, vvhiche is a Mirrour and an excellent president, for all such as shall take in hande to gouerne nevve Discoueries: for here they shall behold, hovv Glorie, Renovvne, and perfite Felicitie, is not gotten but vvith greate paines, trauaile, perill and daunger of life: here shall they see the vvisedome, curtesie, valour and pollicie of vvorthy Captaynes, yea and the faithfull hartes vvhiche they ought to beare vnto their Princes seruice: here also is described, hovv to vse and correct the stubbern & mutinous persons, & in vvhat order

a.ij.

to exalt the good, stoute and vertuous Souldiers, and chiefly, hovv to preserue and keepe that bevvtifull Dame *Lady Victorie* vvhē she is obtayned. And vvhere it vvas supposed, that the golden mettall had his beginning and place in the East and VVeast *India*, neare vnto the hote Zoane, (as moste learned vvriters helde opinion) it is novve approued by the venterous trauellour and vvorthy captaine *Martin Frobisher* Esquire, yea and also through the greate paynes, procurement, and firste inuention of the vvorshipfull *Mychaell Locke* Merchaunt, that the same golden mettall dothe also lie incorporate in the bovvelles of the Norvveast parties, enuironned vvith admirable Tovvers, Pillers and Pynacles, of Rockes, Stone, and Ise, possessed of a people brothe straunge, & rare in shape, attire and lyuing, yea suche a Countrey and people, as all *Europe* had forsaken and made no account of, excepte our moste gratious Queene and hir subiectes, vvhome vndoubtedly God hath appoynted, not onely to be supreme Princesse ouer them, but also to be a meane that the name of Christ may be knovven vnto this Heathenish and Sauage generation.

Not long since (right Honorable) I happened to trauayle from the famous Cittie of *Tolledo* in *Spayne*, tovvarde highe *Castile*, and by fortune ouertooke an auncient Gentlemen, vvorshipfully accompanied, vnto vvhō I vvas so bold as to approch, beseching his vvorship to aduertise me of his iourney: vvho (after he had beheld my white head & beard) answered ful gentlely, that his intēt vvas to trauayle vnto the king

of

of Spaynes Court, and vvelcomied me vnto his company. In shorte space that vve had iourneyed togither, and communed of each other his Countrey, it pleased him to say as follovveth : My good friende, if you knevv my sute vnto the Kings maieſtie, you vvould iudge that I vvere a mad man, and therefore to ſhorten oure vvay, I vvill declare my attempted ſute vnto you. You ſhall vnderſtande, that I am a Gentleman of lxx. yeares of age, and ſometimes I ſerued in the ciuill vvarres of *Pirru*, vvhere I vvas vvounded in diuers parts of my body, and am novv thereby lame in one of my legges and ſhoulder. I haue neyther VVife nor childe, and at this preſente (God be praiſed) I haue in the Contractation houſe in the Citie of *Siuill*, in golde and plate, the ſumme of thirtie thouſande Duckates: and I haue alſo in *Pirru* in good lands and poſſeſſions, the yearely rente of tvvelue thouſande Duckates, vvhiche rentes and readye money is ſufficiente to mainteyne a poore Gentleman. But al this notvvithſtanding, I do novv ſue vnto the Kings Maieſtie, to haue licence and authoritie to diſcouer and conquere a certayne parte of *India*, vvhyche adioyneth vvith *Brazile*, and is part of the Empire of *Pirru*, I pray you novve declare what you thinke of my ſute. By my troth ſir (quoth I) I truſt your vvorſhip vvill pardon a raſh and ſuddaine iudgemēt, which you now demand at my hād: yea truly (quoth he) ſay vvhat you liſt. Then (quoth I) my opiniō is, that you are not wel in your wit, for vvhat vvould you hauev vvil hot reaſon ſuffice you? or elſe would you now in your old days be an Empe-

rour, con-

considering that your Sepulchre attendeth for you.
Novve truly I thanke you (quoth he) for of youre
iudgement are most men: but I say vnto you, considering that all flesh must finish, I seeke for no quiet
rest in this transitorie life: yea the vvise and Christian Doctors do teach and admonish, that euery true
Christian is borne, not for his ovvne priuate vvealth
and pleasure, but rather to help and succoure others
his poore brethren. Likevvise doe I consider the
greate number of Gentlemen, yonger brethren, and
other valiat persons, vvho through vvant of liuing,
do fall into many disorders. VVherefore to accomplish my dutie tovvard God and my Prince, and to
releeue such poore Gentlemen, do I novv attempte
this iourney, vvith the aduenture of my bodye and
goodes, and for that purpose I haue in readinesse
foure tall Shippes, vvell furnished in the porte of
Saint Lucar de Barrameda, hoping assuredlye, that before
the life depart from my body, to heare these valiante
yong Gentlemen (vvhome novv I meane to haue in
my company) say, oh happie day, vvhen olde *Zarate*
(for so is my name) broughte vs from penurie, yea
and from a number of perils that vve vvere like to
fall into. I hope also, that the royall estate of my
Prince shall be by my paynes and poore seruice enlarged: beleeue you me, this is the onely sumptuous
Tumbe that I pretende to builde for my poore car-
kas. But yet I knovv there are some, vnto vvhome
I may compare the Bore that lyeth vvallovvyng
in his Stye, vvho vvill not lette to saye, vvhat neede
vve any other vvorld, honor, or Kingdomes? let vs
be

be contented vvith that vve haue: vvho may eafily
be aunfvvered, Sir glutton, your paunch is full, and
little care you for the glory of God, honor of youre
Prince, neyther the neede and necefsitie of youre
poore neyboures. VVith this conclufion the Gentleman ended his tale, the iudgement vvhereof I leaue
to noble Gentlemen his peeres to be determined.

And vvhere oure Captayne *Hernando Cortez* of
vvhofe valiant actes this hiftorie treateth, hathe de-
ferued immortal fame, eué fo doubtleffe I hope, that
vvithin this happie Realme is novv liuing a Gentleman, vvhofe zeale of trauayle and valiant beginnings dothe prognofticate greate, maruellous, and
happie fucceffe : for perfection of honor and profite
is not gotten in one daye, nor in one or tvvo voyages, as the true hiftories of the Eaft and VVeft Con-
quefts by Spanyardes and Portingalles do teftifye.
And calling to remembrance the greate zeale and
good vvill vvhich your honor hath alvvayes extended to good and profitable attemptes, and efpecially
in the proceedings of the nevv difcouery, youre honor hath not only vfed liberalitie in your aduétures,
but alfo taken greate paynes in Courte, to aduance
and further the voyage, a number I faye of Gentlemen, Marriners, and other artificers, fhal haue great
caufe to pray for your honor. And vvhere I for my
parte haue tafted of your honors goodneffe fundrye
vyayes, I am novve moft humbly to befeech youre
honor to accept this poore gifte, the vvhiche I haue
tranflated out of the Spanifh tong, not decked vvith
gallant couloures, nor yet fyled vvith pleafant phrafe
of

The Epistle

of Rhetorike, for thefe things are not for poore
Marchant trauellers, but are referued to learned
VVriters: yet I truft the Author vvill pardon mee,
bycaufe I haue gone as neere the fenfe of this Hiftorie, as my cunning vvoulde reach vnto. I alfo craue,
that it may pleafe youre honor, vvhen your greate
and vvaightie bufineffe vvill permitte, to beholde
this vvorke, and that fhall be for me an encourage-
mente to take in hande the tranflation of the Eaft
India, vvhiche is novve enioyed by the King of
Portingall. Thus I ende, befeeching
the Almighty to preferue your
honorable eftate.

(?)

Your honors moft ready at commaundement
Thomas Nicholas.

To the Reader.

I Thought it good gentle Reader, to aduertise thée to conſider in reading this hiſtorie, that _Hernando Cortes_ was not the firſt that did diſcouer the newe Spayne, for after the Ilands of _Santo Domingo_ and _Cuba_ were diſcouered, conquered, and inhabited by the Spanyards, _Hernando Cortes_ was then a dweller in the Iland of _Santo Domingo_, and at that time was gouernoure in the Iland of _Cuba_ one _Iames Velaſques_, who had vnderſtanding (by others) that néere vnto thoſe Iſles ſtoode a firme land, riche of gold and plate, whereupon the ſame _Velaſques_ prepared certayne Shippes, and in them ſente for Generall a kinſman of his called _Iohn de Gryalua_, who with one _Franciſco Hernandez de Cordoua_, diſcouered the ſaid firme land in traffike of marchandiſe, and for things of little value, he broughte great treaſure, as ſhall appeare in an Inuentorie placed in this hiſtorie.

This _Gryalua_ pretended not to conquer, nor yet to inhabite, but onely to fill his hungry belly with golde and ſiluer, for if hée had pretended honor, then _Cortez_ had not enioyed the perpetuall fame which now is his, although his corpſe bée clothed in clay.

In this hiſtorie doth appeare the ſimplicitie of thoſe ignorant _Indians_ in time paſt, yea and how they were deluded in worſhipping Idolles and wicked _Mamon_, their bloudy ſlaughter of men in ſacrifice, and now the greate mercie of Ieſus Chriſt extended vpon them in lightning their darkeneſſe, giuing them knowledge of the eternitie, and holy trinitie in vnitie, whereby they are nowe more deuoute vnto heauenly things than we wretched Chry-
b.   ſtians,

To the Reader.

ſians, (who preſume of auntiente Chriſtianitie) eſpe-
ciallye in Charitie, humilitie, and liuely workes of
faith.

And now (gentle Reader) I do for my part but onely craue, that it may pleaſe thee to accept theſe
my paynes taken, in good part, for other
benefyte I ſæke not,
Farewell.

(T. N.)

Stephan Goßon in prayse of the Translator.

THe Poet which sometimes hath trod awry,
And song in verse the force off syry loue,
When he beholdes his lute with carefull eye,
Thinkes on the dumpes that he was wonte to proue.
His groning sprigyt pryickt with tender ruth,
Calles then to minde the follies of his youth.

The harder minde whiche all his honour gotte,
In bluddy fielde by fruyte of deadly iarre,
When once he heares the noyse of thirled shotte,
And threatnyng trumpet sounde the poyntes of warre,
Remembers how through pykes he lodde to runne,
When he the pryce of endlesse glory wonne.

The traueller whiche neare restsrce the parke,
To passe the daunger of the streightes befounde,
But hoysed sayle to searche the golden barne,
Whiche natures crafte hath hidden in the grounde,
When he perceiues Don Cortez here so pearte,
May well be mindefull of his owne deserte.

Then yeelde we thankes to Nicholas for his toyle,
Who brings the Lute that putteth vs in minde,
How dotng dares haue giuen vs all the foyle,
Whilste learned wittes in forrayne landes doe finde.
That labour beares away the golden fleece,
And is rewarded with the flower of Greece.

Loe here the trumpe of euerlasting fame,
That rendes the ayre in sunder with his blaste,
And throwes abroade the prayses of their name,
Which ofte in fight haue made their foes agast.
Though they be dead, their glory shall remayne,
To reare alofte the deedes of haughty Spayne.

Loe here the traueller, whose paynefull quill,
To lyuely paynties the Spanish Indies out,
That English Gentlemen may vew at will,
The manly prowesse of that galant route.
And when the Spaniarde ba vewed his golde,
Their owne renowne in him they may beholde.

FINIS.

In Thomæ Nicholai occidenta-
lem Indiam St. Gosson.

Sordescant Cræsi radiantia tecta Pyropo,
  Et iaceat rutili pompa superba Mydæ.
Aurea fœlici voluuntur secula cursu,
  Pactóli assidue flumina vera tumens.
Terra ferax pandit, sua viscera plena metallis
  Prægnans, divitias parturit illa suas.
India luxuriat, locupleti prole triumphat,
  Pingue solum gemmis, fundere gestit opes.
O vos qui patriæ cupitis fulcire ruinam,
  Et dare mella bonis aurea, mentis apes.
Cortezi hos animo cupidè lustrate labores,
  Postq; reluctanti credite vela salo.

The Conqueſt of the

Weaſt India.

The Byrth and lynage of
Hernando Cortez.

N the yeare of our Sauiour,
1485. being kings of *Caſtill* and
Aragon, the Catholike princes
Fernando and *Iſabell* his wyfe,
was borne *Hernando Cortez* in
a towne called *Medellin*, ſituated in the prouince of *Andalo-
zia*: his father was named
Martyn Cortez de Monroy, & his
mother was called Lady *Katherin Piſarro Altamirano*, they
were bothe of good byrth, and proceeded from foure principall houſes, that is to ſay, the houſe of *Cortez*, the houſe
of *Monroy*, the houſe of *Piſarro*, and the houſe of *Altamirano*, which foure houſes are auncient, noble and honorable:
yet theſe parents but poore in goods, but riche in vertue &
goodlife, for which cauſe they were muche eſteemed and
beloued among theyr neighbours. His mother was of
inclination deuoute, but ſomewhat harde: his father was
charitable and mercyfull, who in his youth applied himſelfe to the warres, and was Liuetenant to a company of
horſemen. *Hernando Cortez* in his childehood was very
ſickely, ſo that many tymes he was at the poynt of death:
And when he came to xiiij. yeeres of age, his parents ſent
him to the Vniuerſitie of *Salamanca*, where he remayned
twoo yeares, learnyng Grammar, and then returned to
Medellin werie of his ſtudie, yea poſſible for want of money: yet his parets were much offended with him for leauing his ſtudie, for theyr onely deſire was to haue had

B.   him

him a student at lawe, whiche is a facultie both riche and worshipfull, consideryng their sonne to be of a good witte and abilitie: Yet he caused muche strife in his Fathers house, for he was a very unhappy ladde, high minded, and a louer of chiualrie, for which cause he determined with himselfe to wander abroad to seeke aduentures. And at that instant happened two iorneys fit for his purpose & inclination   The one of them was to *Naples* wyth *Gonsalo Hernandez* of the Citie of *Cordoua* , who was a worthy man, & named the great captaine. And the other iourney was to the Weast India, with the Lorde *Nicholas de Ouando,* a knight of the order of *Larez,* who was then appointed for gouernour of those parties. And musing with himselfe which waye to take, determined to passe into *India,* chiefly bycause the gouernour was of his acquaintance, and such a one as would haue care of him. And likewise the great desire of gold made him to couet that voyage more than the Iorney vnto *Naples.* Now in the meane while that ý fleet was preparing for *India,* it chaunced, *Hernando Cartez* pretended to go vnto a certaine house in the night season to talke with a woman, and clyming ouer a Wall whyche was of weake foundation, both he and the Wal fell togither: So that with the noyse of hys fall , and ratling of his armoure which he ware, came out a man newly married, and findyng him fallen at hys dore would haue stayne hym, suspecting somewhat of his newe married wife , but that a certaine olde woman(being his mother in lawe) wyth great perswasions stayed him from that fact. Yet with the fall he fell into a grieuous Ague, and continued sicke for a long season, so that he could not procéede vppon his voyage with the gouernour *Ouando* . And when he had obtained and fullye recouered his health, he mynded to passe into *Italy,* And so toke hys way towarde *Valentia,*

wandering

wandering here and there almoste a whole yeare with
much neceſſitye and penurie, and then returned home a-
gaine to *Medellyn*, with determination to proceed vppon his pretended voyage of *India* : Whereuppon hys
father and mother waying their ſonnes eſtate, deſired
God to bleſſe hym, and gaue him money in his purſe for
his iourney.

The age of Cortez vvhen he paſſed
into India.

Ernando *Cortez* was of the age of
nintiene yeares, in the yeare of
Chriſt 1504. and then he went toward *India*, and agreed for his paſſage and victual with *Alonſo Quin-
tez* who went in companie of o-
ther four ſhippes laden with merchandiſe, whiche nauie departed
from ſaint *Lucas de Barramedo*, with proſperous nauigation, vntyll they arriued at the Iland of *Gomera* one of the
Canarie Ilands, where they did prouide themſelues of all
things neceſſarie for ſo long a voyage as they then had
in hand.

Alounſo Quintezo, being greedie of his voyage, and deſirous to come to the Ilande of *Sainte Domingo* before his
fellowes, hoping to ſel his commoditie the better, departed from *Gomera* in the night ſeaſon without knowledge
giuing vnto his company. But incontinent after he had
hoyſed vp his ſayles, aroſe vp ſo great a winde and tempeſt, that his maine maſt brake, whereby hee was forced
to retourne backe againe to the Ilande of *Gomera*. And
he made earneſt requeſte to them of the other ſhyppes
to ſtaye for him, vntyl hee hadde mended his Maſt,
who friendlye and neyghbourlye graunted hys deſire,

B.ij. and

and departed altogither, sayling in sight the one of the other certayne dayes : yet the sayde *Quinters*, seyng the weather stedfast, and harpyng vpon gaynes, flewe from his fellowes agayne. And where as *Frances Ninio de Guelua* his pilote was not experte in that Nauigation, they knew not where they were at length : the Mariners did giue sundzy Judgements : the Pilote was in great perplexitie and sadnesse, their passengers lamented, and bewayled their vnfortunate successe : the Master of the shippe layde the faulte to the Pilote, and the Pilote like-wise charged the Master, for it did appeare that they were fallen out befoze. In this meane time their victuall wared skant, and their freshe water wanted, so that they pzepared themselues to die. Some cursed theyr foztune, others asked mercie at Gods hande, lookyng foz death and to be eaten of the *Carines*. And in this tyme of tribulation came a Doue flying to the shippe, beyng on good Friday at Sunne sette, and satte him on the shippe toppe : whereat they were all comfozted, and tooke it foz a my-racle and good token and some wept with ioy, some sayd y̆ **Comfort of God.** God had sente the Doue to comfozte them, others sayde that lande was neare, and all gaue hartie thankes vnto God, directing their course that way that the Doue flew : and when the Doue was out of sighte, they sozrowed a-gaine, but yet remayned with hope to see shoztlye lande and on Easterday they discouered the Ilande of *Santo Domingo*, whiche was firste discried by *Christopher Zorso*, who cryed, lande, lande, a chéerefull voyce to the saylers. The Pilote looked out, and knewe that it was the poynt, oz cape of *Semana*, and within foure dayes after they arri-ued in the pozte of *Santo Domingo*, whiche was long wi-shed foz, and there they founde the other shippes of their company arriued many dayes befoze.

The

The time that Cortez abode

in Santo Domingo

Done after that the Gouernoure, Ouando was in his regimente and office, Cortez arriued at Santo Domingo: and the Gouernoures Secretarie, called Medina, receyued and lodged him, and also informed him of the estate of the Iland, and aduised hym what was nedefull to doe, wishing that hée would be a dweller there, and that he should haue a plot to build vpon, with certaine grounde for husbandry. But Cortez his thought was cleane contrary, for hée iudged that as sone as he came thither, he should lade with gold, whereby hée did little estéeme his friend Medina his counsell, saying, that he had rather goe to gather gold, than to trauell in husbandrie: Medina yet perswaded him, that he shoulde take better aduisement, for to finde golde, was doubtfull, and very troublesome. This talke ended, Cortez went to kisse the Gouernours handes, and to declare the cause of his comming, with other newes from Estremadure the Gouernours Countrey. The Gouernour friendly welcommed him, and also perswaded him to abide there, the which councell he accepted, and shortlye after wente to the warres, whereof was Captayne Iaymes Velasques, in the prouince of Anagui Aquiq, and Guaca panma, and other Lordships whiche were not as yet pacifyed wyth the late rebellion of Anacauna widdowe, who was a gentlewoman of great liuing. Ouando gaue vnto Cortez certayne Indyans in the Countrey of Daigua, and also the office of publike notarie in Azua, a towne whyche the Gouernour had builded, and there dwelt Cortez fyue or fyue yeares, and began to play the good husband. Now in this meane season he woulde haue gone to Veragua,

which was reputed to bee maruellous riche, with the
Captayn *Iaymes de Nicuesa*: but bycause of an empostume
that he had vnder his righte knée, he went not, and as it
happened, he was therein fortunate, for that thereby hée
escaped great perils and troubles, whiche happened to
them that went on that voyage and iourney.

Things that happened to Cortez in
the Ilande of Cuba.

 He Lorde *Iames Colori* being Admirall
and chiefe Gouernour of the new *India*,
sent one *Iaymes Velasques* to conquer the
Ilande of *Cuba*, in the yeare. 1511. And
gaue vnto him men, Armour, and other
thinges necessarie. And then *Hernando*
Cortez wente to that conquest as a Clearke to the Trea-
sorer called *Michaell de Passamontes*, for to kéepe the ac-
compts of the Kings fiftes and reuenewes, being so intreated and required by the same *Iaymes Velasques*, bycause he was holden for a man both able and diligente.
And it followed, that in the repartition of the lands conquered, *Iaymes Velasques* gaue vnto *Cortez* the Indians of
Manicorao, in coniunct company with his brother in lawe
called *Iuan Xuarez*, whereupon *Cortez* did inhabite in
Saint Iames de Barucoa, whiche was the first place of habitation in that Ilande, whereas he bredde and broughte
vp Kine, Shéepe, and Mares, and was the first that hadde
there any heard or flocke, and with his *Indians* he gathered great quantitie of golde, so that in short time he waxed riche, and ioyned in company with one *Andres de Du-*
ero a Merchaunt, and put in two thousande Castlins for
his stocke. He was also highly estéemed with *Iaymes Ve-*
lasques, and put in authoritie to dispatch businesse, and to
give

giue order for edifices. In his tyme he caused a money
house to be built, e also an Hospital. At that time one *Iuan
Xuarez* naturall of the Citie of *Granada*, carried to the
Isle of *Cuba*, his mother and three sisters; whiche came to
the Ilande of *Santo Domingo*, with that vicequéene the
Lady *Mary* of *Toledo*, in Anno. 1509. hoping to marrie
them there with rich men, for they were very poore. And
the one of them named *Cathelina* was wont to say, That
she shoulde be a greate Gentlewoman: it was eyther by
dreames and fantasies, or else some Astronomer hadde
made hir beléeue so, but hir mother was reported to bée
very cunning. The maydens were beautifull, for which
cause, and also being there but fewe Spanishe women,
they were muche made of, and often feasted. But *Cortez*
was woer to the saide *Cathelina*, and at the ende married
with hir : Although at the first there was some strife a-
bout the matter, and *Cortez* put in prison, bycause he refused hir for his wife, but she demaunded him as hir huf-
band by faith and troth of hand: wherein *Iaymes Velasques*
did stande hir friende, by reason of an other sister of hyrs
which he had, but of an euill name. It so fell out that one
Baltazar Bermudez, *Iuan Xuares*, and the two *Anthony Velasques*, with one *Villegas* accused *Cortez*, that he ought to
marrie with *Cathelina*, yet those witnesses spake of euill
will many things, as touching y affaires committed to his
charge, alleadging y he vsed secret dealing with certaine
persons. The which causes although they were not true,
yet they carried great colour therof. For why: many wét
secretly to *Cortez* his house, complayning of *Iaymes Velasques*. Some bycause they had not iust repertitió of the có-
quered Indiäs, and other some not accordîng to deserte.
Contrariwyse *Iames Velasques* gaue credit to his talebearers, bicause *Cortez* refused to marrie tó *Cathelina Xuarez*,
e vsed vncourteous wordes vnto him in y presēce of many

that rode by, and also commaunded him to warde. And
when Cortez sawe himselfe in the stockes, he feared some
proces of false witnesse, as many times dothe happen in
those parties. At time conueniente he brake the locke of
the stockes, and layde hand vpon the Sword and Target
of the keeper, and brake vp a windowe, escaping thereby
into the stréete, and toke the Church for Sanctuary. But
when Iaymes Velasques had notice thereof, he was great-
lye offended with Christopher Lagos the Jayler, saying, that
for money he had losed him: wherefore he procured by
al meanes to plucke him out of the Sanctuary. But Cortez hauing intelligence of his dealing, did resiste and
withstand his force: Yet notwithstanding one daye Cortez walking before the Churche dore, and being carelesse
of his businesse, was caught by the backe with a Serie-
ant called Iohn Esquier and others, and then was put a-
borde a Shyppe vnder hatches. Cortez was welbeloued
among his neighbours, who did well consider the euill
will that the Gouernour bare vnto him. But nowe Cortez séeing himselfe vnder hatches, despaired of his libertie, and did verily thinke, that he shoulde be sent prisoner
to the Chancerie of Santo Domingo, or else to Spayne, who
being in this extremitie, soughte all meanes to get hys
fote out of the chayne, and at length he gote it out, and
the same nighte he changed his apparell with a ladde
that serued him, and by the Pump of the Shippe he gote

Cortez
escapeth.

out, not heard of any his keepers, climbing softly along
the Shippe syde, he entred the Skiffe and went hys way
therewith, and bycause they shoulde not pursue after
him, he losed the Boate of another Shippe that roade by
them. The Currant of Macaguanigua a riuer of Baruca,
was so fierce, that he could not gette in with his Skiffe,
bicause he had no help to rowe, & was also very werie, fearing to be drowned if he should put himselfe to the land,
where-

wherefore he ſtripped himſelfe naked, and tyed a nyght-
kerchiefe aboute hys head, with certayne wrytings apperteyning to his office of Notarie and Clearkſhippe to
the Treaſourer, and other things that were agaynſt the
Gouernoure *Iames Velaſques*, and in this ſorte ſwamme
to lande, and wente home to hys owne houſe, and ſpake
with *Iohn Xuarez* hys brother in law, and tooke Sanctuarie agayne with Armour. Then the Gouernoure *Iames
Velaſques* ſente hym worde, that all matters ſhoulde bee
forgotten, and that they ſhoulde remayne friendes, as in
tyme paſt they hadde bin, and to goe with hym to the
Warres agaynſte certayne Indians that hadde rebelled. *Cortez* made hym no aunſwere, but incontinent married with miſtreſſe *Catalina Xuarez* accordíng to his promiſe, and to lyue in peace. *Iames Velaſques* procéded on
hys iourney wyth a greate companye agaynſte the Rebelles. Then ſayde *Cortez* to hys brother in lawe *Iohn
Xuares*, bryng me (quoth he) my Launce and my Croſ-
bowe to the Townes ende. And ſo in that euening hée
wente out of Sanctuarie, and taking hys Croſſebowe
in hande, hée wente with his brother in lawe to a certayne Farme, where *Iames Velaſques* was alone, with his
houſeholde ſeruauntes, for hys armye was lodged in a
Village thereby, and came thither ſomewhat late, and
at ſuche tyme as the Gouernoure was peruſing hys
Booke of charges, and knocked at his dore which ſtode
open, ſaying : Hére is *Cortez* that woulde ſpeake with
the Gouernoure, and ſo wente in. When *Iames Velaſques*
ſawe hym armed, and at ſuch an houre, he was maruel-
louſly afrayde, deſiring hym to reſt hymſelfe, and alſo to
accepte hys Supper : No Sir (quoth he) my onely comming is, but to knowe the complayntes you haue of me,
and to ſatiſfye you therein, and alſo to bée youre friende
and ſeruitor. They then embraced eache other in token

The Go-
uernoure
vvas ſore
afrayde.

C.

of

of friendſhip. And after long talke, they lay both in one bedde, where *Iames de Orrelano* founde them, who went to carrie newes to the Gouernoure, how *Cortez* had fledde. After this ſort came *Cortez* agayne to his former friend ſhyppe with *Iames Velaſques*, and proceded with him to the Warres, but afterwarde at his returne, he was lyke to haue bin drowned in the ſea: For as he came from the Caues of *Bani* to viſite certayne of hys Shepheardes and *Indians* that wrought in the Mines of *Barrucoa* where his dwelling was, his *Canoa* or little bote ouerthrew, be yng night, and halfe a league from land, with tempeſte, wherby he was put to his ſhiftes, and forced to ſwimme, and happened to eſpye lyght that certayne Shepheardes had which were at ſupper nére the Sea ſide. By ſuche like perils and daungers, runne the excellente menns their race, vntill that they arriue at the Hauen where their good lotte is preſerued.

The diſcouery of nevv Spayne.

Raunces *Hernandes de Cordoua* did firſt diſ couer *Xucatan*, going with thré Shyps for *Indians*, or elſe to barter. Theſe Shippes were ſet forth forth by *Chriſto pher Morante*, and *Lope Ochoa de Saizedo*, in Anno.1517. And although he broughte home nothing at that time but ſtripes, yet he broughte perfect relation, how the Countrey was rich of gold and ſiluer, and the people of the countrey clothed. Then *Iames Velaſques* Gouernoure of the Iland of *Cuba*, ſent the next yeare folowing his kinſman, called *Iohn de Grijalua*, with two hundred *Spanyardes* in foure Shippes, thinking to ob tayne much gold and ſiluer for his Merchandiſe at thoſe places, which *Fraunces Hernandez* had enformed him: So that

that *Iohn de Grijalua* wente to *Xucatan*, and there soughte with the *Indians* of *Champoton*, and was hurt. From thēce he entred the riuer of *Tauasco*, which *Grijalua* hadde so naꝛ med, in the whiche place he bartered foꝛ things of small value. He had in exchaunge golde, cloth of cotten wooll, and other curious things wꝛought of feathers. He was also at Saint *Iohn de Vlhua*, and tooke possession foꝛ the king, in the name of *Iames Velasques*, and there also exꝛ changed his Haberdaſhe wares, foꝛ Golde, and Couerꝛ lets of cotten, and feathers: and if he hadde consibered his good foꝛtune, he would haue planted habitation in so rich a land, as his company did earneſtly requeſt him, and if he had so done, then had he bin as *Cortez* was. But suche wealth was not foꝛ him which knew it not, although he excused himselfe, saying, he went not to inhabite, but to barter onely in traffike of his Marchandise, and to discoꝛ uer whether that land of *Xucatan* were an Ilande, oꝛ no. And finding it a mayne land, and populous, he left off foꝛ very feare. Likewise, some of his company were desirous to returne to *Cuba*, among whome, was one *Pedro de Alꝛ uado*, who was farre in loue with a woman of that counꝛ trey. So they determined to returne, with relation to the Gouernoure of suche things as hadde happened till that day, and sayled homewardes along the coaſt to *Panuco*, and so came to *Cuba*, to the greate griefe of many of hys company. Yea some of them wept with soꝛrowe, that hée would not abide in that rich countrey. He was fiue moꝛ nethes vpon his voyage homewarde from land to lande, and eyght monethes till his returne to the Citie. But when he came home, the Gouernoure hauing hearde of his pꝛocéedings, would not looke vppon him, whiche was hys iuſt rewarb.

Men tan-gled in foo-lish loue.

C.ij.   The

The Inuentorie of the treafure that

Gryalua brought for his wares.

Iohn de *Gryalua* bought of the Indians of *Potonchan, Saint Iohn de Vlhua*, and other places of that coaft, fuche thynges as made his fellowes farre in loue with the Countrey, and loth to depart from thece.
The wozkmáfhip of many of the things that they bought, was moze wozth than the thing it felfe, as this Inuentozy perticularly doth fhew.

The Inuentory.

A Little Idoll of golde hollowe.

A greater of golde, with hoznes and heare, with a ftring of beadeftones aboute his necke, and a Flyeflappe in his hand, and a little ftone foz his nauell.

A péce of golde, like the patent of a Challice, garni-fhed with ftones.

A Skull of golde, with two hoznes, and blacke heare.

Two and twenty earerings of golde.

Two and twenty péces of an other fafhion.

Foure bzacelettes of golde very bzoade.

A payze of beades of golde, the ftones hollowe, wyth a Frogge of golde hanging at the fame.

Another paire, with a Lyon of golde.

A great paire of earerings of golde.

Two little Eagles of golde hollowe.

A little Saltfeller of golde.

Two earerings of golde with Turkie ftones.

A coller to hang aboute a woomans necke, of twelue péces, with four and twenty ftones hanging thereat.

A great coller of golde.

Sire little collers of golde thinne.

Seauen

Seauen other collers of gold with ſtones.

Foure earerings of golden leafe.

Twentie fiſhinghookes of golde.

Twelue graines of gold, waying fiftie Duckets.

A headlace of gold.

Certaine thinne planches of gold.

A Potedge pot of gold.

An Idoll of golde hollowe.

Certaine thinne brouches of gold.

Nine beade ſtones of gold.

Two payre of gilt beades.

One payre of wodden beades guilt.

A little cuppe of golde, with eighte purple ſtones, and twentie three ſtones of an other collour.

Foure belles of gold.

A little ſauſer of gold.

A little boxe of gold.

Certaine ſmal collers of gold of ſmal value.

A hollow apple of gold.

Fourtie hatchets of gold mixed with copper, valued in two thouſand fiue hundred Duckets.

A whole harneis or furniture for an armed man of gold thinne beaten.

In other whole armour of wood with leaues of golde, garniſhed with little blacke ſtones.

A certaine piece made like vnto a feather, of an hyde and gold ioyntly wrought.

Foure pieces of armour of wood made for the knees, and couered with golden leafe.

Two targets couered with feathers of many and fyne colours.

Diuerſe other targets of gold and feathers.

A tuſſe of feathers of ſundry colours, with a little byrd in the middeſt, very liuely.

C.iij.   A

A wing of gold and feathers.

Two flyflappes of feathers.

Two little chamberpottes of Allabaster, beset with many trimme stones, and some fyne, & among them there was one esteemed at two thousand Duckets.

Certaine beades of tinne.

Fiue paire of woodden beades rounde and couered wyth a leafe of gold very thinne.

A hundred and thirty hollow bead stones of gold.

Many beades of woodde gilt.

A paire of Sissers of wood gilt.

Two gilt vissors.

A vissor of strange gesture of gold.

Foure vissors of wood guilt.

Foure dishes of wood couered with golden leafe.

A dogges head of gold beset with stones.

An other beastes head garnished with gold.

Fiue paire of rush shoes.

Three red hides.

Seuen rasors of flint stone, for to cut up men that were sacrifised.

Two painted dishes of wood with an Ewer.

A garment with halfe sleues of feathers of excéeding fine colours.

A couerlet of feathers.

Many couerlets of cotton very fine.

Many other couerlets of cotten course.

Two kerchiefs of good cotton.

Many perfumes of sweete odor, much of that countrey fruite.

They also brought a gentlewoman that was giuen thē, and other prisoner *Indians*. And for one of them was offered hys weight in golde, but *Grijalua* woulde not take it.

They

They alſo bɜought newes that there were *Amazons* women of warre, in certaine Jlandes, and manye gaue credit, being amaʒed at the things that they had bɜought bartered foɜ things of a vile pɜice: as here vnder appeareth the Merchandice that they gaue foɜ al the afoɜeſaid Jewels.

The Inuentorie of the Spanish Merchandice.

Sire courſe ſhirts.

Thɜée paire of Maryners bɜeeches of lynnen.

Fiue paire of womens ſhoes.

Fiue bɜoad leatherne girdels wɜought with coloured thɜéd, with their purſes.

Manye purſes of ſhéepes ſkinne.

Sire glaſſes a little gilt.

Foure bɜouches of glaſſe.

Two thouſand beadſtones of glaſſe gréene.

A hundɜed paire of beades of diuerſe colours.

Twenty woddencombes.

Sire paire of Siſſers.

Fiftéene kniues great and ſmall.

A thouſand taplers nedels.

Two thouſand pinnes of ſoɜts.

Eight paire of coɜded ſhoes.

A paire of pinſers and a hammer.

Seauen red night cappes.

Thɜée coates of colours.

A freeſe coate with a cap of the ſame.

An old gréene beluet coate.

An olde beluet cappe.

The

The determination of Cortez to prepare a
Nauie for difcouerie.

Ycaufe *Iohn de Grijalua* was abfent a longer feafon than was *Francifco Hernandez de Cordoua*, befoze his returne, oz giuing aduife of his pzocéedings, the gouernoure *Valafques* pzepared a Caruel, and therein fent one *Chriſtofer de Olid*, foz to féeke *Grijalua* with fuccoz if néed wer, and gaue *Olid* great charge, that he fhould returne with newes from *Grijalua* with all fpéede. But this meſſenger taried but a fmall while vpon his voyage, and faw but little of *Yucatan*, and not fynding *Grijalua*, he returned backe againe to *Cuba*, which returne happed not wel foz the gouernour noz yet foz *Grijalua*. Foz if he had pzocéeded foz the on his way to Saint *Iohn de Vlhua*, hee had then mette with whom he fought foz, and likewife caufed him to haue inhabited there. But he excufed him felf, alleaging that he had loft his ankers, and was therfoze foz ced of neceſſitie to returne.

And as foone as *Olid* was departed on that voyage, *Pedro de Aluarado* returned to *Cuba*, wyth full relation of the difcouerie, & bzought many things to hym, wzought in gold, with ftrange coloured feathers, and cotton wool. The gouernour *Iames Valafques* relioyced much to behold thofe pzinciples : And all the Spaniardes of *Cuba* wondered therat, and likewife to heare the whole relatió of the fourney. Yet the gouernour feared the returne of his kinfman, bycaufe fome of his companye that came ficke and difeafed from thofe parties, faide that *Grijalua* meaned not to inhabite there, and that the people and land was great, and alfo how the fame people were warlike : likewife the gouernour feared the wifedome and

courage

courage of his kinsman. Whereuppon he determined to
send thyther certaine shippes, with souldiers and armor
and other trifling things, thinking chiefly to enrich himself by barter, and also to inhabite by force. He requested
one *Baltazer Vermudez* to take that voyage in hand, who
accepted the offer, but he demaunded three thousand duckets for his furniture and prouission. Their gouernour
hearing this demaund, answered, that in suche sorte the
charges, would be more than the profite: And so for that
tyme lefte off the matter, bycause he was couetous, and
loth to spend, thinking to prouide an army at other mens
cost, as he had done before, when *Grijalua* went firste on
that voyage, for at that time one *Francisco de Montezo* did
furnish one shippe. And also certaine gentlemen called
*Alaunso Fernãdez, Porto Carero, Alaunso de Auila & Iames
de Ordas* with manye others, wente with *Grijalua* at theyr
proper costes and charges. It followed that the gouernour brake the matter to *Cortez*, & required that the voyage shoulde be set forth betwixte them, knowing that
Cortez had two thousand Castlyns of gold in the power
of one *Andres de Duero*, a merchaunt, and also that *Cortez*
was a man diligent, wise, and of stoute courage. *Cortez*
being of haughtye stomacke, accepted both the voyage
and the charges, thinking the cost would not be much, &c.
So that the voyage and agræmente was concluded,
wherupon they sent one *Iohn de Sanzedo* to the kings coũ-
sel and chauncery, resident in the Iland of *santo Domingo*,
who were then religyous persons) to haue and obtain
of them licence, frælye to góe and traffike into those
parties of newe discouerie, and also to sæke for
Iohn de Grijalua, for they imagyned that wythout hym
small trafficke woulde bee hadde, whyche was, to exchaunge trifles of Haberdashe-for golde and syluer.
The chiefe rulers of gouernemente at that tyme

D.   in

in ꝑ kings counfell there, were thefe following, *Segnieur Aloufo de Sãto Domingo, Segnieur Luys de Figueroa, & Segnieur Barnardo de Munfanedo*, who graunted the licence, and appointed *Hernando Cortez* foꝛ captaine Generall of the voyage, and fetter foꝛth in company of *Iames Velafques*. They alfo appointed a Treafurer, and Surueꝑour to pꝛocure foꝛ the kings poꝛtion oꝛ parte, whych was accoꝛding to cuftome one fifte parte. In thys meane feafon *Cortez* pꝛepared hymfelfe foꝛ the Iourney, and communed wyth hys efpeciall friendes to fee who woulde beare hym companye: And hee founde thꝛee hundꝛed men that agreed to his requeſt. He then bought a Caruell and Uergantine, and another Caruell that *Pedro de Aluarado* bꝛought home. An other Uergantine he had of *Iames Valefques*: he pꝛouided foꝛ them armour, artillerp, and other Munition: hee bꝛought alfo wyne Oyle, Beanes, Peafe, and other biꝗuals neceffarye: he toke vp alfo vppon hys credite, of one *Iames Sauzedo* muche Haberdaſhe, to the value of feauen hundꝛed Caſtlyns in golde. The gouernour *Velafques* deliue-red vnto hym a thoufande Caſtlyns whyche he poffef-fed of the gods of one *Pamfilo de Naruaiz* in hys abfence, alleaging that he had no other money of hys owne pꝛo-per. And beeyng in thys manner agreed, the Articles and Couenauntes were dꝛawen and fet downe in wꝛyting, befoꝛe a Notarp, called *Aluunfo de Efcalantes*, the thꝛee and twenty day of Oꝗober *Anno*. 1518.

The cõming ome of Griꝑlua.

In this meane time arriued at *Cuba, Iohn de Grialua*, vpon whofe arriuall, the gouernour chaunged his pur-pofe and pꝛetence, foꝛ hee refufed to difburfe any moꝛe money, noꝛ yet would confent that *Cortez* ſhould furniſh his Nauie. Foꝛ the onely caufe was, that he ment to dif-patch backe againe his kinfeman and his army. But to behold the ſtoute courage of *Cortez*, his charges, and li-beraltie beralitie in expences, it was straunge, and to sée how hee was deceiued. And also to côsider, the flatterie and deceite of his aduersarie, yea what complaints were made to the Lozd Admirall, saying that Cortez was subtil, high minded, and a louer of honoz, which were tokés that he wold rebel, being in place conuenient, and that he woulde reuenge olde griefes. Also it grieued Vermudez that he had not accepted ẙ voyage, vnto whô it was once offered, seing the great treasure that Grijalua had bzought, & what a rich land the countrey newely discouered was. Also he pzetended that ẙ gouernoz would be chieftain of ẙ fléet, although his kinesman were not fit foz ẙ rowme. The gouernoz also thought ẙ he being slacke, Cortez would also be slacke. But yet he séeing Cortez earnestly pzocéed, he sent one Amador de Larez a pzincipal mã, to intreate him to leaue off ẙ voyage (côsidering ẙ Grijalua was returned) and ẙ he would pay him al ẙ costs & charges ẙ he had layd out. Cortez vnderstãding the gouernozs minde, made answere vnto Larez, ẙ he wold not leaue of the Jozney, foz very shame, noz yet bzeake the agréement made. And also if Valasques would send a Nauy foz his owne account, he woulde be contente, foz (quoth he) I haue alreadie my licence and dispatch of the fatherǝ gouernours. And thẽ he conferred with his friendes, to knowe their mindes if that they would fauour and beare him côpany, at whose handes he found both ready helpe and friendshippe. Hee sought then foz money, and toke vp vpon his credit foure M. Castlyns in gold, of his friend Andreas de Duero, & of Pedro de Xerez & others. With ẙ which money he bought two ships, 6. hozses, & much apparel, & began to furnish a house & kepe a good table foz cômers & goers: he went also armed like a captaine, & many wayting & attẽding vpon him, whereat diuerse murmured, saying that hee was a Lozd without rente. In thys meane whyle came

The gouernour an old enemy.

Courage of Cortez.

Grijalua to the Cittie of Sainte *Iames de Cuba* : but hys kinseman the gouernour woulde not loke vppon hym bycause he had lefte and forsaken so riche a lande. Also it grieued him inwardlye that *Cortez* proceeded thither ward so strong and mightye, and coulde by no meanes disturbe or lette hym, and to see the greate traine that wayted vppon hym wyth manye of them that had byn the other voyage with *Grijalua* : yea if that he shoulde disturbe him, bloud shedde would follow in the Citie. So that he was forced to dissemble his sorow. Yet (as many affyrme) hee commaunded that hee shoulde haue no victuals solde vnto hym. Nowe *Cortez* departed from thence, proclayming himselfe for General, and that the gouernour *Valasques* had nothing to doe wyth hys Nauie, requesting his soldiers to enbarke themselues wyth such victuals as they had. He also bargayned wyth one *Fernando Alfonso* for certaine Hogges and Sheepe that were prepared for the shambles, and gaue vnto hym a chayne of golde and brouches for payment, and also moneye, to pay the penaltie that the butcher fel into for not prouiding the Citie. And so he departed frō Saint *Iames de Baracoa* the eighteenth of Nouember, with about three hundred Spaniardes in sixe shippes.

The nauie and men that Cortez caried
with him to the Conquest.

Cortez departed from Saint *Iames de Baracoa* with small prouision of victuals for suche a number of men, and also for the nauigation whyche as yet was vncertaine And beeyng out of that parte, he

he ſent *Pedro Xuarez Gallinato* with a Caruell to *Iaymaica*,
for vittailes, commaunding him, that thoſe things which
he ſhould there buy, to goe therwith to *Cape de Corrientes,*
or to *s. Anthonies* point, which is the fartheſt part of that
Iland Weſtward. And he himſelfe wente with his companye to *Macaca*, and boughte there greate quantitie of
bread, and ſome Hogges, of one *Taymaio*. Then he proceeded to the Trinitie Ilande, and there boughte another
Shippe of one *Alonſo Guillen*. And of perticulare perſons he bought thrée Horſes, and fiue hundred buſhels of
Corne. And being there at roade, he had aduice, that *Iohn
Nonez Sedenio* paſſed that way with a Shippe laden with
victuals, for to make ſale thereof at the Mynes. Wherevppon he ſente *Iames de Ordas*, with a Caruel well armed,
for to take him, and to bring him vnto *s. Anthonies* point.
Ordas went and tooke him at the Channell *de Iardines*, and
brought him to the place appointed. *Sedenio* broughte the
regiſter of his marchandiſe, whiche was greate ſtore of
bread, Bacon, and Hennes : *Cortez* gaue him chaynes of
golde, and other pieces for payment, and a bil for the reſt.
In conſideration whereof, *Sedenio* wente with him to the
Conqueſt. In the Trinitie Ilande *Cortez* gathered togyther two hundred men more, who had bin in *Gryalua* hys
company, and were dwellers in that Iland, and in *Ma-
tancas, Carenias*, and other Villages, and ſending his ſhips
forward, he went with his men by land to *Hauana*, which
was then inhabited on the South ſide in the mouth of the
riuer called *Onicaxinall*, but there they would ſell him no
prouiſion, for feare of the Gouernour *Velaſques*. But yet
one *Chriſtopher Galſada* rentgatherer to the Byſhoppe, and
receyuer for the Popes Bulles, ſolde to him great ſtore
of Bacon and bread of that Countrey called *Maiz*, and
other prouiſion, whereby his fléete was reaſonably prouided. &c. And then he beganne to diſtribute his men and

vittayles abworde eache vessell in good order. Then came
Aluarado with his caruell, with his other friendes Christopher de Olid, Alonso de Auila, Francisco de Monteio, & manye others of Grijalua hys company, who had bin to talke
with the Gouernoure Velasques. And among them came
one Garnica so called, with letters for Cortez from Velasques, wherein he wrote, desiring him to abide there, for
that he meant to come himselfe, or else to send vnto hym,
to treate of matters profitable for them both.

Also, the sayd Gouernour sente other secret letters to
Iames de Ordas and others, requiring them to apprehende
and take prisoner Cortez. Nowe Ordas did inuite Cortez
to a banket aboorde his Caruel, thinking by that meanes
to catche Cortez in a snare, and so to carrie him prisoner
to the Citie of Saint Iames de Barocoa, but Cortez vnderstod
the matter, and fayned hymselfe to be very sicke, and also
fearing some vprore, he went aboorde his Shippe Admirall, and shot off a péece of Ordinance, giuing warning
to his Nauie to be in a readinesse to make sayle, and to
follow him to Saint Anthonies poynte, whiche was done
with expedition, and there in the Towne of Guani Guani-
ga he mustered his men, and found fiue hundred and fiftie
Spanyardes, wherof fiftie were Marriners. He deuided
them into eleuen companies, and appointed these persons
following for Captaynes, that is to say, Alonso de Auila, Alonso Fernandez Porto Carrero, Iaimes de Ordas, Francisco de Monteio, Francisco de Morla, Francisco de Salzeda, Iohn de
Escalante, Iohn Velasques de Leon, Christopher de Olid, and
one Escouar, and he himselfe as Generall toke one Company. He made these many Captaynes, bycause his
whole fléete was eleuen sayle, and that eache of them
shoulde seuerally be Captayne, both of Shippe and men.
He also appoynted for chiefe Pilote Antonio de Alami-
nes, who had taken charge befoze with Francisco de Hernandez,

<del>A snare lay de for Cortez.</del>

nandez de Cordoua, and *Grijalua.* &c. He carried also 200 *Indians,* borne in ye Jle of *Cuba,* to serue and to carrie baggage, & also certayne *Negros* with some *Indian* womē, and sixtéene Hozses & Mares, with great pzouision of Bacon, cozne, bisket, hennes, wine, oyle, pease, and other fruittes, to great stoze of Haberdash, as Belles, necklaces, beades of glasse, callers, points, pinnes, purses, nedels, girdels, thzedde, kniues, sissers, pinsars, hammers, hatchets, Shirts, Copses, headkerchiefes, handkerchiefs, bzeches, coates, clokes, cappes, Marriners bzeches, all ye which Merchādise he deuided amōg his nauie. The Ship Admiral was of the burthen of a hūdzed Tunnes. Other thzée Shippes of the burthen of eightie Tunnes the peéce. All the residue were small withoute ouerloppe, and vergan ines. The deuice of his ensigne oz aunciente, was flames of fire in white and blewe, with a redde crosse in the middest, and bozdzed round with letters, in the Lattine and Spanishz tongs, which signified this in effect: friends, let vs follow the Crosse, and with liuely faith with this stanoerde we shall obteyne victozie. The pzemisses (as ye haue hearde) was the furniture that *Cortez* pzouided foz his iourney, and with so small a thing he conquered so greate and mightie an Empire, & strange Countreys, vnknowen at that time. There was neuer Captayne that did with like army ouercome so infinite a people, & bzing both thē and their coūtrey vnder subiectiō. He caried no money to pay his souldiers, but was rather much indebted to others at his departure. And to say the truth, there néeded any money to make pay to those souldiers that went to the Cōquest, foz if they shuld haue serued foz wages, they would haue gone to other places néere hand. But in *India,* euery one pzetēdeth ye state of a noble man, oz else great riches. Now all ye fléete being in readinesse (as ye haue hearde,) *Cortez* began an exhoztation to his cōpany as followeth.

D.iiij. The

The Oration that Cortez made
to his Souldiers.

My louing fellowes and deere friendes, it is certayne that euery valiant manne of stoute courage, doth procure by deedes to make him selfe equall with the excellente men of his time, yea and with those that were before his time. So it is, that I do now take in hãd such an enterprise, as godwilling shall be heereafter of greate fame, for myne heart doth pronosticate vnto mée, that we shall winne greate and rich Countreys, and manye people, as yet neuer séene to anye of oure nation, yea and (I beléeue) greater Kingdomes than those of oure Kinges. And I assure you, that the desire of glory dothe further extend, than treasure, the whiche in sorte, mortall life doth obtayne. I haue now prepared Shippes, Armor, Horses, and other furniture for the warres, with victuall sufficient, and all things that are vsed as necessary in Conquestes. I haue bin at greate costes and charges, wherein I haue not onely employed myne owne goodes, but also the goodes of my friendes, yet me thinketh that the employmente thereof dothe encrease my treasure and honor. We ought (louing fellowes) to leaue off small things, when great matters doe offer themselues. And euen as my trust is in God, euen so greater profite shall come to our kings, and a nation of this oure enterprise, than hath héeretofore of any other. I doe not speake how acceptable it will be to God our sauiour, for whose loue I do chiefly and willingly hazard my goods and trauel. I will not nowe treat of the perils and danger of life that I haue passed since I began this voyage. This I say, that good men doe rather expect renoune, than treasure. We doe now attempt and begin warre that is both good and

iust,

iuff,and the almighty God in whose name and holy faith
this voyage is begonne, will assuredly graunte vnto vs
victory, and the time will shew the end of things well be-
gonne.Therefore we will now haue an other manner in
our proceedings, than eyther Cordoua or Gryalua hadde,
whereof I meane not nowe to dispute, for the presente
time doth hasten vs away,but at our arriuall, we will do
what shall seeme vnto vs conuenient.Heere deere friends
do I lay before you great gaynes,but wrapped in greate
trauell,yet Vertue is an enimie to idlenesse.&c. Therefore
if you will accept hope for Vertue, or Vertue for hope,and
also if ye forsake me not, as I will not forsake you, I
will with Gods help make you in shorte time the richest
men that euer passed this way.I doe see you are but fewe
in number,but yet such men of haughtie courage, that no
force or strength of Indians can offende.   Likewise wee
haue experience, that Christ our sauiour hathe alwayes
fauoured our nation in these parties. Therfore my deere
friendes,let vs now in Gods name depart ioyfull, expecting good successe,according to our beginning.&c.

The entrance of Cortez into the
Iland of Acusamill.

Ith the aforesayd communication, Cortez
gaue great hope to his company of waigh-
tie matters,yea and great admiration of
his person,so that all his company had an
earnest desire to proceede on that iorney.
    And Cortez likewise reioyced, to see his
men so willing:and incontinente, they embarqued themselues, and after their prayers made vnto God, hoysed
vp their sayles, and with faire winde departed the eight-
tenth day of Febrnarie Anno 1519.And beyng at Sea,he
willed all his nauie (as the vse is) to haue S. Peter for
    C.   theit

their patrone, warning them alwayes to follow the Admirall(wherin he went)bycause he carried a light for the night season to guide them the way, whiche was almost East and West from *S. Anthonies* point,being the nerest part of *Cuba* to *Cape de Cotoche*, which is the first lād point of *Yucatan*, whither they were bounde, so ẙ being there, they might run alōg the coast, betwene the North point and the West. The first night ẙ *Hernando Cortez* begā to passe ouer the gulfe betwene *Cuba* & *Yucatan*, being little aboue lr. leagues, the winde rose vp at Northeast with much force, so ẙ all the Fleete were separated without sight ẙ one of the other: yet by the accompt that their Pilots kept, they arriued all sauing one at the Ilande of *Acusamil*, although not at one time, and those that last arriued, wer the Admirall, and Captayne *Morla* his Ship, who had lost his Ruther, but by shoting off a pece, *Cortez* vnderstood his necessitie, and came vering to him, and amayned his sailes to succour him, being in ẙ night season. Yet when the day appeared, it pleased God ẙ the rage of the tempest ceassed, & being cleere day, they found agayne their Ruther, and trimmed the Ship, and made sayle, and sayled that day and the next following, without sighte of land, or any of the Fleete. But the third day they arriued at a cape or point of land, called Womens cape. *Cortez* cōmanded *Morla* to follow him, directing his course to seeke the residue of his Fleete, and arriued in this sorte at the Iland of *Acusamil*, and there found all his nauie excepte one, whereof they hearde no newes in many dayes after. The people of that Ilande beholding suche a straunge

The feare of the Indians of A- cusamil.

sight, were in great feare and admiratiō, so that they gathered their stuffe and wente vp into the Mountaynes. *Cortez* caused a certayne number of his mē to goe a land to a Towne which was neere the place where they were arriued, and they foūd the towne wrought with Masons worke, and good building, but they founde no creature

therein,

therein, yet in some houses they found cloth made of cotte wooll, and certaine Iewels of gold. Also they entred into a high tower made of stoneworke, nære the sea side, and there they founde nothing but Idols of earth and stone. With this newes they returned to *Cortez*, and enformed him what they had sæne, and also many faire sowe fields of *Maiz*, and great store of hiues of Bæs, and many træs of fruites, and also presented vnto him the gold and other things that they had found. *Cortez* reioyced with y newes, but yet maruelled that the people were fledde, considering that when *Grijalua* was there, they had not so done, wherby he iudged, that his nauie bæyng greater, caused them to feare and flie, and likewise he feared least a snare were prepared for him. Then he comanded to vnship his Horses for thrée causes: the one to discouer the Countrey: and the other to fight if nædewere : and also to grase thé, hauing there abundance. Also he vnshipped his mé of warre, and sent them to discouer the land. And in the thickest of the Mountaynes, they found four women, and thrée children, whome they brought to *Cortez*, so that not vnderstanding their language, by signes & tokens they ymagined that one of thé was the mother to the children, & mistresse to the other women. The pore creatures bewayled their captiuitie. *Cortez* made muche of them, & apparrelled the mistresse as wel as he might with Spanish attire: and to hir seruants he gaue loking glasses and sissers: and to the little children other toyes to play withall, vsing no dishonestie towards thé. And thé he determined to send one of the wenches to call hir maister, and to enforme him how well they were intreated. In this meane season came certaine spies lurking a farre off, by the comandement of their Lord, who was called *Calachuni*, to bring newes of his wife, & what else passed. *Cortez* receyued them gétly, & gaue vnto them certayne trifles, and sent others to theyr Lord, and returned thé w embassage on his behalfe & his

Hovv the people vver found

E.ij.   wiues,

wiues, to defire hym to come vnto him, and to fée thofe
folke from whome he had fledde, promifing, that neyther
his perfon, no2 none of his countrey fhould recepue anye
moleftation of him, no2 of any of his company. *Calachuni*
vnderftáding this friendfhippe, and alfo with the loue hée
bare to his wife and childjê, came the next day following
with all the Townefmen, in whofe houfes ý Spanyards
were lodged, who woulde not permitte that their gueftes
fhould giue place. And the Lo2de commaunded, that they
fhould be wel entertayned, and frô that day fo2ward p2o-
uided them of b2ead, fifhe, honey, ¢ fruite. *Calachuni* fpake
and faluted *Cortez* with greate humilitie and ceremonie,
and euen fo was he louingly recepued, ¢ wel entertained.
Cortez did then declare vnto him the commoditie that
would enfue vnto him by that nation. And alfo p2efented
vnto him ¢ his côpany many toyes, which were vnto thê
of fmall balewe, but muche efteemed among them, yea
mo2e than golde. And mo2eouer *Cortez* cômaunded, that

all the golde and other things that his men had taken in
the Towne, fhoulde be b2oughte befo2e him, and placed it
fo, that euery *Indian* knewe his owne, and was refto2ed
vnto them, whereat they were not a little ioyfull, wondering at the liberalitie of the ftraungers, and departed
both merrie and riche with their ftraunge giftes, and
went th2oughout al the Iland, fhewing to their fellowes
their p2efentes, commaunding them in the name of *Calachuni* their Lo2d, to returne euery man to his houfe, with
their wiues and childzen, commending highly the honeft
and gentle nature of the ftraungers. With this newes
and commaundemente, euery man returned to his houfe
and Towne from whence he had fledde. And after thys
fo2t their feare was paft, and they p2ouided the Camp a-
bundantly of honey, b2ead, waxe, fifhe, and frute, all the
time that they abode in that Iland.

A facte
vvorthy of
prayfe.

The

The Indians of Acuſamil gaue nevves
to Cortez of certaine bearded men.

Ow *Cortez* ſeeing theſe *Indians* quiet and
wel pleaſed,and alſo very ſeruiceable , he
did determyne to take away they² Idols,
and to giue them a remembraunce of Ieſu Ch²iſt bo²ne of the Uirgin Mary,by one
Melchior a fiſher man and very ruſtical,who had bin ther
befo²e with *Francifco Hernandez de Cordoua,*who declared
vnto them,that *Cortez* his Lo²d and captaine would en-
fo²me them of a better god,and better lawes,than thoſe
which they maintained.The *Indians* anſwered,that they
were contented therewith , and went with them vnto
their temples , and there b²ake downe their Idols, and
celeb²ated diuine ſeruice , teaching them to ado²e and
wo²ſhippe Ch²iſt crucifyed, ſo that they were verye at-
tentiue to the doctrine,and ceaſed ſacrifiſe of men which
they were wōt to vſe. Theſe *Indians* did wonder much at
the ſhippes and ho²ſes, yea and marueyled as muche at
our colour and beardes, ſo that many times they would
come and fæle them, and ſignifyed vnto them by ſignes
and tokens towardes *Yucatan,*that there were fiue o² ſixe
bearded men. Then *Cortez* conſidering how p²ofitable it
wold be to haue an interp²eter to vnderſtand and to be
vnderſtood, he beſought *Calachuni* that he would appoint
a meſſenger to carrye a letter to the beardes men , who
were in the power of a great Lo²d and Ty²ant,and *Calachuni* found none that durſt take that iourney in hand,
fearing that they ſhould be ſlaine and eaten. *Cortez* ſeing
this, entreated with faire wo²ds,th²ée of the *Indians* that
ſerued him to accept the iourney, and gaue thē rewards
fo² they² labour:yet the *Indians* excuſed them,ſaying that

Nevves of
bearded men.

       E.iii.   **they**

they should be slayne, notwithstanding with faire promises and rewardes, they accepted the voyage, so that *Cortez* wrote with them this letter following.

WOrshipful sirs, I departed from *Cuba* with eleuen saile in my fleete, furnished with fiue hundred and fiftie Spaniardes, and I arriued here at *Acusamil* from whence I write you this letter. The people of this Iland haue certifyed me, that there is in that countrey fiue or sire bearded men, and in al pointes like vnto vs: they can not here enforme me of anye other signes or tokens, but hereby I do coniecture, and certainely beleue that ye be Spaniardes. Both I and these gentlemen of my company do come to discouer and inhabit this land, we hartily pray you y within sire days after the receite hereof, ye come vnto vs, wout any excuse or delay, and if ye so doe, al we of this nauie wil gratifye your gentlenesse & good seruice y ye shal do vnto vs. I do send you a Uergantyn wherin you may come, & two shippes for your safecondua. *Hernando Cortez.*

THis letter being written, there was found an inconuenience, which was, they knew not how to carrye the letter so secretly y it might not be seene, & they taken for espies, wherof the saide *Indians* stwde in great feare. The *Cortez* bethought him, y the letter wold passe wrapped in y haire of the head of one of the, for ordinarily the *Indians* wear logheare, & on their solemn feasts & in wars they vse their haire platted & boud about their forheads. And he appointed captaine of the Uergantine wherin y messegers wet, *Iohn de Escalante*, & *Iames de Ordas* for captaine of the other two ships, with fiftie men if any nede should happen. So shortly after the ships arriued at the place appointed, *Escalante* set a land his messengers, and abode there eight days they returne, although he promised the to abide there but sire dayes. And the seeing that

they

they came not, be surmyſed ẏ they were either ſlaine oʒ taken captiues: ⁊ ſo returned backe againe to *Acuſamill* without his meſſegers, wherof al the army were ſoʒowful, ⁊ chiefly *Cortez*, thinking that the *Indians* had wʒõg enfoʒmed him. Nowe in this meane ſeaſon they trymmed their ſhippes of the hurte receiued by the late tempeſt, ⁊ at the returne of the two ſhips and Mergantyne, they hoyſed vp ſailes and departed.

A miraculous chaunce hovv Geronimo de
Aguilao came to Cortez.

Alachuni and all his ſubiectes were full of heauineſſe(as it ſemed)with the departure of the Chʒiſtians, bycauſe they were wel vſed at their handes. From *Acuſamil* the fleete ſayled to get the coaſt of *Yucatan* tothe cape called Womens point, with pʒoſperous weather, ⁊ there *Cortez* came to an Anker, deſirous to ſee the diſpoſition of the lande, and the manner of the people : but it liked him not,ſo that ẏnext day folowing being ſhʒouetuiſday, he departed, meaning to double the ſayde cape, and ſo to paſſe to *Cotoche* and to biewe it. But befoʒe they hadde doubled the poynte, *Peter de Aluarado* ſhotte off a piece, in token that hee was in great peril, whereuppon the other ſhippes dʒewe neare to knowe what hadde happened : And when *Cortez* vnderſtoode that *Aluarados* ſhippe was in ſo great a leake that with two pumpes they mighte not emptie the water, he found no other remedy but to returne backe again to *Acuſamil* with al his fleet. The *Indians* of ẏ Ilande came incontinent to ẏ water ſide very ioyfull, and to knowe whether they had left any thing behind thẽ. The Chʒiſtiãs enfoʒmed thẽ of their miſhap,and came a ſhoʒe,⁊ in ſhoʒt time found the leake ⁊ amended it. The Saterday following they toke ſhipping again,al the army excepte

Hernando

Hernando Cortez, and fiftie of his company, then the winde arose contrary, and so much, that they could not departe that day: & the furie of the winde endured al that night, but in the morning it waxed calme, so that they myghte proceede on their voyage. But for as much as that was the Sabboth daye, they determined to heare diuine seruice, and after dinner to make saile. When their seruice was ended, and *Cortez* sitting at his meate , there was newes brought him that a little vessell called a *Canoa*, came vnder saile toward the shippes, whiche seemed to come from *Yucatan* : with that newes *Cortez* arose from his meate, to behold whether the *Canoa* went, and perceiupng that she left the way toward the shippes, he sente *Andrew de Tapia* with certaine others, as secrete & closely as might be deuised, to lye in ambushe for their comming a shoare . The *Canoa* arriued in a calme place, out of the whiche came foure men all naked, except their priuie members , and the heare of their heades platted and bound aboute their foreheades like vnto women, with bowes and arrowes in their hands: three of them which were *Indians*, wer afraide when they saw the Spaniards with their drawen swordes, and would haue fled againe to their *Canoa*, but the Christian feared not , and desired his fellowes in the *Indian* tong to abide with hym . And then he began to speake in the Spanish tongue in thys wise: Maisters are ye Christians, yea (quoth they) and of the Spanish nation. Then he reioyced so much, that the teares fell from his eyes, and demaunded of them what day it was, although he had a Primer wherein he dayly prayed.

He then besought them earnestlye to assist him with their prayers & thanksgiuing vnto god for his deliuery, & kneling deuoutly downe vppon his knees, holding vp his handes, his eyes toward heauen, and his face bathed with

with teares, made his humble prayer vnto God, giuing
most hartie thankes, that it hadde pleased hym to deliuer him out of the power of Infidels and infernal creatures, and to place hym among Chꝛistians and men of
his owne nation. *Andrew de Tapia* holpe hym vppe, and
toke hym in hys armes, and so did al ꝑ others embꝛace &   The cōming
louingly salute him. Then he commaunded the other   of Aguilar
thꝛee *Indians* to follow him, and went talking wyth hys   to Cortez.
friendes, where *Cortez* aboade, who recepued him ioyfully, and gaue vnto hym such apparel as he neded, and
wyth great pleasure hauing him in his companye, hee
demaunded the estate of his misfoꝛtune, and what was
hys name, who aunswered befoꝛe them al, saying,
Sir my name is *Geronimo de Aguilar,* I was boꝛne in
the Cittie of *Esja* in the *Andolozia,* and by missoꝛ-
tune I was loste after this soꝛte. In the warres of
Darien and in the time of the contentions and passions of
Iames de Nicuessa, and *Vasco Nonez Balboa,* I came with
Captaine *Valdinia* in a little Caruell, towarde *Santo Domingo,* to giue aduice to the Admirall and gouernour, of
the troubles which had happned, and my comming was
foꝛ men and victuals: and likewise we bꝛought twentye
thousand Duckettes of the kings in *Anno.*1511. And whē
we appoꝛted at *Iamayca,* our Caruel was lost on the shal-
lowes whiche were called the Vipars, and with greate
pain we entred (about twenty persons) into the boate, wȝ
out saple, water oꝛ bꝛead, and weake pꝛouision of oares:
we thus wander thirtéene oꝛ fourtéene dayes, and then
the currant, whiche is there very great & runneth alway
weastward, cast vs a shoare in a pꝛouince called *Maya,* &
traueling on our way, seauen of our fellowes died wyth
hunger & famin. And captain *Valdinia* & other 4. were sacrifised to the ydols by a cruel and cursed *Cacike,* that is to
say, a Loꝛd in whose power we fell. &c.

F   And

And after the sacrifice, they were eaten among the *Indians* for a solemne banket: and I, and other sixe wer put into a Cage or coupe, to be fatned for an other sacrifice. And for to escape suche abhominable death, we brake the prison and fledde through certaine mountaines: So that it pleased God that wee mette with another *Cazike* who was enimy to him that first toke vs, his name was *Quinqus*, a man of more reason and better condition, hee was Lord of *Xamansana*: he accepted vs for his captiues, but shortly after he dyed, and then I aboad with *Taxmar* his heire. Then deceased other fiue of our fellowes, so that there remayned but onely I and one *Gonsalo Guerrer*, a maryner, who now abydeth with *Nachancan* the Lorde of *Chetemal*, and he married with a rich gentlewoman of that countrey, by whom he hath children, and is made a Captaine, and wel esteemed with the *Cazike* for the victories ý he hath had in the wars against the other Lords. I sent vnto him your worships letter, desiring him that he would come with me hauing so fit a passage, but he refused my request, I belieue for verye shame, bycause hee had his nose ful boared of holes, & his eares iagged, hys face & handes painted according to the vse of ý countrey, or else he abode there for the loue he bare to his wife and children. All those whiche stode by & hard this Historie, were amased, to heare *Geronymo de Aguilar* report howe those *Indians* did sacrifise & eate mans flesh. They also lamented the miserie & death of his fellowes, and highly praysed God, to sée him frée from his bondage & from such cruel & barbarous people, & to haue likewise so good an enterpreter with thé, for vndoubtedly it semed a miracle ý *Aluarados* ship fel into a leak, for with ý extremity they returned back again to that Iland, wheras with contrarie winde they were constrayned to abide ý cóming of *Aguilar*. And certainly he was ý mean & spéech of al their
procéedings.

proceedings. And therfore haue I bin so prolixious in ye rehearsal of this matter, as a notable point of this historie. Also I wil not let to tell how the mother of *Geronimo de Aguilar*, became mad. &c.

When she hard ye hir son was captiue among people ye vsed to eate mãs flesh, & euer after whẽ she saw any flesh spitted or roasted, she would make an open outcrie, saying, oh I miserable woman, behold this is the flesh of my dearebeloued sonne who was all my comfort.

The Iland of Acusamil.

The *Indians* naturall of that countrey do cal their Ilande *Acusamil*, & corruptlye *Cosumel. Iohn de Gryalua* was ye first Spaniard that apported there, and named it the holy Roode, bycause hee fell in sighte therof on holy roade daye. It cõtayneth ten leagues in length & three leagues in breadth, although some say more, some lesse: it standeth twentye degrees on this side the equator, and fiue leagues from the womẽs cape: it hath three villages, in ye which liueth nere 3 thousand mẽ. The houses are of stone and brick, and couered with straw & bowes, & some with tile. Their temples and towers are made of lime & stone very wel built: thei haue no other fresh water but out of welles and raine water. *Calachuni* is their chiefe Lord: they are browne people & goe naked: & if any weare cloth, it is made of cotten wool only to couer their priuie mẽbers: they vse lõg heare plated & bound about their foreheads: they are great fishermẽ, so ye fish is their chiefest foode & sustenance, they haue also *Maiz* which is for bread: also good fruites: & hony, but somewhat soure: and plots for bees, which contayn.1000 biues. They knew not to what vse war serued, but whẽ they saw our mẽ make cãdels therof, they wõdred therat.

F. ij.   Their

Their dogges haue ſore faces and barke not, theſe they gelde and fatten to eate. This Iland is ful of high mountaines,& at the feete of them,good paſtures,many Deare, and wilde Boares,Connyes and Hares,but they are not great.The Spaniardes with their handguns and croſſebowes prouide them of that victual, freſh ſalt and dried. The people of this *Iland* are Idolaters,they doe ſacrifice children, but not manye . And many times in ſtead of children they ſacrifice dogges.They are poore people,but very charitable and louing in their falſe religion and beliefe.

The religion of the people of
Acuſamil.

Be temple is like vnto a ſquare Toure broad at the foote,& ſteps round about it, & from y middeſt vpward very ſtraight: the top is hollow & couered with ſtraw: it hath foure windowes with frontals and galleries. In y holow place is their chappel,wheras their Idols do ſtand . The temple that ſtode by the ſea ſide was ſuch a one , in the which was a maruellous ſtraunge Idol, and differed muche from all the reſt,although they haue manye and of diuerſe faſhions.The body of this Idol was great and hollow, and was faſtened in that wall with lime : hee was of earth. And behinde this Idols backe was the Weſterie, where was kept ornaments & other things of ſeruice for y temple.The prieſts had a little ſecret doze hard adioyning to y Idol,by which doze they crept into y hollow Idol, and anſwered the people y came with prayers &peticiõs. And w this deceit y ſimple ſoules beleued at y the Idol ſpake, & honored y god moze thã al the reſt w many perfumes & ſweete

A ſtraunge Idol.

ſwéete ſmelles, and offered bꝛead and fruite, with ſacrifice
of Quayles bloud, and other birds, and dogges, and ſome-
time mans bloud. And thꝛough the fame of this Idoll and
Dꝛacle, many Pilgrimes came to *Acuſamil* from many
places. At the foote of this Temple was a plotte like a
Churchyard, well walled and garniſhed with pꝛoper pin-
nacles, in the middeſt whereof ſtoode a Croſſe of ten
foote long, the which they adoꝛed foꝛ God of the rayne, foꝛ
at all times whē they wanted rayne, they would goe thither on Pꝛoceſſion denoutely, and offered to the Croſſe
Quayles ſacrificed, foꝛ to appeaſe the wꝛath that the
God ſéemed to haue agaynſte them: and none was ſo acceptable a ſacrifice, as the blond of that little birde. They
bſed to burne certaine ſwéete gūme, to perfume that God
withall, and to beſpꝛinckle it with water, and this done,
they beléeued aſſuredly to haue rayne. Suche is the Religiō of thoſe *Indians* of *Acuſamil.* They could neuer know
the oꝛiginal how that God of Croſſe came amōgſt them,
foꝛ in all thoſe partics of *India*, there is no memoꝛie of a-
nye Pꝛeaching of the Goſpell that had bin at any time,
as ſhall be ſhewed in another place.

The God of rayne.

The Battell and vvinning of
Potonchan.

Ortez pꝛocéeded with his Fléete very ioyfull,
bycauſe he had found one of his Ships which
hée thought had bin loſt, & apoꝛted at the riuer
de Gryalua, whiche in the *Indian* tong is called
Tauaſco, and anckred at the riuers mouth, fearing to enter in with the bigger beſſels ouer the barre: and incontinente came manye *Indians* to gaze at them and theyꝛ
Shippes, who were armed with feathers, and ſuche lyke
armour as they bſe, ſéeming a farre off trimme fellowes.

They

They wondered not muche to sée oure Shyppes and menne, bycause they hadde séene before *Iohn de Gryálua* in the same Riuer. The behauiour of that people, and scituation of the Countrey, liked *Cortez* verye well, so that leauyng sufficiente garde in hys Shyppes, he manned hys Uergantynes and Boates, and carried with hym certayne pieces of Ordinance, and with force of oares he entred the Riuer agaynste the streame, whiche was verye greate, and hauyng rowen little moze than halfe a league, they espyed a greate Towne walled wyth Timber, and the houses made of mudwall, couered with strawe. The Towne wall was verye strong, with loope holes to offende withall. And before oure menne came néere the Towne, they mette with manye little Boates, whiche the *Indians* call *Tahucup*, full of armed menne, shewyng themselues desirous of battayle. *Cortez* procéeded forwardes, and made vnto them signes of peace, declaring vnto them by his interpreter, that hys commyng thither was not to molest oz disquiet them, but onely to take freshe water, and to buy victuals, as menne that trauelled by Sea, and stode in néede thereof, promising good paymente for anye thing that they shoulde take. The *Indians* hearyng theyr requesst, promised to shewe theyr message to the Townesmen, and woulde also returne with theyr aunswere and vittayles, and so departed. In shorte space they returned againe, and broughte bread and fruite, and eyght Turkie Cockes, and presented it franckely vnto them. *Cortez*

gaue them thankes, but (quoth he) the prouission that ye haue brought, is very little, for the néede that I and so manye persons which I haue within yonder greate vessels locked and shutte vp, therefore I pray you to bryng me moze vittayles, oz else to permitte and suffer mée and my folkes to come vnto youre Towne to séeke oure remedie.

remedie.

The *Indians* demaunded one nyghtes space to doe the one and the other, and departed towarde the towne. *Cortez* alfo went to a little Iland that ſtandeth in the riuer, to abide their aunſwere, ſo that eache pretended to deceyue the other, foz the *Indians* demaunded that time, to the intent to carrie that night away theyr goodes, and to put in ſafetie their wiues and childzen in the Mountaynes, and likewiſe to gather their men of warre to defende theyr Towne. *Cortez* alſo commaunded his Har-gabuſhiers and Croſſebowmen to goe a lande vppon the Ilande, and cauſed the Riuer vpwardes to bée ſoughte foz way, to wade ouer, ſo that theſe thyngs were done that nyghte without anye knowledge to the contrarye ſyde. And all thoſe whyche abode abozde the Shyppes, came vnto *Cortez*, and thoſe who wente to ſéeke the paſſage, founde within leſſe than halfe a league vpwardes, a place that was of depth to the girdle of a manne. And likewiſe founde ſuche couerte of woodes, that they myghte come néere vnto the Towne, and not to bée ſéene.

Diligence of a good Captayne.

Thys newes lyked well *Cortez*, wherevppon he appoynted two Captaynes, whoſe names were *Alonſo de Auila*, and *Peter de Aluarado*, and to eache of them fiftie menne. The ſame nyghte hée ſente certayne Souldyers wyth a ſea compaſſe, to lye in ambuſhe in the woode whyche ſtode betwéene the riuer and the towne, foz two conſiderations. The one, bycauſe the *Indians* ſhoulde ſée, that there were no moe Spanyardes in the Ilande, than were the daye befoze. And the other was, that hys menne hearing their watchwozd, ſhoulde aſſaulte the towne on the land ſide. And as ſone as the day appeared, came eight boates of *Indians* armed, where-as oure Campe was pitched, who bzoughte a little

F.iiij. victuall,

victuall, saping they could get no moze, bycause that the
inhabitantes of the Towne were fledde, with feare of
them, and their deformed vessels, desiring them to returne abozde their Shippes, and not to disquiet the people of that Countrey. The interpzeter aunswered, that
it was against humanitie to suffer them to perishe wyth
hunger, yea and if they woulde heare the cause of theyz
comming, they should shoztly sée what pzofite would re-
dound vnto them. The *Indians* replyed, that they woulde
take no counsell of straungers and menne whome they
knewe not. Lykewise, they thoughte not good to lodge
suche guestes in their houses, foz they séemed terrible,
and such as would be commaunders. But if they woulde
nædes haue water, they mighte take riuer water, oz elle
make welles on the shoze, foz so dyd they at theyz næde.

Then *Cortez* séeyng that wozdes pzeuapled not, hée
signifyed vnto them that he woulde enter their Towne
by foze, to sée it and their Countrey, foz to giue thereof
relation to the greatest Pzince in the wozlde, who hadde
sent them thither: requesting them to be therewith contented, considering he meante not to disquiet them: and
if they would not permitte the same, he would commend
himselfe to his God, and to the strength and foze of hys
men. The *Indians* aunswered agayne, that they shoulde
depart, and not thus bzagge in other mens land, foz in no
wise they woulde permitte them to enter their Towne.
And if with this warning they would not departe, they
meante to kyl both him and as many as were with him.
Yet *Cortez* ceassed not to vse all humanitie with those
barbarous people, accozding to the commaundements
and instructions giuen vnto him by the King of *Castill*,
whiche was, to require those people oftentimes with
peace, befoze the attempting of warre, oz entring per-
foze into their Townes and Countrey, so that yet a-
gayne

gayne he conuited them with peace, promising them libertie with good entertainement, assuring them of things
profitable both for body and soule, and that they myghte
accompt themselues happie with the knowledge thereof:
but if now they would refuse his offer, he did then warne
them to make them ready for the euening, for before the
going downe of the Sunne, he did hope with the help of
his God, to rest and take vp his lodging in the Towne,
in despite of all the inhabitants thereof, who had refused
his offer.

The *Indians* laughed at his talke, and skorning at him,
they returned to the Towne, to enforme their fellowes
of the pride and madnesse that they thought they hadde
hearde. Then the Spanyardes wente to dinner, and hauing well refreshed themselues, they putte on their Armour, and went aboord their Boates and Uergantines,
loking for some aunswere from the *Indians*, and seyng
the Sunne decline apace, and no aunswere, *Cortez* aduised
the Spanyardes that lay in ambushe in the woodde, to
giue assault, and he embarqued himselfe with his rapier
and Targett, goyng likewise assaulte with neere two
hundred men, who comming neere the Towne walles,
discharged his Ordinance, and lept into the water to the
knees, and began valiantly to assault the walles and bulwarkes. The *Indians* seyng their enimies so nigh vnto
them, beganne to fighte with courage, shooting arrowes,
throwing of dartes and stones, wherewith they hurte a-
bout twenty Spanyardes: yea, and though the fearefull
noyse of the Ordinance did many times so annoy them,
being things so straunge, and neuer before seene of them,
yet they fledde not from the walles, but resisted the Christians valiantlye, and suffered them not to enter the
Towne that way, if they had not bin assaulted in another place. But when the Company that lay in ambush

G.   heard

hearde the shooting of their fellowes, they began likewyse theyr onsette. The *Indians* knowyng nothyng what was prepared behynde theyr backes, and hauing also theyr handes full in defending the entrance by the Riuer: and the Chrisstians fyndyng that parte of the Towne without resistance, entred in wyth a terrible noyse, killing as many as they mette. Then the Townesmen vnderstode theyr ouersyghte, and woulde haue remedyed it, and fledde from the place where *Cortez* was gyuing combat, whereby *Cortez* and hys Company entred the Towne at ease, without contradiction, so that hee and the other Companye of his Souldyers mette togither at the Markette place, and expulsed all the *Indians* out of the Towne, excepte those that were taken prisoners, and the carkases of the deade. Then the Chrysstians soughte the spoyle, and founde nothyng but Turkie Hennes, and some thyngs wrought of Cotten wooll, but verye little Golde.

There was that daye aboue foure thousande *Indians* in fyghte and defence of the Towne: There was much *Indian* bloud shedde, bycause they fought naked, manye were wounded, and fewe Captiue.   *Cortez* lodged himselfe wyth hys armie in the chiefest Temple of the Idolles, where was rome sufficiente. They kepte that nyghte good watche, as in a house of enimies, but the poore *Indians* durst not once interrupte them.   After thys sorte was *Potonchan* taken, béyng the fyrste Cytie that *Cortez* wanne by force in all hys Conquest.

The Battell of Cintla.

A L ẏ nighte *Cortez* flept not, but rather oc=
cupped himfelfe in carrying the wounded
men, & other ſtuffe abozd ẏ Shyps, & alfo
to difenbarke thirtéene Họzfes, & the reſi=
due of his mẽ ẏ he had left abozd,ẏ which
he bzought to paſſe befoze the ſunne riſing, although the
Tauaſcans had notice therof. Whẽ the ſunne was riſen,he
had with his company made vnto God their pzayers,and
muſtered his men, where were at that time in Campe
néere fiue hundzed Spanyardes, thirtéene Họzfes , and
ſire péeces of ozdinance : Theſe Họzfes were the fyzſte
that euer came into that Countrey,whych now is called
new *Spayne*. He planted his men and munition in good oz=
der,and thus marched fozwardes toward *Cintla*.The *Indians* féepng this pzeparation, began alfo to make readie,
and to place in good ozder fortie thoufand men in fyue cõ=
panies:their méeting was in ploughed lande among ma=
nye déepe lakes and pondes, very daungerous to paſſe,
fo that our men by reafon thereof were bzought out of
ozder. And *Hernando Cortez* with his họzfemen wente to
féeke a better paſſage, and to encloſe himfelfe among cer=
tayne trées on their left hand, foz to fet vpon the enimies
when time ſhould ſerue. The footemen pzocéeded on,and
paſſed many mariſhe groundes, vntill they came to the
tilled land.The *Indians* were expert in thofe places wher
they beganne the battayle , ſhoting with their bowes
and ſlings,and thzowing of dartes. And although our mẽ
did fome hurt among them with their Croſſebowes, hãd=
gunnes,and Ozdinance,whẽ they were in place to ſhote,
yet the *Indians* purſued our men fo thicke,that they could
not put them off, foz by pollicie, the *Indians* of *Potonchan*
hadde foughte out that place : and it is to bée thoughte

that

Care of a good Cap=tayne.

Fortye thoufande Indians.

that they were not barbarous, nor of small vnderstanding in warres, yet notwithstandyng wyth muche
payne, oure men gate out of that place, and obtayned a-
nother somewhat better, and more playner grounde,
whereas they myghte vse their Ordinance, and fyghte
with their weapons bodye to body. But the *Indians* béeyng so greate a number, draue our men to so narrowe a
place, that they were fayne to ioyne backe to backe
for theyr owne defence, yea & for all that were in maruellous greate daunger, for they hadde no roome to vse their
Ordinance, nor yet Horsemen to make them waye.
They béeyng in thys perplexitie, and readie to flye, suddaynely appeared a Horseman with a speckled Horse,
whome they iudged to be Captayne *Morla*, whych Horsemanne sette vppon the *Indians*, and made them retyre:
and hauyng more space than befor̄e, they sette afresh̄e
vppon the enimies, and slewe some of them. In thys
meane tyme the Horsemanne vaded away, and was
not séene, and wyth hys absence the *Indians* begann̄e a-
fresh̄e, and enclosed the Chrystians in the same daunger that they were in before: then the Horsemanne appeared agayne néere oure menne, and made maruellous
way among the enimies, wherevpon our menns séeyng
this succoure, gaue the onset agayne with great courage,
and slewe and hurt many *Indians*, but at the best season,
the Horseman vanished away cleane out of sighte, and
when the *Indians* sawe not the Horseman, with feare
of whome they fledde, thinkyng that he hadde bin a *Cen-
taure*, and that the Horse and man was all one incorporate, they returned agayne with liuely courage, and v-
sed our Chrystians worse than they hadde done before.
Then the Horseman returned the third time, and putte
the *Indians* to flight with great hurte, whom our footemé
pursued with great slaughter.

Perill of
the Chri-
stians.

A miracle.

Nowe

Now at this instant came *Cortez* with al his company
of horsemen, being wearied with the tranaile in passing
such strange lakes and wildernesse, wherof the countrey
is replenished. Our men being ioyful of his comming,
they began to enforme him what wonders they had sene
a horseman do, which came to succour them, demanding
of him which of their company it was. *Cortez* answered
and faithfully assured them, that it was none of their cōpany, bicause it was not possible for any of them to come
any sooner: Then they al gaue God praise, belieuing that
it was a helpe sent from heauen. *Cortez* said (my deare
fellows) forwards, for god is with vs. Then the horseme
set vpon the *Indians*, and with force of lance droue them
out of the marish ground, and brake their mayne battel.
The *Indians* incontinent left the fielde, and fled into the
thicke woodes, the footemen followed them, and slue a-
boue three hundred *Indians*, besides many other that were
hurt. There wer aboue seauenty Spaniardes wounded
with arrowes and stones.

And whether it were with labour of the battel, or with
excessiue heate, or with drinking the water of that place,
there fel such a stitch in their loynes, that about a hūdred
of them fel flat vpon the groūd, not able to go nor stand.
their fellowes being forced to carry thē on their backes,
But it pleased god that the same night the payne wente
fro them, being in the morning wel againe. Who seyng
themselues deliuered from so manye perils, gaue moste
humble thankes to the almightye god that had miracu-
loufly deliuered them. They all agreed that three times
they had sene the straunge horseman, with the speckled
horse, fight in their fauour, as is aforesaid, beléeuing generally it was a miracle, as certainely it did appeare, for
the Christians did not alone sée this thing, but also the
Indians dyd muche note it, for the maruelous fiercenesse

margin note: A sodaine disease.

wherwith

wherwith he came vppon them, with ſuch great murder,
that they were amaſed, and almoſte blynde with hys
bꝛyghtneſſe, being ſo trodden vnder hys féete . The
captiue *Indians* after the battayle declared the circum-
ſtance therof.

The Lord Tauaſco ſubmitteth
himſelfe to the *Chriſtians.*

Ortez releaſed ſome of hys
pꝛiſoners and ſent them to
their Loꝛde, ſaying that it
grieued him the hurt done
on both parties , but the
fault was theirs. And that
god was witneſſe of hys
innocencie and alſo of hys
curteſie offered vnto thẽ.
But notwithſtanding all
that was paſſe, he pardo-
ned their errour with ſuche condition, That if in continent oꝛ within two dayes , theyꝛ Loꝛde woulde come
vnto him , to yélde ſatiſfaction of their malice and
ſtubboꝛneſſe, and to treate of peace and friendſhip, warning and aduiſing them , that if they came not wythin
the time appointed , bee woulde enter into his countrey, burning and ſpoyling with ſlaughter both great &
ſmal, armed and vnarmed: with which meſſage the meſſengers departed, and *Cortez* returned to the towne to
cure his wounded men. The next day came fiftie auncient Jndians to craue pardon foꝛ their offence, and alſo
licence to bury the dead , with likewiſe ſafeconduct that
their rulers and pꝛincipal perſons, mpght ſafely come
vnto

The Ca-
zike enbaſ-
ſadours.

vnto the towne. *Cortez* graunted their requeſt, warning them to make any lyes or yet to conſpire againe: and alſo if their lords came not perſonally,he would not heare any more embaſſadors: with this rigorous commaundemēt & proteſtation they departed. Theſe *Indians* feeling their ſtrength woulde not preuaile, thinking the chriſtians to be inuincible,their Lords and chiefeſt perſons did determine to goe and viſite the chriſtians and their captaine. And according to the time appointed, the Lorde of that town and other foure Lords his neyghbours came vnto *Cortez* with a good trayne of their veſſals andſeruitours, and preſented vnto him,bread,turkie hennes, & fruites, with other like prouiſion for his hoſt,with four hundred piecesof gold of ÿ value of 400. double duckets,wt other ſmall iewels, and certaine turkie ſtones of ſmall value. And twentie women ſlaues,to ſerue to make breade and dreſſe meate for ÿ whole army. He craued and beſeeched *Cortez* to pardon his former offence. And to accept and receiue them into hys friendſhippe. And in token of his obedience, hee and his fellowes dyd willinglye deliuer their bodies, landes and goods into his handes and power.*Cortez* did louingly receiue them, and gaue vnto them certaine trifles of his wares, whiche they eſtemed much. And thoſe *Indians* hearing the horſes and mares ney, they maruelled at their neying, thinking that the horſes could ſpeake,& demaunded of the Chriſtians what they ſayd,(mary quoth they) theſe horſes are ſore offended with you bycauſe ye fought with them,& wold haue you corrected and chaſtened for your ſo doing. The ſimple *Indiās* hearing this,preſented roſes and Gynea Hens vnto the horſes,deſiring them to eate and to pardon thē.

Certaine

Certaine queſtions that Cortez de-
maunded of the Cacike Tauaſco.

Any things paſſed betweene our men & the *Indians*: for where the *Indians* vnder-ſtood thẽ not, their behauiour was much to laugh at. And vſing conuerſation with our men, & ſeeing they receiued no hurts of them, they brought to the towne their wiues and childzen, which were no ſmal number. And a-mong many matters that *Cortez* communed with *Tauaſ-co* by the mouth of *Ieronimo de Aguila* his enterpreter:

The firſt queſtion was: Whether there wer mynes of gold oz ſiluer in that countrey, and from whẽce they had that ſmall quantitye that they hadde broughte vnto them?

The ſecõd queſtion was: Why they denyed him their friendſhippe, moze than the other captaine that had bin there the yeare befoze?

The third was : Why they being ſo many in nũber, fled from them being ſo fewe?

The fourth was: To giue thẽ to vnderſtãd the migh-tie power of the king of Caſtill. And laſt of all to giue them knowledge of the faith of Ieſu Chziſt.

The an-ſvvere of the Cacike.

As touching Sir (quoth he) the Mynes of gold and ſiluer in our country, we ſéeke for none, for we ſéeke not after treaſure and riches, but we pzocure and deſire a quiet life. And that golde whiche we haue, was founde by chaunce: for we know not what Mynes do mean. Yet notwithſtanding further within the lande, whereas the ſunne doth hide himſelfe, ther the people do finde muche gold and are giuen to ſéeke the ſame.

And

And as touching the captaine that was here of late, we seeing the men and shippes to be such as we had neuer before seene, spake vnto them and demaunded what they would haue, they sayde that their comming was, to chaunge their merchandice for gold and nothyng else, wherefore we graunted to their request. But now seeing greater vessels and moe in number, wee feared least ye came to take our substance. And I knowing my selfe nothing inferiour to any of my neyghbours, would not permit any iniurie to be offered me, and that he and his subiectes did esteeme themselues the most valiant of men of warre in all these parties, and that none durste take away their goods, women, and children, to be sacrificed by force, wherevpon he thought to withstande those fewe Christians, but (quoth he) I founde my selfe deceiued, seeyng we could not kill any of your companye. And likewise the brightnesse of youre weapons dyd blynde vs, and the woundes you made were incurable.

But the noyse and lightning of your ordinance dyd more amase vs, than either thunder-clappes or tempest: and also the great spoyle that you made among vs therwith: likewise your straunge horses made vs greatly to wonder, to behold their open mouthes, wee feared to be swallowed. And then to consider their swiftnesse in running, we knew no creature could escape them. But ẙ first horse that fought with vs, put vs in marueylous feare, being but one, but when we espyed many, then all oure helpe was past, for we belieued that the horse and man was al one incorporate.

Hovv the Indians of Potonchan brake
downe their Idols, and worshipped Christ crucified.

Ith the relation of *Tanasco Cortez* sawe that the countrey was not fo2 Spaniardes, no2 yet he toke it a thing conueniente to settle themselues where no golde no2 siluer was, o2 other riches. And so p2etended to passe fo2wardes to discouer westward the lande endewed with golde. But befo2e his departure, he declared to those new conquered *Indians*, that the Lo2d in whose name he and hys company had taken that iourney was king of Spayne and Emperour of Ch2istians, and the greatest P2ince in the wo2lde, vnto whom many kings and P2inces dyd homage and obey. And that hys rule and gouernemente in iustice p2oceeded from God, beeing iust, holy, peaceable, and sweete, and also the *Monar-chie* of the vniuersall did appertaine vnto him. And fo2 these causes he required them to yelde themselues as his subiectes. And if they would doe so, there shoulde ensue vnto them great p2ofite, lawes and pollicie. And as touching their religion, he declared their blindnesse & greate abuses which they vsed in wo2shipping many Gods, and in making sacrifice vnto them with mans blood, yea & thinking that those images and Idols, did o2 coulde doe good o2 euill vnto them, being dúbe, without life o2 soule, yea and ý wo2ke of their owne hands. He certifyed them of one god maker of heauen and earth, and all creatures whom the Ch2istians did wo2shippe and serue, and that

all

all creatures ought to doe the same. In conclusion with thys doctryne they brake downe their Jools, and receyued the crosse, *Cortez* hauing first declared vnto them the great miseries that the son of God suffered on ỳ Crosse for mankynde. And in the greatest temple of *Potonchan*, set vp a Crosse in remembrance of the death of Christ and celebrated the feast vpon their knees, and the multitude of *Indians* likewise, and departed to their meate. *Cortez* desired them within two dayes to come agayne to theyr diuine seruice. And that day was Palme sunday. And so they did and brought an infinite number of men women and children of other villages with them whych was straunge to behold. And there generally gaue theyr vassalship to the king of Spaine into the handes of *Hernando Cortez*, with protestation of perpetuall friendship with the Spanish nation. So that these were the fyrst vassals that the Emperour had in the new Spayne. And this feast and ceremony ended, our men toke shipping with the palme boughes in their handes. In this doyng *Cortez* deserued no lesse prayse than in his victorie, for he vsed wisedome with manhode in all his doings: he lefte those *Indians* with a newe faith, and the towne free and without hurt, he toke none for slaues, nor yet any spoyle nor exchaged his merchaundice for any thing although he aboade there twentye dayes. The towne is called in the *Indian* tongue *Potonchan*, that is to saye, a place that stincketh, and our menne named it, the victorie.

The Lord (as ye haue heard) was called *Tauasco*, and therefore the first Spaniardes that came thyther, named the riuer *Tauasco*, but *Grijalua* called it after hys owne name, whose name and remembraunce will not so sonne be forgotten. And truely all those that do discouer

H.g.   new

newe countreys, ought to make perpetuall their owne names. This town doth containe neare fiue and twentye thousand houses(as some say)but as euery house standeth by himselfe like an Iland, it seemeth much bigger than it is in deede. The houses are great, made of lime stone, & bricke:others there are made of mud wal, and rafters & couered with straw oz bozdes. Their dwelling is in the vpper part of the house, foz the greate moystnesse of the riuers and lakes, and foz feare of fier, they haue theyz houses separated the one from the other. Without, the towne they haue moze fairer houses than wythin foz their recreation and pleasure. They are browne people, and go almost naked, and eat mans flesh sacrificed. Their weapons are bowes and arrowes, slyngs, darts, and lan-

The armor of the Indi-ans.

ces. The armour wherwith they defend themselues, are Targets and skulles made of wodde oz barke of trees, and some of gold very thinne. They haue also a certayne kinde of harneis made of cotten woll wrapped aboute their stomacke.

The good entertainement that
Cortez had in Saint Iohn de Vlhua.

Aptaine *Cortez* and his company beeyng embarked, sayled weastwards as nye the shoar as thei might. And this coast hauing no harbozs, they founde no place where they might Anker safely with their grea-ter vessels, vntill they arriued vpon Maudie thursday at *Saint Iohn de Vlhua*, whiche seemed a good harboz foz them. The *Indians* of this place call this harbour *Chalchi-coeca*, there the fleete came to Anker . They were not so sone at Roade, but incontinente came two
little

little boates named *Acalles*, enquiring for the Generall
of the Fléete, who when they came to hys presence,
dyd humble reuerence vnto him, and sayde vnto hym
that *Teudille* the Gouernoure of that Prouince sente to
knowe what people they were, and what they woulde
haue, and whether they meante to ſtay there or procéde farther. *Aguillar* dyd not well vnderſtande that
language. *Cortez* cauſed them to come aboorde hys
Shyppe, geuyng them thankes for theyr paynes and
viſitation. Hée made vnto them a banket of Wyne and
Conſerua, and ſayde vnto them, that the nexte day followyng hée woulde come alande, and talke with the
Gouernoure, whome hée beſoughte not to alter him nor
hys people wyth hys commyng a ſhore, for he meant not
to moleſt hym, but rather to pleaſure and profyte hym.
So that theſe meſſengers were rewarded wyth certayne gyftes, they eate and dranke, but yet ſuſpected
euill, although they lyked the Wyne well, wherefore
they deſired to haue thereof, and alſo of the Conſerua,
to preſente vnto theyr Lorde, whyche was giuen them,
and ſo departed.

The nexte daye béeyng good Friday, *Cortez* came
alande wyth hys Boates full of menne, and broughte
hys Horſes and artillerie aſhore by little and little,
wyth all hys menne of warre, and two hundred *Indians* of *Cuba*, whyche ſerued to toyle and laboure.
Hée planted hymſelfe in the beſt ſcituation that hée
coulde fynde among the Sandy bankes on the Sea
ſyde, and there pytched hys Campe, and hauyng
néere that place manye trées, they builte them Cotages
with boughes.

From a little Village that was at hand, came many
Indians to gaze at things ſo ſtraunge, and the like neuer
ſéene vnto them, and broughte wyth thé gold to barter for

suche toyes, as the two little Boates had broughte from
them before. They brought also bread and meate readie
dressed after their vse likewise to sell. Oure men chaunged wyth them beadestones of glasse, loking glasses,
sissers, kniues, pinnes, and suche other wares, whereof
the *Indians* were not a little glad, returning home to
their houses, shewing their neighbours. The ioy and
pleasure that these simple soules toke with these trisles,
was so greate, that the nert day they came agayne wyth
other *Indians* ladē with Jewels of gold, Turkie Hennes,
bread, meate, and fruite, that suffised for all the Campe,
and for the same they receyued nedels, and beadestones
of glasse, but the poore soules thought themselues therewith so riche, that they knewe not where they were
with ioy and pleasure, yea and they thoughte that they
hadde deceyued the Straungers. Nowe *Cortez* seeyng
the greate quantitie of golde broughte and bartered so
foolishly for trifles of no valewe, proclaymed throughout
all hys host, that no Christian shoulde take any golde

VVise-
dome.

vppon greate penaltie, and that they shoulde all shewe,
as though they knewe not to what purpose the golde
serued, and that they passed not for it, bycause they
shoulde not thynke that the desire thereof had broughte
them thyther, and so they did dissemble that great demonstration of golde, to see what was meante thereby,
and whether the *Indians* hadde brought that golde, to
proue whether theyr comming was for that or no. On

The com-
ming of the
Gouernor.

Easter day in the morning, came *Teudilli* the Gouernour
to the Campe, from *Cotosta* hys dwelling place, whyche
was eyght leagues from thence. He brought attendyng
vpon his person foure thousande men without weapon,
and the most part well clothed, some of them with garments of Cotton, riche after their manner. And others
naked, laden with victuals in great abundance, whiche
was

was ſtraunge to ſée. *Teudilli* accozding to their vſance, did his reuerence to the Captaine, burning frankinſence, and little ſtrawes touched in blouð of his owne boðye, he pzeſented vnto him the victuals, and certayne Iewels of golde very riche and well wzought, and other things made of feathers very curious ſtraunge and artificiall. *Cortez* embzaced him in his armes, and receyued hym ioyfully, ſaluting all hys company. He gaue to *Teudilli* a coate of ſilke, a bzoche, and a coller of glaſſe, with many other péeces of Haberdaſhe wares, whiche was highly eſtéemed of him.

^{A ſtraunge ſalutation.}

The talke of Cortez vvith
Teudilli.

L the fozmer talke was had without an Interpzeter, bycauſe *Ieronimo de Aguillar* vnderſtoode not thys language, bycauſe it differed muche from the ſpæche of the other *Indians,* whereas hée hadde bin captiue : foz whyche cauſe *Cortez* was ſomewhat carefull, bicauſe he would largely haue diſcourſed with *Teudilli.* It chanced that among thoſe twentie women giuen hym in *Potonchan,* one of them ſtode talking with a ſeruaunte of *Teudilli,* bycauſe ſhe vnderſtode them as menne of hir owne language. *Cortez* eſpying this, called hir aſide, and pzomiſed hir moze than libertie, ſo that ſhe woulde bée a truſtie and faithfull interpzeter betwixte hym and thoſe *Indians,* and that hée woulde eſtéeme hir as his Secretarie. And further demanded of hir of what lignage ſhe was, then ſhe aunſwered, that ſhe was naturall of the Countrey that bozdered vpő *Xalixco,* and of a towne

^{A maruelous happe.}

called *Viluta*, daughter vnto riche parentes, and of the kinrede of the Lorde of that lande. And béyng a little girle, certayne Merchantes dyd steale hir away in tyme of warre, and brought hir to be solde at the fayre of *Xicalanco*, whyche is a greate Towne néere *Coasaqualco*, not farre distant from *Tauasco*: and after this sorte shée came to the power of the Lord of *Potonchan*. This woman was Christened *Marina*. She and hir fellowes were the first Christians baptised in all the newe *Spayne*, and the onely with *Aguilar*, were Interpreters betwixt the *Indiãs* and our men.

Nowe *Cortez* béyng assured of hys true Interpreters, hée celebrated hys accustomed deuine seruice, and *Teudilli* wyth hym, and after they hadde dyned in *Cortez* hys Tente in presence of many *Spanyardes* and *Indians*, *Cortez* enformed *Teudilli* howe that hée was vassall to the Lord *Charles* of *Austria* Emperour of the Christiãs, and Kyng of *Spayne*, and Lorde ouer a greate parte of the worlde, whome great Kings and Princes dyd serue and obey: and that all Princes were glad to bée hys friendes for his Vertue and myghte. And hée hauyng aduertisemente of that Countrey and Lorde thereof, had sente him thyther to visite hym on hys behalfe, and to enforme hym of certayne secrete matters, the effecte whereof he hadde in wrytyng. Sir (quoth *Teudilli*,) I am

very glad to heare the Maiestie and Vertue of the Emperours youre maister, but you shall vnderstande, that my Lorde the Emperoure *Melzuma* is as greate and as good a Prince as hee. And I doe muche maruell, that there shoulde bée anye so greate a Prince in the whole worlde, but yet accordyng to youre request, I wyll certifye hym, and knowe hys pleasure, for I trust (quoth he) in the clemencie of my Prince, that youre newes and message shall bée acceptable vnto him,
and

and you well recompenfed fo2 your paynes. *Cortez* then
commaunded al his men to fet themfelues in o2der of bat=
tayle with fife and d2umme, and to fkirmifhe befo2e *Teudilli.* And that the ho2femen fhoulde runne, and the o2di=
naunce fhotte of ,to the entent that *Mutezuma* fhoulde
be aduertifed thereof. The *Indians* did much beholde the
gefture, apparell and beardes of our men, they wondered
to fæ the ho2fes runne, they feared the b2ightneffe of the
fwo2des, and at the noyfe of the o2dinaunce they fell flatte
to the ground, thinking that the heauens did fall. And the
fhippes, they held opinion was the God of the ap2e called
Quezalcouale, whiche came with the temples on his backe,
fo2 they dayly loked fo2 him. *Teudilli* difpatched the pofte
to *Mexico*, to *Mutezuma*, aduifing him of all that he had
féene, and demaunded golde of him fo2 to giue vnto the
Captayne of that newe people. Bicaufe *Cortez* had inqui=
red of him, whether *Mutezuma* had gold o2 no, he anfwe=
red(yes)mary quoth *Cortez*, I and my fellowes haue a
certayne difeafe of the harte, and golde helpeth vs. This
meffage wente from the campe to *Mexico* in one day and
a night, whiche is 210. myle, and the pofte caried paynted
the ho2fes and ho2femen vpon them, the maner of they2
armour, and howe many péeces of o2dinaunce they had, &
what number of bearded men there were : and as fo2 the
fhippes he had giué aduife as fœne as they arriued, fhew=
ing the greatneffe and quantitie of them. All thefe things
afo2efayde, *Teudilli* caufed to be paynted in cloth of Cotten
very liuely, that *Mutezuma* mought fée it. The caufe that
this meffage wente fo farre in fo fho2te a fpace, was, they
had certayne places that poftes attended, as we may fay
ho2fepoftes which gaue alwayes from hand to hande the
paynted cloth: they doe runne on fœte fafter in this fo2te,
than by ho2fepoft, and is mo2e of antiquitie than ho2fe=
poft: Alfo *Teudilli* fent to *Mutezuma* the garments & many

The difeafe of the Spa-niardes.

I. other

other things whiche Cortez had giuen him, whiche things were afterwardes founde in the treasorie of Mutezuma.

The present and ansuvere that
Mutezuma sente vnto Cortez.

Fter the message sente, and the answere promised, Tendilli toke his leaue, and within two flight shote of Cortez his campe, he caused a thousande cotages of boughes to be made, & lefte there two principall men as Captaynes ouer two thousande persons men and women, and then departed for Cotosta hys dwellyng place. The two Captaynes had charge to prouide the Christians of all things necessarie, and the women serued to grynde their corne and make bread of Maiz, and to dresse theyr fishe and flesh and other victuals, and the men serued to carrie the dressed meate to the Christians cãpe, and wod, water, & grasse for the horses and al other necessaries, and this they passed eight dayes. In this meane season returned the poste with a riche and gentle present, whiche was many couerlets and clothes of cotton, white, and of other colours wrought, many tuffes of feathers very fayre, and some things wrought with golde and feathers, quantitie of Iewels and péces of golde and siluer, two thinne whéeles, the one of siluer whiche wayde. 2 5. markes with the signe of the Mone, and the other whéel of golde which wayed a hundreth markes, made like vnto the Sunne, with many leaues and beasts, a very curious péce of worke : these two things they helde for Gods in that countrey, & giueth thé the colours of the metall that is likest thé, euery whéele was two yardes & a half broade, and so proportionally in compasse round aboute, this present was estéemed at 20900. Ducates. This present shold
                                                            haue

haue bene giuen to *Grijalua*,if he had not so sone departed
as the *Indians* reported.He also gaue vnto *Cortez* this an=
swere, that *MuteZumas* his Lorde was very gladde to
know,& to be friend to suche a mighty Prince as the king
of Spayne was,and that in his time should arriue in his
countrey such new people, & the like neuer sœne befoze, &
that he was readie to shew them al pleasure & honour,re=
questing him to sœ what things he stœde in nœde of foz ye
time that he meant to abide there,as well foz himselfe as
foz his ships,army and dcceasse, and it should be pzouided
abundantly : yea & also if he could finde any thing in that
countrey to his contentment, to pzesent to the Empcrour
of Chzistians,he would willingly pzouide it. And as tou= The ex=
cuse of
Mutezuma
ching the desire that *Cortez* had to come to visite & to haue
cōmunication with him,he thought it vnpossible, bycause
that he was sickly and could not come vnto the sea coast,
and likewise foz *Cortez* to come where he did abide,it was
harde,troublesome and difficill,as well foz the many and
cragged mountaynes,as also the countrey, wilde,desert &
without habitation, and shoulde be constrayned to suffer
hunger,thirst,and other necessitie : and mozeouer the en=
habitaunts of much part of the way that he should passe,
were his enimies, both cruell & cursed people, and know=
ing thē to be his friendes,they should not escape with life.

All these excuses did *MuteZuma* by the mouth of *Teudilli* declare vnto *Cortez*,thinkyng to dziue him frō his pur=
pose & pzetēded iourney,alleaging the fozesayd difficulties
and perils,the *Indians* did also hope that with some cōtra=
ry weather they should be fozced to leaue that coast & cou=
trey. Notwithstāding this cōtradiction,so much the moze
desire had *Cortez* to visite *MuteZuma*,who was so great a
pzince in that parties,& thzoughly to discouer the treasure
which he imagined to be there.And hauing receiued ye pze=
sent,& also ye answer, he gaue vnto *Teudilli* a garmēt of his

I.ij.   owne

owne wearyng,and many other trifles of his Haberdaſh,
to be ſente vnto *Mutezuma*, ſaying that if it were foꝛ no
other purpoſe but onely to ſée ſo mightie and vertuous a
Pꝛince, it ſhould be requiſite and iuſte to trauayle vnto
his Court,how much the moꝛe, he was of duetie cóſtray-
ned to doe the Embaſſage which the Emperour of Chꝛiſtians had willed and commaunded him to doe, foꝛ other-
wyſe he ſhoulde incurre the diſpleaſure of the Ring his
mayſter, wherefoꝛe he beſought *Teudilli* yet once agayne
to aduertiſe *Mutezuma* of his conſtant determination,by-
cauſe hée ſhoulde vnderſtande that he would not leaue off
hys pꝛetended purpoſe foꝛ any inconuenience that was
obiected vnto him. Alleagyng moꝛeouer,that he who had
cómen 2000. leagues by ſea,mought well goe 70.leagues
by lande,and conſideryng that he had many at his charge
with ſmall pꝛouiſion, and likewiſe his ſhippes in daunger,he required that with all expedition the meſſengers
ſhould be diſpatched. *Teudilli* deſired him to recreate himſelf, ⁊ not to take any grief,foꝛ as much as he himſelf did
dayly aduertiſe *Mutezuma* of his pꝛocédings, euen ſo
with all expedition the full reſolution ſhould come from
Mexico,although it were ſomewhat farre off. And as foꝛ
his victuals, he ſhoulde take no care, foꝛ abundantly he
ſhould be pꝛouided.And alſo deſired him foꝛ ſo much as he
was not well placed among thoſe ſandy bankes,that it
might pleaſe him to goe with him to certayne townes a-
boute ſire oꝛ ſeuen leagues frō thence. *Cortez* refuſed that
offer,wherevpon *Teudilli* departed, and he abode there ten
dayes looking foꝛ anſwere from *Mutezuma*.

Hovv

Hovv Cortez knevv of difcorde and
diffention to be in the Countrey.

In this meane feafon certayne *Indians* were efpied, that went lurkyng a farre of among the fandy hilles. And thofe came not neare the *Indians*, that ferued the Spaniarde, *Cortez* demaunded what people they were, & for what caufe they went lurkyng fo farre off, and came no néerer vnto them.

The two Captaynes anfwered, that they were hufbandmen, that went aboute theyr hufbandry. *Cortez* lyked not theyr anfwere, but fufpected that they had tolde hym a lye: for it féemed vnto hym that thofe people defired to come among the Chriftians, and that they durfte not with feare of the *Indians* of *Teudilli*, and fo it was in very déede. For all that coafte and mayne lande within, as farre as *Mexico*, was full of the newes and ftraunge things that our men had done in *Potonchan*. Wherefore they all defired to fée them and to talke with them, but they durfte not for feare of the *Indians* of *Culhua*, who are fubiectes vnto *Mutezuma*, wherevpon *Cortez* fente fiue Spaniardes to call them with fignes and tokens of peace. This company of *Indians* were in number twentie, and were gladde to beholde thofe fiue men commyng towardes them, and were defirous to fée fuche ftraunge people and fhippes, wherefore they came willingly altogither vnto *Cortez* his Tente.

Thefe *Indians* dyd differ muche from all the other *Indians* yet féene, for they were hygher of perfon, and had the gryftels of theyr nofes flitte, hangyng ouer their mouths, and rings of Jette and Amber hanging thereat. The Indiã attyre. They had alfo theyr neither lippes bored, and in the holes rings of golde and turky ftones, whiche wayed fo muche,

that

that their lippes hanged downe ouer they꞊ chinnes, and their tæth remayned bare:The whiche cuſtome although they vſed fo꞊ a b꞊auery, it ſæmed a faule and vgly ſighte in the Spanyardes eyes,and very lothſome.

The other *Indians* of *Mutezuma*, had they꞊ lippes and eares bo꞊ed, with reunde ſtones hangyng at the iagges thereof, yet they had not ſuche foule ſlittes in their noſes, but they had ſuche bo꞊ed holes that a manne myght put any finger of his hande th꞊ough them, with rings of golde and ſtone hanging thereat,the euill fauou꞊ red ſighte of they꞊ faces made our men to muſe.

Cortez commuued with them by hys interp꞊eter *Ma= rina*, to knowe from whence they were,they anſwered, that they were dwellers in *Zempoallan*,a Cittie diſtant from thence one dayes iourney,ſituated vpon a riuer ſide, and bo꞊dered vpon the Countrey of *MuteZumazin*, and that their *CaZique* o꞊ Lo꞊de had ſente them, to ſæ what Goddes were comen in thoſe *Teucallis*, that is to ſay, Temple,ſaying, alſo that they durſte not come ſœner,not knowyng what people they were.

CorteZ made muche of them and ſhewed a chærefull countenaunce vnto them, fo꞊ they ſæmed very beſtiall, he declared vnto them that he was gladde of they꞊ com= myng, and to knowe the good will that they꞊ Lo꞊de bare vnto him, a꞊d gaue them Haberdaſhe toyes, and ſhew= ed them the Ho꞊ſes and Armour, a ſtraunge ſighte fo꞊ them . And ſo they wente th꞊ough the army lœkyng and gaſing here and there as menne ama꞊ed. And in all the tyme they abode there,they vſed no conuerſation with the other *Indians*. *Cortez* enquired of *Maryna* the cauſe thereof, and ſhæ ſayde that thoſe menne did not onely ſpeake an other languague, but alſo did appertayne to another Lo꞊de, who was not vaſſall to *MuteZuma*,but by fo꞊ce and exto꞊tion.

CorteZ

Cortez was very glabbe of that newes, for hée conjectured by the talke of *Teudilli* that *Mutezuma* had warres and eniimies, wherevppon hée tooke afide thrée of thofe *Indians* whiche ſéemed moſte wyſeſt, and demaunded of them by *Maryna* what Loꝛdes there were in that Countrey: they anſwered that *Mutezuma* was Loꝛde ouer all, although in euery Cittie and Pꝛouince was a Loꝛde, yet neuertheleſſe all in generall dyd paye tribute and ſerue him as vaſſals, nay rather lyke ſlaues.

But yet many of them of late dayes did reknowledge hym by foꝛce of armes, and payde vnto him ſuche tolle and tribute that they were not accuſtomed to pay, of whiche number their Loꝛde of *Zempoallan* was one of them, and other his neyghbours, who many tymes helde him warre to be frée from his tiranny and bondage, but yet ſayde they, it pꝛeuayled not, foꝛ his hoſte was greate and his warriers valiant.

Cortez receyued greate pleaſure to finde in that countrey diſſention and diſcoꝛde among ſome Noble menne, and at deuiſion among themſelues, thynking thereby the better to bꝛyng his purpoſe to paſſe. He gaue thanks vnto thoſe *Indians* foꝛ their aduiſe, offeryng vnto them his fauour, helpe and friendſhippe, pꝛaying them to come often to his campe, and ſo tooke his leaue of them, with his commendations to their Loꝛde, and ſente him certayne pꝛeſents, with aduertiſement, that ſhoꝛtly he would come and ſée him, yea and alſo ſerue him.

Hovy

Hovv Cortez vvent to furuey the
Countrey with foure hundreth men.

 T the ende of tenne dayes came *Teudilli*
backe againe, and brought certaine cloth
of Cotten, and other things made of feathers well wrought for recompence of
the thyng sente vnto *Mexico*, and warned *Cortez* to departe, for at that tyme
there was no remedie to see *Mutezuma*, and to loke what
was necessary for his prouision and furniture, and it
shoulde be prouided, offeryng the same seruice at any time
that hee shoulde happen to come that way. *Cortez* would
not accept the offer, saying : That he would not departe
from that countrey, vntill he had bothe seene and talked
with *Mutezuma*. The gouernour *Teudilli* yet agayne replied, that he shoulde not contende therein, and with those
wordes departed from hym. The nexte night followyng
he with all those *Indians* as well men as women whiche
attended to serue and prouide the Spanishe campe, wente
from thence : so that in the mornyng all the cotages were
emptie, where those seruitors had bene.

Cortez suspecting this alteratió prouided himselfe with
preparation for battayle, & finding the matter contrary to
his expectation, he deliberated to seeke a sure roade or harbor for his nauie, & also a good plotte or situation to buylde
vpon, for then he fully meant to obtayne perpetuitie & to
conquere the lande, considering ý he had found such great
tokens of gold, plate, & other riches, & thereaboute within
a whole league cópasse was no fit place for ý purpose: for
why? all was sandy ground, & such as tossed to & fro with
the winde, with other morish groúd not meete for habitation. In consideration wherof he sent *Francisco de Monteio*,
with two vergantines, and fiftie men, to runne along the
coast,

Coaſt, vntill they ſhould finde ſome reaſonable poart and good ſcituation to build vpon.

Monteio proceeded on his voyage, and ſayled in ſighte of lande, vntill he came to Panuco, withoute finding anye port or harbor, ſauing the ſhadowe of a Rocke, whyche ſtode ſomewhat diſtant from the land a ſea bord, ſo that at three weekes ende he returned backe agayne with the foreſayde newes. Hauing runne ſo little a way, he fell in- to ſuche terrible currants, that although he made waye wyth oares and ſayles, yet the ſayde Currant forced hym backe agayne. Alſo he broughte newes, that the Indians of that coaſt did let themſelues blaud, offering the ſame vnto them vpon little ſtrawes, in token of friendſhip or deitie.

The relation of Monteio contented not Cortez, yet notwithſtandyng he pretended to goe to the ſhade or ſuccoure of the Rocke, bycauſe hee was enformed, that neere that place, was two fayre Riuers, wyth ſtore of woddes, neceſſarye for tymber and fyre wodde, greate quantitie of ſtones to builde with, fayre paſtures, and ground for tyllage, although the harbour was not ſufficiente for hys Nauie and contratation, bycauſe that roade was without defence, and open vppon the Northe, which is the winde that moſt ruleth with greateſt hurte vpon that coaſt.

And alſo conſidering that Teudilli and hys menne were departed, fearing alſo the want of victuals, and likewiſe, that hys Shyppes myghte periſhe vppon the ſhore, he commaunded to lade aboorde all they ſtuffe, and hee wyth foure hundred menne, and all his Horſes, followed on the hygh way that the Indians hadde gone.

After hee hadde iourneyed three leagues, hee came to a fayre badeable Riuer, and paſſing ouer the Riuer, hee

K.   founde

found a towne not inhabited, for the inhabitantes thereof were fledde with feare : he entred into a great house, which seemed the place of the Lorde of the Towne, built with timber and earthen walles, the foundation whereof was raysed with handie worke, about a fadome high: the roofe was couered with strawe, but of a fayre & strange workemanshippe inwardes, with many greate pertitions, some full of pottes of honey, and Maiz, with other grayne whiche they keepe in store all the yeare: other roomes had cloth of Cotten wool, wrought with feathers, golde and siluer.

Cortez commaunded Proclamation to be made, that none of his company shoulde take any thyng away, vppon payne of deathe (onely victuals excepted) to the intente to obtayne the good will and friendship among the *Indians.*

There was in that Uillage a Temple, whiche hadde a little Tower with a Chappell on the toppe, and twentie steppes to come vnto the Chappell, where they found some Idolles, and many bloudy papers, and much mans bloud of those which hadde bin sacrificed, as *Marina* dyd certifie.

They found also the blocke whereuppon they vsed to cutte open the menne sacrificed, and the razors made of Flint, wherewyth they opened theic breastes, and plucked out their heartes beyng aliue, throwing them vppe toward Heauen as an offering, and after this done, they annoynted their Idolles, and the papers they offered, and then burned them.

This sight put a great compassion, yea and a feare among our *spanyards,* who did beholde these things. From this Uillage they went to other three or foure, and found none aboue two hundred houses, and all without people, yet well prouided with victuall, as the firste towne was.

Cortez

Cortez returned from thence to discharge his Shippes, and to take order to sende for moe men : and with desire to beginne habitation, in these affaires he occupyed hymselfe tenne dayes.

Hovv Cortez rendred vp his charge
and office with pollicie.

Hen *Cortes* was come where his Ships were, and the residue of his company, hǣ began this talke, saying :

Now my louing friends and fellowes, ye doe sǣ what greate mercy God hathe shewed vnto vs, in bringing vs safe and in health to so good and riche a Countrey, as by manifest signes and tokens we haue alreadye sǣne, yea and howe plentifull of meate, inhabited of people, better clothed, and of more iudgement and reason,than the others which ye haue sǣne, since your firste comming : also better buildings,fieldes of grayne and corne;yea and it is to be thought, that the things not yet sǣne, doe surmount all that hithervnto ye haue playnely sǣne. Wherefore wǣ ought to giue most hartie thankes vnto God, and to beginne oure habitation hǣre, whereas we shall enioy the grace and mercy of God. And to bryng this matter to passe, me thinke best that we abite hǣre, vntill we may finde a better port or scituation. Also that we make a wall or Castell for oure defence,if nǣde shou'de happen, for the people of this land hath little ioy of our comming and abiding hǣre.

It was then considered that frō that place they might the soner haue friendshippe and contradation with the *Indians* and Townes nexte adioyning, as *Zempoallan*, and others whyche were enimies to *Mutezuma,* and bǣyng in this order once placed , they myghte

B.y.   discharge

discharge their Shyppes, and sende them incontinent to
Cuba , Santo Domingo , Iamayca, Borriquen, and other J-
landes, o2 elfe to *spayne* fo2 mo2e men, armour and Ho2-
ſes, and fo2 clothing and bictuals.

Mo2eouer, it was thought iuſt and méete, to ſende relation of all their p2océdings to the Emperoure they2
King and maiſter, with the demonſtration of golde, ſyl-
uer, and other riches, which they had in their power.

And bycauſe all theſe things ſhould be done in god o2-
der, *Cortez* determined as Captayne generall, to appoint
a Counſell, Aldermen, and Judges.

And alſo o2deyne all other offices that ſhoulde be neceſſary and nédefull to rule and gouerne a Citie, whych
he then p2etended to edifie and erede, the whiche Magi-
ſtrates ſhould fully commaund, bntill ſuch time that the
Emperour ſhould otherwiſe p2ouide in matters conuenient fo2 his ſeruice.

After this diligence put in bre, he ſolemnely tooke poſ-
ſeſſion of all ẙ land, in the name of the Emperour *Charles*
King of *Caſtill,* with all the ades and ceremonies, as to
ſuch a matter apperteyned. And demaunded of *Franciſco
Fernandez* notarie appoynted, that he ſhoulde gyue bnto
him by teſtimonie in w2iting, all the ades done therein.
All his company aunſwered, that they did bery well al-
lowe hys p2océdings and p2ayſed, and alſo app2oued
hys determination, beſieching hym to p2océde acco2-
dingly, ſithence they were come to ſerue and obey hym.
Then *Cortez* named Judges, Aldermen, Atto2ney, Ser-
ieant, Notary, and Towneclearke, and all other officers
apperteyning to the god gouernement of a Citie, in the
name and behalfe of the Emperoure hys naturall Lo2d,
and delyuered incontinent to the Judges white roddes
to beare in their handes in token of Juſtice, and named the newe Citie to be built. The ryche Towne

De la

Policie.

A good
ſubiede.

De la vera Crux, bycause that one goodfriday they had entred into that land. After these things finished, *Cortez* began before ȳ saide Notary, another act in presence of the iudges, who were *Alounso Fernandez Portocarero,* and *Frācisco de Monteio,* in whose handes he made cession, and dyd despst from all rule and offices whiche heretofore he had receiued, whiche was his gouernership, captaineship and general discouerer, receiued in the Chauncerie of *Santo Domingo,* at the handes of the presidentes, who were there chiefe of the kings counsell, and presidents, likewise he protested not to vse the power and audority of the gouernour of *Cuba,* Admirall of *India,* for so much ȳ now none of them had any rule or gouernement in that Countrey which he and his fellowes had newely discouered, and begun to enhabite in the name of the king of Castil, as his naturall subiectes. The which audoritie he likewise required to be set downe in recorde, and to haue a copie of the same.

Hovv the soudiours chose Cortez
for Captaine generall, and chiefe ruler in Iustice.

 L the newe officers toke possession and charge of their offices, and entred into the towne house to counsel according to the vse and custome of Castill. In the which congregation or counsel then holden, many matters were had in question as touching the good gouernemente of the common weale. And among many other things, they al agréed to electe *Hernando Cortez* for captaine generall and chiefe Iustice, and to giue vnto him full power and authority

for all matters appertayning to the wars and conquest,
vntill such time as the Emperour should otherwise prouide: with this determination the next day following al
the Aldermen, Judges, and Counsellers, went vnto *Cor-*
tez, and sayde vnto him : Sir we haue greate néede of a
guide and captaine for the warres to procéede vppon the
conquest of this countrey, wherfore vntil such time as ẙ
Emperour shall prouide therein, they all besought hym
to accepte that office and charge, approuing him a man
most fit for the same, both to rule and gouerne, for ẙ great
experience that they had séene of his courage, wisdome,
and pollicie, and by vertue of their offices, did command
him to accept the same, saying, that in so doing, God and
the king shoulde bee faithfully serued. And they woulde
thankfully gratify the same, knowing that at his hands
they should be ruled with iustice, vsed with humility, ɛ
be preserued with diligence and strength . And for that
purpose, they had chosen him for that office , giuing vnto him their ful ɛ whole authority, submitting théselues
vnder his hands, iurisdiction ɛ defence. *Cortez* accepted ẙ
charge at smal entreating, for he desired nothing so much.

And being in this sort elected general, the counsel said
vnto him. Sir you do wel vnderstād, that vntil such time
as we shal bee better planted in this countrey, we haue
not wherwith to maintaine our selues but only w suche
things as are abord our shippes. Therfore it may please
you to commaund it to be brought ashore, and that you
take therof what shal seme good vnto you, for your houf-
hold and familie, and the residue may be tared at a reasō-
nable price, and so to be deuided among them: ɛ for payment they wold al binde théselues , or else ẙ presently it
should be deducted out of the stocke, after that the kings
fift parte were subtracted. Likewise they desired him to
value his ships and artillery, bycause they would make
like

like payment foz the same, and that frō thence foztwards
the ships should serue in common, foz to paſſe to the I-
lāds foz bzead, wine, clothes, weapons, hozſes, and other
things which should be nædeful foz the new towne and
army, foz therby they mought be better cheape pzouided
than if merchants should pzouide them, conſidering alway they ſeke foz exceſſiue gaine, ſaying that if it would
pleaſe hym to accepte thys offer and requeſt, they would
thankfully requite the ſame. *Cortez* aunſwered, that at y̆
time he made his pzeperation and furniture in *Cuba*, he
ment not to ſel his pzouiſion as others vſed to do, but he   Liberalitŷ
would and did frankely giue it vnto them, although hee
had ſpent his gœds and indetted himſelfe therin. And incontinent he commaunded the maiſters of the ships and
purſers, to bzing a lād al their victual to the town houſe,
requiring the Aldermen to deuide it equally, to euerye
man his part, without making any difference of him oz
of any other, foz (quoth he) in time of nede of victuals y̆
pongeſt hath as muche allowaunce as the eldeſt. And although J am indetted and do owe moze than ſeauen M̃.
Duckets, J giue this victuall al franckly vnto you. And
as cōcerning the ships, J wil do y̆ which ſhal be moſt cō-
neniēt foz you al. And (quoth he) J wil determin nothing
to be done with thē, but wil firſt giue you aduertiſemēt
of the ſame.

Al this did *Cortez* foz to get their loue and fauour, bp-
cauſe there were many that loued hym not, althoughe in
very trouth he was of his own nature liberal and large
in experiences with al his ſouldiers in the warres.

The receiuing of Cortez into
Zempoallan.

Dz as much as the situation there was not conuenient to place the newe wozke, they determined to go from thence, to *Aguiahuiztlan*, which standeth nere the shadowe of the rocke that *Monteio* had infozmed them of, whereuppon *Cortez* commaunded the shippes to depart, foz that place. And he with his foure hundzed men and hozses would goe by land, and there mete thẽ, which may be about ten leagues iozney. In this ozder the fléete departed, and likewise *Cortez* with his company toward *Zempoallan* which stcode directly weastward. And after he had iourneyed thzee leagues he came to the riuer which deuided the Lozdshippe of *Mutezuma* and *Zempoallan*, ẽ coulde finde no passage, wherefoze he was fozced to returne to the seaside, where with muche adoe they passed ouer, and so trauayled on that side of the riuer, ẽ found cotages of fishermen and other poze houses, and some sowen ground, and pzocéding on their iozney at length they came into very faire balleys, wher was great stoze of deare, and stil they went along the riuer side, hoping to finde some god towne, and in shozt space, they espied neare twenty persons uppon the toppe of a hill, *Cortez* commauuded foure of his hozsemen to fetch them vnto him, willing thẽ to make signes of peace vnto them, but if they flie (quoth he) then follow them, vntill you ouertake them, foz they shall stand vs in steade, as wel to lead vs the way as to serue vs foz enterpzeters.

                                                    The

The horsemen tooke on theyr way, and when they came to the hill toppe, they made signes of peace vnto them, but the poore and fearefull *Indians* fledde with spéede, yea being amased and in great feare to beholde suche a monsterous thyng as a horseman, beleuyng assuredly, that horse and man was one thing incorporate, but in theyr flight they were soone ouertaken, and they yéelded themselues, and so were all brought vnto *Cortez*.   Simplicitie.

These men had in theyr eares and noses bored holes, with rings of golde hangyng thereat, for so was the vse of *Zempoallan*, they enformed *Cortez* that the Cittie was neare at hande. *Cortez* demaunded the cause of their commyng thither, they answered to behold and sée so straunge a sight, but why fledde you then (quoth he?) For feare only sir sayde they, of people which we knew not. Then *Cortez* willed them to put all feare aside, and tolde them that he with his small company woulde goe vnto their Cittie to visite their Lorde, and to be acquaynted with him: the *Indians* sayde, that the day was farre spent, and that it was late to goe that night to *Zempoallan*, but if it pleased hym they would conduct him to a village whiche stoode on the otherside of the Riuer and within sight, and although it were but a small village, yet there was reasonable lodging with meate sufficiente for his armie: their counsell séemed well, so they wente to that village, and when they were comen thither, the *Indians* craued licence to goe & to aduertise their Lorde how the straungers abode in that place, promising to returne the nexte day with answere. Some of the *Indians* had licence to do the message, the others abode there, attendyng and prouiding for the newe géstes, & in this order they were al lodged and their supper abundantly prouided. That night *Cortez* fortified himselfe as strong as mought be, and the nexte morning came a hundreth men laden with Hennies, saying that

L.   they

their Lord much reioyced of their comming, and bicause
he was so grosse and vnwealdie, he came not personallye
vnto him, but yet notwithstanding he aboade in the cittie
expecting his comming. *Cortez* friendly welcomed them,
and with that presente, he and his company brake their
fasse, and then proceeded with his guides in good order
with two fauconets in readinesse, if neede should happen:
and: from that passage of the riuer they had a faire way
vntil they came to another riuer, which being likewise
waded ouer, they discried *Zempoallan*, whiche stode a
myle distant from them, all be set wyth fayre Orchardes
and Gardens, verye pleasaunte to beholde: they vsed alwayes to water them with sluses when they pleased.

There proceeded out of the Towne many persons, to
behold and recepue so strange a people vnto them. They
came with smiling countenance, and presented vnto the
diuers kinde of Floures, and sundry fruites, which none
of our menne had heeretofore seene. These people came
without feare among the Ordinance, with this pompe,
triumph and ioy they were receiued into the Citie, which
seemed a beautifull Garden: for the trees were so graene
and high, that scarsely the houses appeared.

At the Citie gate stode many graue persons of nobilitie, as Magistrates of the Citie, who solemnely welco-
Mens folly
vvith a
great lyr. med the Strangers. Sixe Horsemen, which hadde gone
before the army to discouer, returned backe as *Cortez*
was entring into the Citie, saying, that they had seene a
great house and Court, and that the walles were garnished with siluer. *Cortez* commaunded them to proceede
on, willing them not to shew any token of wonder of a-
ny thing that they should see. All the streetes were replenished with people, whiche stode gaping and wondering
at the horses and straunges. And passing through a great
market place, they saw on their right hande, a great walled

led house made of lyme and stone, with loupe holes and towers, whited with playster that shined lyke siluer, being so well burnished and the sunne glistering vpon it. And that was the thing that the Spaniards thought had bene walles of siluer. I doe beleeue that with the imagination and great desire whiche they had of golde and siluer, all that shined they deemed to be the same mettall.

Within this great house was a long rew of lodgings, and on the other side sixe or seuen Towers one higher than another. They proceeded on, dissimulyng the errour of the siluer walles, and followed their guide vntill suche time as they came to the Lordes lodging, who came forth accompanied with many auncient persons, and better attired then the other Citizens were, with two Gentlemen that ledde him by the armes. They saluted eche other according to the vse of their countreys, and then entred into the pallayce, where certayne principall men conducted *Cortes* and all his trayne to their lodgyng, and Captayne *Cortes* was lodged in the house whiche had the glisterpng walles, situated in the markette place, whiche house was sufficient for him and all his company. And when they were placed, and behelde the walles, they were ashamed of their owne folly: for where they thought those walles had bene adorned with siluer, they founde them cleane contrary. *Cortes* deuided his men, caused his horses to be trimmed, and planted his ordinaunce at his dore, making himselfe as strong as though he had bene in campe and neere his enimies. And commaunded, that none of his men shoulde goe out of the house without his expresse licence vpon payne of death, the officers of the Lorde prepared a plenteous supper for them, and bedding accor̄ding to their vse.

A vigilant Captayne.

The talke that the Lorde of Zem-
poallan had with Cortez.

He nexte day in the mornyng came the Lorde, to visite *Cortez* with an honorable company, and presented vnto him many garmēts wrought of Cottē wolle, accordyng to their fashion, with a knot on the shoulder like vnto the Egiptian garments, and certaine iewels of golde that might be worth two thousande Ducates, besechyng both him and his cōpany to recreate themselues and take their reste, and at that present he meante not to trouble him with any matters: And so toke his leaue for that time as he had done the day before, willing him to demaunde and call for any thing that he should néede. *Cortez* gaue him hartie thāks, and so departed.

Then came moe *Indians* in number then were there Spaniardes, with their courses & seruice of meate ready dressed, and many boughes of daintie fruits. In this sorte they were feasted & bāketed fiftene daies most plētuously. The next day folowyng, *Cortez* sent vnto the Spaniardes certaine olde garments of the Spanishe fashion, and many other trifles, besechyng him to appoynt a day of conference at his owne pallayce: worde was sent agayne that he was ready and very well contented. Wherevpon *Cortez* toke with him fiftie of his men all armed, and left the residue at his lodgyng in a good readinesse, and appoynted an vnder Captayne to gouerne them. The Lorde hearing of his comming, came out of his Courte into the streate to receyue him. And hande in hand they entred togither into a lowe hall, whiche they vse for the extremitie of heate in that countrey, the plotte that they buylde vpon is raysed a fadome from the grounde, so that they ascende vpon

vpon ſteppes, and the walles plaiſtered with very white
lime, their tile is eyther of ſtraw oʒ leaues of trées, very
beautifull and ſtraungely wʒought, and a good defence a-
gainſt the rayne. The Loʒde and *Cortes* ſatte them downe
vpon thʒée footed ſtooles made all of one péece, the Loʒde
commaunded his ſeruitours to ſtande aſide, and by their
interpʒeters they began to common of their affayʒes a
great ſpace, in demaundes and anſweres, bicauſe *Cortes*
deſired to be well inſtructed of the affayʒes of that countrey, and lykewiſe of that mightie kyng of *Muteʒuma*.

This *Cacike* oʒ Loʒd although he were huge and laden
with fleſhe, yet in his demaundes and queſtions ſéemed
very wiſe. The ſumme of all *Cortes* his talke was to
ſhewe the cauſe of his comming thither, and who had
ſente him, euen as he had done in *Tabaſco* to *Teudilli* and
others.

This *Cacike* after he had heard *Cortes* attentiuely, he began a long communication, makyng his complaynt and
opening his griefe in this ſoʒte.

Ightie Sir, my Anteceſſoʒs liued a long tyme in
great peace, libertie and quietneſſe, but of late yéeres
my countrey and Cittie was deſtroyed by tiranny, bycauſe the Loʒdes of *Mexico Tenuchtitlan* with their men
of *Culhua* did not only vſurpe my Cittie, but alſo my lands
by foʒce of armes, in ſuche ſoʒte that my power coulde
not reſiſte them. And in the beginnyng thoſe Pʒinces
beganne theyʒ vſurpation by way and colour of religion
and holineſſe, and afterwardes with foʒce of armes, and
with this title became Loʒdes ouer vs.

And nowe we ſeyng our errour, haue thought it to
late to pʒeuayle agaynſt them to take away our yoke of
ſeruitude and bondage, although we haue attempted it.
And as often as we haue ſo done, ſtill the victoʒie was
theyʒs, and the ouerthʒowe ours. Nowe all ſuche as doo

ſubmitte

The Indiãs complaynt.

Vnder colour of hoʒ lineſſe.

submitte themselues vnto them, are taxed with certayne tributes,and reknowlegyng them for Lordes, are defended by them,and esteemed as frendes. But if after such submission made, any chaunce to speake agaynst them, or rebell, then they are terribly corrected,yea murdered, and after Sacrifice made to the Goddes of warre, called *Tezcatlipuca* and *Vitzilopuchtli* of theyr carkasses,then is theyr fleshe eaten in banquet, and those who remayne a lyue, doe serue for slaues, yea and the Fathers, Mothers and Children, are compelled to labour and toyle from the Sunne rising to the Sunne settyng, with confiscation of all theyr goodes and landes. And besides all this crueltie and vituperie,they sende theyr officers and Serieantes to execute the premisses, who without eyther pittie or mercie many tymes suffereth them to sterue with hunger. And beyng this cruelly punished of *Mutezuma*,who nowe raigneth in *Mexico*, who woulde not suffer to bée Vassall willingly to so good a Prince as you enformed me of the Emperour.Although it were but onely to bée frée from suche vexation and robbery whiche suche a mighty King coulde doe. And with these wordes the teares gushed out of his eyes, and pawsing a whyle, he beganne to extoll the strength, magnificence and situation of *Mexico* planted in a greate lake of water, also exalted the riches, courte,Maiestie and mightie power of *Mutezuma*. Hée sayde also howe *Tlaxcallan*, *Huexocinco* and other prouinces thereaboute, as also the people called *Totonaquez* of the Mountaynes were of contrary opinion to the *Mexicans*, yea enimies vnto them, who had intelligence what had happened in *Tauasco*, Yea sir (quoth hée) if it please you, I will treate suche a compact with this people that *Mutezuma* with al his power shall not preuayle agaynst vs.

Cortes reioyced in harte to heare this newes, and
sayde

fayde vnto him . It grieueth mée to heare of the euill vfage of *Mutezuma* towarde his countrey and fubiectes. But I aſſure you with Gods helpe I will deliuer you, yea and reuenge all your iniuries, fo2 my commyng hi= ther is to take away all euill cuſtomes, and to helpe the opp2eſſed, to fauour the p2yfoner, and comfo2te the af= flicted, and chiefly to abolifhe ty2annie . And fo2 the good entertaynement that I haue recepued at your handes, I doe remayne yours to doe you any pleaſure, and to defende you agaynſt your enimies, and the lyke will I doe fo2 your friendes, wherefo2e I p2ay you ad= uertife them thereof as many as are of our confederacie.

Cortes then toke hys leaue, faying that he had bene many dayes there, and that he had greate néede to goe vifite his fhippes and menne, who muche defired his re= turne : And abode in *Aquiahuiztlan*, where hée meante to foiourne fo2 a certayne feafon, and from thence day= ly they mighte conferre of their affay2es . The Lo2de of *Zempoallan* fayde, that if it pleafed hym to abyde with him hée woulde gladly accept it, and if his bufineſſe were fuche that he might not, that then he befought him to re= member him.

Then the Lo2de commaunded eyght maydens to be An other gifte. called, who were very well apparelled after they2 maner, they2 attyre was muche lyke the *Morifca* fafhion , the one of them was mo2e coſtely apparelled than the o= thers . And fayde vnto *Cortes*, all thefe maydens whiche you here fée are Gentlewomen, noble and riche, and this mayden whiche is beſte attired, is a Lady of Maf= fals, and my b2others daughter, I doe p2efente hy2 vnto you, meaning that *Cortes* fhoulde marrie with hy2, and the others you may beſtow vpon the Gentelmen in your company, in a perpetuall token of loue and friendfhip.

Cortes recepued the p2efente with thankes, bycaufe he
                                                            woulD

woulde not offende the giuer thereof. And so departed with their women ridyng behinde them, with many *Indian* women to wayte vpon them, and many *Indian* men to beare them company, and to puruey all things necessarie.

Things that happened to Cortez in *Chiauiztlan*.

He same day that they departed fró *Zempoallan* they came to *Chiauiztlan*, and yet the shippes were not arriued. *Cortes* marueyled at their long tarying in so shorte a iourney, there was a village within shotte of a hargabushe from the rocke called *Chiauiztlan* standyng vpon a litle hill. *Cortes* hauing little to do, went thither with his men, and the *Indians* of *Zempoallan*, who certified *Cortes* that the village was appertayning to a Lorde oppressed by *Mutezuma*. They came to the foote of the hill, without sighte of any man of the towne, excepte twoo, that *Marina* vnderstoode not, and going vp the hill, the horsemen to fauour their horses would alight, bicause the ascending was cragged and euill way. *Cortes* commaunded that they shoulde not alight, bycause the *Indians* shoulde thinke that there was no place highe nor lowe, but that these horses shoulde and coulde come vnto it. So by litle and litle they came into the towne, and finding no creature there, they feared some deceyte, yet approchyng further, they mette with twelue auncient men, whiche brought with them an interpreter who vnderstoode the languague of *Culhua* and the speache of that place, whiche is the language of the *Totonaquez*, or inhabitauntes of the Mountaynes. These auncient menne declared that the cause of theyr goyng out of the

the towne, was bycause that they had neuer séene anye such men as the Spaniardes were, no? yet heard that any such had passed that way, wherefo?e with feare they had fledde from thence. But (quoth they) when the Lo?d of *Zempoallan* aduertised vs, how you did hurt no bodye, but rather being a people good and peaceable, then wee were well assured who ye were, when we saw you come towar? vs. And wee are nowe comen vnto you on the behalfe of the Lo?de, to b?ing you to your lodging.

Cortez gaue them thankes, and went with them to a certaine place where the Lo?d was abydyng their comming wel accompanyed: he shewed vnto the Ch?istians great good wil, and maruelled to sée those straungers with their long beardes.

The Lo?d toke a little chafyngdishe in his hande, and cast into it a certaine gumme, whych sauoured in swéet smel much like vnto frankinscence. And with a sencer he smoked *Cortez* with this ceremony they vse their salutations to they? gods and nobilitie. A straunge salutation.

This done they set them down, and *Cortez* enfo?med him of the cause of their comming into that countrey as he had done in all other places where he had bin. A straunge hap.

The *Casike* certifyed *Cortez* euen as the Lo?d of *Zempoallan* had done, but he stood in great feare least *Mutezuma* should be offended fo? recepuing and lodging him within that towne, without his commaundement, and being in thys communication, sodenly appeared twentye men entring where they sate, w? certain wads like cudgels in their hads, which did signify ? they were rent gatherers & in ech other hand, a fly flap of feathers, the *Cacike* & hys company were soare afrayde. *Cortez* demaunded where-fo?e he so altered himself, he answered, bicause those twéty *Indians* were collecters of *Mutezuma*, and that he feared that they would complayne of him, hauing founde those

M.   Ch?istians

Chriſtians there, he feared likewiſe cruell puniſhment
foꝛ the ſame. *Cortes* comfoꝛted him, ſaying that *Mutezuma*
was his friende, and that he would ſo vſe the matter that
he ſhoulde receyue no blame at all, but rather that *Mutezuma* ſhoulde giue him thankes foꝛ that whiche he had
done : And if *Mutezuma* did not, oꝛ would not ſo accept it,
that then he would defend both him and his ſubiects, foꝛ
(quoth he) euery one of my men is ſufficient foꝛ a thouſand
Mexicans, as *Mutezuma* himſelfe was well enfoꝛmed by
the late warres at *Potonchan.*

Yet foꝛ and notwithſtanding all this talke, the Loꝛde
and all his folke were in great feare, and meante to ariſe
and to lodge the recepuers. *Cortes* woulde not ſuffer him,
and bycauſe (quoth he) thou ſhalte ſée what I and my men
can doe, commaund thy ſeruaunts to appꝛehend and take
pꝛyſoners theſe recepuers of *Mexico*, and I wil abide here
with thée, in ſuch ſoꝛte that *Mutezuma* with all his power
ſhall not offende thée.

With the courage that he receyued at theſe woꝛdes,
he commaunded to lay hande vpon the *Mexicans*, and bycauſe they defended themſelues, they were ſoꝛe beaten,
and layde euery one in a ſeuerall pꝛiſon, and bounde them
The re-
ceyuers put
in pryſon. to a great poſte whereat they were tied by the thꝛoate,
féete, and handes, and beyng in this ſoꝛte impꝛyſoned, they
aſked of *Cortes* whether they ſhould kill them. *Cortes* requeſted that they ſhould not be ſlaine, but that they might
remayne as they were, with good watch that they might
not eſcape: Then they were bꝛought into a hall in the
Spaniardes lodging, and were placed rounde aboute a
good fire, but yet bounde hande and foote with garde of
watchmen. *Cortes* alſo appoynted certaine of his men to
watch the hall doꝛe, and then went to his lodging to ſupper, where he and his company was well pꝛouided at the
Caziks furniture.

                                                                    The

The meſſages ſent by Cortez
vnto Mutezuma.

Þe nighte beyng farre ſpent, and the *In-dians* that kepte the watch being aſléepe, Cortes ſente vnto the Spanyardes that watched at the hall doȝe where the pȝyſoners were, and commaunded them to let goe twoo of the pȝyſoners, as ſecretly as they might, and to bȝing them vnto him. The Spaniardes handled the matter ſo well,that they fulfilled his deſire, and bȝought twoo of them to *Cortes* his chamber, who loked vppon them as though he had not knowen them,and willed *Aguillar* and *Maryna* to demaunde who they were, and what they would haue, and why they had bene in pȝyſon. They anſwered,that they were baſſals of *Mutezuma,* and that they had the charge to recepue certayne tributes,that thoſe of that towne & pȝouince payde vnto their Loȝde. And alſo(quoth they)we know not foȝ what cauſe we are nowe impȝyſoned and ſo euelly vſed. We rather woder to ſée this new cuſtome and madneſſe, foȝ in time paſt theſe men were wont to méete vs and receiue vs with great honour & curteſie, ſhewing all ſeruice and pleaſure. Therefoȝe we thinke that the cauſe of this alteration is thȝough the fauour of you and your cõpany, who beare the name of immoȝtalitie. We alſo fearc leaſt our felowes which are in pȝiſon ſhal be ſlaine,befoȝe *Mutezuma* haue knowlege therof. Alſo ſaid they,theſe barbarous people dwelling in the Mountaynes, would be glad to rebel if they foũd any ſuccour oȝ ayde,only to put their Pȝince to coſt and charges, as herefoȝe they haue done. Therefoȝe they moſte humbly beſought *Cortes* that hée ſhoulde not permitte them and their fellowes to be ſlaine, nor yet to abide in the handes of their enimies wherein he should do singular pleasure to *Mutesuma* their lord, & otherwise if they should perish, their Lord would be very sorowfull that his olde faithful and trustie seruaunts shoulde haue such a reward for their good seruice.

A wyse Captaine. *Cortez* aunswered that it grieued him much, that *Mutesuma* his friend should be misvsed wher he was, no nor yet his seruauntes euill entreated, and that hee woulde haue as muche care ouer them as of his owne, willing them to prayse the god of heauen, and to be thankful vnto him that had commaunded them to be set at libertie, in the grace and friendshippe of *Mutesuma* : he certifyed that in all haste they shoulde be dispatched, for *Mexico* with certaine busynesse therefore (quoth he) get you to meate, and make you strog to take in hand that iourney, trusting to your fæte least ye should be taken againe to your greate perill and daunger, Iwis their meate was soone eaten with the great haste they had to be gone.

Cortez brought them out of the towne and gaue them victuall to carry with them. And charged for the liberty and curtesie shewed vnto them, that they should signifye to *Mutesuma* their Lorde, howe that he was his assured friend, and that after he had vnderstanding of his fame, goodnes and mighty power, he much desired to serue him yea and that he helde himselfe happy, to fynde himselfe at such a time & season to loose those his seruaunts, and to shew therin his good wil, likewyse he woulde do all that lay in him to preserue the honour and audority of so gret a Prince as hee was, & also to defende his subiectes and to loke to his affaires as his owne proper, although his highnesse dyd little esteeme hys friendshippe as appeared by *Teudilli*, who departed from him without bidding him farewell, and likewise absenting all the people of the sea coaste : yet thys notwithstanding he would not
let

let to do him ſeruice at all times when occaſion ſhoulde
ſerue, and to procure by all meanes poſſible his grace, fauour, and friendſhip, and that he was fully perſwaded,
that his hyghneſſe woulde not refuſe his good will and
friendſhip, conſidering that with his acquaintance, God
had done much for him, to meete with a ſeruaunte of the
Emperoures, for thereby he might know great ſecretes
of holy things, and alſo recepue greate benefytes, if then
he would refuſe the ſame, the fault ſhoulde be his: but yet
notwithſtanding he truſted in his wiſedome, that conſidering the thing well, he woulde be glad both to ſee hym,
and talke with him, and alſo to be friende and brother
with the King of *Spayne,* in whoſe moſt happie name,
both he and his company were come thither. And as
touching his ſeruauntes that remayned in priſon, hée
woulde ſo vſe the matter, that they ſhould eſcape all perill, promiſing alſo to ſet them at libertie to pleaſure him,
and that incontinente he woulde haue done it, but onely
bycauſe he woulde not offende the Lorde of the Towne,
who had friendly entertayned him with greate curteſie,
for which cauſe he would not preſume to controll him in
his owne houſe, nor yet to ſhewe himſelfe vnthankefull.
The meſſengers departed with this meſſage very glad
and ioyfull, promiſing to accompliſhe faithfully ý charge
committed vnto them.

The confederacy and rebellion
done by the induſtrie of *Cortez.*

Hen the *Cazike* founde miſſing the two
priſoners, he blamed muche the guarde or
watch, and pretended forthwith to murther thoſe that remayned. Then came
Cortez, and requeſted that their deathe
ſhoulde be pardoned, for ſo muche as they

were

were but officers obediente to their Lozde and maiſter, and accozding to iuſtice they had committed no offence, noz yet deſerued anye cozrection in the facte, whiche was ſeruice to their Bing: but foz ſo muche as they ſhall not flæ as the other two haue done, deliuer them vnto me, and I will take them to my cuſtody and charge.

Vpon this requeſt the eyghtæne prisoners were delyuered vnto *Cortez*, who ſent them abozde his Shyppes, and there commaunded them to be put in prons, The Lozde and his counſellozs fearing what mighte followe, entred into councell what was beſt to doe, conſideryng that they certaynely belæued that the two prisoners whiche were eſcaped, would certifie in *Mexico* the ſhame and cruell entertaynemente done vnto them. Some replyed that it was iuſt and requiſite to ſende vnto *Mutezuma* hys tribute, with other preſentes, to mitigate hys anger, and to excuſe them, and accuſe the Chriſtians, who were the cauſes of the apprehenſion of his officers, and to craue pardon of their erroure and ouerſighte whyche they hadde committed as madde men, in diſhonoz of the maieſtie of *Mexico*. Others aunſwered agayne, that it were muche better to caſt off that yoke of bondage and ſlauery, and to giue no longer obedience to the *Mexicans*, who were both cruell and wicked tyzants, and alſo conſidering that now they had on their ſide thoſe halfe Gods, and inuincible hozſemen, ſaying likewiſe that they ſhould not wante many others their neyghbours and bozderers to help and ſuccour them.

Diuers opinions in counſell.

In this ſozte they reſolued themſelues fully to rebell, and not to loſe ſo good an occaſion, wherevppon they beſoughte *Hernando Cortes* to bæ their defendoz and Captayne, conſidering that foz his ſake they had begun that enterprise, and whether *Mutezuma* ſhoulde prepare hys army againſte them oz no, yet they on their parte were fully

fully pretended to hold hym warre, and to defiff from ſervitude.

God knoweth how glad *Cortes* was to heare this matter, foz he well wayed that it was the high way to hys iourneys ende : yet diſſimuling the cauſe, he anſwered that they ſhould well looke to the thing which they meant to take in hande, bycauſe (quoth he) I vnderſtande that *Mutezuma* is a mightie Pzince, but if ye will valiantly pzocæde, I will be youre Captayne, and ſafely defende you, foz I do moze eſtæme your friendſhip,than the good will of *Mutezuma*, whyche I nothing care foz : therefoze lette me knowe what number of men of warre pæ are able to make. Sir(quoth they)among all our friends wæ are able to make a hundzed thouſande menne of warre. I lyke that well quoth *Cortez*, wherefoze incontinente ſende poure poſtes, with aduiſe vnto all your friendes in league againſte *Mutezuma*, and certifie them of this agræemente and ſuccoure of the Chziſtians, not (quoth he) that I ſtande in næde of your help,foz I alone with my company are able to ſtande againſte thoſe of *Culhua*, although they were as manye moze, but reaſon required that they ſhoulde be warned of your pzetence, and to be in readineſſe foz the ſame, fearing leaſt *Mutezuma* mighte ſende his army vpon a ſuddayne,and finde you vnpzouided.

With this aduiſe and encouragement of *Cortez*, & alſo they themſelues being a people heady and of ſmall conſideratió,they diſpatched incótinent their meſſegers to all the Townes and Uillages of neyghbours and friendes, aduertiſing them what they hadde determined, exalting the ſtrangers aboue the cloudes.

And by this meanes rebelled many *Cazikes* & townes, and all the whole Mountaynes, ſo ÿ there was not left any collectoz oz other officer of *Mexico* in al thoſe bozders,

with

with open proclamation of warres againſte *Mutezuma,* and all his adherentes.

Cortez his intēt was on the other ſide, to ſtirre vp theſe Indians, to get both their goodes, willes, and landes, for otherwiſe, he could not well bring his matter to paſſe: he only cauſed the officers of *Mutezuma,* to be taken priſoners, and to be louſed agayne, he fayned a greate loue to *Mutezuma,* and ſtirred his ſubiectes agaynſte him, he offered to be their defendor, and lefte them rebelled, to the intent that they ſhould ſtand in næde of him.

The foundation of the riche
Towne called Vera Crux.

 T this inſtant the Fléete was arriued at the port, then wente *Cortez* to viſit them, and carried with him many *Indians* of the Rebels, both of that Towne, and alſo of *Zempoallan,* who did good ſeruice to cutte downe timber, and to carrie ſtones to the place appoynted, for the building of the Citie, named the riche towne of *Vera Crux,* accordyng to the determination, when the officers were appoynted for the ſame, and choſen in S. *Iohn de Vlhua,* and in good order made repertition to the inhabitants of the ground, and plottes to builde vpon.

They appoynted alſo a place for the high Churche, a Market place, a Towne houſe, a Gayle, ſtore houſes, a kay or Wharfe, to lade or vnlade, a butcher row, & other places neceſſary to the good gouernement and pollicie of a Towne. They alſo drew out a plot to build the Caſtel or Fort on, nére the roade in a place conueniente, and in this ſort began theyr worke, and their houſes made with mudwall, for the earth there is good for that purpoſe. And euery man being this occupyed in this new worke,

came

came from *Mexico* two kinsmen of *Mutezuma* , with
other four graue learned menne for Councellors, and
many seruing men that attended vppon them, as Ambal-
sadors from *Mutezuma*, they presented vnto *Cortez* certayne cloth of Cotten well wouen, and feathers curiously and fynely wroughte, other pæces of golde and filuer wrought, and a Casket of graynes of golde, as they
were founde in the Mynes not molten, which wayed al-
togyther two thousand & ninetie Casttins, & fayd, ŷ *Mutezuma* hadde sente hym the golde in the Casket, to cure
theyr disease, and woulde gladly knowe howe they fa-
red, giuing also vnto him most hartie thankes, for losing
his two housholde seruauntes, and preseruing the others
from slaughter, besiechyng hym to make accompte, that
hæ woulde doe the lyke in anye affayres of his, desiring
hym also to procure the libertie of the other eyghtæne
Prisoners : and bycause those *Indians* hadde entertayned
hym well in their houses, he did pardon their vproze,
yet notwithstanding he knewe very well that they were
suche a kynde of people, that in shorte space they woulde
committe some other offences, whereby they myght bæ
chastned for all togyther , euen as a Dogge deserueth
stripes . And as concernyng the rest of hys request,
theyr Lorde was not well at ease, and also occupyed in
matters of warre of greate importance , whereby at
that presente, there was no remedie to visit eache other,
but in procesle of tyme his desire shoulde be accompli-
shed.

Cortez welcommed them friendly and ioyfully, and also lodged them in Cotages nære vnto the water side, and
sent forthwith for the Lorde of *Chiautztlan*, that had rebelled, who came at his commandement. *Cortez* sayd vnto
him, lo sæ what troth J haue vsed with thæe, for *Mutezuma* dareth not to send any army, no nor yet displease anye

perſon where J am. Therefore from this daye forwarde you and all youre lignage and friendes maye accompte youre ſelues frée and exempt from the ſeruitude of *Mexico*, without rendꝛyng the tributes accuſtomed. He re⸗ queſted to ſet at libertie the pꝛiſoners, and to reſtoꝛe thé to the Ambaſſadoꝛs of *Mutezuma*. Thys *Cazike* wplled *Cortez* to doe what pleaſed him, foꝛ ſayde he, euen as wée haue choſen you foꝛ oure Captayne, we will not excéede one iote of youre commaundemente: whereuppon hée re⸗ turned home to his towne, and the Ambaſſadoꝛs toward *Mexico*, all well pleaſed and content.

Nowe fame flew abꝛoade, blaſing that *Mutezuma* fea⸗ red the Chꝛiſtians, whereupon all the *Totonaques* pꝛepa⸗ red themſelues foꝛ the warres, taking cleane awaye from *Mexico* their tribute and obedience.

The Ambaſſadoꝛs departed from *Cortez* with theyꝛ pꝛiſoners, and manye other things that were giuen thé, of linnen, wollen, ſkynnes, glaſſe, and pꝛon, being greately amaʒed at the things which they had ſéene.

Hovv Cortez tooke by force of
armes Tizapanſinca.

Ot long after that theſe things had happe⸗ ned, the *Indians* of *Zempoallan* ſente vnto *Cortes*, to deſire him of ſuccour againſt the garriſo of *Culhua*, which *Mutezuma* main⸗ teyned in *Tizapanſinca*, who did greately a⸗ noy them, in ſpoyling, burning, and deſtroying theyꝛ coꝛne in the fieldes, and flew their huſbandmen, and toke many pꝛiſoners. The Towne of *Tizapanſinca* doth confins with the *Totonaquez*, and with the grounde of *Zempoallan*, and is a good ſtrong Towne, ſcituated néere the Riuer, and hath a foꝛt ſtanding vpon a high rocke. And bycauſe
this

this Towne was strong, and planted among them who were alwayes seditious and Rebelles, *Mutezuma* placed there his garrison, who séyng the officers of recepuers and auditors come flying thyther for helpe, béyng persecuted of the Rebels, they wente out to pacifie the Rebellion, and for to chasten them, they burned and destroyed whatsoeuer they found, and also had taken many prisoners,

Cortez hearing this newes, departed towarde *Zempoallan*, and from thence in two dayes iourney with a greate armye of *Indians* to *Tizapansinca*, whiche stode eyghte leagues and more from that Citie.

The garrison of *Culhua* came into the fielde, thinkyng to haue hadde battayle onely with those of *Zempoallan*, but when they saw the Horsemen and the bearded men, they lost theyr courage, and beganne to flye as fast as they myghte possible : theyr succoure béyng nére, they were sone in holde : they woulde haue entred into theyr Castell, but for the swiftnesse of the Horses which stopped theyr way.

And when the Horses coulde not ascende vp vnto the forte, *Cortes* alighted with other foure of hys men, and among the preasse of the Townesmen gote into the forte, and béyng within, they kept the dore tyll theyr companye came wyth manye friendes, vnto whome hée delyuered the forte and Towne, desiring to do no hurte to the inhabitantes, but to suffer them to depart fréely without weapon and standerde. It was a newe worlde to those *Indians*, who did fulfyll *Cortes* hys commaundemente in all poyntes. Thys done, *Cortez* returned agayne to the Sea coast, by the same way whiche hée hadde come.

This was the firste victory that *Cortes* had among the subiectes of *Mutezuma*, whereby all the Mountaynes remayned

The valiant courage of Cortes

remayned frée from the vexations of the *Mexicans*, and all our men with great fame and reputation, as well among their friendes, as among their enimies, in so much that afterwardes when any néede did happen among the *Indians*, they would immediatly sende vnto *Cortes* for one of his men, saying, that one man alone of the Chrystians, was sufficient to be their Captayne and securitie.

Thys was a good begynnyng for the pretence of *Cortes*. Now when he came to *Vera Crux* wyth hys company triumphantly, he founde there *Francisco de Salzeda*, who was come with his caruell which he had boughte of *Alonso Cauallero*, a dweller in *Saint Iames de Cuba*, and was left there to be grounded and dressed at his departure from thence. He brought with him .70. Spanyardes, and nine Horses and Mares, wherewith they all maruellously reioyced.

The presents that Cortez sent to
the Emperour for his fifte.

Ortez made greate hast in building vp the new town and the Castell, bycause the Citizens and souldiers mighte haue succoure againste winde and rayne, and commoditie of householde, and lykewise to bée assured of defence againk enimies if néede shoulde happen, pretending lykewise with all expedition, to enter within the land toward *Mexico*, to visit *Mutezuma*, and to leaue in that newe worke all thing in good order, he finished many thinges, touching as well the peace as the warre.

He

He commaunded to be brought a lande out of his shippes all the armour & other furniture for the warres, with the Merchandise, victuall and other prouision, and to deliuer it to the rulers of the newe Cittie, accordyng to his promisse. He also signified vnto all his company that it was méete and conuenient, to sende relation to the Kyng of all theyr procéedings and dealings in that countrey, with demonstration of Golde and Siluer there founde.

And (quoth he) to deale vprightly in this case, it is necessary to deuide equally our treasure to euery man his portion, accordyng to the vse of the warres, the deuision beyng made, then firste and principally lette vs deduct the Kings fifte parte. And for the better performance therof, I doe name and appoynt *Alounso de Auila* Treasurer for the King, and also I doe elect *Gonsalo Mexia* Treasurer of the armie.

All the newe Magistrates ratified his sayings, and allowed his discretion and wisedome, praysing the election of the newe officers as men moste méete for suche an office, and besought them to accept theyr charge.

This diligence done, he commaunded to bring forth into the markette place all the goodes and treasure which they had gotten, as well cloth of Cotten, Feathers, Golde, and Plate, whiche mought amount vnto in value the summe of. 27000. Ducates: The same he caused to be deliuered vnto the newe elected treasorers by account, requestyng the whole counsell of the Cittie that they shoulde make deuision therof. The counsellours and communaltie replyed, saying : Sir here is nothing to deuide, for deductyng the fifte parte whiche appertayneth to the King, all the reste shall be to make payment for the furniture whiche you prepared for this voyage, and you beyng satisfied, then the shippes, munition and furniture shall

P.iij.

ſhall ſerue in common foʒ vs all,beſéching him with one
aſſent to take all the treaſure,and to ſende vnto the kings
maieſtie his poʒtion oʒ fifte parte, euen as ſhoulde ſéme
moſt conuenient vnto him.

Liberalitie
of Cortez.

Cortes replied and ſayde,that time hereafter ſhoulde
ſerue to pay him accoʒding to their gentle offer: But foʒ
this pʒeſent time my louyng felowes (quoth he) I will
recepue no moʒe than the ſhare oʒ poʒtion that appertay=
neth vnto my office of generall Captayne, and all the re=
ſidue ſhal be foʒ the Gentlemen of my company, where=
with yé may beginne to make payment of your debtes,
whiche ye ought when ye made your pʒouiſion to come
with me on this voyage.

And where I haue appoynted certayne things to ſend
to the King,of moʒe value than his fifte parte, it mighte
pleaſe them, foʒ as muche as they were ſuche things as
coulde not be well deuided, and likewyſe the firſte fruite
of that Conqueſt,fréely to giue him libertie to vſe his diſ=
cretion in that onely poynt.They al in generall graunted
to his requeſt,wherevpon he toke out of the ſtocke,theſe
things followyng.

Inuentary.

Irſte the twoo whéeles of Golde
and ſiluer, whiche *Heudilli* pʒe=
ſented vnto him on the behalfe
of *Mutezuma.*
A coller of golde of eight péeces,
whereat hanged a hudʒeth and
four ſcoʒe and thʒée little Eme=
raldes,and twoo and thirtie lit=
tle

ble redde stones, lyke vnto Rubies, of small value: there hanged at the same coller seauen and twentie little beiles of Golde, and certayne heads of pearle.

Another coller of foure doubled twisse, with a hundreth and two Rubies, and a hundreth and seuentie and two Emeraldes, and tenne good pearles well sette, and for border or fringe sire and twentie belles of golde: both those collers were beautifull to beholde, and had many other fine thyngs wrought in them, than is here declared.

Many grapnes of golde of the bignesse of a pease, euen as they were founde.

A Casket of grapnes of golde of the same sorte.

A Helmet of woodde champed with golde and besette with stones, and at the beuier fiue and twentie belles of golde, and vpon the toppe a gréene birde, with his eyes, beake, and féete of golde.

A sallet of planches of golde, and belles rounde aboute it, decked with stone.

A bracelet of golde of small weight.

A rodde lyke vnto a roiall Scepter, with two rings of golde hangyng thereat, garnished with pearle.

Foure forkes with thrée shepehookes at ech, couered with feathers of sundry colours.

Many papres of shoes made of Déere skinnes, sowed with golde thréede, and in the soales were sette certayne stones of colour white and blewe whiche shyned fayre.

Sire papre of letherne shoes of diuers colours, garnished with golde, siluer, and pearle.

A Targatte of woodde couered with leather, beset rounde about with belles of Latton, and the basse in the midst was

was planched with gold, and there was engraued vpon the fame *Vitſilopucthli*, God of the warres, and alſo
foure heads ſet croſſewiſe, whiche heades were of a
Lion, a Tigre, an Eagle, and an Owle, verye liuely
made with feathers.

Many ſkinnes of beaſt and foule, coꝛried and dꝛeſſed in
their feathers and in haire.

Foure and twenty targets of gold feathers, and ſet with
pearle both curious and gallant to behold.

Fiue Targets of feathers and ſiluer.

Foure fiſhes of gold wel wꝛought.

Two birdes called Auades, and other birdes of gold.

Certaine Hatchets and a rod of latten.

Diuerſe loking glaſſes garniſhed with gold.

Many Myters and crownes of gold & feathers wꝛought
of many colours beſet with pearle and ſtone.

Many faire feathers of ſundꝛy colours.

Many tuffes of feathers adoꝛned with ſiluer and gold.

A garment like a coape of cotten, wouen of ſundꝛy cou-
lours, and in the middeſt a blacke whele made of feathers.

Many ſurplices, beſtments, palles, frontals and oꝛna-
ments of Idols alters and temples.

Many couerlets of cotten of diuerſe colours, whyche
ſhewed like vnto vnſhoꝛne veluet.

Manye ſhirtes, Jackettes, headclothes and other nape-
ric.

Many Carpets and hangings of cotten.

Al theſe things wer moꝛe beautiful than rich, although
the wheeles were very rich, the woꝛkmanſhippe of al the
reſt, was moꝛe woꝛth than the thing it ſelfe. The colours
of the cloth of cotten wool was exceeding fine, and the fe-
thers natural.

The pounced woꝛke in gold and ſiluer did exceed our
gold-

goldſmithes, of whiche things we wil wꝛite in an other place . They ioyned with this pꝛeſent certaine *Indian* bꝛkes of figures which ſerue to their vſe foꝛ letters:theſe bꝛkes are folden like vnto clothes, and wꝛitten on both ſides.Some of theſe bꝛkes were made of cotten & glewe, and others were made of leaues of a certaine trǽ called Melt, whyche ſerue foꝛ theyꝛ paper, a thyng ſtraunge to behold. Straunge Paper.

At that time the *Indiãs* of *Zempoallan* had many pꝛiſoners to ſacrifice. *Cortez* demaunded them to ſend vnto the Emperour, but the *Indians* deſired him to pardon them, foꝛ if we ſo do(quoth they)we ſhall offend our gods,who will take awaye our coꝛne and childꝛen from vs,yea and alſo our liues in ſo doing.

Yet notwithſtanding,*Cortez* twke foure of them,and two women which were al yong and luſtie.

But it was very ſtrange to ſǽ thoſe that ſhold be ſacrificed,how they wer trimmed and deckt with feathers, and went dauncing thꝛough the Cittie,aſking almes foꝛ their ſacrifice & death. It was alſo ſtrange to ſǽ the offerings ẏ were giuen thẽ.They had at their eares hanging rings of gold beſet with turkie ſtones, & likewiſe other rings at their lippes, whiche ſhewed their tǽth bare, a grieſely ſight to ſǽ,but yet eſtǽmed among them a thing beautifull.

Letters from the army and magiſtrates of
the new towne directed to the Emperour.

 Hen this pꝛeſent and fift part was layde aſide foꝛ the king,*Cortez* required the magiſtrats to name and appoint two atturneyes, to carry the Emperoꝛs poꝛtion vnto Spayne. And that he foꝛ his part wold

D. giue

giue vnto them his full power, and letter of attourneye, with also one of his beste Shippes for that voyage.

The Counsell of the newe towne chose *Alounso Fernandez Portocarero*, and *Francisco de Monteio* for that iourneye: whereof *Cortez* was verye glad, and gaue them *Antonio de Alominos* for their pilot, with golde and plate sufficiente for tourne and retourne of the voyage. *Cortez* gaue them instructions, what they shoulde doe particularlye for hym, in the Courte of Spaine as also in Ciuil, and the towne where he was borne. Hee sente to his Father and Mother certaine money, with newes of his prosperitye: hee sente also with them the ordinaunces and actes instituted, and wrote by them a large letter to the Emperour, in the whiche hee gaue full aduertisemente of all things whyche hadde passed from the time of his departure from the Ilande of *Cuba* vntil that day, and of the discord betwéene hym and *Iames Valasques*, and of their greate traueyle and paynes, with the greate good will whiche they all bare vnto hys royall seruice: hee certified likewise of the riches of that countreye, with the maiestie and power of *Mutezuma.* Hee offered to bring in subiection vnto his royall Crown and state of Castil, al that Empire, & to winne also the greate Citie of *Mexico*, and to bring that mightie king *Mutezuma* to his handes quicke or deade.

Beséeching the Emperours maiestie to haue hym in remembraunce when offices and prouisions shoulde bee sente vnto that newe Spayne latelye discouered at hys great costes, and in recompence of hys paines and trauell.

The Counsell and magistrates of *Vera Crux* wrote also

alſo two letters to the Emperour, the one was touching the ſucceſſe of their pꝛocædings in his royall ſeruice. In that letter, went onely the Aldermens firmes,
and Iudges,

The other letter was firmed by the generalitye and
chiefeſt of the army, the contentes whereof was in ſub-
ſtance, that they would holde and kepe that towne and
countrey wonne, in his royall name, oꝛ ende theyꝛ ly-
nes in the quarrel, if his maieſtie did not otherwiſe determyne.

They alſo moſte humblye beſought him, that the gouernement thereof, and of al that hereafter ſhoulde bee
conquered, might be giuen to *Hernãdo Cortez* their guide,
generall captaine, and chiefe Iuſtice by them electe
and choſen, ſaying, that wel he had deſerued the ſame, foꝛ
that he alone ſpent moꝛe than the whole army vpon that
iourney. And that it might pleaſe his maieſty to confirm
that, which they generally of fræwill had done foꝛ theyꝛ
owne ſafegard and ſecuritye, in the name of his royall
maieſtie.

And if by chaunce his maieſtie had already giuen the
ſayde office of gouernement to any other perſon, that it
might pleaſe him to reuoke it.

Foꝛ ſo ſhould it be expedient foꝛ his ſeruice, and quietneſſe of the countrey. And thereby might be excuſed, ru-
mours, ſlanders, perils, and ſlaughters, that myght enſue, if any other ſhould gouerne and rule as captaine
general.

And moꝛeouer they beſoughte hys maieſtie to
graunte them aunſwere with bꝛenity, and gꝺ diſpatch
of theyꝛ attourneys, who departed from the poꝛte of
Aguiahuiſtlan in a reaſonable ſhippe the twenty ſire day
of Iuly. *Anno.*1519.

D. y.   They

Thep touched by the way at *Marien* a poztof *Cuba*,de=
claring that they went to *Hauana* : they paſſed thzough
the chanell of *Bahama* without diſturbaunce, and ſapled
with a pzoſperous winde,till they arriued in Spayne.

The cauſe why the generaltye had wzitten theſe let=
ters was,ſuſpecting *Iames Velaſques*, who had frends and
great fauour in the Court and counſel of *Indias*,and alſo
ſome ſecrete friendes in *Cortez* his campe . Foz *Franciſco
Salzeda* bzought newes that *Iames Velaſques* had already
obteyned a graunt of the Empeoz foz the gouernment
of that land by the meanes of one *Bonito Martinez* going
into Spayne.And although they knew not the certainty
thereof, yet it was moſt true,as ſhal appeare in another
place.

An vproare among the ſouldiers againſt
Cortez,and the puniſhment for the
ſame.

Here wer ſome in the hoſt ẏ murmured
againſt the election of *Cortez*,foz thereby
was excluded *Iames Valaſques*, vnto whõ
they bare good wil.

Some were *Valaſques* friends, and o=
ther ſome his kineſſolkes,who letted not
to ſay openly, that *Cortez* by flattery, ſuttcltie and giftes
had gotten and obtayned his purpoſe.

And that the diſſymulation in makyng hym ſelfe to
bee entreated and pzayed to accepte that charge and
office,was a thing craftily fayned , whereby ſuche
election coulde not bee of anye value, and chieflye
without any ſuch authozity of the Ierome Friers dam,
who

who ruled and gouerned the *Indians* as chiefe pꝛeſidents: how muche moꝛe they hadde newes that *Iames Velaſques* had alreadꝪ obteꝪned the gouernement of that land, and *Yucatan.* Then *Cortez* began to vnderſtande in thoſe mat-ters, and made infoꝛmatiō who had raꝪſed vp this ru-moure, and bæing knowen, he appꝛehended the chie-feſt, and ſent them pꝛiſoners abwꝛde his Ship: and to mo-liſꝪe their wꝛath, he ſhoꝛtly releaſſed them agaꝪne, the which afterwards was cauſe of moꝛe miſchief, foꝛ theſe his enimies woulde haue fledde with a Vergantine and killed the maiſter, pꝛetending to flꝪe vnto the Ilande of *Çuba,* foꝛ to aduertiſe *Iames Velaſques* of the great pꝛeſent ſent vnto the Emperour, to the intent it ſhoulde be taken from their attoꝛners paſſing nære the poꝛte of *Hauana,* with all the letters and relations of their buſineſſe, by-cauſe the Emperoure ſhoulde not ſæ it, to conceꝪue well of their pꝛocædings. Then *Cortez* began to be agræued in earneſt, and appꝛehended diuers of them, whoſe con-feſſions being taken, the matter was manifeſtly knowen to be true, and therebppon accoꝛding to the pꝛoceſſe, hæ condemned thoſe that were moſt culpable, and cauſed foꝛthwith two of them to be hanged, who were *Iohn Eſ-cudero,* and *Iames Cermenio* pilot, and condemned *Gonſalo de Vmbria* and *Alonſo Penate* to be whipped, and incontinent execution was done, all the reſt being pardoned.

With this coꝛrection *Cortez* was moꝛe feared, and al-ſo eſtæmed, than befoꝛe he was, foꝛ certainely if he hadde vſed gentleneſſe, he ſhould neuer haue tamed them, yea and if he had not loked to them in time, he had bin ſpoꝪ-led : foꝛ their pꝛetence was, to haue aduertiſed *Iames Ve-laſques,* who would haue pꝛeuented them of their Shyps and pꝛeſent, and yet afterwarde he ſente a Caruell after the ſaꝪd Ship, although it were two late.

D.iij. *Cortez*

Miſchefe.

Tvvo han-ged, and tvvo vvhip-ped.

Cortez caused all his Shippes to be
sunke, and broken vpon the shore, a
most worthy facte.

Ortez purposed to goe vnto *Mexico*, and woulo not gyue his Souldyers to vnderstand it, bycause they shoulde not refuse the iourney, through the talke of *Tendilli*, especially hearing that the Citie of *Mexico* was situated vpon water, whyche they imagined to be excœding strong, as in effect it was: and to the intent that they shoulo all follow hym, although againste their willes, he detearmined to spoyle all his Shyppes, which was a strange case, perillous, and a great losse. His intent throughly weyed, he little estœmed the losse of his Shippes to withstand his men from disturbance of his enterprise, for doubtlesse they woulde haue stayed him, yea and rebelled, if they hadde knowen his minde and pretended purpose. He did secretly accord with one of the Maisters of hys Flœte in the nighte season to boze holes in them, that thereby they myghte synke, wythoute anye remedie to recouer them againe.

Also he requested the other Maisters and Pylots to publish among the army, that the Shyppes were so rotten and wormeaten, that they were not fytte to goe to sea agayne, and that they shoulde, when they chanced to espye him and many of his Souldies togither, come and certifie him openly of the estate and force of the sayde Shippes, bycause that afterwardes they shoulde not laye any fault to his charge.

According to this instruction, the Pylots and Maisters did accomplish his commaundemente: for shortlye after they espyed him among a flocke of his companye, and then came they vnto him, saying: Sir, your nauie is not

A famous facte.

not

not to make any moe voyages, by reason that they are
all leake, and spoyled, rotten, and worme eaten, wherfore
according to our duetie, we to certifie you thereof, to prouide therein as you shall see cause. All the Souldiers
gaue credite to their tale, because the Shippes had bin
there more than three monethes. And after long talke a-
boute the matter, *Cortez* commaunded that they shoulde
profite themselues of them the best that they myght, and
as for the Hulles, let them sinke or runne a shore, fayning
great sorrow for so great a losse, and want of such prouision. And in this manner they lette runne a shore fyue of
the best Shyppes, sauyng theyr Ordinance, vittayles,
sayles, Cables, Ankers, ropes, and all other tacle :
and shortely after they spoyled other foure vessels, but
that was done wyth some difficultie , because they
beganne to surmise the intente of *Cortez*, and beganne
openly to saye, that *Cortes* meant to carrie them to the
slaughter house. He then pacifyed them wyth gentle
wordes, saying, what is he that will refuse the warres
in so riche a Countrey: if there be any of you that wyll
leaue my companye, hee or they may (if please them) returne to *Cuba* in a Shyppe that yet remayneth. And
this hee spake, to knowe howe many were the cowards,
meanyng in tyme of neede to haue no trust or confidence
in them. Then dyuers shamelesse persons demaunded
licence to returne to *Cuba*, but they were suche as loued
no warres. There wer also others that said nothing, who
woulde gladly haue retourned , seeyng the greatenesse
of the Countrey , and the multitude of the people,
but yet they were ashamed to shewe cowardise o-
penlye.

   Cortez knowing his souldyers mindes, commanded the
other Ship to be sunke, so that then they were all without hope to goe out of that Countrey at ye time, exalting
and

and praysing the noble minde of *Cortes* shewed in that worthy facte. Certaynely it was a déede necessary for the present time, and done by the iudgement of a stout Captayne, although he lost much by his Shyppes, and abode without succour of the sea. There are few of these examples, which are not of valiant personages, as was *Gmiez Barbaroza* with the cut arme, who a few yeares past brake seauen Galleys and Foystes, to winne thereby *Bugia*, as largely I do write thereof in battayles of ẙ sea in our dayes.

Hovv the inhabitants of Zempoallan
brake downe their Idolles.

Uery day séemed long to *Cortes*, with the desire to sée *Mutezuma*. He nowe began to publishe openly his iourney and departure, and chose out of the body of his host a húdred and fiftie mé, which he thought sufficient to leaue for safegard of the new towne and fort, which was almost finished, and appoynted *Pedro de Hircio* their Captaine, leauing with them two Horses, and two small péces of Ordinance, wyth many *Indians* to serue them, and fiftie Townes round about them in faithfull friendship and league, out of the which Townes they might alwayes haue at their néede fiftie thousande men of warre: and he departed with the residue of his Spanyardes towarde *Zempoallan*, whyche mighte be foure leagues from thence, and was scarcely come to the Towne, when newes was broughte hym that foure Shippes of *Francisco Garray* sayled along hys coast, and were in sight of *Vera Crux*. With this newes he returned incontinent with a hundred of his men, suspecting euill of those Shippes. At his comming to *Vera Crux,*

Nevves.
for Cortez,

Crux,his Captaine there enfozmed him how he had gone himselfe to know what they were,and from whence they came,and what they would,but coulde speake with none of them. *Cortes* beyng infozmed how they roade at anker, toke Captaine *Hircio* and certaine of his company to expect their commyng ashoze, suspectyng them muche,bicause they roade so farre off,being by signes and tokens willed to come into the harbor. *Cortes* hauing wandered neare thzée miles, mette with thzé Spaniardes whiche came from the shippes,the one of them sayde that he was a Notary,and the other two were to serue foz witnesses in their affayzes,which was,to ascite and notifie certaine wzytings, whiche they shewed not:and also to require *Cortes* by vertue of the same,to come and make repartitió of that countrey with captayne *Garay* their generall, foz theyz sayd Captaine pzetended that conquest (as first discouerer of the same,) certifying mozeouer that hée was determined to inhabite twentie leagues distát from that place westwarde neare vnto *Nahutlan*, whiche nowe is called *Armeria*. *Cortes* answered,that they should returne vnto their shippes, and to will theyz Captayne to come to *Vera Crux* with his nauie, and there they woulde commune togither aboute his comming, and if he stode in néede of any thing it shoulde be pzouided. And if it were (as they repozted)that he was comen on the kings affaires, he woulde gladly fauour his pzocédings, considering that he and all his were there in seruice of his highnesse,how muche moze beyng all of one nation.

They answered,that in no wise their captaine noz none of his army woulde come ashoze, noz yet come where as *Cortes* was. With this answere *Cortes* vnderstod the matter,and layde holde of them, and went and placed himself in ambushe behinde a little hill of sande, whiche stode right ouer agaynst the shippes, beyng neare sunne sette,&

P.   slepte

stepte there that night till daye approched, and the mor:
nyng farre spent,hopyng that Garay his Pilote o2 some of
his company woulde come ashoze, meanyng likewise to
appzeheade them fo2 to be certified what courfe they had
made, and what hurte they had done, and findyng them
guiltie,to sende them prisoners into Spayne: likewise he
desired to knowe whether they had spoken with any vas:
fals of *Mutezuma*, and feyng they came not a laude his
suspition was the greater.

A vvife
practife.
Cortes commaunded three of his men to chaunge appa:
rell with the three messengers that came from Garay, and
this done,caufed them to goe to the Sea side, wauyng
with they2 clokes,and callyng fo2 the shippe boate. Now
thofe of the shippes thought by they2 apparell that they
were their owne menne, and came with a do2en perfons
in the skiffe with Croffeboes and Handgunnes. Then
Cortes his men whiche were clothed in other mens gar:
ments hidde themfelues among bushes, as who woulde
fay,they were gone into the shadowe, fo2 to flee from the
great heate of the Sunne,being at that time highe noone,
and bicaufe they should not be knowen.

The Mariners of the skiffe fet a laude two men with
Hargabushes,and other two mé with Croffebowes, and
an *Indian* who went straight way to the bushes,thinkyng
to finde their fellowes.Then stept fo2th *Cortes* and caught
them befo2e they coulde gette abo2de the skiffe,although
they meant to haue defended themfelues,fo that one of
them who was a Pilote, hauing his Hargabushe ready
charged,& would haue shot at captaine *Hircio*, & affuredly
if his match and pouder had bene good he had flayne him:
When the general abo2de the ships perceiued this deceit,
he would abide no lóger,& cómaûded to make faile,not ta:
rying fo2 his skiffe.By thefe feuen mé taken at two times
Cortes was fatiffied,& alfo certified how captain Garay had
sayled

ſayled along the coaſt ſéeking *Florida,* and arriued in a riuer (the King of that prouince was called *Panuco,*) where they founde little golde, barteryng aborde their ſhippes: all their golde paſſed not thrée thouſande Caſtelins, but in exchaunge of things of ſmall value: nothing contented *Garay* on that voyage, bycauſe the quantitie of golde was ſmall and not fine.

With this newes *Cortes* returned to *Zempoallan* with his men which he brought in his company: and there concluded and fully agréed with thoſe *Indians* to pull downe their Idols & ſepulchres of their *Caſſikz,* whiche they did reuerence as Gods, perſwading them to worſhip the God of heauen. And after this doctrine their league of friendſhip was effectually eſtabliſhed, and with other townes adioyning againſt *Mutezuma.* Thoſe *Indians* gaue vnto him gagues to be alwayes faithfull of worde & promiſſe, and offered vnto him as many men fitte for warre & ſeruice as he would require. *Cortes* receiued the gagues which were of the principalleſt perſons of the townes, as *Mamexi, Teuch,* and *Tamalli,* he toke alſo a thouſand *Tamemes,* that is to ſay, men that are carriers, who ordinarily taketh his burden vpon his backe which is halfe a hundred waight, and thoſe fellowes followe the campe with their bagge & bagage: Theſe men ſerued for horſes to draw the ordinance, and to carrie other munition and victuals.

Hovv Olintlec exalted the mightie
povver of Mutezuma.

Ortes departed fró *Zempoallan* (leauing that towne named *ſinillia,*) toward *Mexico,* the ſirtenth day of Auguſt of the ſame yére, with 400. Spaniardes and fiftene horſes, & ſire péces of ordinance, and 1300. *Indians* to the carriers & mé of *Cuba.* And whé *Cortes* departed fró

Zempoallan he had not one vaſſall of *Mutezuma* in his campe to leade them the way towarde *Mexico*, foʒ al were fledde, ſeing the new league, oʒ elſe by commaundement of their Loʒd: and the *Indians* of *Zempoallan* knew not well the way.

The firſt thʒæ dayes iourney the army paſſed thʒough the countrey of their friendes, & were louingly recepued and lodged, eſpecially in *Xalapan*. The fourth day they came to *Sicuchimatl*, whiche is a ſtrong place ſituated on a hill ſide very craggy, and the way to paſſe therevnto is made with foʒce of mans hande as a ſtayʒe. And if the inhabitants thereof would haue reſiſted the entraunce, with great difficultie bothe fœtemen & hoʒſemen mought haue entred the towne, but as afterwarde appeared, they were commaunded by *Mutezuma* to lodge them and alſo to honour them. The rulers of that towne ſayde to *Cortes*, that foʒ as muche as he wente to viſite their Pʒince *Mutezuma*, he ſhould aſſure himſelfe that they were and would be his friendes. This towne hath many villages and farmes beneath in the playne, foʒ *Mutezuma* was alwayes pʒouided there of. 5000. men of warre.

Cortes gaue great thankes to the Loʒde foʒ his curteſſe and gœd entertaynement, muche eſtæming the gœd will of this Loʒd *Mutezuma*, and ſo departed from thence, and wente to paſſe ouer a mountayne very high, the paſſage whereof he named *Nombre de dios*, bycauſe it was the firſt that he had paſſed, beyng ſo aſperous and highe, that there is none ſuche in all Spayne, foʒ it conteyned directly vpright thʒæ leagues, and hath in many places grapes and træs with hony. And diſcendyng downe on the other ſide of that hill, they came to a towne called *Theuhixuacan*, whiche is a foʒte and friende to *Mutezuma*, where our army was recepued and entertayned as in the other towne behinde.

Ayd

And from thence he traueled thzée dayes in a countrey inhabitable,and paſſed ſome neceſſitie of hunger,& much moze of thirſt,bicauſe all the water that they founde was **Troubles.** ſaltiſhe, and many of his men foz wante of other dzanke thereof,whereof they fell into ſickeneſſe:and ſodainely fel a inernaplous Hayle with great colde, whiche increaſed their griefe,yea and the *Indians* of their company thought there to ende theyz liues,& ſome of the *Indians* of *Cuba* died there through nakedneſſe,not being accuſtomed to ſo cold a countrey. After the fourth iourney of euill way they aſcended vp an other hil,and vpon the toppe therof,(to their iudgement) they founde a thouſande carte loade of wood ready cut,neare to a little tower of idolles : they named that place the pozte of wood:& hauing paſſed two leagues from the pozte of wood, they founde the countrey barren and poze,but ſone after the army came to a place whiche they named white Caſtell,bicauſe the Lozdes houſe was of ſtone very white and newe, and the beſte that they had ſéene in all that countrey, and ſo curiouſly wzought,that they meruayled thereat : that towne in their language is called *Zaclotan*, and the valley neare vnto it is named *Zacatami*, and the Lozdes name is *Olintlec*, who recepued *Cortes* honozably, and pzouided foz him and his company abundantly, being ſo commaunded by *Mutezuma*, as hée repozted afterwarde.

And in token that he had recepued that comiſſion from **A ſtraunge** his Lozde, he commaunded fiftie men to be ſacrificed foz **ioy.** ioy,whoſe bloud they ſawe newe and freſhe. The townes men of that towne caried the Spanyardes on their ſhoulders,on ſuche beares as we carry dead men to Churche. *Cortes* enfozmed them(by his enterpzeters)of the cauſe of his comming into that countrey,as he had vſed in other places,& demaunded whether he the Lozde of this towne were tributary to *Mutezuma*.This *Cazike* being amazed

at

at his queſtion, anſwered, ſaying: What is he that is not eyther ſlaue oʒ vaſſall to the great *Mutezuma*. Then *Cortes* certifi ed him, who and what the Emperour king of Spayne was, willing him to be his friend and ſeruitour, & further enquired if he had any golde to ſende him ſome. This *Cazike* anſwered, that he would do nothing without the commaundement of his Loʒde, noʒ yet ſende his king any golde although he had inough. *Cortes* diſſimuled the matter, and helde his peace, yet by and by he deſired to knowe the Maieſtie and mightie power of *Mutezuma*: the *Cazike* anſwered, that *Mutezuma* was Loʒde of the whole woʒlde, and that he had thirtie Uaſſals who were able to make a.100000.men of warre: eche one of them he alſo certified that he ſacrificed. 20000, men yerely to his Goddes : And alſo his dwellyng was in the moſt beauty-fulleſt and ſtrongeſt citie of al that euer was enhabited, likewiſe (quoth he) his houſe and courte is moſte greate, noble, and repleniſhed with Gentlemen, his riches incre-dible, and his charges exceſſiue. And truely therein he ſayde the very troth, excepte in the ſacrifice wherein he ſomething enlarged, although the ſlaughter of men foʒ ſa-crifice in euery temple was very great, yea and ſome hold opinion, that ſome yéeres were ſacrificed aboue. 50000. men. Being in this conuerſation, came two Gentlemen of that valley to ſée the Spanyardes, and eche of them pʒe-ſented vnto *Cortes* foure women ſlaues, & certayne collers of golde of ſmall pʒice. *Olintlec* although he was vaſſall to *Mutezuma*, was a greate Loʒde, and had. 20000. paſ-ſals, and thirtie wiues altogither in his houſe, beſide a hundʒeth other women that attended vpon them. And had foʒ his garde and houſhold, 2000. perſons, his towne was great, & had. 13. temples in it, & eche temple many idolles of ſtone of diuers faſhiós, befoʒe whom they ſacrificed men, doues, quayles, & other things in perfumes & great bene-ration.

ratió. In this place and territorie, *Mutezuma* had, 5000. souldiers in garrison, and ordinarie postes from thence to *Mexico*. Untill this time, *Cortez* had not so amply vnderstoode the mighte and power of *Mutezuma*, yea and though many inconueniences, difficulties, feare, and such like, did represent it selfe vnto him in his iourney to *Mexico*, whiche perhaps would haue amazed some valiãt persons, yet he shewed not one iote of cowardise, hauyng hearde suche a reporte of that mightie Prince, but rather his desire was so much the more to see hym.

Considering now that he shoulde passe through *Taxcallan* to goe to *Mexico*, *Taxcallan* being a greate & strong Citie, and warlike people: he dispatched four *Zempoallanezes* to the Lordes and Captaynes of that Citie, on the behalfe of *Zempoallan* and his owne, offering vnto them his friendship and fauour, giuing them to vnderstande, that those few Christians woulde come vnto their Citie to serue thé, desiring thé to accept the same, thinking assuredly that those of *Taxcallan* would haue done with him as the *Zempoallanezes* had done, which were both good and faithful, who had always vsed treuth with him, eué so he thought that now he moughte credite them, for they had enformed him, that the *Tlaxcaltecas* were their friendes, and so would be his, considering that they were vtter enimies to *Mutezuma*, and willingly would goe with him to the siege of *Mexico*, with desire of libertie, and to reuenge olde iniuries and griefes, whiche they had susteyned many yeares before of the people of *Culhua*. *Cortez* refreshed himselfe in *Zaclotan* fiue dayes, where is a fresh riuer and quiet folke, pulling downe the Jdolles, and placed a remembrance of Christ crucifyed, as he hadde done in all the Townes that he had passed.

He toke his leaue of *olintlec*, leauing him wel pleased, & went to a town two leagues frõ théce along ý riuer side, where-

whereof was Lorde *Iztacmixtlitan*, one of the Gentlemen who had giuen him the slaues and collers of golde.

This towne standeth in a playne grounde of two leagues compasse, which is replenished with so many houses
as doth séeme to touche one another, in that way that
our army passed: and the towne it selfe doth contayne fiue
thousande householdes, standing on a hill, and on the one
side thereof is the Lordes house with a strong forte, being the beste yet séene in those parties, walled with good
stone with barbucan and déepe ditche. There *Cortes* rested himselfe thrée dayes, abiding the foure messengers
whiche he sent from *Zacloton*, to knowe the answere that
should be brought.

The first encounter that Cortez had
with the men of *Tlaxcallan*.

Ortes seyng the long tarying of the messengers, he departed from *Zaclotan* without
any intelligence from *Tlaxcallan*. Our cáp
had not marched much after their departure from that place, but they came to
a great circuite of stone made without lyme or morter,
being of a fadom and a half high, and twentie foote brode,
with loupe holes to shoote at : that wall crossed ouer all
the valley from one mountayne to another, and but one
onely entraunce or gate, in the whiche the one wall doubled against the other, and the way there was fourtie
paces brode, in such sort, that it was an euill and perilous
passage, if any had bene there to defend it. *Cortes* demaunded the cause of that circuite, and who had buylte it,
Iztacmixtlitan that wente to beare him company, tolde
him that it was but a deuision from their countrey and
Tlaxcallan, and that their antecessors had made the same
to

A straunge
vvall.

to diſturbe the entrance of the *Tlaxcaltecas* in time of
warre, who came to robbe and murther them, bycauſe of
the friendſhip betwixte them and *Mutezuma,* whoſe vaſſals they were.

That ſtrange and coſtly wall, ſeemed a thing of greate
maieſtie to our Spanyardes, and moʒe ſuperfluous than
pʒofitable, yet they ſuſpected that the *Tlaxcaltecas* were
valiant warriers, who had ſuche defenſe made agaynſt
them. And as *Cortes* and his army ſtoode beholding thys
woʒke, *Iztacmixtlitan* thought he had bin afrayde to pʒo-
ceede foʒward, and pʒayed him (foʒ ſo much as he was his
Loʒdes friend) not to paſſe that way, noʒ yet thʒough the
Countrey of *Tlaxcallan,* foʒ ſo muche as he wente to viſite
his maiſter, foʒ (quoth he) if they knowe you to be my
Loʒdes friende, they will ſeeke youre diſpleaſure, as they
haue done to others, and I will pʒouide you of guides to
leade you continually thʒough the dominion of *Mutezuma,* where you ſhall be well recepued and pʒouided, vntil
you come to *Mexico.*

But *Mamexi* and the others of *Zempoallan* willed hym
to refuſe that offer and counſell in any wiſe, alleadgyng
that it was an onely pʒetence to ſeparate them from the
friendſhip of that pʒouince, whoſe people were good, ho-
noʒable, and valiant, and that *Iztacmixtlitans* perſwaſſion
was to pʒohibite theyʒ helpe and ſuccoure agaynſt *Mutezuma,* willing hym earneſtly to giue no credite vnto
hys ſayings, foʒ he and his allyes are falſe Traptoʒs,
and meante to bʒyng hym into ſome ſnare, where they
myghte kill both him and his company, and feede vppon
theyʒ fleſhe.

Cortes foʒ a ſpace was amazed at ẏ talke of ẏ one and
the other, but in concluſion he accepted the councell of
Mamexi, foʒ that he hadde concepued a better opinion of
the *Zeampoallaneʒes* his allyed friendes, than of the o-
ther.

Q.   thers.

thers. And setting all feare asyde, he toke the way to *Tlaxcallon,* byddyng *Iztacmixtlitá* farewell, and with thrée hundred Souldyers on a ranke, he entred the way in the wall, and procéeded in good order all the way forwardes, carrying the Ordinance ready charged, and he himselfe the leader of all his army, yea and sometimes he woulde be halfe a league before them, to discouer and make the way playne.

And hauing gone the space of thrée leagues from that circuite, he commaunded his fotemen to make hast, bycause it was somewhat late, and he with his Horsemen went to descrye the way forwardes, who ascendyng vp a hyll, two of the formost horsemenne mette with fiftéene *Indians* armed with swordes and Targets and tuffes of feathers, whiche they vse to weare in the warres. These fiftéene were spyes, and when they sawe the Horsemen, they beganne to flye with feare, or else to gyue aduise,

Then approched *Cortez* with other thrée horsemen, calling to them to stay, but by no meanes they woulde abyde: then fyre Horsemen ranne after them, and ouertoke them, & ioyned all togither, with determination rather to dye than to yéelde, shewing them signes to stande still: yet the Horsemen comming to lay handes on them, they prepared themselues to battayle, and foughte, defendyng themselues for a whyle. In thys fyghte the *Indians* slewe two of theyr Horses, and as the *Spanyardes* doe witnesse, at two blowes they cutte off a Horsehead, bridle and all. Then came the rest of the Horsemenne, and the army approched, for there were in syghte néere fiue thousande *Indians* in good order, to succoure theyr fiftéene fyghting menne, but they came too late for that purpose, for they were all slayne wyth the anger that was taken for the killyng of the two Horses,

Ho2ſes, and woulde not render themſelues in tyme : yet notwythſtandyng theyz fellowes foughte, vntyll they eſpyed oure armye commyng, and the Ozdinance, then they returned, leauyng the fielde to oure menne, but oure Ho2ſemenne followed them, and ſlewe a=boute 70. perſons of them, withoute receyuing anye hurte.

Thys done, the *Indians* ſente vnto *Cortes* two of the foure meſſengers whiche hadde bin ſente thither befoze wyth other *Indians*, ſaying, that the *Tlaxcaltecas* knewe nothyng of the thynges that were happened, certifying lykewyſe that thoſe with whome hée hadde fought were of other comunities, and not of their iuriſdiction, bée=yng ſozowfull foz that whyche hadde paſſed : and foz ſo muche as it happened in theyz Countrey, they woulde willingly pay foz the two Ho2ſes whyche were ſlayne, pzaying them to come in good time to theyz Towne, who woulde gladly recepue them, and enter into theyz league of friendſhippe, bycauſe they ſéemed to bé vali=ante menne : but all was a fayned and a falſe meſ=ſage:

A ſubtill meſſage.

Yet *Cortes* beléeued them, and gaue them thankes foz theyz curteſie and good will, and that accozdyng to theyz requeſt he woulde goe vnto theyz Towne, and accepte their friendſhippe. And touchyng the deathe of his Ho2=ſes, he required nothyng, foz within ſhozte ſpace he expec=ted many moe : but yet God knoweth how ſozowfull he was foz the want of them, and not only ſo muche foz thē, as that the *Indians* ſhoulde thinke that Ho2ſes could dye, oz be ſlayne.

Cortez pzocéeded fozwardes aboute two leagues where the Ho2ſes were kylled, although it was almoſt Sunneſette, and his men wéeried, hauing trauelled farre that day.

Q.ij.   His

His will was, to haue pitched his Camp in a strong place of water: wherefore he planted his army by a Riuer side, whereas they remayned all that night with good watche both of footemen and horsemen, fearing some assault: but there was no attempt giuen that night, whereby they might haue taken better rest, than they were aware of.

Hovv there ioyned a hundred and fiftie
thousand men against Cortez.

THe next morning at Sunne rising, *Cortez* departed with his army in good order, and in the middest of them wente the fardage and artillerie, and as soone as they were come to a little Uillage there néere at hande, they mette with the other two messengers of *Zempoallan,* who departed from them at *Zaclotan:* they came with pitifull chéere, exclayming of the Captaynes of the power of *Tlaxcallan,* who had bounde them, and deteyned them from returning: but with good fortune, that nighte they hadde broken loose, and escaped, for otherwise in the morning follewing, they had bin sacrificed to the God of Uictory, and after the sacrifice, to be eaten, for a good beginning of their warres, protesting the like to be done with the berded men, and with as many as came with them.

They had no sooner tolde their tale, when there appeared behinde a little hill about a thousande *Indians,* verye well appoynted after their fashion, and came with suche a maruellous noyse and crye, as though theyr voyces shoulde haue pearced the Heauens, hurling at oure menne stones, dartes, and shotte wyth bowes and arrowes.

Cortez

Cortes made many tokens of peace vnto them,and by
his interpreters deſired them to leaue the battell. But ſo
much the moꝛe as he entreated foꝛ peace, the moꝛe haſtie
and earneſt were they,thinkyng either to haue ouercomen them,oꝛ elſe to holde them play, to the entēt that the
Spanyardes ſhould haue folowed them to a certaine ambuſhe that was pꝛepared foꝛ them, of moꝛe then.80000.
men,whiche they had planted in a crække of a riuer which
abutted vpō the high way. Then our men began to ceaſe
from woꝛdes, and to lay hande vpon their weapons, foꝛ
that company of a thouſande were as many,as on oul
ſide were fighting men, they were well pꝛactiſed in the
warres,very valiāt, and alſo pitched in a better place foꝛ
fight . This battell endured certaine houres,and at the
ende the *Indians* being eyther wearied,oꝛ elſe meanyng to
take our men in the ſnare appointed,began to flie towarð
theyꝛ maine battell, not as ouercome, but to ioyne with
their owne folke . And our men being hote in the fight
and ſlaughter whiche was not litle, followed them with
all their fardage,and vnwares fell into the ambuſhe a-
mong an infinite number of *Indians* armed, they ſtayde
not bycauſe they would not put themſelues out of oꝛder,
and paſſed thꝛough their campe with great haſte ꝼfeare.
The enimies began to ſette vpon the hoꝛſemen,thinkyng
to haue taken their lances from them,their courage was
ſo ſtoute:many of the Spaniardes had there periſhed, had
it not bin foꝛ the *Indian* friends. Likewiſe the courage of
Cortes did much animate them, foꝛ although he ledde his
army making way yet, diuers times, he turned him
backe to place his men in oꝛder and to comfoꝛte them,
and at length came out of that daungerous way into the
playne fielde,where the hoꝛſes mought helpe, and the oꝛ-
dinaunce ſtande in ſtæde, whiche two things did greatly
anoy the enimie to their great wonder and maruell, and

D.iij. at

at the sight thereof began to flie.

In bothe encounters remayned many *Indians* slayne and wounded, and of the Spaniardes some were hurt, but none killed, giuyng moste hartie thankes vnto God for their deliuery from so great a multitude of *Indians* their enimies with muche ioye and pleasure of the victory. Then they wente to pitche their campe in a village called *Teoacazinco*, where was a little Tower and a Temple, and there fortified themselues, and buylte cotages of bowes and strawe. The *Indians* of *Zeampoallan*, and those of *Iztacmixtlitan* did play the valiant men that day, wherfore *Cortes* honoured them with harty thankes.

The care of good souldiers.

This day was the first of September. The night following our men slepte not quietly with feare of inuasion of their enimies, but they came not, for they neuer vse to fighte in the nighte season. And as soone as it was day *Cortes* sente to the Captaynes of *Tlaxcallan*, to requyre them of peace and friendshippe, willyng them quietly to suffer the passage through their countrey to *Mexico*, for that they meant them no hurte but rather good will. This done, hee lefte two hundreth Spanyardes and the Carreirs in the campe. And toke with him other two hundreth, with seuen hundreth *Indians*, and wente with them abroode to skirmishe in the face of their enimies, and at that tyme burned fiue or sixe villages, and returned with foure hundreth pryfoners, without receyuyng any hurte, although they followed him to his campe. At his returne he founde the answere of the Captaynes his enimies, whiche was, that the next day they would come and talke with him and declare theyr mindes.

Cortes was well preuented that night, for the answere liked him not, but rather seemed braue, and a matter determined to be done as they had sayde: lykewise those whiche were taken pryfoners, certified that his enimies were

were ioyned togither to the nũber of a. 150000, mẽ to giue
him battaile the next day folowing, ᚱ to ſwallow thẽ aliue $\underset{men.}{150000.}$
whom ſo moztally they did hate, thinking thẽ to be friẽds
to *Mutezuma*, vnto whom they wiſhed all euil ᚱ miſchief.

It was moſte true that the *Tlaxcaltecas* had gathered
all their whole power to apprehende the bearded menne,
and to make of them a moze ſolemne ſacrifice vnto their
Goddes, than at any time heretofoze they had done, with
a generall banquet of their fleſh, which they called Cele-
ſtial. The Captaines of *Tlaxcallan* deuided their ſouldiers
into foure battayles, the one to *Tepeticpac*, another to *O-
cotelulco*, the thirb to *Tizatlan*, and the fourth to *Quiahuiztlan*, that is to ſay, the men of the Mountaynes, the men
of the Lymepittes, the men of the Pinetrẽs, and the water men, euery of theſe had their Lardes and Captaynes
whome they ſhoulde repayze vnto and obey, and all theſe
foure ſoztes of men dothe make the body of the common
weale and cittie, and alſo commaunde both in tyme of
warre and peace. So that euery of theſe Captaynes had
his iuſt poztion oz number of warriers, but the generall of
al the whole army was called *Xicotencatl*, who was of the
Limepits: and he had the ſtandart of the cittie, which is a
Crane of gold with his wings ſpzed, adozned with Emeralds ᚱ ſiluerwozke, which ſtandart is accozding to their
vſe, either caried befoze the whole hoſt oz elſe behinde thẽ
all. The ſecond Captaine oz Lieutenant was *Maxixca-
zin*, ᚱ the number of the whole army was. 150000. men.
Such a great number they had ready againſt. 400. Spaniardes ᚱ yet at length ouercome: neuertheleſſe after all
this bzoyle, they were moſt greateſt friends. Theſe foure
captains came wᵗ their cõpany that the fields where they
were ſẽmed a fozeſt. They were trimme felowes ᚱ well
armed accozding to their vſe, although they were paynted
ſo that their faces ſhewed like diuels with great tuffes of
feathers,

Indian ar∫
mour.

feathers and triumphed gallantly. They had also ∫linges,
∫taues, ∫peares, ∫wordes, bowes and arrowes, ∫kulles,
∫plintes, gantlettes all of wood, gilte or el∫e couered with
feathers or leather, their cor∫elets were made of cotten
woolle, their targettes and bucklers gallant and ∫trong,
made of woode couered with leather, and trimmed with
laton and feathers, their ∫wordes were ∫taues with an
edge of flint ∫tone cunningly ioyned into the ∫taffe, which
woulde cutte very well and make a ∫ore wounde.

The ho∫t (as is declared) was deuided into foure parts,
their in∫trumentes of warre were hunters hornes, and
drumnes called attabals made like a caldron and couered with vellam. So that the Spanyardes in all the di∫-
couery of *India* did neuer ∫é a better army togither nor
better ordered.

The threatning of the Indian campe
agayn∫t the Spanyardes.

These *Indians* were great braggers, and
∫ayde among them∫elues, what madde
people are the∫e that threatneth vs and
yet knoweth vs not. But if they will be
∫o bolde to inuade our countrey without
our licence, let vs not ∫ette vpon them ∫o
∫oone, it is méete they haue a litle re∫te, for we haue tyme
inough to take & binde them, let vs al∫o ∫ende them meate
for they are commen with empty ∫tomackes: And againe
they ∫hall not ∫ay that we do apprehende them with wea-

A pre∫ent.

rine∫∫e and hunger. Wherevpon they ∫ent vnto the Chri-
∫tians thré hundreth Gynnea cockes, and two hundreth
ba∫kets of bread called *Centli.* The whiche pre∫ent was a
great ∫ucker for the néde that they ∫tode in. And ∫oone after (quoth they) nowe let vs goe and ∫ette vpon them, for
by

by this time they haue eaten their meate, and nowe wée
will eate them, and so shall they pay vs the victuals that
we sent : likewise we wil know if *Mutezuma* commaunded them to come into our countrey, or who else. And if he
sente them, then let him come and deliuer them : and if it
be their owne enterpryse, they shall receyue they reward
accordingly. These and such like bragges they vsed, seing
so fewe Spaniardes before them, and not knowyng their
strength. Then the foure Captaynes sente twoo thousande of their valiantest men of warre and olde Souldiers, to take the Spanyardes quietly, with commaundement that if they did resist, either to binde them or else to
kill them, meanyng not to sette their whole army vpon
them, saying that they shoulde gette but small honour for
so great a multitude, to fight agaynst so fewe. The twoo
thousande Souldiers passed the trench that was betwixt
the twoo campes, and came boldely to the Tower where
the Christians were . Then came forth the Horsemen, and after them the footemen, and at the first encounter they made the *Indians* féele howe the yron swordes
woulde cutte : and at the seconde, they shewed of what
force those fewe in number were, of whome a little before they had so iested : But at the thirde brunte they
made those lusty Souldiers fly, who were come to apprehende them, for none of them escaped, but onely suche as
knewe the passage of the trenches or ditche.

Then the mayne battell and whole army sette forth
with a terrible and maruellous noyse, and came so fierce
vppon our menne, till they entred into our campe without any resistaunce, and there were at handye strokes
and wrastlyng with the Spanyardes, and in a good space
coulde not gette them out, killyng many of them whiche
were so bolde to enter: and in this sorte they faught
foure howers , before they coulde make way among

their

A reckning made be-fore the hoste.

Battayle.

their enimies. And then the *Indians* began to faynt, feyng so many dead on theyr side, and the greate woundes they had, and that they coulde kill none of the Chzistians: yet the battayle ceased not till it dzewe neare night and then they retyzed. Whereof *Cortes* and his Souldiers were exceedyng gladde, foz they were fully weried with killyng of *Indians*, so that all that nighte our men triumphed with moze ioy than feare, considerynng that the *Indians* fought not by night, they slepte and toke their reste at pleasure, whiche they had not done til that tyme, but alwayes kept bothe watche and warde.

The *Indians* finding many of their hoste missyng, yet they would not yeelde themselues as ouercome, as after did appeare. They coulde not well tell howe many were slayne, noz yet our men had leasure to count them.

Cortes vvas a pain full man. The nexte day in the moznyng *Cortes* wente fozth to runne the fieldes as he had done befoze, leauing halfe his menne to keepe the campe, and bicause he shoulde not be espied he departed befoze day, & burned aboute .x. townes, and sacked one towne, whiche was of thze thousande houses, in the whiche were founde but few folke of fight, bycause the moste of them were gone to their campe: After the spoyle, he set fire on the towne and came his way to his campe with a great pzay by noone time. The enimies pursued thinkyng to take away their pzay, and followed them into the camp, where they fought fiue houres and could not kill one Spaniarde, although many of their side were slayne: foz euen as they were many and stode on a thzong togither, the ozdinaunce made a wonderfull spoyle among them, so that they lefte off fighting, and the victozy remayned foz our men. The *Indians* thought that the Spanyardes were inchaunted bycause their arrowes coulde not hurte them.

The nexte day followyng, the foure Captaynes sente
thze

thꝛée ſeuerall things in pꝛeſent to *Cortes*, and the meſſen⸗ gers that bꝛought them ſayd: Sir behold here fiue ſlaues, and if thou be that rigoꝛous God that eateſt mans fleſhe and blouo, eate theſe whiche we bꝛing vnto thée, and we will bꝛing thée moe. And if thou be the gentle and méeke God, beholde here Franckinſenſe and Feathers. And if thou be a moꝛtal man, take here foule, bꝛead, & Cherries.

A ſtraynge preſente,

Cortes anſwered, that both he and his were moꝛtal men euen as they were. And bicauſe that alwayes he had vſed to tell them trouth, wherfoꝛe did they vſe to tell him lies, and lykewiſe to flatter him, foꝛ he deſired to bée their friende, aduiſing them not to be madde and ſtubboꝛne in their opinion, foꝛ if they ſo did, aſſuredly they ſhoulde re⸗ ceyue great hurte and dammage. Likewiſe (quoth he) it is apparant vnto you how many of youꝛ ſide are ſlayne without the loſſe of one of mine, and with this anſwere ſent them away. Notwithſtanding the anſwere ſent, there came aboute. 30000. of them euen to *Cortes* his campe to pꝛoue their Coꝛſelettes, as they had done the day befoꝛe, but they returned with bꝛoké pates. Here is to be noted, that although the firſt day the whole hoſt of *Indians* came to combat with our men, & finally all they came to fight, yet the next day they did not ſo, but euery ſeueral captaine by himſelfe, foꝛ to deuide the better the trauayle & paynes equally amóg them: & bicauſe that one ſhould not diſturbe another thꝛough ỹ multitude, conſidering that they ſhould fight but with a few, & in a narrow place, & foꝛ this conſi⸗ deration, their battayles were moꝛe freſher & ſtronger, foꝛ eche captaine did contende who ſhould do moſt valiantly, foꝛ to get honour, & eſpecially in killyng one Spaniarde, foꝛ they thought that all their hurtes ſhoulde be ſatiſfied with the death of one Spaniarde, oꝛ taking one pꝛiſoner.

Likewyſe is to bée conſidered, the ſtraungeneſſe of their battayle, foꝛ not withſtandyng their controuerſie

Indian po-
licie.

all thofe fiftene dayes that they were there, whether they
fought o2 no. The *Indians* fente vnto the Spanyardes
cakes of b2eade, Gynnea cockes and Cherries. But this
polycie was not to giue them that meate fo2 good will,
but onely to efpie and fée what hurte was done amongſt
them, and alfo to fée what feare o2 ſtomacke they had
to p2océde: but the Spanyardes fell not into that recke-
nyng, fo2 the efpies of *Tlaxcallan* fayde, that none had
fought with them but certayne outlawes and knaues
called *Otomies*, who lyued as vagaboundes without a
Lo2de o2 other ruler: And that they were théeues, who
had they2 abyding behinde a hill, whiche they poynted vnto with they2 hande.

Hovv Cortez cut off the handes
of fiftie Indian efpies.

The nexte day after thefe p2efentes were
fente vnto them as Goddes, whiche was
the firte of September, there came to the
Campe fiftie *Indians* of *Tlaxcallan*, whiche
féemed after they2 fo2te honeſt menne, and
gaue vnto *Cortes* b2ead, cherries, & Gynnea cocks, as they
o2dinarily vfed to do, enquiring how all his Spaniardes
did and what they meant to doe, and whether they ſtode
in neceſſitie of any thing. And after this communication
they went vp and downe the camp, gafing and beholding
the ho2fes, armour and artillery, and féemed amafed to
fée fuch things. But the effect of their cóming was the office of efpies.

Teuche of *Zempoallan* marking thefe things, who being
of a childe b2ought vp in wars, by reafon wherof he was
erpert and wife, came vnto *Cortes*, faying, fir it femeth not
well, ÿ thefe *Tlaxcaltecas* wander vp & downe your campe
behol-

beholding the entrance and going out of the same, to be
holde likewise the fortitude and weakenesse of youre po
wer, I like it not: It may please you to make enquirie
whether they be espyes or no. *Cortez* hauing heard hys
tale, gaue him hartie thankes for his good aduice, yea
and maruelled, that neyther he himselfe, nor none of his
Spanyardes had noted the thing, the *Indians* hauing so
many dayes come vnto them after this sort, yea and that
only *Indian* of *Zempoallan* had considered it.

Nowe the originall cause was not bycause *Teuch* was
more wise than the Christians, but by reason that hée
had séene and heard those *Indians* commune with the subiectes of *Iztacmixtlitan* to féele their mindes, and wyth
craft and subtiltie to obteyne their desire: whereby *Cortez* vnderstoode that those fellowes came not to any good
purpose: he apprehended that *Indian* whiche stoode nexte
vnto him, and hauing him alone from his fellowes, by
his interpreters examined him effectually, who incontinent confessed that he was a spye, and that his comming
thither was to view the way how to enter their Campe
for to spoyle and burne their Tentes: and for so much as
they hadde proued fortune all the houres of the day, and
all happened contrary to their desire, against their auncie
ent fame and glory which they hadde obteyned by noble
exploytes in warres, they now meant to proue their successe by nighte, hoping of better fortune: and also bycause
their souldiers shoulde not feare the Horses, with the
darkenesse of the nighte, nor the blowes or stripes of the
bright swordes, nor yet the fire and terrible noyse of the
Ordinance: and that Captayne *Xicotencatl* was alreadye
appoynted for that enterprise, with prouision of manye
thousand souldiers which lay in ambush in a vale behind
certayne hilles, right ouer against their Campe.

After this confession taken, *Cortes* full prudently com-

R.iij.   maun-

maunded to take alfo the feuerall confeffions of other foure o2 fyue, who likewife confeffed that they were all efpies, vppon whofe confeffions they were al fiftie taken p2ifoners, and iudgemente giuen, that their one hande

A good correction.

fhould be cut off, which was fo2thwith executed, and then were returned to their Camp, fignifying vnto them that the like iuftice fhould be executed vpon as many efpyes as they might take. And alfo they were charged to fhew vnto their Generall who had fente them, that both daye and night he would be ready fo2 them.

When the *Tlaxcaltecas* fawe their efpyes come in thys pickle, they were in a maruellous feare, and it féemed a newe wo2ld vnto them : they alfo beléeued that oure men hadde fome familiar fpirites that did inftructe them of their thoughtes, and with feare of cutting off hads, there went no moe efpies with victuals.

An embaffage that Mutezuma fente
to Hernando Cortez.

Hen thefe efpyes were gone, oure men ef pyed out of our Campe a great multitude of men goe croffing ouer a hill, and it fée med that they were thofe that the Cap tayne *Xicotencatl* hadde in ambufh: and al though it was néere night, *Cortes* determi

A carefull Captayne.

ned to followe them, and not to abide their comming, fearing that at the firft b2unt they mighte fet fire among his cotages, as was p2etended among them, whiche p2e tence hauing taken effecte, myght haue bin the deftructi on of all his men, eyther by the fier o2 otherwife : where fo2e he put all his men in good o2der, and commaunded the Ho2femenne to decke the b2eft plates of hys Ho2fes with belles, and then p2océded towarde their enimies,
who

who durſt not abide their comming, hauing intelligence
of the cutting of their eſpyes hands, and likewiſe hearing
the new noyſe of belles: yet oure men followed them tyll
two houres within night, through many ſowen fieldes of
Centli, and ſlew many of thẽ, and then returned with victozie to the Campe.

At that ſeaſon were come ſixe noble men from *Mexi-* Ambaſſage
co, who brought two hundzed ſeruing men to wayt vpon from Mu-
them. They brought vnto *Cortes* a pzeſent, whiche was a
hundzed garments of cotten, and ſome of feathers, and a
thouſand peeces of golde.

Theſe ambaſſadozs on the behalfe of *Mutezuma,* declared, that their Lozd would be friende with the Emperoure, and alſo with him, and his company, requeſtyng
to knowe what tribute he woulde yearely demaunde, in
golde, plate, pearles, ſlaues, oz garments, oz of any other
thing that was within his kingdome, and the ſame tribute he woulde well and truly pay withoute delay, wyth
ſuch condition, that neyther he noz his company ſhoulde
come vnto *Mexico.* And this requeſt (quoth they) is not
only bycauſe you ſhould bee diſturbed to come into hys Excuſes.
countrey, but chiefly bycauſe the waye is euill, barren,
and full of euill rockes, whyche lette dothe greeue *Mu-*
tezuma, that ſuche valiant menne as ye be ſhoulde ſuffer
in his Countrey, lying not in hys power to remedie
it.

Cortez dyd thankefully receyue the pzeſent and gentle
offer foz the Emperoure King of *Caſtile,* but (quoth hee)
my earneſt deſire is, that you depart not til ye ſee the end
of theſe warres whyche I haue nowe in hande, bycauſe
yee ſhall carrie newes thereof to *Mexico,* what I pze-
tende to doe againſte theſe moztall enimies of *Mute-*
zuma.

Then *Cortez* fel into an ague, foz which cauſe he went
not

not out to skyrmish as he was wonte to do, but only prouided to make his Camp strong against certaine flockes of *Indians*, whiche came dayly to skirmishe, for that was as ordinarie, as the meate that was wont to be broughte to thẽ: but yet these skirmishes nor furie of ỹ *Indiãs* were not like to their fierce beginning.

Cortez now meaneth to take a purgation for his ague: and tooke certayne pilles whiche he broughte with him from *Cuba*, at suche houre of the nighte as is vsed for purgations.

It happened that the nexte daye following, before hys purge had wrought, came three great companies of *Indians* to besiege his Camp. It should seeme that those *Indians* had some intelligence of his sicknesse, or else thinking with feare that he durst not come abroade as he was wont to doe.

A valiant Captayne.

Cortes being aduertised of this newes, withoute anye more respect to his purgation taken, tooke his horse, and with his menne came to the encounter, and foughte with his enimies all day till it was nighte, and draue them a good way off, to their great hurt, and then returned to his Camp, and the next day following, he purged as fresh, as though it had bin newly taken. I doe not rehearse thys for a miracle, but to declare what he passed: for *Hernando Cortez* was a greate sufferer of trauell and paynes, and one of ỹ firste that alway was at any assay or brunt of enimies, and he was not onely a good man of his handes, but also graue in counsell. And hauing thus purged hym selfe, and taken rest those dayes, he watched euery night that fell to his lotte, as well as any other souldier, and so continually he vsed to do. He was not for this the lesse esteemed, but rather muche the more beloued among hys men.

How

Hoyv Cortez vvan a great Citie
called Zimpanzinco.

IN an euening *Cortes* went vp to the toppe of his Tower, and looking rounde aboute hym, he espyed aboute foure leagues diſtant in the Mountaynes among rockes and proceeding out of a woode dyuers smokes, whereby he ymagined people to be there : he opened not his minde to anye man, but commaunded two hundred of his men to followe hym, and some *Indians* hys friendes, and within three or foure houres of the nyghte he toke hys iourney towarde the Mountaynes, beeing very darke. He had not fully gone a league, when suddaynely appeared the lykeneſſe of a great Bull whiche ouerthrewe them that they could not ſtirre. The firſte Horseman beeing fallen, they aduyſed *Cortez* thereof, who aunſwered, that he ſhoulde returne wyth hys Horſe to the Campe : and incontinente fell another, *Cortez* commaunded hym the lyke: and when three or foure were fallen, his company retyred, ſaying, it was an euill token, deſiring him to returne and abyde the morning, that they myghte ſee whether they wente. He aunſwered, ſaying, yee oughte to gyue no credite to witchcraftes or fantaſies, for God, whoſe cauſe we take in hande, is aboue all nature: wherefore I will not leaue my pretended iourney, for I doe ymagine that of thys nyghtes trauell ſhall come greate eaſe and pleaſure, ſaying, that the Deuill hathe in this forme of a Bull appeared, to diſturbe vs. He hadde no ſooner ended his talke, when hys Horſe fell likewiſe : then counſell was taken what was beſt to be done.

It was determined that the Horſes which were falle,

S. ſhould

[marginal notes:]
An euill Spirite appeared.

A couragious Captayne.

ſhould be returned to the Campe, and that of the reſidue, eache Horſeman ſhoulde leade hys Horſe by the bridle, and ſo procæde on theyr way, and ſhortly after the Horſes were well agayne, but they neuer knewe of what motion they hadde fallen : wyth the darkeneſſe of the nyghte they loſt theyr way to the Mountaynes, and chanced into a cragged rockie waye, that they thoughte neuer to haue come out thereof.

And after a whyle that they had gone this euill waye, wyth their heare ſtanding with very feare, they eſpyed a little lyghte, and tooke the way thyther, where they founde a little houſe, wherein were two Women, and thoſe Women, with other two women that afterwards they mette, conducted them to the Wildernesſſe, where they had eſpyed the ſmoke, and before day they ſette vppon certayne Uillages, and ſlewe many, yet they burned not thoſe Uillages, bycauſe they ſhould not be perceyued through the lyght thereof. They receyued there aduyſe, that néere at hand were great populations, and ſoone after he came to *Zimpanzinco*, a towne of twenty thouſand houſes, as after dyd appeare by the viſitation of *Cortes*. Theſe inhabitantes béyng vnaduiſed of this ſuddayne happe, were taken in their beddes, and came out all naked through the ſtrætes to knowe what the great mourning and lamentation meante: at the firſt entrance many were ſlayne, but bycauſe they made no reſiſtance, *Cortez* commaunded to ceaſſe from killyng, nor yet to take any of theyr goodes, or women.

A famous Cortez.

The feare of theſe poore inhabitantes was ſo greate, that they fledde without reſpect of the father to the child, or huſbande to the Wyfe, or yet eyther of houſe or goodes.

Cortes commaunded ſygnes of peace to be made vnto them, and with that they ſtayed, and before the Sunne riſing.

rifing, the Towne was pacifyed.

Cortez went vp into a Tower to defcry the Countrey, and there efpyed a mofte greate population : he then demaunded what it was: aunfwere was made that it was called *Tlaxcallan*, and the Townes therebnto appertey-nyng. Then he called hys Spanyardes, and fayd vnto them: beholde, what woulde it haue preuayled vs to kyll thefe poore foules, hauyng yonder fo manye emmies? and wythoute doyng anye more hurte in that Towne, hée wente to a fayre Fountayne there at hande, and thyther came the Rulers of that Towne, and other foure hundred menne wythoute weapon, and broughte wyth them muche victuall, mofte humbly they befought Cortes to doe them no more hurte, gyuing hym likewife greate thankes, that hée hadde fo fauourablye vfed them, offering both to ferue and obey hym, and from that daye forwarde they woulde not onely kéepe hys friendfhippe, but alfo trauell wyth the Lordes of *Tlaxcallan* and others, that they fhoulde doe the fame. Cortez replyed, that fure he was, howe they had foughte agaynfte hym before that time, although that nowe they broughte hym meate, yet notwithftandyng hée pardoned them, and alfo receyued them into hys feruice and friendfhippe, to the vfe of the Emperoure.

Wyth thys communication he departed from them, and returned to the Campe verye ioyfull wyth fo good fucceffe, hauyng fuche a daungerous beginning, wyth the fuddayne fall of theyr Horfes, wherein the Pro-uerbe is fulfylled, whyche fayeth, Speake not euill of the daye, till it be at an ende.

They hadde alfo a greate hope, that thofe newe friendes woulde bée a meane, to caufe the *Tlaxcalte-cas* to leaue from Warre, and to become theyr friendes.

S.ij.   From

From that day forward he commaunded that none of hys Campe shoulde doe any hurte to any *Indian*, and certifyed his men that the same daye his warres were at an ende with that prouince.

The desire that some of the Spanyardes
had to leaue the warres.

Hen *Cortez* was returned so ioyfull to his Camp, he founde some of his men discouraged with the suddayne mishappe of the Horses, fearing that likewise some misfortune hadde happened to *Cortes*, but when they sawe him come well and with victorie, their ioy was great, although true it is that manye of his men were not well pleased, but desired muche to leaue the warres, and to returne to the coast, as they had often requested, but nowe chiefly seeyng such a great Countrey, and full of people, who woulde not permitte theyr abiding there, and they beeyng so fewe in number in the middest among them withoute hope of succoure, certaynely things to be feared. With this murmuration they thought it good to talke with *Cortes*, & also to require him to proceede no further, but returne backe agayne to *Vera Crux*, from whence by little and little they mighte haue intelligence with the *Indians*, and therevppon proceede accordyng to tyme, and that he mighte prouide more Horses and men, whiche was the chiefest prouision of the warre.

Murmuration.

And although some secretely enformed *Cortes* of thys matter, yet he gaue no eare to their talke, but on a night as hee came out of hys Tower to ouerlooke the watche, hee hearde a loude talke out of one of the Cotages, and beganne to hearken what theyr communication was,

was : and the matter was, that certaine fouldiers fayde
thefe wozdes: If our Captayne be madde, and go where
he may be flayne, let him goe alone, what néede we to fol‐
low him. *Cortez* hearyng this talke, called two of his
friendes foz witneffe, willyng them to harken his fouldi‐
ers talke, foz he that durft fpeake fuche wozdes would be
ready to doe it. Alfo he hearde others fay, what fhall our
iourney be as *Pedro Carbonerotes* was; who went into *Bar‐
baria* to take Mozes, and he and all his were there flayne,
wherefoze fayde they let vs not follow him but turne in
time. It grieued *Cortez* muche to heare this talke, who
would fayne haue cozrected them but it was not then
tyme, wherefoze he determined to leade them with fuffe‐
raunce, and fpake vnto them as followeth.

The Oration made by Cortez
to his Souldiers.

Aifters and louyng friendes, I did chofe
you foz my fellowes, and ye chofe me foz
your captaine, and all was foz the feruice
of God, and the augmenting of his holy
faith, & alfo the feruice of our foueraigne
Lozd the King now Emperour: and next
foz our owne commoditie, I (as yée haue féene) haue not
fayled noz yet difpleafed yée, noz yée likewife haue other‐
wife done to me vnto this day. But now I do féele faint‐
neffe in fome, yea and an euill will to goe fozwarde in the
warres whiche we haue in hande: but (God be pzayfed) it
is now finifhed, at the leaft the ende is vnderftod, what it
may be, and alfo the wealth that may follow, as partely
you haue féene, but much without comparifon of that you
haue not féene, whiche is a thing that doth excéede the
greatneffe of our wozdes oz thoughts.

S.iij.   Feare

Feare not my louyng fellowes to goe and abide
with me, God forbidde that I should thynke, yea or that
any shoulde reporte, that feare bereth my company,or
elſe diſobedience to their Captayne,whiche is a perpetuall infamie, if wee shoulde leaue this Lande, this
Warre,this way already made, and returne as ſome doe
deſire,ſhall wee then lyue at reſte,loytring as well and
loſſe folke : God forbidde, that euer oure nation shoulde
haue ſuche a name,hauyng warres of honour. And whether (I pray) ſhall the Ore goe where he ſhall not helpe
to ploughe the grounde:doe pee thinke peraduenture that
pee ſhall finde leſſe people, worſe armed, and not farre
from the ſea ? I doe aſſure you, that in ſo thynkyng pee
ſeeke after fiue feete for a Catte, yea and you ſhall trauell no way, but that you ſhall meete ſome euill paſſage
(as the Prouerbe ſayth) yea and farre worſer than this
that we haue in hands. For why (God be thanked)ſince
wee came into this Countrey, we neuer wanted meate,
friendes, neyther money nor honour. For nowe pee
ſee that pee are eſteemed more than menne, yea as perſons immortall, and Goddes, if it mighte be ſpoken, for
theſe *Indians* beyng ſo many and without number, and
ſo armed as ye your ſelues affirme, yet can they not kyll
one of vs:and as touchyng theyr weapons, you ſee that
they are not poyſoned, as the *Indians* of *Cartagena*, *Veragua*, and the *Caribez* doe vſe, whiche haue killed many of our nation therewith, dying as madde menne ra-
gyng.

And if there were no other cauſe than this onely,you
ſhoulde not ſeeke others with whome to warre : I doe
confeſſe that the Sea is ſomewhat farre from vs, and
neuer Spaniarde trauelled ſo farre into the mayne lands
of *India*, as wee haue done : for why:nowe we leaue the
Sea a hundreth and fiftie myles behinde vs,nor yet euer
                                                        any

any hath come so neare *Mexico* where *Mutezuma* dothe reside, from whome suche messages and Treasure wee haue receyued. It is nowe but thrée score myles thyther, and the woꝛste is paste, as you doe sée, if we come thither, as I truste in Iesus wée shall, then shall we not onely gette and winne foꝛ the Emperoure oure naturall Loꝛde a riche Lande, greate Kingdomes, infinite Vassalles, but lykewyse foꝛ oure selues muche riches, as Golde, Siluer, Pꝛetious stones, Pearles, and other commoditie, and besides thys, the greatest honour that euer any nation did obtayne. Foꝛ loke howe great a King this is, howe large his countrey is, and what greate multitude of peoplehée hath, so muche the moꝛe is our gloꝛy.

Besides all this, wée are bounde as Chꝛistians to exalte and enlarge oure Catholyke fayth, as wée haue begonne, abolishyng Idolatrie and blasphemie agaynst our Sauiour Chꝛiste, takyng away the bloudɒy Sacrifice and eatyng of mannes fleshe, so hoꝛrible and agaynste nature, and many other grieuous sinnes so muche here vsed, foꝛ the foulenesse whereof I name them not.

And therefoꝛe (I saye) feare you noꝛ yet doubte you the victoꝛie, consideryng that the woꝛste is paste. Of late wée ouercame the *Indians* of *Tabasco*, and also an hundꝛeth and fiftie thousande this other daye of the *Tlaxcaltecas*, who haue the onely name of bꝛeakers of Lyons sawes: so with Gods helpe you shal be Conquerers of the reste, if ye faynt not and folowe me.

All hys company was pleased and contente with this comfoꝛtable erhoꝛtation, and those that were faynt harted recouered strength. And hys valiaunt Souldiers recouered double courage, & those who hated him began to honour him: and in conclusion he departed from thence
                                                                  erceding

exceding welbeloued of all his company. But all his for=
mer talke was very nædefull as time then requyred: for
why?some of his(as you haue heard) were desirous to re=
turne:likewise vpon dissention, rebellion mought haue
growen,and he forced to returne to the sea coaste,where
all his toyle and trauell taken had bene loft.

Hovv Xicotencatl came for Embaſ=
ſadour to Cortez his Campe.

Ortez had not so sone made an ende of his
talke,when *Xicotencatl* came entryng into
the campe, who was chiefe and generall
captayne in *Tlaxcallan*,& of all the warres:
he brought in his company fiftie persons
of audoritie to kæpe him cōpany. They approched neare
where *Cortes* was,and saluted eche other accordyng to the
vse of their countrey. Theic salutations ended and the
parties setten dowle,*Xicotencatl* began the talke, saying:
Sir J am come on mine owne behalfe and also of my
fellow Captaine, and Lieuetenant *Maxixca*, and in the
name of many other noble personages, and finally in the
name of the whole state and common weale of *Tlaxcallan*,
to besæche and pray you to admitte vs into your friend=
shippe, and to yælde our selues and countrey vnto your
King,crauyng also at your hande pardon for our attempt
in takyng armes agaynst you, wé not knowyng what
you were,nor what you sought for in our countrey. And
where we presumed to resiste and defende your entrance,
we did it as agaynst straungers whome we knewe not,
and suche menne as we had neuer here tofore sene : and
fearyng also that you had bene friendes to *Mutezuma*,
who is and alwayes hath bene our mortall enimy . And
these things wé suspected,seyng *Mutezuma* his seruaunts

to

in your company; oʒ elſe we imagined that you were comen to vſurpe our libertie, the whiche of tyme without memoʒy we haue poſſeſſed, as our foʒefathers did with the ſhedyng of their bloud. And of our owne naturall pʒouiſion we wante cotten woolle to clothe vs, wherfoʒe in tyme paſſe we wente as naked as we were boʒne, but ſome of vs vſed other clothe to couer our nakedneſſe, made of the leaues of the trée called *Metl*: and Salte alſo wée wanted, of which two things ſo neceſſarie to humayne lyfe, *Mutezuma* had greate ſtoʒe, and other our enimies,with whome we are rounde aboute enuironed. And lykewiſe where wée haue no golde,ſtones of value, oʒ any riche thyng to barter with them, of very pure neceſſitie many times we are foʒced to ſell our owne bodies to buy theſe wantes. And this extremitie(ſayde he) wée néeded not,if that we woulde be ſubiectes and vaſſalles to *Mutezuma*. But yet had we rather all in generall to ende our lyues, than wée woulde putte oure ſelues in ſuche ſubiection,foʒ we thynke our ſelues as valiaunt menne in courage as our foʒefathers were, who alwayes haue reſiſted agaynſt him and his grandfather,who was as mightie as nowe is he : wée woulde alſo haue withſtoode you and your foʒce, but wée coulde not,although we pʒoued all our poſſibilitie by night and day,and founde your ſtrength inuincible, and we no lucke agaynſt you. Therefoʒe ſithence our fate is ſuch, we had rather be ſubiect vnto you than vnto any others. Foʒ wée haue knowen and hearde by the *Zeampoallanezer*, that you doe no euill, noʒ came not to vexe any, but were moſte valiaunt and happie,as they had ſéene in the warres, beyng in your companie. Foʒ whiche conſideration,we truſte that our libertie ſhall not be diminiſhed,but rather our owne perſons, wyues,and familie better pʒeſerued, and our houſes and huſbandʒy not

T.   deſtroyed.

destroyed. And in summe of all his talke, the teares trick=
ling downe his cheekes, he besought Cortes to wey that
Tlaxcallan did neuer at any tyme rcknowledge any supe=
riour King or Lorde, nor at any time had commen any
person among them to commaunde, but onely he, whome
they did voluntarily electe and chose as their superiour
and ruler.

It can not be tolde, howe muche Cortes reioyced with
this Embassage, and to see such a mighty Captayne come
vnto his campe to submitte himselfe: and also it was a
matter of great wayght to haue that Cittie in subiection,
for the enterprice whiche he had in hande, whereby he ful=
ly made an account that the warres were at an ende, to
the great contentation of him and his company, and with
great fame and reputation among the Indians.

Cortes with a mery and louing countenaunce answe=
red, laying to their charge the hurte and damage whiche
he had receyued in their countrey, bycause they refused at
the firste to harken vnto him, and quietly to suffer him
to enter into their countrey, euen as he had required and
desired by his Messengers of Zeampoallan sente vnto them
from Zaclotan. Yet al this notwithstandyng, he did both par=
don the kyllyng of his two horses, the assaultyng of him
in the highe way, and the greate lies whiche they had
moste craftily vsed with hym, (for where as they them=
selues fought agaynst him, yet they layde the faulte to o=
thers) likewise their pretence to murder him in the am=
bush prepared for him, (enticing him to come to their Ci=
tie,) without makyng firste defiance accordyng to the law
of armes.

These causes notwithstanding, he did louingly recepue
their offer made in subiection to the Emperour, and in
this sorte departed, saying, that shortely hee woulde be
with him in Tlaxcallan, and presently he coulde not goe
with

with him for the dispatche of the Ambassadours of *Mutezuma.*

The receyuing and entertaynement
of Cortez in Tlaxcallan.

T grieued muche the Embassadours of *Mutezuma,* to sée *Xicotencates* in the Spanishe Campe, and the offer made vnto *Cortes* in the behalfe of his King, of their persons, Cittie and goodes, aduising *Cortes* to gyue no credite vnto them, for all their saying (quoth they) is treason and lies, and to the entent to locke you vp in their Cittie.

Cortes answered, that although their aduise were true, yet he did determine to go thither, for that he feared them lesse in the towne than in the fielde. They hearyng this answere and determination, besought him to giue vnto one of them licence to returne vnto *Mexico,* to aduertise *Mutezuma* of all that was past, with an answere to their Ambassage, promising within sire dayes to haue newes from *Mexico,* and till then prayed him not to departe with his Campe.

Cortes graunted their request, and abode there the time appointed, expectyng the answere. In this meane season came many of *Tlaxcallan* to the camp, some brought Ginnea cockes, other brought bread and Cherries, and gaue it for nothyng in comparison, with merry countenaunce, desiryng them to goe home with them vnto their houses.

The sirth day the *Mexican* came, accordyng to promise, and brought vnto *Cortes* tenne Iewelles of Golde, bothe riche and well wrought, and a fiftene thousand garments of Cotten excéeding gallant, and moste earnestly besought

A riche present.

T.ij.   him

hym on the behalfe of *Mutezuma*, that he shoulde not daunger himselfe in trustyng to the wordes of the *Tlaxcaltecas*, who were so poe y with necessitie they would robbe him of the thyngs whiche his mayster had sente him, yea and lykewise murder him, knowyng of the friendshippe betwéene his mayster and him: likewise all the chiefest Lordes of *Tlaxcallan*, came to intreate hym to goe with them to *Tlaxcallan* where he shoulde be cherished, lodged, and well prouided. For it was a greate dishonour and shame for them to permitte suche personages to abyde in suche vyle cotages as they were in. And if (quoth they) you trusse vs not, that then wée are ready to gyue you for your securitie what soeuer gages you shall demaunde: notwithstandyng they dyd bothe sweare and faithfully promise, that they might safely goe with them, saying also that the Othe and fayth of theyr common weale should neuer be broken for all the goodes in the worlde.

Wherevpon *Cortez* seyng the good will of so many Gentlemen his newe friendes, and lykewise the *Indians* of *Zeampoallan*, of whome he had good credite, did so importune him and assure him of his goyng, he commaunded his fardage to be laden and also his ordinaunce, and departed towarde *Tlaxcallan*, whiche was sire leagues from that place, with as good order as it had bene to a Battayle: And at the Tower where he had pitched hys campe, he lefte certayne Crosses for a memorie, with a greate heape of stones, and entred into *Tlaxcallan* the eightenth of September. There came out such a multitude of people to sée him and to méete him in the way, that it was a wonder to sée.

Entraunce into Tlaxcallan.

He was lodged in the greatest temple, which had many great and fayre lodgyngs, sufficient for hym and all his companie, except the *Indians* hys friends which were lodged

lodged in other Temples. He set certayne limittes, out
of the whiche he commaunded straightely that none of
hys company should passe, vpon payne of deathe, and also
commaunded that they shoulde take nothing, but what
shoulde be giuen them. His commaundement was well
obserued, for none presumed to goe a stoanes cast without his licence. The *Indian* Gentlemen shewed greate
pleasure and curtesie to the strangers, and prouided thē
of all things necessarie, and manye of them gaue theyr
daughters vnto them, in token of true friendshippe, and
likewise to haue fraite of their bodyes, to be brought vp
for the warres, beyng such valiant men.

This Countrey lyked well oure men, and the greate
loue of the people. They abode there at their pleasure
twenty dayes, in whiche time they did procure to knowe
particularly the estate of their common weale and secretes, and also were sufficiently instructed of the estate
of *Mutezuma*.

The description of Tlaxcallan.

Laxcallan is properly in the *Indian* tong
as much to say, as bread well baked, for
there is more grayne called *Centli* gathered, than is in all ẙ prouince round about.
In times past the Citie was called *Tex-*
callan, that is to say, a valley betwixt two
hilles. It is a greate Citie, and planted by a riuer side,
whiche springeth out of *Atlancatepec*, and watreth the
most parte of that prouince, and from thence issueth out
into the South sea, by *Zacatullan*. This Citie hathe foure
goodly streetes, whiche are called *Tepeticpac, Ocotelulco, Ti-*
zatlan, Quiahuiztlan. The firste streete standeth on hygh
vpon a hyll, farre from the riuer, whiche maye be aboute

halfe a league, and bycause it ſtandeth on a hill, it is calꝉ led *Tepeticpac*, that is to ſay, a hyll, and was the firſte po- pulation which was foūded there on high, bycauſe of the warres.

An other ſtréete was ſcituate on the hill ſide towarde the Riuer, bycauſe at the building thereof, there were many pyne trées:they named it *Ocotelulco*, which is to ſay, a pine apple plot. This ſtréete was beautifull, and firſte inhabited of all the Citie, and there was the chiefeſt Market place, where all the buying and ſelling was v- ſed, and that place they called *Tianquiztli* : in that ſtréete was the dwelling houſe of *Maxixca*. Along the Riuer ſide in the playne ſtandeth another ſtréete called *Tizatlan*, bycauſe there is muche lyme and chalke. In this ſtréete dwelled *Xicotencatl*, Captayne generall of the common weale. There is another ſtréete named by reaſon of the brackiſh water, *Quiahuiztlan*, but ſince the Spanyardes came thither, all thoſe buildings are almoſt altered, af- ter a better faſhion,and built with ſtone. In the plaine by the riuer ſide, ſtandeth the Towne houſe, and other offices, as in the Citie of *Venice*. This *Tlaxcallan* was go- uerned by noble and riche men : they vſe not that one a- lone ſhould rule,but rather flye from that order, as from tyrannie.

In their warres (as I haue ſayde before) they haue foure Captaynes, whiche gouerneth eache one ſtréete, of the whiche foure,they do elect a Captayne generall.Alſo there are other Gentlemen that are vndercaptaynes,but a ſmall number. In the warres they vſe their ſtanderde to be carried behynde the army,but when the battayle is to be fought, they place the ſtanderde where all the hoſte may ſée it, and he that commeth not incontinent to hys auntient,payeth a penaltie. Their ſtanderd hathe two croſſebowe arrowes ſet thereon, whiche they eſtéeme as
                                                            the

the relikes of their auncetors. Thys standerd two olde souldiers and valiant menne, being of the chiefest Captaynes, haue the charge to carrie, in the which standerde an abusion of southsaying, eyther of losse or victory is noted. In this order they shote one of these arrowes against the fir st enimies that they meete, and if with that arrow they doe eyther kill or hurte, it is a token that they shall haue the victorie, and if it neyther kill nor hurt, then they assuredly beléeue that they shall lose the field.

This prouince or Lordship of *Tlaxcallan*, hath. 28. Villages and townes, wherein is contepned 15 0000. households. They are men well made, and good warriors, the lyke are not among the *Indians*. They are very poore, and haue no other riches, but only the grayne or corne called *Centli*, and with the gayne and profite thereof, they doe both cloth themselues, and paye their tributes, and prouide all other necessaries. They haue many market places, but the greatest and most vsed dayly, standeth in the stréete of *Ocutelulco*, whiche is so famous, that 30000. persons come thither in one day to buy and sell, whyche is to say, changing one thing for another, for they know not what money meaneth.

A strange contradiction.

They sell such things in that market, as héere we vse, & al thing vnto them néedeful to eate, and cloth for themselues and necessaries for building.

They haue all kinde of good policie in the Citie: there are Goldsmithes, fetherdressers, Barbors, hotchouses, and potters, who make as good earthen vessel, as is made in *Spayne*. The earth is fat and fruitefull for corne, fruite, and pasture, for among the pine trées groweth so muche grasse, that our men féede their cattell there, whiche in *Spayne* they can not do.

Within two leagues of that Citie standeth a rounde hill of sire miles of heigth, and fiue and fortie myles in compasse, compaffe, and is now called Saint Bartholmewes hill, where the snow freeseth. In times past they called that hill *Matealcucie*, who was their God for water. They had also a God for wyne, who was named *Ometochtli*, for the great dronkennesse whiche they vsed. Their chiefest God was called *Cumaxtlo*, and by another name *Mixcauatl*, whose Temple stode in the streete of *Ocotelulco*, in the whiche temple there was sacrifised some yeares aboue eyghte hundred persons. In *Tlaxcallan* they spake three languages, that is to saye, *Nahualth*, whiche is the courtly speech, and chiefest in all the land of *Mexico*: another is called *Otomir*, which is most commonly vsed in the Uillages: There is one onely streete that spake *Pinomer*, which is the grosest speache. There was also in that Citie a common Jayle, where fellons lye in prons, and all things which they held for finne, was there corrected.

Correctió.   It chanced at that time a Townesman to steale from a Spanyard a little golde, whereof *Cortes* complayned to *Maxixca*, who incontinent made such enquirie, ý the offender was found in *Cholollа*, whiche is another Citie fyue leagues from thence: they brought the prisoner with the golde, and deliuered him to *Cortez*, to doe with him hys pleasure: *Cortes* woulde not accepte him, but gaue hym thankes for his diligence: then was he carried wyth a Cryer before hym, manifestyng hys offence, and in the Market place vppon a skaffolde they brake hys ioyntes with a cudgell: our men maruelled to see suche straunge Justice.

The

The aunſvvere of the Tlaxcaltecas
touching the leauing of their Idolles.

Hen Cortes ſaw that theſe people exercuted Iuſtice, and liued in Religion after theyr manner, although abhominable and diuelliſh: and alwapes when he deſired them to leaue off from their Idolatrie and that cruell vanitie, in killing and eating men ſacriſiced, conſidering that none among them how holly ſoeuer he were, would willingly be ſlayne & eaten, required them to beléeue in the moſt true God of the Chriſtians, who was the maker of Heauen and earth, the giuer of rayne, and creator of all things that the earthe produceth only for the vſe and profite of mortall man.

A godly perſvvaſion

Some of them aunſwered, that they woulde gladly do it, onely to pleaſure him, but they feared that the commons would ariſe and ſtone them. Others ſayde, that it was an hard matter to vnbeléeue that which their foreſathers had ſo long beléeued, and that it ſhoulde be a cauſe to condemne their forefathers and themſelues.

Others ſayde, that it mighte be in time they woulde conuert, ſéeing the order of the Chriſtian Religion, and vnderſtanding the reaſons and cauſes to turne Chriſtians, and likewiſe perceyuing thoroughly the manner and life of the Chriſtiās, with theyr lawes and cuſtoms: and as for warlike feates, they were ſatiſſyed, & had ſéene ſuche tryall, that they helde them for men inuincible in that poynte, and that their God did help them.

Cortes promiſed them, that ſhortlye he woulde bring them ſuche men, as ſhoulde inſtruct and teache them, and then they ſhould ſé which way was beſt, with the greate ioy and fruits that they ſhoulde féele. They accépting
U.
that

that councell which he like a friende had giuen them, and
for as much as presently it could not be brought to passe
by reason of his iourney to *Mexico*, he desired them, that
the Temple wherein he was lodged, shoulde be made
a church for him and his company, and if it pleased them,
they mighte also come to sée and heare their diuine seruice.

The *Indians* graunted to his request, and dayly came
among them all the time of their abode there, and some
came and dwelte with the *Spanyardes*, but the chiefest
friende was Captayne *Maxixca*, who neuer went from
Cortez.

The discord betyveene the
Mexicans and *Tlaxcaltecas*.

Cortez being throughly satisfyed of theyr
hartie good wylles, he demaunded of them
the estate and riches of *Mutezuma*.
They exalted him greately, as men that
had proued his force.   And as they affyr-
med, it was nére a hundred yeares that they mainteyned warre with him and his father *Axaiaca*, and others
his Unckles and Grandfathers. And saide also, that the
golde and treasure of *Mutezuma*, was without number,
and his power and dominion ouer all the lande, and hys
people innumerable: for (quoth they) he ioyneth sometime
two hundreth thousand men, yea and thrée hundred thousande for one battayle. And if it pleased hym, he woulde
make as manye men double, and thereof they were good
witnesse, bycause they had manye times fought with thé.

Maxixca desired that *Cortes* should not aduenture himselfe into the power of the men of *Culhua*, wherat some
of the *Spanyardes* feared and suspected euill of the matter.

Cortes

Cortes tolde him, that notwithstanding all those things whiche they had tolde him, he was fully minded to goe to Mexico, to visit Mutezuma, willing him to aduise hym what hethought do, or bring to passe for them with Mutezuma, for he woulde willingly do it, for the curtesie shewed vnto him, and that he beleeued Mutezuma woulde graunt him any lawfull request.

Then they besought him to procure for them a licence to haue cotton wooll and salte out of his Countrey, for (sayd they) in time of the warres we stoode in great neede thereof, and that they had none but suche as they boughte by stealthe of the Comercans verye deere, in change of golde: for Mutezuma had made a straight lawe, whereby all suche as carried anye of those commodities to them shoulde be slayne. Then Cortez enquired the cause of their disorder and euill neyborhood. They aunswered, that their griefes were olde, and cause of libertie: but as the Ambassadors did affyrme, and Mutezuma afterward declare, it was not so, but for other matter farre differente. So that eache partye alleadging their causes, they reasons were, that the yong menne of Mexico and Culhua dyd exercise and bryng them vppe in warlike feates neere vnto them, and vnder they noses, to theyr greate annoyance, whereas they moughte haue gone to Panuco and Teocantepec, hys frontiers a farre off.

Lykewyse they pretence was, to haue warre wyth them beyng they neyghbors, onely to haue of them to sacrifice to their Gods: so that when they would make any solemne feast, then would they send to Tlaxcallan for men to sacrifice, with such a great army, that they might take as many as they needed for that yeare: for it is most certayne if Mutezuma woulde, in one daye he moughte haue broughte them in subiection, and slayne them all, ioyning his whole power in effect: but his purpose was, to keepe them for a pray to hunt withall, for men to be sacrificed to his Goddes, and to eate, so that hée woulde neuer sende but a small armye againste them: whereby it did chance that sometimes those of *Tlaxcallan* did ouercome.

Cortez receyued great pleasure to heare these discordes betwixt his newe friendes and *Mutezuma*, whiche was a thing fitte for his purpose, for by that meanes he hoped to bring them all vnder subiection, and therefore hée vsed the one and the other secretely, to build his pretence vpon a good foundation.

At all this communication there stode by certayne *Indians* of *Vexozinco*, whiche had bin against our men in the late warres, the which Towne is a Citie as *Tlaxcallan*, and ioyned with them in league of friendship against *Mutezuma*, who oppressed them in like effect of slaughter for their Temples of *Mexico*, and they also yéelded themselues to *Cortes* for vassals to the Emperoure.

The solemne receyuing of the
Spanyardes into Chololla.

 He Ambassedors of *Cortes* séeyng the determination of *Cortes* to procéde on his iourney towarde *Mexico*, they besoughte him to goe by *Chololla*, whiche stode fiue leagues from thence, certifying that *Chololla* was a Citie in their friendship, and that there he might at his pleasure abide the resolution of their Lord *Mutezuma*, whether it were his pleasure that he should enter into *Mexico* or no. This requeste was onely to haue him from thence, for truly it gréeued much *Mutezuma* of theyr newe friendshippe and league,

fearyng

fearyng that thereof woulde some great displeasure happen towardes him, and therefore procured all that was possible to haue him from thence, sending him alwayes presents to allure him to come fró thence the soner. But when the *Tlaxcaltecas* saw that he would goe to *Chololla*, it grieued them muche, saying vnto *Cortes*, that *Mutezuma* was a liar and fraudelent person, and that *Chololla* was a cittie his friende but not constant, and it mighte happen that they would displease him, hauyng him within their Cittie, wishyng him to looke wel to himself: And if néedes be would goe thither, yet they woulde prouide. 20000. men to kéepe him company.

A gentle offer.

The women that were giuen to the Spaniardes at their firste entraunce, had vnderstandyng of a snare that was layde to murder them at their commyng to *Chololla*, by meanes of one of the foure Captaynes, who had a sister which discouered the thing to *Pedro de Aluarado* who kepte hir. *Cortes* incontinent called that Captayne out of his house, and caused him to be choked, and so was the matter kepte close that his death was neuer knowen, whereby the snare was vndone without any rumour. It was a wonder that all *Tlaxcallan* had not made an vprore seyng one of their greatest Captaynes dead. There was inquirie made of that snare, and the truth being knowen, it was approued that *Mutezuma* had prepared. 30000. Souldiers who where in campe for that purpose within two leagues of the Citie, and that the streates in *Chololla* were stopped vp with timber and rayles, and the toppes of their houses prouided with stones, whiche houses are made with playne rooffes or sotties, and the highe way stopped vp, & other false bywayes made with déepe holes pitched ful of stakes very sharpe, to spoyle and lame both horse and man: these engines were finely couered with sande, and coulde not be espied, although the skoute had

Correction of treason.

U.iij.   gone

gone before on foote to discouer. The matter also was very suspitious, for these Citizens of *Chololla* had not at any time come to visite hym, or sente any presente. vnto him as others had done.

Wherevpon *Cortez* consulted with the *Tlaxcaltecas* to sende certayne messengers to *Chololla*, to request their Captaynes and rulers to come vnto him, who did their message accordingly, and the *Chollollans* woulde not come, but yet they sent three or foure persons to excuse them, saying ý they were not well at ease, praying him to signifie vnto them what he woulde haue: the *Tlaxcaltecas* enformed *Cortes* that those messengers were menne of small credite and of lowe degrée, wishyng hym not to departe till their Captayne came. In this sorte *Cortes* returned their messengers backe agayne, with commaundement written, declaring that if they came not within three dayes, hée woulde proclayme them rebelles and his vtter enimies, and as suche would he chasten them with all rigour.

When this commaundement came vnto them, the next day followyng came many Lordes and Captaynes to make their excuse, saying, that the *Tlaxcaltecas* were their enimics, and that through them they coulde not liue in safetie: lykewise they knewe of the euill reporte whiche they had made agaynst them : wherefore they besought him to giue no credite vnto them, for why, they were both false and cruell menne : beséechyng him also to goe with them to their Citie, and then he shoulde sée that all was but a mockery that had bene tolde him, and they his good and faythfull friends: and laste of all they offered to serue him as tributary subiectes.

Cortes commaunded that all this talke shoulde be sette downe in wryting before the Notary and his interpreters, and so tooke his leaue of the Citizens of *Tlaxcallen*. *Maxixca* wepte at his departure, but there wente in his com

pany a hundreth thousande men of warre: there were a-
mong them many Marchantes that wente to bartet for
salte and Mantels.

Cortes commaunded that those hundreth thousande
men should go alwayes by theselues: that day he reached
not to *Chololla*, but abode by a broke side, and thither came
many of the citie, to desire him that the *Tlaxcalsecas* should
not doe any hurte in their countrey: wherevpon *Cortes* comaunded them to returne backe againe all sauing. 5000.
or there aboute, much against their willes. But they stil
required him to take good heede of those euill folke, who
be not (quoth they) men of warre, but pedlers, and men of
double harte: and they of their partes would be very loth
to leaue him in any peril or daunger, hauing giuen themselues to be his true and faithfull friendes.

The nexte day in the morning the Spaniardes came
to *Chololla*, and there came out neere. 10000. *Indians* to recepue him with their Captaynes in good order: many of
them presented vnto him bread, foule, & roses, and euery
Captayne as he approched welcomed *Cortes*, and then
stode aside that the reste in order mighte come vnto him.
And when he came entring into the Citie, all the other
Citizes recepued him, marueling to see such men & horses.

After all this came out all the religious menne, as
Priests, and Ministers to the idols (who were many and
straunge to beholde,) and all were clothed in white lyke
vnto surplices, and hemmed with Cotten threede: some
brought instrumentes of musicke like vnto Cornettes,
other brought instrumets made of bones, other an instru-
met like a ketel couered with skin, some brought chafing
dishes of coales with perfumes, others brought idols couered, and finally they al came singing in their language,
which was a terrible noyse, and drew neere *Cortes* and his
copany, sensing them with sweete smelles in their sensers.

With

With this pompe and solemnitie(whiche truely was great)they brought him into the Cittie,and lodged him in a house where was roume inough for him and his, and gaue vnto eche of them a Gynnea cocke, and his *Indians* of *Tlaxcallan*,*Zempoallan* and *Iztacmixtlitan*,were prouided by themselues.

The conspiracie of the Cholollans
to kill *Cortes* and his men.

 L that night following *Cortes* was vigilant with all his company, for bothe in the way and in the towne they had found some of the things wherof they had bene aduised before in *Tlaxcallan*,and although their firste present was a Gynnea cocke to eche mans allowance, other thre dayes following they gaue them nothing almost to eate, and very seldome the Captaynes came to visite them, whereof *Cortes* had great suspition.

And in this meane while the Embassadours of *Mutezuma* entreated him to leaue of his iourney to *Mexico*, alleaging that their great king woulde die in beholdyng their beardes & gesture: other times they sayde that there was no passage, other times they woulde say that they wanted wherewith to sustayne them. And seyng them fully and in euery respecte answered to all these poyntes, they caused the Townes menne to enforme them, that where *Mutezuma* his abiding was, were menstrous Lysardes, Tigers, Lions, and many other fierce beastes, the whiche when *Mutezuma* commaunded to be losed, were sufficient to plucke in péces, and to destroy those fewe straungers: and seyng that all these pollicies auayled not, they consulted with the Captaynes and chiefe Citizens to

murder

murder the Christians. And bycause they shoulde to
bʒyng it to passe, the Embassadours pʒomysed the Citizens greate rewardes on the behalfe of *Mutezuma*, and
pʒesented to theyʒ generall a dʒumme of Golde, and pʒo-
mised to bʒyng the thirtie thousande souldiers whiche lay
aboute two leagues from thence: the *Chololans* pʒomysed to deliuer them bounde hande and fote. But yet they
woulde not consente that those Souldiers of *Culhua* shoulde
come into their Cittie, fearyng that they (vnder colour
of friendshippe) woulde remayne with the towne, for
why, the *Mexicans* had vsed the lyke sleyght. And in this
soʒte they with one bolte meante to kill two byʒdes at a
shote, foʒ they thought to take the Spaniardes sléepyng,
and then to remayne with the Towne of *Chololla*. Also it
was determined, that if all these pʒetences coulde not be
bʒought to passe, that then they shoulde be conducted a contrary way to *Mexico* vpon the left hande, in the whiche
were many daungerous places, bycause the way was all
sandy, with many sluces, diches, and holes of thʒée fadome
déepe, meanyng there to méete them and to carry them
bounde to *Mutezuma*: this matter being fully agréed, they
beganne to take away theyʒ householde stuffe, and to carry it with their wiues and chyldʒen vp into the mountaynes.

Many pe-
rils.

And our men beyng also readye to departe from thence
foʒ theyʒ small chéere with euill countenaunce, it happened, an *Indian* woman (beyng wife to one of the pʒincipa-
lest Cittizens,) hauing some affection to the bearded men,
saydé vnto *Marina*, that shée shoulde abide there with hyʒ,
foʒ that she loued hir well, and that it woulde grieue hir
that she should be slayne with hir maystter. *Marina* dissimulyng the matter, pʒocured to knowe what they were
that had conspired the thing, and hauing knowledge therof, she ranne to séeke *Aguillar* hir fellow interpʒeter, and

Helpe from
God.

          X.   bothe

both togither enformed Cortes of the whole matter.

Cortes hearyng this newes, slepte not, but incontinent examined twoo of the Citizens, who confessed the thyng euen as it passed, and as the Gentlewoman had declared: wherevpon Cortes stayed his iourney twoo dayes, to mollifie the matter and to disapoynt them of that euill pretended purpose, and also to correcte their offences, he commaunded their rulers to be called, saying that he had to talke with them, and when they were comen he requyred them neyther to vse lies nor deceytes with hym, but rather lyke menne to defie him to the fielde and battayle, for (quoth hée) honest menne vse rather to fighte than to lie. They all answered that they were his friendes and seruitours, and no liars, and that it mighte please him to shewe them when he woulde departe, for they woulde goe armed to kéepe hym company. He answered that he woulde departe the nexte day followyng, and that he required but onely some of their slaues to carry his fardage, bycause his owne *Tamemez* or Carriars were weried: lykewise he requyred some prouision of vignall.

At this laste requeste they smyled, saying among themselues, to what purpose will these men haue victuals, for shortly they themselues shalbe boyled and eaten with the sause called *Axi*, yea, and if *Mutezuma* had not pretended their bodies for his owne dishe, they had bene eaten here before this tyme.

The

The punishment that Cortez executed for conspiracie.

He nexte day in the mozenyng the *Cholol-lans* thinkyng that they had their deter-minate purpose in good readinesse, they came and bzought many to carry their fardage, & other some to carry the Spa-niardes vppon their backes, hopyng to appzehed them in the same ozder. There came also many armed men of the most valiantest, to kill him that should disozder himselfe. Likewise that day their Pziests sacri-ficed ten childzen of thzee peaₑes of age to their God *Que-zalcouatl,* fiue of these childzen were menne, and the o-ther fiue wemen, whiche was their custome when they began their warres: the Captaynes placed themselues at the foure dozes of *Cortes* his house with some armed men. *Cortes* earely in the mozenyng had secretely in a readi-nesse the *Indians* of *Zempoallan* and *Tlaxcallan,* and other friends: he comaunded his horsemen to take their horses, giuing them this watche wozde, that when they hearde the noyse of the shotte of a handgun, that then they should play the mē, foz it impozted all their liues. And he seing the townes men appzoch nære his lodging, commaunded ȳ captaynes & chiefest of them to come vnto him, saying, ȳ he would take his leaue of them: there came many, but he would not suffer aboue thirtie persons to come in, who were the pzincipallest, and declared vnto thē, that alwaies he had dealte truly with them, & they with him nothing but treason and lies. Likewise they had vnder colour re-quested that his friēds the *Tlaxcaltecas* shuld not come vn-to their towne, & that he fulfilled there in their desire, & al-so comaunded his own men in no wise to be hurtful vnto thē, yea & although they had not pzouided him of victuals

O vvorthy Cortes.

as reason did require, yet he would not permit any of his men to take the value of one henne from them, so that in recompence of all his gentle dealings and good will, they had moste wickedly procured the death of him and all his companie. And bycause they coulde not perfo2me it in their owne towne, they had prepared the slaughter in the high way, at those daungerous places whiche they had determined to leade them vnto, pretendyng also the helpe of thirtie thousand men, Souldiers of *Mutezuma*, whiche army stode not fully two leagues from thence. And fo2 this ho2rible and detestable wickednesse yée shall all die, and in memo2y of trayto2s J will destroy this cittie, and turne the fundations vpwardes, so that there shall remayne no remembraunce of you.

Their offence beyng manifest, coulde not be denied, and lookyng one vpon an other, their colours wared pale and wanne, saying, this man is lyke vnto our Goddes, who knoweth all things, therefo2e lette vs not denie the truth, and openly befo2e the Embassadours of *Mutezuma* confesse their erreur and euill facte.

Then sayd *Cortes* to the Embassadours, you do sée that we should haue bene slaine by the *Chololans*, and th2ough the procurement of *Mutezuma*, but yet J beleue it not, considerying that he is my friende and a mightie P2ince, saying also that Noble men vsed neyther treason no2 lyes, wherefo2e feare not you, but these dissemblyng Trayto2s shall be punished, fo2 you are persons inuiolable and messengers of a P2ince, whome he meante to serue and not offende, bicause he had an assured opinion in *Mutezuma*, to be a vertuous P2ince, and one that woulde not committe villanie.

All these wo2des he spake, bycause he woulde not fall out with *Mutezuma*, vntill he sawe himselfe within the Cittie of *Mexico*.

Incontie

Incontinent he commaunded some of those Captaines to be slayne, and kepte the residue bounde. Then he shotte off hys handgun, whiche was the watch vnto his armye, who forthwith sette vppon the Townesmen, and within two houres slewe sire thousand persons and more.

Cortes commaunded that they shoulde kill neyther woman nor childe: they foughte welnere fyue houres : they sette fire on all the houses and Towers that made resistance, and draue all the inhabitantes out of the Towne. The dead carcases lay so thicke, that of force they must treade vpon them.

There were twentie Gentlemen, and many Priestes, who ascended vp to the high tower of the temple, whiche hath a hundred and twenty steppes, from whence wyth arrowes and stones they did muche hurt, and woulde not yéelde, wherevpon oure men set fier to the Tower, and burned them all. Then they erclaymed on their Goddes, who woulde neyther helpe them nor their Citie and holy sanctuary.

The Citie being sacked, oure men toke the spoyle of golde, plate, and feathers, and the *Indians* their friendes toke clothes and salte, which was the treasure that they desired.

Cortez commaunded to ceasse the spoyle. The other Captaynes that lay bounde, hearing of suche a greate destruction and punishment, most pitifully besought *Cortez* to loase some of them, for to sée what was become of their Gods and cómó people. Likewise they humbly besought hún te pardon them, who had not so muche faulte as *Mutezuma*, who perswaded and entised them to that pretended treason.

Upon their lamentable requeste, he leased two of them, and the nert day following the Citie was as ful of people agayne, that there séemed not one to be wanting.

X.iij.   At

At the sute of the *Tlaxcaltecas* who were put for mediators, *Cortes* pardoned them all, and sette his prisoners at libertie, assuring them that the like correction he woulde do vppon al them that should dissemble or shewe an euil countenance, or make lyes, or fynally vse anye kinde of treason toward him: wherevpon they all abode in greate feare. He made the knot of friendship betwéene them and the *Tlaxcaltecas*, which in time past had bin betwixt them, for *Mutezuma* and his auncetors made them enimies, with fayre promises, words and also feare.

The Citizens hauing their generall slayne, chose another with licence of *Cortes*.

The Sanctuary or holy place among
the Indians was Chololla.

Hololla is a city as *Tlaxcallan*, and hathe but one person who is gouernour and general Captayne, chosen by the consente of all the Citizens. It is a Citie of twentie thousande households within the walles, and in the suburbes as muche more. It sheweth outwardes verye beautifull, and full of towers, for there are as manye temples as dayes in ye yeare, & euery temple hath his tower. Our men counted foure hundred towers. The men and women are of good disposition, well fauoured, and very wittie.

The women are Goldsmithes and also Caruers, the men are warriers, and light fellowes, and good maisters for any purpose : they goe better apparelled than anye other

ther *Indias* yet ſéene. They weare foꝛ their vtter garmẽt clokes like vnto Moꝛiſcos, but after an other ſoꝛt. Al the Countrey rounde aboute them is fruitefull and eareable grounde, well watered, and ſo full of people, that there is no waſt grounde, in reſpect whereof, there are ſome pooꝛe, whiche begge from dooꝛe to dooꝛe. The *ſpanyardes* hadde not ſéene any beggers in that Coũtrey befoꝛe they came thither.

Chololla is a Citie of moſt deuotion and Religion in all *India*, it is called ẏ Sanctuary oꝛ holy place among ẏ *Indians*, and thither they trauelled from many places farre diſtante on pilgrimage, and foꝛ this cauſe there were ſo many temples.

Their Cathedꝛall Temple was the beſt and hygheſt of all the new *Spayne*, with a hundꝛed and twenty ſteppes vppe vnto it.

The greateſt Idoll of all their Gods was called *Quezalcouately*, God of the ayꝛe, who was (ſay they) the founder of their Citie, being a Virgin of holy lyfe, and great penance. He inſtituted faſting and dꝛawing of bloud out of their eares and tongs, and lefte a pꝛecepte, that they ſhoulde ſacrifice but onely Quayles, Doues, and other foule.

He neuer ware but one garmente of Cotten, whyche was white, narrow, and long, and vpon that a mantle beſette with certayne redde croſſes.

They haue certayne gréene ſtones whiche were hys, and thoſe they kéepe foꝛ relikes. One of them is lyke an Apes head. Héere they abode twentye dayes, and in thys meane whyle there came ſo manye to buy and ſell, that it was a wonder to ſée. And one of the things that was to bée ſéene in thoſe fayꝛes, was the earthen veſſell, which was excéeding curious and fine.

The

The hill called Popocatepec.

Here is a hill eyght leagues from *Chololla*, called *Popocatepec*, whiche is to say, a hill of smoke, for manye tymes it casseth oute smoke and fier. *Cortez* sente thither tenne *Spanyardes*, with manye *Indians*, to carrie their victuall, and to guide them in the way. The ascending vp was very troublesome, and full of craggie rockes.   They approched so nigh the toppe, that they heard such a terrible noyse which proceeded fro thence, that they durst not goe vnto it, for the grounde dyd tremble and shake, and great quantitie of Asshes whyche disturbed the way: but yet two of them who seemed to be most hardie, and desirous to see straunge things, went vp to the toppe, bicause they would not returne with a deuellesse aunswere, and that they myghte not be accompted cowardes, leauing their fellowes behinde them, proceeded forwards. The *Indians* sayd, what meane these men? for as yet neuer mortall man tooke suche a iourney in hande.

These two valiât fellowes passed through ye desert of Asshes, and at length came vnder a greate smoke verye thicke, and standing there a whyle, the darkenesse vanished partly away, and then appeared the vulcan and concauetie, which was about halfe a league in compasse, out of the whiche the ayre came rebounding, with a greate noyse, very shrill, and whistling, in sort that the whole hil did tremble. It was to be compared vnto an ouen where glasse is made. The smoke and heate was so greate, that they coulde not abide it, and of force were constreyned to returne by the way that they had ascended: but they were not gone farre, whê the vulcan began to lash out flames

of

of fier, aſhes, and imbers, yea and at the laſt ſtones of burning fire: and if they had not chanced to finde a rocke, where vnder they ſhadowed themſelues, vndoubtedlye they had there bin burned.

When with good tokens they were returned where they left their fellowes, the other *Indians* kiſſed their garments as an honor due vnto Gods. They preſented vnto them ſuch things as they had, and wondred much at their facte.

Thoſe ſimple *Indians* thoughte, that that place was an Purgatory. infernall place, where all ſuche as gouerned not well, or vſed tyrannie in their offices, were puniſhed when they dyed, and alſo belæued, that after their purgation, they paſſed into glory.

This vulcan is like vnto the vulcan of *Cicilia*, it is high and round, and neuer wanteth Snowe about it, and is ſéene a farre off in the nighte, it laſheth out flames of fire.

There is néere aboute this hyl many Cities, and *Huexozinco* is one of the nigheſt.

In tenne yeares ſpace this ſtraunge hill of worckyng dyd expell no vapoure or ſmoke: but in the yeare.1540. it beganne agayne to burne, and with the horrible noyſe thereof, the neyghbours that dwelte foure leagues from thence were terrifyed, for the eſpeciall ſtraunge ſmokes that then were ſéene, the like to their predeceſſors hadde not bin ſéene.

The aſhes that procéded from thence came to *Huexozinco, Quelaxcopan, Tepiacac, Quauhquechollâ, Cholollâ,* and *Tlaxcallan,* whiche ſtandeth tenne leagues from thence, yea ſome ſay, it extended fiftéene leagues diſtant, and burned their hearbes in their gardens, their fieldes of corne, trées, and clothes that lay a drying.

Y.   The

The confultation that Mutezuma had,
concerning the comming of Cortez into Mexico.

Ortez pꝛetended not to fall out with *Mu-tezuma*, befoꝛe his comming to *Mexico*, and yet he vnderſtoode all *Mutezuma* hys pꝛetence, wherevppon he complayneth to the Ambaſſadoꝛs, ſaying that he muche maruelled that ſuche a mightie Pꝛince, who by ſo manye Gentlemen had aſſured his friendſhip vnto him, ſhoulde nowe pꝛocure his totall deſtruction , in not keeping hys pꝛomiſe and fidelitie, In conſideration whereof, where he meant to viſit him as a friend, that now he would goe to his Courte as an enimie. The Ambaſſadoꝛs excuſed their maiſters cauſe, beſieching him to withdꝛawe hys furie, and to giue licence to one of them to goe to *Mexico*, who woulde bꝛyng aunſwere from thence with all ſpeede.

Cortes graunted vnto the requeſt, the one of them went, and returned agayne within ſixe dayes in company of a-nother meſſenger that hadde gone thither befoꝛe, who bꝛoughte tenne platters of golde , and a thouſande fiue hundꝛed mantels of cotten, with much victuall, and *Cacao* whiche is a kinde of fruite that ſerueth foꝛ currant mo-ney among them. Likewiſe they bꝛought a certaine kind of wine oꝛ licoure made of *Cacao* and *Centli*. They en-foꝛmed *Cortes*, that *Mutezuma* was innocente of the con-iuration in *Chololla*, noꝛ by anye meanes pꝛiuie to their dealings, affyꝛming moꝛeouer that the garriſon of ſoul-dyers did apperteine to *Acazinco*, and *Acazan*, who were neyghboꝛs to *Chololla*, who by inducement of ſome naugh-tye perſons, had pꝛocured that thing, ſaying that he ſhuld both ſee and vnderſtand him to be his faithful and louing
friend,

friend,p;aping him to come fo;warde on his iourney, fo;
he would abide his comming in *Mexico.*

This ambaſſage pleaſed well *Cortez,* but *Mutezuma*
feared, when he hearde of the ſlaughter, and burning of
Chololla, and ſaide to his friends, theſe are the people that
our Gods ſaid ſhould come and inherite this land.

Prophecie
of the Di-
uell.

Mutezuma went incontinent to his O;ato;ie, and ſhut
in himſelfe alone, where he abode in faſting and p;ayer
eyght dayes, with ſacrifice of many menne, to aſſlake the
fury of his Idolles, who ſeemed to be offended.

The voyce of the Diuell ſpake vnto him, bidding him
not to feare the Ch;iſtians, ſaying they were but fewe,
and when they were come, he ſhoulde doe what he lyſtcd
with them, willing him in no wiſe to ceaſſe from the
bloudy ſacrifice, leaſt ſome miſchance might happen vnto him. And aſſured hym that he ſhould haue the Goddes
Vitzipuchtli, and *Teſcatlipuca* to p;eſerue and keepe hym.
And bycauſe *Quezalcouatle* was agrieued fo; wante of
bloudy ſacrifice, he permitted the Straungers to puniſhe
them of *Chololla.* And *Mutezuma* hearing this dyueliſhe
O;acle, and likewiſe *Cortez* hauing warned him that hee
would viſite hym as an enimie, he was by this perſwa-
ſion of Sathan, the better willing to receyue hym into
Mexico.

Likewiſe *Cortes* when he came to *Chololla,* was ſtrong,
and hadde at commaundemente a mightie power, and
there made hymſelfe ſtronger, the fame whereof, was
blowen ab;oade, th;oughout all the dominions of *Mutezuma.* And whereas the poo;e *Indians* hadde but onely
marnelled at their perſons and furniture, nowe they began to tremble and to feare at his doings, ſo that where-
ſoeuer he came, they opened him the gates with pure
feare, mo;e than fo; any loue.

Mutezuma at the beginning, p;etended to feare *Cortes*

with the fearefull paſſages and other perils and danger, as the foztitude of *Mexico*, with his greate multitude of ſubiectes, and the great number of Pzinces that dyd both ſerue and obey him: and ſæyng that all theſe things pzofited not, he thoughte to haue ouercome him with gyftes and treaſure, knowyng that he hadde required golde: yet he ſawe that nothing woulde pzenaple, foz that *Cortez* woulde nædes come to ſæ hym. wherevppon, he tæke

An euill counſellor.

counſell of the Diuell what he ſhoulde doe in that caſe, vpon which counſell he was ſatiſfyed by hys Pzieſts and Captaynes, that he ought not to warre againſt ſo fewe ſtraungers, foz if he ſo did, the diſhonoz would be his, and chiefly, bycauſe *Cortez* certifyed that he was an Ambaſſadoz, and vſing hym otherwiſe, it myghte ſo fall out, that hys owne ſubiectes would rebell againſte him theyz Lozde and Pzince, ſaying likewiſe that it was manifeſt that the *Otomies* and *Tlaxcaltecas* woulde fauour his ſyde, and alſo manye others, foz to deſtroy and ſpoyle *Mexico*, vpon which conſultation it was openly pzoclaymed, that his will was that the ſtraungers ſhould enter into *Mexico* fræly, thinking that if at anye time they ſhoulde diſpleaſe hym, to make a bzeakefaſt of them the nexte day.

Things that happened to Cortez in
his iourney to Mexico.

Cortez hauyng ſo god an aunſwere of the Ambaſſadozs, he gaue licence to as manye of the *Indians* hys friendes, as liſted to departe home to their houſes, and he likewiſe depated from *Chololla* with ſome bozderers that would nædes follow him.

He lefte the way that the *Mexicans* had perſwaded him
to come, foz it was bothe euill and daungerous, as the
Spaniarde whiche went to the vulcan had ſéene, he went
another playner way and moze nearer. That day he traueled but foure leagues, bicauſe he meant to lodge in the
villages of *Huexozinco*, where he was friendly receyued,
and they pzeſented vnto him ſlaues, garments, and golde,
although but little, foz they are pooze by reaſon that *Mutezuma* hath enuironed them aboute, bicauſe they were of
the parcialitie of *Tlaxcallan*. The nert day in the mozning
he aſcended vp a hill couered with ſnowe, which was ſire
myles of heigth, where if the .30000. Souldiers had wayted foz them, they might eaſily haue taken them, by reaſon
of the great colde: and from the toppe of that hill, they diſcouered ye land of *Mexico*, and the great lake with his villages rounde about, whiche is an erceeding goodly ſight.
But when *Cortes* ſaw that beautifull thing, his ioy was
without comparifon, and he tooke not ſo much pleaſure,
but ſome of his men feared as muche, and there was a
murmuration among them to returne backe againe, yea
and like to haue bene a mutinie among them. But *Cortes*
with his wiſedome and diſſimulation did pacifie the matter, with courage, hope, and gentle wozdes, and they ſeing that their Captayne at all aſſayes was the firſt himſelfe, they feared the leſſe the things that they imagined.
And diſcending downe into the playn, they found a great
large houſe, ſufficient foz him and all his company, with
ſire thouſande *Indians* of *Tlaxcallan*, *Huexozinco*, and *Chololla*. And ye ſeruants of *Mutezuma* made cotages of ſtraw
foz the *Tamemez* oz carriers, who were lade with the fardage, and victuals: there was a good ſupper pzepared foz
them, and great fires to warme them, and all things neceſſary. Thither came many pzincipall perſons from *Mexico* to viſite him, among whome was a kinſman of *Mutezuma,*

Oh wiſe
Cortes.

P.iij.

tezuma, who prefented vnto *Cortes* the value of thꝛee thow
fand Ducates in gold, ɇ befought him to returne backe a
gaine, and to haue confideration of the pouertie, hungꝛ,
ɇ euill way, yea and to paffe in litle boates in daunger of
dꝛowning. And as foꝛ tribute to be giuen to the Empe
rour, a greater fumme ſhould be appointed the though he
went perſonally to *Mexico,* yea and that it ſhould be payde
at what place he would apoint. *Cortes* welcomed them, as
reaſon did require, and pꝛefented vnto them haberdaſhe
toyes, which they eſtemed in much, ɇ chiefly he did louing
ly entertayne *Mutezuma* his kinefman, vnto whome he
made this anſwere, faying, I woulde gladly ſerue ɇ plea
fure fuch a mightie pꝛince as your foueraigne *Mutezuma*
is, if it lay in my haudes without offence of the King my
mayſter, and concerning my goyng to *Mexico, Mutezuma*
ſhall recepue both pleafure and honour rather than other
wiſe, ɇ after I haue talked with him I will fone returne,
likewife hunger I feare not, neyther yet doubt that I noꝛ
none of mine ſhall wante, and foꝛ my paſſage on the wa
ter, I fay it is nothing in compariſon of two thouſande
leagues, which I haue fayled onely to come and vifit him.
      But yet foꝛ all this talke, if they had founde him care
leſſe, they would haue pinched him as fome doth fay, foꝛ
he gaue them to vnderſtand that he noꝛ his men ſlept not
by night, noꝛ yet vnarmed themfelues, yea and alfo if it
chanced the to finde in the night feafon any that were not
of their company, they ſlew them out of hād, defiring him
to aduife his men thereof, leaſt any of them ſhould happen
to fall into that daunger, which would much grieue him,
and with this talke they went all to take their reſte.
      The next day in the moꝛning he pꝛoceded foꝛward and
came to *Amaquemecan* which is two leagues frō thence, ɇ
ſtandeth in the pꝛouince of *Chalco,* a towne that cōtayneth
20000. houſeholders. The Loꝛde of that towne pꝛefented
                                                          to

to *Cortes* fourtie women flaues,and.3000. Ducats in gold, with meate abūdantly foz two dayes, and fecretely made complaynt vnto him of *Mutezuma*. And from thence he went to another towne foure leagues from thēce,the one half therof was builte vpon the lake, and the other halfe vpon the lande at the foote of a ragged hill. There went in his company many fubiectes of *Mutezuma* foz purueyers, but yet both they and the townes men would fayne haue layde hand vpon the Spaniardes, and euery night would fende their fpies to fée what the Chziftians did, but the watch flew about twentie of them, wherbpon the matter ftayed and their pzetence toke no effect: fure it is a thing to laugh at,foz at euery fancie they woulde pzone to kill them,and yet they were not foz the purpofe.   The nexte day in the moznyng came twelue Lozdes from *Mexico*, among whome was *Cacama* Neuew to *Mutezuma*, who was Lozde of *Tezcuco* a yong man of.xxv. yeares of age, whom the *Indians* did much honour: he was carried vpon their fhoulders, & when they fet him downe one went be- foze with a bzome to fwéep the duft out of his way.Thefe Gentlemen came to accōpany *Cortes* excufing *Mutezuma*, faying that he was not well at eafe & therfoze he came not perfonally to receiue him.And yet they entreated *Cortes* to returne backe againe, & not to come vnto *Mexico*, gyuing him to vnderftand by fignes, ȳ they would there difpleafe him,yea & alfo defend the paffage & entrance, a thing eafie to be done,but they were either blinded oz elfe they durft not bzeake the Calfey. *Cortes* entertayned the like noble mē,& gaue vnto thē of his haberdafhe, & departed from ȳ towne wt many graue perfonages who carried with thē a great trayne,whiche filled vp the way well nigh as they fhould paffe,wōdzing at their beardes, harneys,apparell, hozfes & ozdinaunce,faying to themfelues,thefe be Gods. *Cortes* gaue them warning not to come among the hozfes,

nor among his men, for feare they would kil them. This
he made them beléeue bicause he would not haue his way
stopped, for ý the number of thē was so great. They then
came to a towne buylte vpon the water of two thousand
houses, and before they came thither they had gone more
than halfe a league vppon a fayre Calsey, whiche was
twentie foote brode: the towne had fayre houses and many
towers: the Lord of the towne did receyue them worship-
fully, and prouided all things plentifully, desiryng him to
abide there that night, and secretly made complayntes a-
gainst *Mutezuma*, of many wrongs and exactions done by
him, and certified him, that from thence the way was very fayre to *Mexico*, and al the like calsey as he had passed.
With this newes *Cortes* was very glad, for he meant to
haue stayed there for to haue buylte barkes and foystes,
& yet he feared least they woulde breake the calsey, wherfore he had alwayes a care ouer *Cacama*, who with the o-
ther Lordes desired him not to abide there, but to proceede
forward to *Iztacpalapan*, which was but two leagues off,
and that the Lorde thereof was another Neuew to *Mutezuma*. To admit their request he wēt with them to that
towne, and from thence to *Mexico* was but two leagues,
the which the next day he might goe at pleasure, and come
timely into the Citie, & in this order came to *Iztacpalapan*.

Euery fiue houres came messengers betwixte *Cortes*
and *Mutezuma*: then came *Cuetlauac* Lorde of that towne,
with the Lorde *Cullouacan* his kinsman to receyue him,
who presented vnto him, slaues, garments, and feathers,
and to the value of foure thousande Ducates in golde.
Cuetlauac receyued al the Spaniards into his own house,
whiche hath very fayre lodgings all of stone and Carpenters worke exceeding well wrought, with high & lowe
roumes, with all kinde of seruice: The chambers were
hanged with cloth of Cotten, very rich, after their maner.
                                                                There

There were fayre gardés repleniſhed with many ſwéete floures, and ſwéete trées garniſhed with netwozke, made of Canes, and couered with roſes and other fine hearbes, with ſundzy pondes of ſwéete water. There was an other garden very beautifull of all ſoztes of fruptes and hearbes, with a great ponde walled with lyme and ſtone, and was foure hundzeth paces ſquare, made with fayre ſteppes to diſcende vnto the bottome in many places, and was full of diuers kindes of fiſhes, and many kinde of water birds, which ſomtimes couered ý pond, as Gulles. Mewes, and ſuch like. *Iztacpallapan* is a towne of. 10000. houſcholds, ¶ is pláted in a lake of ſalt water, the one half of the towne buylt on the water, ¶ the other on the lande.

The Solemne pompe vvherevvith
Cortez was receyued into *Mexico.*

From *Iztacpalapan* to *Mexico* is two leagues all vpon a fayre calſey, vpon the which eight hozſemé may paſſe on rāke, and ſo directly ſtraight as though it had bene made by line. And who ſoeuer hath good eieſight might diſcerne the gateſof *Mexico* from thence. *Coyoacan* is a towne of ſixe thouſande dwellers, *Vizilopuchtli* is of fiue thouſand. Theſe townes are planted in the lake, and are adozned with many temples, whiche haue many fayre towers, that doe beautifie exceedingly the lake. There is great contractatió of Salte, which is made there, and from thence is carried abzode to fayzes and markets, whiche thing was a greate rente to *Mutezuma.* Vpon this Calſey are many dzawe bzidges buylt vpon fayre arches that the water paſſeth thzough.

Cortes paſſed this calſey with. 400. Spaniardes, ¶. 6000. *Indians* his friends: theyz paſſage was with much ado, by

Z. reaſon

reason of the great multitude of *Indians* which came to sée
him, & cóming neare the citie, there adioyned another calsey with a bioder passage, where standeth a strong bulwarke of stone of the heigth of.ij.fadom, with two towers
on eche side, and two gates very strong. Here at this
foite came thiée thousande Courtiers and Citizens to receyue him, & euery of them touched the grounde with his
right hand and kissed it, and passed foiwards in the oider
as they came. These salutatiós endured an houre & moie.
From the bulwark the calsey lieth directly, and befoie the
entraunce into the streate there is an other diawebiidge
made of timber ten paces bioade, vnder the which the water passeth to and fro. At this biidge came *Mutezuma* to
receyue *Cortes* vnder a Canapie of gréene feathers & golde
with much argentery hangyng thereat, whiche Canapie
foure noble men did carry. And the two piinces *Cuetlauac*,
and *Cacama* his neuewes, did leade him by eache arme: all
thiée were riche appareled & al of one fashion, except *Mu-*
tezuma, whiche had a payie of shoes of golde besette with
pietious stones, and the soles were tied to the vpper part
with latchets, as is painted of the Antikes. His Gentlemen wente by two and two laying downe and taking vp
mantels and couerlets vpon the ground, bicause his féete
should not touche the same: then followed him as in pio-
cession.200.noble men barefooted, with garments of a ri-
cher liuery than the first thiée thousand. *Mutezuma* came
in the middest of the streate, and the others came behinde
him as nigh the wal as they mought, their faces towards
the grounde, foi it was a great offence to loke him in the
face. *Cortes* alighted from his hoise, and accoiding to our
vse went to embiace him, but the Piinces who led him by
the armes would not suffer him to come so nigh, foi they
held it foi sin to touch him, but yet saluted ech one ý other.
Cortes put about *Mutezuma* his necke a coller of Mar-
                                                    garites,

garites, Diamondes, & other ftones al of glaffe. Mutezuma receyued it thankfully, & wente before with one of the
princes his Neuewes, & comaunded the other to lead Cortes by the hand next after him in the middeft of the ftreat:
and proceeding forwarde in this order, then came the Gē-
tlemen in the richeft liuery to welcome him one by one,
touchyng the grownd with their handes, & after returned
to their ftandyng. And if the Citizens had come as they
requeffed, all ý day would not haue ferued for falutatiōs.
The coller of glaffe pleafed well Mutezuma, and bycaufe
he woulde not take without giuyng a better thing as a
great prince, he commaunded to be brought two collers
of redde prawnes, which there are muche effeemed, and at
euery one of them hanged eight ſhrimpes of gold of excellent workemanſhip, & of a finger length euery one, he put
thefe collers with his owne hands about Cortes his necke,
the which was effeemed a moft great fauour, yea and the
Indians marueled at it. At this time they were come to
the ftreate ende, whiche was almoft a mile long, broade,
ftraight and very fayre and full of houfes on eche fide, in
whofe dores, windowes and tops was fuch a multitude of
Indians to beholde the ftrangers, that I knowe not who
wondered moft, our men to fee fuch a number of them, or
elfe they to fee our men, their ordinance & horfes, a thing
fo ftraunge vnto them. They were brought vnto a great
court or houfe of idols, which was ý lodging of Axaiaca,
at the doze whereof Mutezuma toke Cortes by the hande
and brought him into a fayre hall, and placed him vpon a
riche carpet, faying vnto him, Sir nowe are you in your
owne houfe, eate and take your reft & pleafure, for I wil
ſhortly come and vifite you againe. Such (as you heare)
was the receiuing of Hernando Cortes by Mutezuma a moft
mightie King, into his great and famous Citie of Mexico,
the eight day of Nouember, 1519.

The Oration of Mutezuma to
the Spanyardes.

He houſe where the Spaniardes were lodged was great and large, with many fayre chambers ſufficient for them all: it was nete, cleane matted, and hanged with cloth of Cotten, and feathers of many colours, pleaſant to behold. When *Mutezuma* was departed fró *Cortes*, he began to ſette his houſe in order, and placed the ordinaunce at his doze, and hauing all his things in good ſorte, he went to a ſumptuous dinner that was prepared for him. As ſoone as *Mutezuma* had made an ende of his dinner hearyng that the ſtraungers were ryſen from the table, and repoſed a while, then came he to *Cortes*, ſalutyng him, and ſatte downe by him. He gaue vnto him diuers iewels of gold plate, feathers, and many garméts of Cotten, both riche, well wouen, & wrought of ſtraunge colours, a thing truely, that did manifeſt his greatneſſe, and alſo cófirme their imagination. This gifte was deliuered honozably, and then began his talke as foloweth: Lozde and Gentlemen, I doe much reioyce to haue in my houſe ſuch valiant men as ye are, for to vſe you with curteſie, and entreate you with honour, accozding to your deſerte and my eſtate. And where heretofoze I deſired that you ſhoulde not come hither, the onely cauſe was, my people had a greate feare to ſée you, for your geſture & grimme beards did terrifie them, yea, they repozted that yée had ſuch beaſtes as ſwallowed men, and that your cóming was fró heauen, bzinging with you lightning, thunder & thúderbolts, wherwith you made the earth to tréble & to ſhake, and that yée ſlew therewith whom ye pleaſed. But now I do ſée & know that you are moztall mé, & that ye are quiet & hurt no man: alſo I haue ſéene your hozſes, which

which are but your seruauntes, and youre Gunnes lyke
vnto shootyng Trunkes. I do now hold all for fables and
lyes which hath bin reported of you, and I do also accept
you for my néere kinsmen. My father tolde me that hée
had heard his forefathers say, of whome I doe discende,
that they helde opinion howe they were not naturals of
thys lande, but come hither by chance, in companye of a
mighty Lorde, who after a while that they hadde abode
héere, they returned to their natiue soyle : After manye
yeares expyred, they came agayne for those whome they
had left héere behind them, but they woulde not goe wyth
them, bycause they had héere inhabited, and hadde wyues
and children, and great gouernement in the land. Nowe
these myghtie Lords séeyng that they were so stubborne,
and woulde not returne with them, departed from them
sore displeased, saying, that he woulde sende his children
that should both rule and gouerne them, in iustice, peace,
and auntient Religion, and for this consideration, wée
haue alwayes expected and beléued, that suche a people
should come to rule and gouerne vs, and considering from
whence you come, I doe thinke that you are they whome
we looked for, and the notice which the greate Emperour
Charles had of vs, who hath now sent you hither. Therefore Lorde and Captayne, be well assured, that we wyll
obey you, if there be no fayned or deceptefull matter in
your dealings, and will also deuide wyth you and youres
all that we haue. And although this which I haue sayde
were not only for youre vertue, fame, and déedes of valiant Gentlemen, I would yet do it for your worthinesse
in the battayles of *Tauasco*, *Teocazinco*, and *Chololla*, béeyng
so few, to ouercome so many.

Now agayne, if ye ymagine that I am a God, and the
walles and roufes of my houses, and all my vessell of seruice to be of pure golde, as the men of *Zempoallan*, *Tlax-*
callan,

Z.iij.

A strange
opinion.

callan, and *Huexozinco* haue enformed you, it is not so, and I iudge you to be so wise, that you giue no credit to such fables. You shall also note, that through your commyng hither, manye of my subiectes haue rebelled, and are become my mortall enimies, but yet I purpose to breake their wings. Come féele you my body, I am of fleshe and bone, a mortal man as others are, and no God, although as a King I doe estéeme my selfe of a greater dignitie and prehemiuéce than others. My houses you do also sée, which are of tymber and earthe, and the principallest of Masons worke, therefore nowe you do both knowe and sée what odious lyars those talebearers were. But troth it is, that golde plate, feathers, armour, iewels, and other riches, I haue in the treasory of my forefathers a long time preserued, as the vse of Kings is, all the which you é yours shal enioy at all times. And now it may please you to take your rest, for I know that you are wéery of your iourney. *Cortez* with ioyfull countenance humbled himselfe, séeyng some teares fall from *Mutezuma* his eyes, saying vnto him, vppon the trust I haue hadde in youre clemencye, I insisted to come both to sée and talke wyth your highnesse, and now I know that all are lyes which hath bin tolde me. The like youre highnesse hath bearde reported of vs, assure youre selfe, that the Emperoure Kyng of *Spayne* is your naturall Lorde, whome yée haue expected for, he is the onely heyre from whence youre lynage dothe procéede, and as touching the offer of youre highnesse treasure, I do most hartyly thanke you.

　　After all this communication, *Mutezuma* demaunded whether the bearded men whiche came with him, were eyther his vassals or his slaues, bycause he would entertayne eache one accordíng to his estate. *Cortes* aunswered, that they were all his bréethren, friendes, and fellowes, except some that were his seruauntes.

A louing
aunswere.

Then

Then he departed, and wente home to his Pallace, and there enformed himselfe particularlye who were Gentlemen, and who were not, and accozding thervnto, sent euery one particular gift oz pzesent. To the Gentlemen he sente the rewarde by his Controller, and to the Marriners & other seruitozs, by a Page of his houßholde.

The Maieſtie and order, vvherevvith
Mutezuma was ſerued.

Mutezuma was a man of a ſmall ſtature and leane, his couloure tawnie as all the *Indians* are. He hadde long heare on hys heade, ſixe little heares vppon him, as though they hadde bin put in with a bodkin. His thinne bearde was blacke. Hee was a man of fayze condition, and a doer of Iuſtice, well ſpoken, graue and wiſe, beloued and feared among his ſubiectes. *MuteZuma* doth ſignifie ſadneſſe.

To ý pzoper names of Kings and Lozds, they do adde this ſillable C. whiche is foz curteſie and dignitie, as we vſe Lozd. The Turke vſeth *Zultan.* The Moze oz Barbarian calleth his Lozde *Mulley,* and ſo the *Indians* ſay *MuteZumaZin.* His people hadde him in ſuch reuerence, that he permitted none to ſit in his ſight, noz yet in his pzeſence to weare ſhoes, noz loke him in the face, except very few Pzinces. He was glad of the conuerſation of the *Spanyardes,* and would not ſuffer them to ſtande on fote, foz the great eſtimation he had of them, and if he lyked any of the *Spanyardes* garments, he woulde exchange his apparell foz theirs.

He changed his owne apparell foure times euery day, and he neuer clothed himſelfe agayne with the garmentes whiche he hadde once wozne, but all ſuche were kepte

kept in his Guardrobe, for to giue in presents to his seruantes and Embassadors, and vnto valiante souldyers
which had take any enimie prisoner, and that was esteemed a great reward, and a title of priuiledge.

The costly matels wherof had bin diuers sent to *Cortes*,
were of the same Guardrobe.

Mutezuma went alwayes very net and fine in hys attire. He bathed him in his hotehouse foure times euerye
day. He went seldoome out of his Chamber, but when hee
went to his meate. He eate alwayes alone, but solemne-
lye and with great abundance. His table was a pillowe,
or else a couple of coulloured skynnes. His Chayre was
a fourefooted stole made of one peece, and hollowe in the
middest, well wroughte and paynted. His table clothes,
napkins and towels were made of Cotten woll, verye
white and newe, for he was neuer serued but once wyth
that naperie. Foure hundred Pages broughte in hys
meate, all sonnes of greate Lordes, and placed it vppon a
table in his greate Hall. The meate beyng broughte in,
then came *Mutezuma* to beholde the dishes, and appoynted those dishes that liked him best, and chafing dishes
were prepared to keepe that meate warme, and seldoome
would eate of any other dish, except the Lord Stewarde
or Controller should highly commende any other dishe.

Before he sate downe, came twentie of his wines of
the fayrest and best esteemed, or else those that serued
weekely by turne, broughte in the bason and ewer, wyth
greate humblenesse. This done, he sate him downe, and
then came the Lord Steward, and drewe a wooden netts
before him, bycause none shoulde come nigh his table.
And this noble man alone placed the dishes, and also
toke them away, for the Pages who broughte in the
meate came not neere the table, nor yet spake any word,
nor no man else.

Whyle

While the Lord *Mutezuma* was at his meate, excepte
some Iester, they al serued him barefoted. There assisted
alwayes somewhat a farre off, sixe auntiente and noble
men, vnto whome he vsed to giue of the dish that best lyked him, who recepued the same at his hande with greate
reuerence, and eate it incontinent, without loking in his
face, whiche was the greatest humilitie that they coulde
vse before him. He had musike of Fiocle, Flute, and of a
Snayle shell, and a Caudron couered with a skinne, and
suche other strange instrumentes. They hadde very euill
voyces to sing. Always at dinner time he had Dwarfes,
crokebackes, and other deformed counterfets, all for
maiestie and to laugh at, who hadde their meate in the
Hall among the Iesters and Ioyots, whiche were fedde
with parte of the meate that came from *Mutezuma* hys
table, all the rest of the meate was giuen to three thousand of the Guard, who attended ordinarily in the parde
or court, and therefore they say that there was broughte
for his table three thousande dishes, and as manye pottes
of wine, suche as they vse, and that continually the but-
trey and Pantrey stode open, whiche was a wonder to
see what was in them. The platters, dishes, and cuppes,
were al of earth, whereof the king was serued but once,
and so fro meale to meale new. He had likewise his seruice of golde and plate verye riche, but he vsed not to bee
serued with it, (they say) bycause he woulde not be serued
twice therewith, the whiche he thoughte a base thing.
Some affirme, that yong children were slayne and dressed in diuers kind of dishes for *Mutezuma* his table, but
it was not so, only of mans flesh sacrifised he fedde nowe
and then. The table being taken vp, then came againe
the Gentlewomen to bring water for his hands, with the
like reuerence as they vsed at the first, and then went they
to dinner with the other wiues, so that then the Gentle-

Aa.   men

men and Pages waited as their course fell.

The footeplayers that played
before Mutezuma.

Hen his table was taken vp, and his ſer-
uitoʒs gone to meate, *Mutezuma* ſate ſtil:
then came in the ſuiters that hadde any
affayʒes to deale with him, barefoted, foʒ
all the perſons did vſe that reuerence, excepte ſome Pʒinces his kinſmen, as the
Loʒdes of *Teſcuco,* and *Tlacopan,* and a fewe others : and
being colde weather, they vſed to weare olde ragged
clothes vppon theyʒ riche garmentes. Al ſuiters vſed to
make thʒee oʒ foure curteſies, not loking towaʒd his face,
and ſpeaking vnto him their heads downewardes, and in
that oʒder retyʒed backe agayne. *Mutezuma* aunſwered
his ſuiters very grauely, with lowe voyce, and in fewe
woʒds, and not to al ſuiters, foʒ others his ſecretaries oʒ
counſellers that ſtode vp, anſwered foʒ him, and hauyng
their aunſwere, they returned backewardes, not turning
their tayles to the pʒince. After theſe buſineſſes done, he
vſed ſome recreation, hearing Jeſters oʒ ſongs, wherein
he delighted much, oʒ elſe to loke vpon the players, who
play with their fete, as we doe with oure handes. Theſe
haue a cudgell like vnto a paſtlers rowler, whiche they
toſſe high and lowe, as it were a bal in the ayʒe, ſtraunge
to beholde.   They vſe other playes to paſſe the tyme, in
ſuch an oʒder, that it ſemed maruellous to the lokers on.
Cortez bʒoughte into *Spayne* ſome of theſe players. Alſo
they vſe *Matachines,* in ſuche ſoʒte they do play, that they
ſtand each vppon others ſhoulders, and he that ſtandeth
higheſt, ſheweth many feates.   Sometime *Mutezuma*
did beholde the players, who played at a game called *Pa-*
                                                   toliztli,

toliztli, whiche is muche like oure Tables, and they play with beanes, squared like dice, which they call *Patolli,* and throw them out of both their hands vpon a matte, or else vpon the ground, where are made certaine strikes, vpon which they set downe the chance that is throwen: and at this game they play all that they haue, and many tymes they valew theyr owne bodyes, and play that into capti-vitie, and to remayne a slaue, I meane such as are com-mon gamesters of small estate.

The Tennis play in Mexico.

Sometimes *Mutezuma* went to the Tennis Courte. Their ball is called *Villamaliztli,* and is made of the gumme which commeth from a tree called *Vlli.* This tree groweth in a hote Countrey. The gumme being kneded togither, and so made round, is as blacke as pitch, and somewhat heauie, and very harde for the hande, but yet good and light to rebound, and better than our winde-balles. They play not at chases, but at bandie, or at checke, that is, if the ball touch the wall it loseth. They maye strike the ball with any part of their body, but there is al-wayes a penaltie if they only strike not with the buttoke or side, whiche is the finest play: wherefore they vse a skynne vpon eache buttocke. They play so many to so many for a packe of mantels, or according to the abilitie of the players. Also they play for golde and feathers, and sometime for their owne bodyes, as they vse at *Patolli,* which is there permitted & lawfull. The Tennis Court is called *Tlachtli,* and is a Hall long and narrow, but wy-der vpwards, than downewardes, and higher on the sides than at ý ends, which is an industrie for their play. The house is always white and smooth in the side walles: they haue certain stones like vnto mylstones, wt a little hole in the middeſt that paſſeth through the ſtone, the hole is ſo ſmall, that ſcarcely the ball maye paſſe through, but hée that chanceth to ſtrike the ball into the hole, whiche ſeldome happeneth, winneth the game, and by an auntiente lawe and cuſtome among Tennis players, he ought to haue the clokes of all thoſe that ſtande and beholde the play, on that ſide that the ball went in, and in ſome Tennis Courtes, the halfe of the garmentes of them that ſtande lꝏkyng on. The winner is then bounde to make certayne ſacrifice to the God of the Tennis play, and to the ſtone where the ball entred. The beholders of the play woulde ſaye, that ſuche a wynner ſhould be a thiefe and an adulterer, or elſe that he ſhoulde dye quickly.

They vſed in the Temple of the Tennis play two Images of the God of the ball, which ſtꝏde vpon the two lower walles.   Their Sacrifice was celebrated at midnighte, with many Ceremonies and Witchcraftes, and ſongs for that purpoſe. Then came a Prieſte from the Cathedrall Churche, wyth other Religious perſons to bleſſe the Sacrifice, ſaying certayne diueliſhe prayers, and throwing the ball four tymes in the Tennis Court. In thys order was the Tennis play conſecrated, and after thys conſecration it was lawfull to play, or elſe not, for this dilligence was firſte to be done when any Tennis Court or play was newly built.

The owner of the Tennis Courte alſo woulde neuer ſuffer any to play, vntill he had firſt offered ſomething to the Idoll, theyr ſuperſtition was ſo great.

Mutezuma broughte the *ſpanyardes* to behold this paſtyme, and gaue the to vnderſtande, y he delyghted much in thys game, and alſo to ſée our men play at Cardes and Dyce.

The

The number of vviues that Mutezuma
had in his houfe.

Vtezuma had many houfes as wel in *Mexico* as without, fo2 his recreation and pleaſure, as alfo fo2 his o2dinary dwelling. To w2ite of al it ſhould be tedious, but where his continual abyding was, he named *Tepac*, that is to fay, Pallace. And that Pallace had twenty do2es o2 gates which had their outcomming into the cōmon ſtreates.

It hath th2ée courtes, and in the one ſtandeth a fay2e fountaine, many halles, and a hund2ed chambers of twentie-th2ée, and thirtie fote long, an hundered bathes ⁊ hot houſes : and although the building was without naples, yet very god wo2kmanſhip.

The walles were made of maſons wo2k, and w2ought of Marble, Jaſpe, and other blacke ſtone, with vaines of redde, like vnto rubies and other ſtones, whiche gliſtered very fay2e: the Rofes wer w2ought of Tymber, and curiouſly carued : the Timber was Ced2e, Cipers, ⁊ Pyne tree: the chambers were painted and hong with cloth ſt cotten, and clothe made of Conneys haire and feathers. The beddes were po2e and of no ballew, fo2 they were nothing but Mantels layde vpon mattes, o2 vpon Hay, o2 elſe mades alone: fewe men lay within thoſe houſes.

There were a thouſande women, and ſome affy2me y there were th2ée thouſand, accounting gentlewomen, ſeruaunts and ſlaues: the moſt were noble mens daughters, *Mutezuma* toke of them fo2 himſelfe, thoſe that liked him beſt, and the others he gaue in mariage to Gentlemen his feruaunts.

Aa.iij. The

The saying was that he had at one tyme a hundreth & fiftie women hys wiues with childe, who through the perswasion of the Deiull tooke Medicines to caste theyr creatures, bycause they knewe that they should not inherite the state: these hys wiues had many olde women for their Guarde, for no man was permitted to looke vpon them.

The shielde of armes, that is sette in his pallayce, and likewyse carried to the warres, is an Eagle soryng vpon a Tiger hys talents bente as takyng pray. Some thynk it is a Gryphon and not an Egle. The Gryphons in tune passe, say they, did cause the vale of *Auacatlan* to be dispeopled, for they were greate deuourers of menne, and that they abidyng was in the Mountaynes of *Teoacan*: they approue that these Mountains were called *Cuitlachtepelt*, of *Cuitlachtli*, which is a Gryphon bigger than a Lion: but the Spaniardes dyd neuer see any of them.

The *Indians* by theyr olde Pictures doe paynt those Gryphons to haue a kynde of heare and no feathers, and also affirme, that with theyr talandes & teeth they breake mens bones. They haue the courage of a Lion and the countenaunce of an Egle: they paynte him with foure feete, and teeth, with a kinde of downe more lyke woolle than feathers, with his beake, talandes and wings.

And in all those things the picture agreeth with our paynting and wryting, in suche sorte that a Gryphon is no approued naturall Foule, nor yet beast. *Plinie* iudgeth this tale of Gryphons to be lies. There are also other Lordes that giue the Gryphon in their armes, flying with a harte in his Talandes.

A

A houſe of Foule, vvhiche vvere onely

preſerued for their feathers.

Ꝓtezuma had another houſe, with
very good lodgings and fayꝛe gal-
laries, buylt vpõ pillers of Iaſpe,
whiche ꝛtendeth towarde a goodly garden, in the whichethere are
ten pondes oꝛ moe, ſome of ſalte
water foꝛ ſea foule, ¢ other ſome
of freſh water foꝛ riuer ſoule and
lake ſoule, which pondes are deuiſed vᵒ ſtupſes to emptie
¢ to fill at their pleaſure foꝛ the cleanneſſe of the feathers.
There is ſuch a number of foule, that ſcarcely the ponds
may holde them, and of ſuche diueꝛs kindes bothe in feathers and makyng, as ſure it was an admiration foꝛ the
Spaniardes to beholde, foꝛ the moſte of them they knew
not, noꝛ yet had at any tyme ſeene the lyke. And to euery
kynde of foule they gaue ſuche bayte as they were wont
to feede of in the fieldes oꝛ Riuers. There did belong to
that houſe thꝛee hundꝛed perſons of ſeruice: ſome were to
clenſe the pondes: other ſame did fiſhe foꝛ bayte: other
ſome ſerued them with meate: other did loſe them and
trimme theyꝛ feathers: others had care to looke to their
egges: others to ſette them abꝛode: others cured them
when they were ſicke: and the pꝛincipalleſt office was
to plucke the feathers: foꝛ of them was made riche Mantels, Tapiſſarie, Targattes, Cuſſes of feathers, and many other things wꝛought with Golde and Siluer, a moſt
perfite worke.

A houfe of foule for havvking, and other
ſtraunge things.

Here is another houfe with large quarters & lodgings, which is called a houfe
for foule, not bycaufe there are more thã
in the other, but bycaufe they bee bigger
and to hauke withal, and are foule of rapine, wherfore they are eſtæmed as more
nobler than al the others.

There are in this houfe many high halles, in the whiche are kept men, women and Children: in fome of them
are kept fuche as are borne white of colour, which doth
very feldome happen: in other fome are dwarfes, crokebackes, burſtenmen, counterfaites, and monſtrous perfons, in greate number: they fay that they vfed to de-
forme them when they were children, to fette forth the
kings greatneſſe: euery of thefe perfons were in feuerall
Halles by themfelues.

In the lower Halles were greate Cages made of
Tymber: in fome of them were Lyons, in other Tygres,
in other Ownzes, in others Wolues: in conclufion, there
was no foure footed beaſte that wanted there, onely to
the effect that the mightie *Mutezuma* might fay that hee
had fuch things in his houfe.

They were fed with their ordinary, as Gynea cockes,
Deare, Dogges, and fuch like.

There was alfo in other Halles great Earthen vef-
fels, fome with earth, and fome with water, wherin were
fnakes, as groffe as a mans thigh, Vipers Crocodilles,
whiche they cal *Caymanes*, or *Lizarts* of twenty foote long,
wyth fuche Scales and head as a Dragon hathe: Alfo
other little Lifarts, and other venemous beaſtes and
Serpents

Serpentes as well of the water as of the land, a terrible
ſight foz the lokers on.

There were alſo other Cages foz foule of rappne of
all ſoztes, as Hawkes, Kpghtes, Boyters, and at the
leaſt nine oz ten kind of Haukes. This houſe of foule had
of daply allowance fiue hundzed Gynea cockes, and thzée
hundzed men of ſeruice, beſides the Falconers and Hunters, which are infinite. There were many other ſoztes of
Foules that our men knowe not, which ſéemed by theyz
beake and talents good to Hauke withal.

To the Snakes and other venemous beaſtes they
gaue the bloude of men ſacrifiſed, to féede them, and ſome
ſape they gaue vnto them mannes fleſhe, whych the
greate Lyſarts doe cate berp well. The Spaniardes
ſaw the floure couered with bloud like a ſcalp in a ſlaughter houſe, it ſtonke hozribly.

It was ſtraunge to ſée the officers in this houſe
howe euery one was occupied. Our men toke greate
pleaſure in beholding ſuche ſtraunge thyngs, but they
coulde not awape wyth the roarpng of the Lyons,
the fearefull hiſſing of the Snakes and Adders, the
dolefull howling and barking of the Wolues, the ſozowfull pelling of the Ownzes & Tigres, when they would
haue meate.

Moſte certaine, in the nighte ſeaſon it ſémed a
Dongeon of Hell, and a dwelling place of the Deuill,
and euen ſo it was in déede, foz neare at hande was a
Hall of a hundzed & fiftie fote long, and thirtie fote bzoad,
where was a Chappel with the Rofe of ſiluer and gold
in leafe Wainescottes, and decked with greate ſtoze
of pearle and ſtone, as Agattes, Coznerines, Emeraldes,
Rubies, and diuerſe other ſoztes, and thps was the
Ozatozy where *Mutezuma* pzayed in the nighte ſeaſon,
Bb. and

and in that chappell the Diuell did appeare vnto hym, and gaue him anſwere accoꝛdyng to his pꝛayers.

He had other houſes lyke vnto Barnes, onely foꝛ the feathers of foules, and foꝛ mantels whiche pꝛoceded of his rentes and tributes, a thing muche to be ſéne: vpon the doꝛes was ſette his armes, whiche was a Connie.

Here dwelled the chiefe officers of his houſe, as Treſoꝛer, Controller, Recepuers and other officers appertaynyng to the Kings reuenewes. *Mutezuma* had no houſe wherein was not an oꝛatoꝛy foꝛ the Deuill, whome they woꝛſhipped foꝛ the Iewels there. And therefoꝛe thoſe houſes were great and large.

The Armory of Mutezuma.

Vtezuma had ſome houſes of Armour, vpon the doꝛes wherof ſtode a bow and arrowes. In theſe houſes was greate ſtoꝛe of all kinde of munition whiche they vſe in their wars: as Bowes, Arrowes, Slings, Launces, Dartes, Clubbes, Swoꝛdes and Bucklers, and gallant Targettes moꝛe trimme than ſtrong, Skulles and Splintes, but not many, and al made of woodde, gilte oꝛ couered with leather. The woodde whereof they make their Armour and Targettes, is very harde and ſtrong, foꝛ they vſe to toaſte it at the fire, and at their arrowe endes they incloſe a litle péce of ſlinte ſtone, oꝛ a péce of a fiſhe bone called *Libiſa*, and that is venemous, foꝛ if any bé hurte therewith and the
head

head remayne in the wounde, it so festereth, that it is almost incurable.

Theyr swordes are of woode, and the edge thereof is flint stone, inclosed or ioyned into a staffe, with a certaine kynde of glew whiche is made of a roote called *Zacolt* and *Teuxalli*, whiche is a kinde of strong sande, whereof they make a mixture, and after kneade it with bloud of Battes or Kearemice and other foule, which doth glewe maruelous strong, and lightly neuer bncleaueth: of this stuffe they make naples, peareers, & ogars, wherwith they bore timber & stone: with theyr swordes they cut speares, yea and a horse necke at a blowe, and make dentes into iron, whiche seemeth a thing bnpossible and incredible. In the Citie no man may weare weapon, but onely in warres, huntyng, and among the kings Guarde,

The Gardens of Mutezuma.

Esides the foresayde houses hee had many others for hys onely recreation and passetyme, with excellent fayre gardens of medicinall hearbes, sweete floures, and trees of delectable sauour, whiche were many, and a thing to gyue prayse to God the maker and creator of all.

In that Garden were a thousande personages, made and wrought artificially of leaues and flowers. *Mutezuma* woulde not permitte that in this Garden shoulde be any kynde of potte Hearbes, or thyngs to be solde, saying, that it dyd not appertayne to Kings to haue thyngs of profite among theyr delytes and pleasures, for suche thyngs (sayde hee) dyd appertayne to Merchants.

Pet notwithſtanding he had Oꝛchards with many and
ſundꝛy fruites, but they ſtode farre from the Cittie, and
whyther ſeldome times hee wente : he had likewiſe out
of *Mexico* pleaſaunte houſes in woodes and foꝛreſtes, of
greate compaſſe, enuyꝛoned with water, in the which he
hadde fountaynes, riuers, pondes with fiſhe, warrantes
of Conneys, rockes & couert where were Harts, Buckes,
Hares, Foxes, Wolues, and ſuch like, with wilderneſſe
foꝛ euery ſoꝛt.

To theſe places the Loꝛds of *Mexico,* vſed to goe and
ſpoꝛte themſelues , ſuche and ſo manye were the houſes
of *Mutezuma* , wherein fewe kings were equall with
him.

The court and Guarde of
Mutezuma.

E had dayly attending vp-
pon hym in hys pꝛiuye
garde ſire hundꝛed noble
men and gentlemen, and
eche of them thꝛæ oꝛ foure
ſeruants, and ſome hadde
twenty ſeruaunts oꝛ moe,
according to his eſtate: and
in this maner he had thꝛæ
thouſand menattendant in
his court, and ſome affirm
moꝛe, al the which were fed in his houſe of the meate that
came from his table.

The ſeruing men alwayes abode belowe in the court
all the daye, and wente not from thence tyll after Supper.

It

It is to be thought that his Guard was the greater, bycause the ftraungers were there, although in effecte of troth it is moft certayne, that all the Lozds that are vnder the *Mexicall* Empire (as they fay) are thirtie perfons of high eftate, who are able to make each of them a hundzed thoufand men. There are thzee thoufand Lozdes of Townes, who haue many vaffals.

Thefe noble menne did abide in *Mexico* certayne tyme of the yeare, in the Court of *Mutezuma*, and could not departe from thence without efpeciall licence of the Emperoure, leauing each of them a fonne oz bzother behinde them foz fecuritie of Rebellion, and foz this caufe they had generally houfes in the Citie : fuch and fo great was the court of *Mutezuma*.

The great fubiection of the Indians
to their King.

Here is not in all the dominions of *Mutezuma* any fubiect that payeth not tribute vnto him. The noblemen paye theyz tribute in perfonall feruice. The hufbandmen called *Maceualtin*, with body & goodes. In this fozt they are eyther tenanntes, oz elfe heyzes to their poffeffions. Thofe which are heyzes, do pay one third part of all their fruite and commoditie that they doe reape oz bzing vp, as Dogges, Hennes, Foule, Conyes, Gold, Siluer, Stones, Salt, Ware, Honey, Mantels, Feathers, Cotten, and a certayne fruite called *Cacao*, that ferueth foz money, and alfo to eate. Alfo all kinde of grayne, and garden Herbes and fruites, whereof they do maynteyne themfelues.

The Tenantes doe paye monethly oz yearely as they can agree, and bycaufe their tribute is greate, they are

called slaues, for when they maye haue licence to eate egges, they thinke it a greate fauour. It was reported that they were taxed what they shoulde eate, and all the residue was taken from them. They went very poorely clothed, yea and the most of their treasure was an earthē potte, wherein they boyled theyr herbes, a couple of Mil stones to grinde their Corne, and a matte to lye vppon. They did not onely pay this rente and tribute, but also serued with their bodyes at all times when the great King shoulo commaunde. They were in such great sub iectiō to their prince, that they durst not speake one word, although their daughters shoulde be taken from them to be vsed at their pleasure. It was reported, that of euerye thrée sonnes, they deliuered one to be sacrifised, but ỹ re port was false, for if it had bin true, the Townes had not bin so replenished with people as they were: and also the noble men did not eate mans flesh, but only of those whi che were sacrifised, and they were slaues or prisoners ta ken in the warres. Assuredly they were cruell butchers, and slewe yearely for that bloudy sacrifice many menne, and some children, but not so many as was reported. All the aforesayde rentes they brought to *Mexico* vpon theyr backes and in boates, I meane so much as was necessary for the prouision of the house and Courte of *Mutezuma*, all the residue was spente among souldyers, and bartred for golde, plate, precious stones, and other riche Jewels, esteemed of Princes, all the whiche was broughte to the treasory. In *Mexico* was large and greate barnes and houses to receyue and képe the Corne for prouision of the Citie, with officers and vnderofficers, who did re ceyue the same, and kepte accompte thereof in bokes of paynted figures. Also in euerye Towne was a recey uer, who bare in his hand a rodde or a bushe of feathers, and those gaue vp their accomptes in *Mexico*. If any such
had

had bin taken with deceypt and falsehoode,death was his reward, pea and his kinred punished with penalties, as of a lignage of a Traytor to his Prince. The Husband-menne, if they payd not well their tribute, were apprehended for the same, and if they were founde to bee poore through sicknesse and infirmitie, then they were borne withall, but if they were found to be lazie and slouthfull, they should be vsed accordingly:but in conclusion, if they payde it not at a daye appoynted, then they shoulde bee solde for slaues to pay their dette,or else be sacrificed.

There were many other prouinces, whiche paid a certayne portion,and reknowledged seruice,but this tribute was more of honor than profite. In this sort Mutezuma had more than sufficiente to prouide his house & warres, and to heape vp great store in his treasory. Moreouer,he spente nothing in the buildings of his houses, for of long time he had certayne townes that payd no other tribute, but only to worke and repayre continually his houses at their owne proper cost, and payde all kind of workemen, carrying vpon their backes,or drawing in sleddes,stone, lyme, timber, water, and all other necessaries for the worke. Likewise they were bounde to prouide all the fierwood that should be spent in the Court, whiche was a great thing,and did amount to 230.hundred waight a day, which was fiue hundred mens burthens,and some dayes in the winter much more. And for the kings Chimneys they brought the barke of Oke trées, whiche was best e-steemed for the light thereof, for they were greate sorcerers. Mutezuma had 100. cities, with their prouinces, of whome he receiued rentes,tributes,& vassalage,where he mainteined garrison of souldiers,& had treasorers in each of thé. His dominió did extend from the North sea to the South sea,& 600.miles in lógitude within the maine lãd, although in very déd ther were some towns,as Tlaxcallã, Mechuacan,

Mechuacan, Panuco, and *Teoantepec,* whiche were his enimies, and payde him neyther tribute no² seruice : but yet the ranſome was muche, when any of them were taken.

Also there were other kings and noble men, as of *Tezcuco* and *Tlacopan,* which were not in ſubiection ꝟnto him, but onely in homage and obedience, fo² they were of his owne lignage , ꝟnto whome *Mutezuma* married hys daughters.

The ſcituation of Mexico.

Exico at the time when *Cortes* entred, was a Citie of ſixtye thouſande houſes. The kings houſe and other noble mens houſes were great, large, and beautifull , the others were ſmall and roynish, without eyther do²es o² windowes: and although they were ſmall, yet there dwelled in ſome of them two, th²ee, yea and tenne perſons, by reaſon whereof, the Citie was wonderfully repleniſhed with people.

This Citie is built ꝟpon the water, euen in the ſame o²der as *Venice* is. All the body of the Citie ſtandeth in a greate large lake of water. There is th²ee ſo²tes of ſtreetes very b²oade and fay²e, the one ſo²te are onely of water, with many b²idges, an other ſo²t of onely earth, and the thirde of earth and water, that is to ſaye, the one halfe earth to walke ꝟpon, and the other halfe fo² boates to b²ing p²ouiſion of all ſo²ts. Theſe ſtreetes are kepte alwayes cleane, and the moſte parte of the houſes haue two do²es, the one towarde the calſey, and the other towarde the water , at the whiche they take boate to goe
where

where they lift. And although this Citie is founded vppon water, yet the same water is not good to drynke,
wherefore there is broughte by conduit water from a
place called *Chapultepec*, three mples distant from the Citie, which springeth out of a little hill, at the foote whereof standeth two Statues or couered Images wrought
in stone, with their Targettes and Launces, the one is
of *Mutezuma*, and the other of *Axaiaca* his father.

The water is broughte from thence in two pypes or
Canalls in greate quantitie, and when the one is foule,
then all the water is conuayed into the other, til the first
be made cleane. From this fountayne al the whole Citie
is prouided, so that they goe selling the same water from
stréete to stréete in little boates, and doe paye a certayne
tribute for the same.

This Citie is deuided into two stréetes, the one was
called *Tlatelulco*, that is to say, a litle Iland, and the other
Mexico, where *Mutezuma* his dwelling and courte was,
& is to be interpreted a spring. This stréete is the fayrest
and most principall, and bycause of the Kings pallace
there, the Citie was named *Mexico*, although the old and
first name of the Citie was *Tenuchtitlan*, whiche doth signifie fruite out of stone, for the name is compounded of
Tetl, which is, stone, and *Nuchtli*, which is fruite, called in
Cuba, *Tunas*. The trée that beareth this fruite, is named
Nopal, and is nothing almost but leaues of a foote broade
and round, and thrée ynches thicke, some more, and some
lesse, accoroing to the growth, full of thornes whiche are
venemous: the leafe is gréene, and the thorne or pricke
russet. After that it is planted, it encreaseth, growing
leafe vnto leafe, and the foote thereof commeth to bée as
the body of a trée, and one leafe dothe not onely produce
another at the poynt, but at the sides of the same leaues
procéedeth other leaues: And bycause hére in *Spayne* is

of the same trées and fruite, it néedeth no further descrip-
tion.

In some prouinces where water is scante, they vse to
drynke the iuice of these leaues. The fruite thereof called *Nuchtli*, is lyke vnto fygges, and euen so hathe hys
little kernels or graynes within, but they are somewhat
larger, and crowned lyke vnto a Medler. There are of
them of sundrye coloures, some are gréene without, and
Carnationlike within, which haue a good tast. Others
are yellowe, and others white, and some speckled: the best
sort are the white: it is a fruite that will last long.

Some of them tasteth of peares, and other some of
Grapes: it is a colde and a fresh fruite, and best estéemed
in the heate of Sommer. The *Spanyardes* doe more e-
stéeme them than the *Indians*. The more the grounde is
laboured where they growe, the fruite is so muche the
better.

There is yet another kinde of this fruite redde, and
that is nothing estéemed, although his tast is not euill,
but bycause it dothe coloure and dye the eaters mouth,
lippes, and apparell, yea and maketh his bryne looke like
pure bloud. Many *Spanyardes* at their first comming into
India, and eating this fruite, were in a maze, and at their
wittes ende, thinking that all the bloud in their bodyes
came out in bryne: yea and manye Phisitions at theyr
first comming were of the same beliefe: for it hathe happened, when they haue bin sent for vnto such as haue eaten this fruite, they not knowing the cause, and beholding the bryne, by and by they ministred medicine to
staunch bloud: surely a thing to laugh at, to sée the Phisitions so deceyued. Of this fruite *Nuchtli* and *Tetl*, which
is a stone, is compounded *Tenuchtlitan*. When this Citie
was begunne to bée founded, it was placed néere vnto
a great stone that stoode in the middest of the lake, at the
foote

fœte whereof grewe one of thefe *Nopal* trées, and therefoze *Mexico* giueth foz armes and deuife the fœte of a
Nopal trée fpzinging from a ftone, accozding to the Cities name.

Others to affirme, that this Citie hathe the name of
his firft founder, called *Tenuch*, béepng the feconde fonne
of *Iztacmixcoatl*, whofe fonnes and defcendentes did firft
inhabite thys lande of *Ananac*, called nowe newe
Spayne.

Howfoeuer the opinions are, certayne it is that the
fcituation is called *Temichtitan*, and the dwellers there
Tenuchca Mexico.

Mexico is as much to fay, as a fpzing oz fountayne, accozding to the pzopertie of the bowell and fpéech.

Others doe affirme, that *Mexico* hathe his name of a
moze auntiente time, whofe firfte founders were called
Mexiti, foz vnto this day the *Indian* dwellers in one ftrete
of this citie are called of *Mexica*. The *Mexiti* tœke name
of their pzincipalleft Idoll called *Mexitli*, who was in as
greate veneration as *Vitzilopuchtli*, God of the warre.

Mexico is enuironed with fwéete water, and hathe
thzée wayes to come vnto it by calfey, the one is from
the Weft, and that calfey is a mile and a halfe long.
Another from the Nozth, and conteyneth thzée myles
in length. Eaftwarde the Citie hathe no entrye. But
Southwarde the Calfey is fyre myles long, whyche was the waye that *Cortez* entred into the Citie.

The lake that *Mexico* is planted in, although it fée-
meth one, yet it is two, foz the one is of water faltifhe,
bitter, and peftiferous, and no kinde of fyfhe lyueth in
it. And the other water is wholefome, good and fwéete,
and bzingeth fozth fmall fifhe.

The falte water ebbeth and floweth, accozdyng

to the winde that bloweth. The sweete water standeth higher, so that the good water falleth into the euill, and reuerteth not backward, as some hold opinion. The salt lake conteyneth fifteene miles in breadth and fifteene in length, and more than fiue and fortie in circuite, and the lake of sweete water conteyneth euen as muche, in such sort, that the whole lake conteyneth more than thirtie leagues, and hath about fiftie townes scituated round about it, many of whyche Townes doe conteyne fiue thousand housholdes, and some tenne thousande, yea and one Towne called *Tezcuco*, is as bigge as *Mexico*. Al this lake of water springeth out of a Mountayne that standeth within sight of *Mexico*. The cause that the one part of the lake is brackishe or saltish, is, that the bottome or ground is all salte, and of that water greate quantitie of salt is dayly made.

In this greate lake are aboue two hundred thousande little boates, which the *Indians* call *Acalles*, and the *Spanyardes* call them *Canoas*, according to the speeche of *Cuba* and *Santo Domingo*, wrought like a kneding trough: some are bigger than other some, according to the greatenesse of the body of the tree whereof they are made. And where I number two hundred thousand of these boates, I speake of the least, for *Mexico* alone hathe aboue fiftie thousande ordinarily to carrie and bring vnto the Citie victuall, prouision, and passengers, so that on the market day all the streetes of water are full of them.

The Market place of Mexico.

 He Market is called in the *Indian* tong *Tlanquiztli*: euery parish hath his Marketplace to buy and sel in: but *Mexico*, and *Tlatelulco* only, which are the chiefest cities, haue great fayres and

and places fitte for the same, and especiallye *Mexico* hath one place where most dayes in the yeare is buying and selling, but euery fourth day is the greate Market ordinarylye: and the like custome is vsed throughout the dominions of *Mutezuma.*

This place is wide and large, compassed round about with dores, and is so great, that a hundered thousand persons come thither to choppe and change, as a Cittie most principall in all that region. Wherefore the resort is frō farre parties vnto that place. Euery occupatiō and kinde of Marchādise hath his proper place appointed, which nō other may by any means occupy or disturbe. Likewise ponderous wares haue their place accordinglye, (that is to say) stone, timber, lyme, bricke, and all kinde of stuffe vnwrought, being necessarie to buylde withall. Also mattes both fine and course of sundry workemanship, also coles, woodde, and all sorts of Earthen vessell glazed and painted very curiously: Deare skinnes both rawe and tanned in haire and without haire, of many colours, for shoomakers, for bucklers, Targets, Jerkins, and lyning of wooden Corselets: also skinnes of other beastes and foule in feathers ready dressed of all sortes, the colours and straungnesse thereof was a thing to behold. The richest Marchandise was salte, and mantels of Cotten wolle of diuers colours, both great and small, some for beddes, others for garments and clothing, other for Tapissarie to hang houses, other cotten clothe for linnen breaches, shirtes, table clothes, towels, napkins, and suche like things.

There were also Mantels made of the leaues of the trée called *Metl*, and of Palme trée, & Connie heare, which are wel esteemed, being very warm, but ȳ couerlets made of feathers are the best: they sell thréede made of Connie heare, péeces of linnen clothe made of cotten wolle, also shapnes of thæde of all colours: also it is straunge to sée the great store of poultrie that is brought to that market,and although they eate the fleshe of the foule, yet the feathers serue for clothing, mixyng one sorte with another.There are of these foule so many sortes and seuerall colours,that I can not number them:some wilde,some tame,some water foule,and other some of rapine. All the brauery of the market,is the place where golde and feathers ioyntly wrought is solde,for any thyng that is in request is there liuely wrought in golde and ieathers and gallant colours. The *Indians* are so expert and perfite in this science, that they will worke or make a Butter flie, any wilde beaste,trées,roses,floures, hearbes, rootes or any other thyng so liuely,that it is a thyng maruelous to beholde. It hapneth many tymes that one of these workemen in a whole day will eate nothyng, onely to place one feather in his dew perfection,turnyng and tossing the feather to the lighte of the Sunne, into the shade or darke place,to sée where is his moste naturall perfection, and till his worke be finished he will neyther eate nor drinke. There are few nations of so muche steame or sufferance. The Arte or Science of Goldsmiths among them is the moste curious, and very good workemanship engrauen with toles made of flinte,or in moulde. They will caste a platter in moulde with eight corners,and euery corner of seuerall mettall,that is to say,the one of golde, and the other of siluer,without any kinde of sowder:they will also founde or cast a litle caudron with lose handles hangyng thereat, as we vse to caste a Bell:they will also caste in mould a fish of mettal with one scale of siluer on his back and another of gold: they will make a Parret or Popingay of mettall,that his tongue shall shake,and his head moue,& his wings flutter: they wil caste an Ape in molo, that both hands & féete shall stirre, & holde a spindle in his

hande

hande séeming to spinne, yea and an apple in his hande as
though he would eate it. Our Spaniardes were not a litle
amazed at the sight of these things, for our Goldsmithes
are not to be compared vnto them. They haue skil also of
Amell worke, and to sette any pretious stone. But now
as touchyng the markette, there is to sell Golde, Siluer,
Copper, Leadde, Latton, and Tinne, although there is
but little of the thrée laste mettals mentioned. There are
Pearles, Pretious stones, diuers and sundry sortes of
Shelles, and Bones, Sponges, and other pedlers ware,
whiche certainely are many and straunge sortes, yea and
a thing to laughe at their Haberdashe toyes and trifles.
There are also many kinde of hearbes, rootes, and séedes,
as well to be eaten as for Medicine, for bothe men, wemen and chyldren haue great knowledge in hearbes, for
through pouertie and necessitie, they séeke them for theyr
sustenaunce and helpe of theyr infirmities and diseases.
They spende little among Phisitions, although there are
some of that Arte, and many Poticaries, who doe bryng
into the markette, oyntments, Siroppes, waters, and
other drugges fitte for sicke Persons : they cure all diseases almost, with hearbes, yea as muche as for to kill
lyse they haue a proper hearbe for the purpose.

The seuerall kyndes of meates to be solde is without
number, as Snakes without head & taple, little Dogges
gelte, Moules, Rattes, Long wormes, Lyse, yea and a
kinde of earth, for at one season in the yére they haue
Nettes of mayle with the which they rake vp a certayne
dusse that is bredde vpon the water of the lake of *Mexico*,
and that is knéeded togither like vnto oas of the sea: they
gather much of this victuall, & képe it in heapes, & make
therof cakes like vnto brickebats: they sell not only this
ware in ȳ market, but also send it abroad to other fayres
& markets a far of: they eat this meate w as good stomake
as

as we eate chéese, yea and they holde opinion that this skūme or fatnesse of the water, is ẏ cause that such great number of foule cōmeth to the lake, which in the winter season is infinite.

They sel in this market venison by quarters or whole, as Does, Hares, Connies, and Dogges, and many other beastes, whiche they bring vp for the purpose, and take in huntyng. There are a great number of shoppes that sell all kinde of ozfall and tripes. It is a wonder to sée how so much meate ready dressed coulde be spent. There is also fleshe and fishe rosted, boyled and baked, Pies and Custardes made of diuers sortes of egges, the great quantitie of bread is without number. Also corne of all sortes threshed and vnthreshed. The greate store of sundry kyndes of fruytes is maruellous whiche are there solde, bothe gréene and ripe: there is one sorte as bigge as Almondes called *Cacao*, whiche is bothe meate and currant money. There are diuers kind of colours to be solde, whiche they make of Roses, floures, fruites, barkes of trées, and other things very excellent : they sell there Honie of sundry kindes, oyle of *Chian*, made of a séede like vnto mustarde séede, and oynting any paynted clothe therewith, the water can not hurte it, they also dresse therwith their meate, although they haue both butter and larde. They sundry sortes of wines shalbe declared in an other place: it woulde be a prolirious thing to rehearse all the things that are to be solde in that markette. There are in this fayre many Artificers, as Packers, Barbars, Cutlers, & many others, although it was thought that among these *Indians* were none such. All the things recited, and many others which I speake not of, are solde in euery market of *Mexico*, all the sellers paye a certaine summe for their shops or stādings to the King, as a custome, & they to be preserued and defended from théeues: and for that cause

there

there goe certayne Sergeants o2 officers vp & downe the
market to espie out malefactours. In the middest of the
market standeth a house whiche may be seene throughout
the fayre, & there sitteth twelue auncient men fo2 iudges
to dispatch lawe matters: their buying and selling is to
chaunge one ware fo2 another, as thus, one giueth a hen
fo2 a bundell of *Maiz*, other giue mantels fo2 salte, o2 money whiche is *Cacao*, and this is they2 o2der to choppe and
chaunge: they haue measure and strike fo2 all kynde of
co2ne, and other earthen measures fo2 Hony and Wine,
and if any measure be falsified, they punish the offenders
and b2eake their measures.

The great Temple of Mexico.

He Temple is called *Teucalli*, that is to say,
Gods house, *Teurl* signifieth God, & *Calli* is a
house, a vowell very fitte, if that house had
bene of the true God. The Spaniards that
vnderstãd not the language, do p2onounce
and call those Temples *Cues*, and the God *Vitzilopuchtli*,
Vchilobos. There are in *Mexico* many parishe churches,
with tow2es, wherein are chappels and Altares where
the images & idols do stande, & those chappels do serue fo2
burial places of their founders, and the Parishioners are
buried in the Churchyarde. All their teples are of one fashion, therefo2e it shal be nowe sufficient to speake of the
cathed2al church. And euen as those teples are al in generall of one making in that citie. I doe beleue that the lyke
was neuer seene no2 heard off. This temple is square, &
doth containe euery way as much ground as a crossebow
can reach leuell: it is made of stone, with foure do2es that
abutteth vpon the th2ee calseys, and vpon an other parte
of the Cittie, that hath no calsey but a fay2e streate.

Dd. In

In the middeſt of this Quadern ſtandeth a mount of
earth and ſtone ſquare lykewiſe, and fiftie fadom long e-
uery way, buylte vpward like vnto a pyramide of Egipt,
ſauyng the toppe is not ſharpe, but playne and flatte, and
tenne fadom ſquare : vppon the weaſt ſide, were ſteppes
vp to the toppe, in number an hundꝛeth and fourtene,
whiche beyng ſo many, high, and made of god ſtone dyd
ſéeme a beautifull thing. It was a ſtraunge ſight to beholde the Pꝛieſtes, ſome goyng vp, and ſome downe with
ceremonies, oꝛ with men to be ſacrificed. Vpon the toppe
of this Temple are two great Alters, a god ſpace diſtant
the one from the other, and ſo nigh the edge oꝛ bꝛimme of
the wall, that ſcarcely a man mought go behind them at
pleaſure. The one Alter ſtandeth on the right hande, & the
other on the left, they were but of fiue fote highe, eche of
them had the backe part made of ſtone, paynted with mō-
ſtrous and foule figures, the Chappell was fayꝛe & well
wꝛought of Maſons woꝛke & timber, euery Chappell had
thꝛée loftes one aboue another, ſuſteyned vpon pillers, &
with ẏ height thereof it ſhewed like vnto a fayꝛe tower,
and beautiſied the Cittie a farre of : from thence a man
mought ſée all the cittie and townes rounde aboute the
lake, whiche was vndoubtedly a godly pꝛoſpect. And bycauſe *Cortes* & his company ſhould ſée the beautie thereof,
Mutezuma bꝛought him thither, and ſhewed hym all the
oꝛder of the Temple, euen from the fote to the toppe.
There was a certaine plot oꝛ ſpace foꝛ the idoll pꝛieſts to
celebꝛate their ſeruice without diſturbance of any. Their
general pꝛayers were made toward ẏ riſing of the ſunne.
Vpon ech alter ſtandeth a great idoll. Beſide this tower
that ſtandeth vpō the pyramide, there are fourtie towers
great & ſmall belonging to other little téples which ſtand
in the ſame circuite, the which although they were of the
ſame making, yet theyꝛ pꝛoſpect was not weſtwarde, but
other-

otherwayes,bicause there should be a difference betwixt
the great temple & them. Some of these Temples were
bigger than others, and euery one of a seuerall God, a-
mong the whiche there was one rounde temple dedicated
to the God of the ayre called *Quecalcouatl,* for euen as the
ayre goeth rounde about the heauens,euen for that consideration they made;his temple rounde.The entraunce of
that Temple had a dore made lyke vnto the mouth of a   A straunge
Serpent, and was paynted with foule and Diuelish ge-   dore.
stures,with great teeth & gummes wrought,whiche was
a thing to feare those that should enter in thereat, & especially the Christians vnto whom it represented very Hel
with that ougly face and monsterous teeth.

There were other *Teucalles* in the citie,that had the ascending vp by steps in three places : all these temples had
houses by theselues with all seruice & priests & particular
Gods.At euery dore of the great temple standeth a large
Hall & godly lodgings, both high and lowe round about,
which houses were common armories for the Citie,for the
force and strength of euery towne is the temple,and therfore they haue there placed their storehouse of munition.
They had other darke houses full of idols,greate & small,
wrought of sundry mettals, they are all bathed and washed with bloud,and do shewe very blacke through ther
dayly sprinklyng and anoynting them with the same,when
any man is sacrificed:yea & the walles are an inche thicke
with bloud, and the grounde is a fote thicke of bloud, so
that there is a diuelish stench. The Priests or Ministers
goe daylye into those Oratories, and suffer none o-
thers but great personages to enter in.Yea and when any
such goeth in,they are bounde to offer some man to be sacrificed, that those bloudy hangmen and ministers of the
Diuell may washe their handes in bloud of those so sacrificed,and to sprinkle their house therewith.

For their seruice in the kitchin they haue a ponde of water that is filled once a yeere, which is brought by conduct from the pryncipal fountayne. All the residue of the foresayde circuite serueth for places to breede foule, with gardens of hearbes and sweete trees, with Roses and floures for the Altars. Such, so great & straunge was this temple of *Mexico*, for the seruice of the Diuell who had deceiued those simple *Indians*. There dothe reside in the same temple continually fiue thousand persons, and all they are lodged and haue theyr liuing there, for that teple is maruellous riche, & hath diuers townes onely for their maintenaunce and reparation, and are bounde to sustayne the same alwayes on foote. They doe sowe corne, and maintayne all those fiue thousande persons with bread, fruyte, flesh, fishe, and firewoodde as much as they neede, for they spende more fire woodde than is spent in the kings courte: these persons doe liue at their hartes ease, as seruauntes and vassals vnto the Goddes. *Mutezuma* brought *Cortes* to this temple, bicause his men shoulde see the same, and to enforme them of his religion and holinesse, wherof I will speake in an other place, being the most straunge and cruellest that euer was heard off.

The Idols of Mexico.

He Gods of *Mexico*, were two thousand in number, as the *Indians* reported, the chiefest were *Vitcilopuchtli* and *Tezcatlipuca*, whose images stode highest in the Temple vppon the Altars : they were made of stone in ful proportion as bigge as a Gyant. They were couered with a lawne called *Nacar*. These images were besette with pearles, precious stones, & peeces of gold, wrought like birds, beasts, fishes, and

and floures, adozned with Emeralds, Turquies, Calce-
dons, and other little fine ſtones, ſo that when the lawne
Nacar was taken away, the Images ſeemed very beautifull to beholde.

The Image had foz a girdle great ſnakes of gold, and　*A vvicked*
foz collozs oz chaynes about their neckes, ten hartes of　*attire.*
men, made of golde, and each of thoſe Idolles had a coun-
terfaite viſoz with eies of glaſſe, and in their necks death
painted: eache of theſe things hadde their conſiderations
and meanings. Theſe two Goddes were bzethzen, foz
Tezcatlipuca was the God of Pzouidence, and *Vitcilo-*
puchtli God of the warres, who was wozſhipped and
feared moze than all the reſt.

There was another God, who hadde a greate Image
placed vppon the toppe of the Chappell of Idols, and hée
was eſtéemed foz a ſpeciall and ſingular God aboue all
the reſt. This God was made of all kinde of ſéedes that
groweth in that Countrey, and being ground, they made
a certayne paſt, tempered with childzens bloud, and Vir-
gins ſacrifiſed, who were opened with their razures in
the bzeaſtes, and their heartes taken out, to offer as firſt
fruites vnto the Idoll. The Pzieſtes and Miniſters doe
conſecrate this Idoll with great pomp and many Ceremonies. All the *Comarcans* and Citizens are pzeſente at
the conſecration, with great triumph and incredible deuotion. After the conſecration, many deuoute perſons　*A madde*
came and ſticked in the dowy Image pzecious ſtones,　*offering.*
wedges of golde, and other Iewels. After all this pomp
ended, no ſecular man mought touche that holye Image,
no noz yet come into his Chappell, nay ſcarcely religious
perſons, excépt they were *Tlamacaztli*, who are Pzieſtes
of ozder. They doe renue this Image many times wyth
new dough, taking away the olde, but then bleſſed is hée
that can get one péece of the olde ragges foz relikes, and

chiefly

chiefly for souldyers, who thought themselues sure therewith in the warres. Also at the consecration of thys Idoll, a certayne vessell of water was blessed with manye wordes and ceremonyes, and that water was preserued very religiously at the foote of the altar, for to consecrate the King when he should be crowned, and also to blesse any Captayne generall, when he shoulde be elected for the warres, with only giuing him a draught of that water.

The Charnell house or place of dead
mens sculles for remembrance of death.

Without the temple, and ouer againste the principall dore thereof, a stones cast distant, standeth the Charnell house onely of dead mens heads prisoners in warres and sacrifised with the knife.

This monument was made like vnto a Theatre, more larger than broade, wrought of lyme and stone, with ascending steppes, in the walles whereof was graffed betwixt stone and stone a skul with the teeth outwards.

At the foote and head of this Theatre, were two Towers, made only of lime and skulles, the teeth outwarde, and this wall hauing no other stuffe, seemed a straunge sight. At and vppon the toppe of the Theatre, were 70. polles, standing the one from the other foure or fiue foote distant, and eache of them was full of staues from the foote to the toppe. Each of these staues had others made fast vnto them, so that euery of them had fiue skulles broched through the temples. *Andrewe de Tapia* did certifie me, that he and *Gonsalo de Vmbria* dyd recken them in one daye, and founde a hundred thirtie and sixe thousande skulles on the polles, staues, and steppes. The other Towers

wers were replenished out of number, a most cruell cu
stome,being only mens heads slaine in sacrifice,although
it hath a shewe of humanitie for the remembrance there
placed of death. There are also men appoynted, that
when one skull falleth, to set vp another in his place, so
that the number may neuer want.

Hovv Cortez tooke Mutezuma
prisoner.

Ernando *Cortez* and his companye, were fire
dayes in beholding and perusing the scituati
on of the Citie,and secretes of the same, with
the notable thinges before rehearsed : they
were often visited by *Mutezuma,*& the Gentlemen of hys
Courte, and abundantly prouided of things necessarye
for his vse,and the *Indians* of his company.

Likewise his Horses were cherished and serued with
gréene barley and grasse, whereof there is plentie all the
yeare:Likewise of corne,meale, roses, and of all thynges
that their owners would requeste, in so much that beddes　*A svveete*
of floures were made for them in place of litter. But yet　*bedde.*
notwithstanding, although they were in this sorte cheri
shed, and also lodged in so riche a Countrey, where they
mighte fyll their purses, they were not yet all contente
and merrie,but rather with great feare and care, especi
ally *Cortes*, who hadde the onely care as head and chiefe
Captayne for the defence of hys fellowes, hée (I saye)
was pensiue, noting the scituation of the Citie, the in
finite number of people, the state and maiestie of *Mexico*, yea and some disquietnesse of hys owne compa
nye, who woulde come and laye vnto hys charge the
snare and nette that they were in , thynkyng it a
thyng vnpossible that anye of them coulde escape,

if *Mutezuma* were therevnto determined, or elſe with the leaſt muteny in the worlde, that mought be rayſed in the Citie, although that euery inhabitant ſhoulde throw but one ſtone at them, or elſe to breake vp the drawbridges, or withdrawing their victuals, things verye eaſie to be done. With this greate care that he had of the preſeruation of his felloures, and to remedie the perill and daunger that he ſtode in, he determined to apprehend *Mutezuma*, and to builde foure Foyſtes to haue the lake in ſubiection, which he hadde tofore ymagined, and without the apprehenſion of the King, he coulde not come by the Kingdome: he would very gladly haue buylt the Foyſtes out of hand, but he left off that pretence, only bycauſe he would not delay the empriſonment of *Mutezuma*, wherein conſiſted the effect of all his buſineſſe, ſo that forthwith he minded to put in execution his intent, without gyuing any of his company to vnderſtand thereof.

The quarrell wherewith he had armed himſelfe for that purpoſe, was, that the Lorde *Qualpopoca* hadde ſlayne nine *Spanyardes*: likewiſe encouraged him the greate preſumption of his letters written to the Emperour *Charles* his king, wherein he wrote that he would take *Mutezuma* priſoner, and diſpoſſeſſe him of his Empyre. Theſe cauſes conſidered, he toeke the letters of *Pedro Hircio*, wherein was written, howe *Qualpopoca* was the cauſe of the death of nine *Spanyardes*, and put thoſe letters into his pocket, and walking vp and downe his lodging, toſſyng too and fro theſe ymaginations in his brayne, full of care of the great enterpriſe that he had in hande, yea he hymſelfe iudging the matter doubtfull, and his head beeyng in this ſort occupyed, he chanced to eſpye one wall more whiter than the reſt, and beholding the ſame, he ſawe that it was a dore lately dammed vp, & callyng vnto him two of his ſeruaunts (for all the reſidue were aſleepe) bycauſe

Determination of Cortez.

cause it was late in the nighte, he opened that doze, and went in, and there found sundzy halles, some with Idols, some with gallant feathers, Iewels, pzecious stones, plate, yea and such an infinite quantitie of golde, that the fight thereof amazed him, and other gallant things that made him to maruell. He shutte thys doze agayne as well as he mought, without touching any part of that treasure, bycause he woulde not make any vpzoze therabout, noz yet to delay the empzisonment of Mutezuma, foz that treasure was alwayes there to be had.

The nexte daye in the mozning came certayne Spanyardes vnto hym, and manye Indians of Tlaxcallon, saying that the Citizens did goe about to conspire their deathe, and to bzeake downe the bzidges of the calseys, to bzyng their purpose the better to passe. So that with this newes, béeyng true oz false, Cortes left the one halfe of his men to defende and kéepe his lodging, and at euery crosse stréete he planted mé, and the resioue he sent to the Court by two and two, and thzée and thzée, and he hymselfe came to the pallaice, saying that he must talke wyth Mutezuma of matters that did empozt their liues. Cortes was secretely armed. Mutezuma hearyng howe Cortez attended foz hym, came fozth and receyued him, taking him by the hand, and placed him in his seate. Thirtie Spanyardes wayted vpon Cortez, and the resioue abode without at the doze.

Cortez saluted Mutezuma accozding to his accustomed manner, and began to iest and talke merily as hée was wont to do. Mutezuma béeyng carelesse of the thing that Foztune hadde pzepared agaynste hym, was also very merrie, and pleased with that conuersation. He gaue vnto Cortes Iewels of golde, and one of his daughters, and other noble mens daughters to others of his company. Cortes receyued the gift, foz otherwise it hadde bin

a frent

a frent vnto *Mutezuma*. But yet he enfozmed him, that
he was a married man, and that he coulde not marrie
with his daughter, foz the Chziſtian law did not permitte
the ſame, noz yet that any Chziſtian mought haue moze
than one wife, vppon payne of infamy, and to be marked
in the fozehead.

After all this talke ended, *Cortez* toke the letters of
Pedro Hircio, and cauſed them to be interpzeted vnto *Mutezuma*, makyng bys grieuous complaynte agaynſte
Qualpopoca, who hadde ſlayne ſo many *Spanyardes* thzough
bys commaundement, yea and that his ſubiectes had publiſhed, that they woulde kill the *Spanyardes*, and bzeake
downe the bzidges.

Mutezuma excuſed himſelfe earneſtly, as well of the
one as of the other, ſaying, the repozt giuen out agaynſte
bys ſubiectes was falſe and vntrue, and as foz *Qualpopoca* who had ſlayne the *Spanyardes*, he was innocent thereof : and bycauſe that he ſhoulde ſée the troth, he called incontinent certayne of his ſeruauntes, commaunding thē
to goe foz *Qualpopoca*, and gaue vnto them his ſeale, whiche was a ſtone that he ware at his wzeſt, engraued with
the figure of the God *Vitzilopuchtli*, and the meſſengers
departed therewith incontinent.

Cortez replyed and ſayd: My Lozd, your highneſſe muſt
goe with me to my lodging, and there abide, vntill youre
meſſengers returne with *Qualpopoca*, and the certaynetie
of the deathe of my men : In my lodging youre highneſſe
ſhall rule and commaund as you do héere in Court, your
perſon ſhall bée well vſed, wherefoze take you no care,
foz I will haue reſpecte vnto youre honoz, as to myne
owne propper, oz the honoz of my Kyng, beſéeching you to
pardon me in this my requeſt, foz if I ſhoulde doe otherwiſe, and diſſemble with you, mine own company would
be offended with me, ſaying that I doe not defende them,

accoz-

accozding to duetie. Wherefoze commaund your householde seruauntes to repose themselues without alteration, foz be you assured, that if any hurte come vnto me, oz
vnto anye of mine, youre person shall pay the same with
life, considering that it lyeth in youre hand to goe quietly
with me.

Mutezuma was soze amazed, saying, Sir, my person is
not fytte to be a pzisoner, yea, and though I woulde permitte the same, my subiectes would not suffer.

They abode arguing the matter neare foure houres,
and at length *Mutezuma* was content to goe, hauing pzo-
mise that he should rule and gouerne as he was wont to
do. *Cortes* comaunded a place in his lodging to be trimmed foz him, and he went fozthwith thither with *Cortes*.
There came many noble men barefooted, weeping and
lamenting the case, carrying their best garmentes vnder
their armes, and bzought a rich seate, whereon *Mutezuma* was placed, & they carried hym vpon their shoulders.

When it was blowen abzoade in the Citie that *Mutezuma* was carried pzisoner to the *Spanyards* lodging, all
the Citie was on an vpzoze: but yet *Mutezuma* did com-
foz the Gentlemen that carried and followed him weeping, pzaying them to ccasse their lamentation, saying
that he was not pzisoner, noz yet went with the Chzysti-
ans againste his will, but foz his onely pleasure. *Cortes*
appointed a *Spanish* garde foz him, with a Captayne, the
which he dayly changed, and had *Spanyards* alwayes in his
copany to make him pastime. Also poze *Mutezuma* was ⟨A sorow-
cotented with their conuersation, & gaue the stil rewards. ⟨ful pastime.
He was serued with his owne seruãts *Indias*, as at home
in his pallace. *Cortes* always intreated him to put off sad-
nes, & to be merrie, permitting him to dispatch suters, & to
deale in all affayzes of his estate, & to comune and talke
openly oz secretely with his noble mẽ as he was wont to

do, and that was but onely a bayte to bring them to the
boоke. There was neuer Greeke nor Romayne, nor any
other nation since the name of kings was ordeyned, dyd
gyue ý lyke enterpzise, as *Hernando Cortez* did, in taking
Mutezuma pzisoner in his owne house, bæing a most
mighty King, & in a most strong fort among infinite people, he hauyng but only 450. companions.

The recreation of Hunting, vvhiche
Mutezuma vsed.

Mutezuma had not only al the libertie that
he desired in the Citie, bæyng pzisoner a-
mong the *Spanyardes*, but also *Cortes* permitted him to hunt and hauke, or to go to
the temple, for he was very deuoute, and
a great hunter.

When he went a hunting, he was carried vpon mens
shoulders with eyght or ten *Spanyards* in his guard, and
thrée thousande *Mexicans*, who were Gentlemen, his seruants, and hunters, of whome he hadde a great number,
some to sæke the game, others to beate the couertes, and
others to marke. Some of those Hunters were only for
hares and connyes, other for all sorts of Dære, Wolues,
foxes, and such like. They were very perfite with theyr
bowes, and good markemē, for he that missed his marke
at fourescore pases distant was punished. It was strange
to sæ the number of people that wente with him on hunting, and to sæ the slaughter of beasts killed, with hande,
staues, nettes, and bowes, some of those beastes were
tame, and other braue and fearefull, as Lyons, Tigers,
and Ounces. It is a harde thing to take a fierce Lion in
hunting as they do, being in manner a naked people, and
the beast couragious and strong, but yet the Pzouerbe
saith, sight and cunning is better than strength.

Jt

It is a moze ſtraunge thyng to take any foule that flieth in the ayze as their Fauconers doe, foz after they haue once marked and ſet eye vpon any foule, the Faulconers of Mutezuma will vnder take to catch him, although the foule be neuer ſo ſwifte of wing, beyng at the leaſt ſo commaunded by the King. It happened one day that Mutezuma ſtode in his gallerie with his Guarde of Spanyardes, who had eſpied a fayze Hauke ſozyng in the ayze, oh quoth they what a fayze Hauke flieth yonder, Mutezuma hearyng their talke, called vnto him certayne of his Faulconers, commaundyng them to followe that Hauke & to bzing him vnto him. The Faulconers wente to fulfill his requeſt, and followed that foule with ſuch diligence, that in ſhozte ſpace they bzought the Hauke vnto him, who pzeſented the ſame vnto the Spanyards, a thing truely almoſte incredible, but yet certified by wozde and wzytings of the pzeſent witneſſes. Their chiefeſt and moſt pleaſant paſtime of Hauking was, of Kightes, Rauens, Crowes, Pies, and other birdes of hardie ſtomake and ſlowe in flight, greate and ſmall of all ſoztes, foz the which he had Egles, Buyters, and other foule of rappyne marueylous ſwifte of wing, and ſuche as woulde mounte very high in the ayze, with the whiche they murdered Hares, Wolues, and (as ſome ſay) Hartes.

He had other foulers, that vſed Nettes, Snares, and ſundzy engins. Mutezuma vſed much to ſhote in a tronke, and with his bow killed many wilde beaſtes. His houſes of pleaſure as I haue befoze declared, ſtode ſire myles from the Citie in pleaſant woddes : and alwayes when he went a huntyng after the tyme that he was pzyſoner, the ſame day he would returne agayne to Cortes his lodging, although he banketed & feaſted with the Spaniardes at his places of ſpozting and paſtime, and would alwayes at his returne to his lodgyng giue ſome pzeſent vnto the,

that

that had accompanied him that day.

Cortes seyng the liberalitie of Mutezuma, sayde vnto him : sir, my company are vnruly fellowes, and as I vnderstand, they haue founde out some of your treasure, and haue made spoyle thereof: wherfore I would know your pleasure what shal be done with the. And in effect it was the treasure that Cortes himselfe had founde out. Mutezuma answered, saying, sir that treasure which they haue founde, did appertayne vnto the Goddes: But yet notwithstandyng, let them leaue the feathers, and all suche things as are neyther golde nor siluer, and all the residue take for you and them, and if you will haue more, I will prouide it for you.

Hovv Cortez began to plucke dovvne the Idols of Mexico.

Hen Mutezuma went vnto the temple, he went leaning vpon a noble mans arme, or else was leade betwéene two, and a noble personage wente alwayes before him with thrée small wandes in his hande, signifying thereby that the King in person was there at hand, and in token also of iustice and correction. If he had bene carried vpon mens shoulders then at his alighting downe he tooke one of those roddes into his owne hand. He was a Prince ful of ceremonies in al his doings, but the substaunce of his estate is already declared, from the time that Cortes entred into Mexico vntil this present. Those first dayes that the Spaniardes came to the Citie, & as often as Mutezuma went to the temple, Indian men were slayne in sacrifice. And to prohibite suche abhominable crueltie & sinne, committed in the presence of the Christians who wét in company of Mutezuma, Cortes

required

required *Mutezuma*, to commaunde that no mans fleshe
should be any moze spoyled, oz bloud shedde in facrifice,
and in not fulfilling his requeſt, he would deſt, op liothe
the temple and Cittie. Also he ſignified vnto him, that he
himſelfe woulde thzow downe the idols, befoze his pze
ſence and all the Citizens.

Mutezuma replied to his demaūd,ſaying:It may pleaſe
you to leaue of your determination, leaſt that in ſo doing
all the Cittie fall into an vpzoze and rebellion to defende
their god Gods, and auncient Religion, the which Gods
had alwayes pzouided them of water, bzead,health,light,
and all other things nædefull. This notwithſtanding,the
firſt time that *Mutezuma* wente to the temple after his
impziſonment, *Cortes* and his company wente with him,
and euery of them layde handes vpon the idols, & thzewe
them downe headlong from their ſeates,and Altars, and
other Chapels. *Mutezuma* with this ſight was in great
agonie,yea and his ſubieds ready to take weapon to ſlay
them there pzeſent, but yet *Mutezuma* commaunded his
ſubiedes to ſtay from their pzetence: beſæchyng *Cortes*
to ſtay from his pzocædings, at whoſe requeſt *Cortes* ceaſ
ſed, foz he thought,as yet time ſerued not foz the purpoſe
and pzetence : but he declared vnto them by his interpze
ters as followeth,

The exhortation that Cortez made
*to Mutezuma and to the Citizens of Mexico,
concerning their Idols.*

LL creatures in the wozld (mightie pzince,
and yæ Gentlemen and religious perſons
whether it be yæ here oz wæ in Spayne,
oz whatſoeuer other nation that it may
be) haue I ſay, all one begynnyng and
ending

ending of moꝛtall lyfe, whiche is had from God: we are al foꝛmed and made of one mettall, and haue all soules and senses, euen so doubtlesse as we are like in pꝛopoꝛtion of body and soule, yea and kinsfolke in bloud, although that by the pꝛouidence of the same our God, some are boꝛne fayꝛe and beautifull, and other some fowle and disfigured: some of one colour, and some of another: some pꝛudent and wise, and other some fonde and foolishe, without eyther iudgement oꝛ vertue: in the which his maruellous woꝛks God sheweth himselfe iuste, holy and almightie, giuyng those seuerall giftes, to the entent that the wise and lear-ned mought teache the rude and ignoꝛant, and to guyde the blinde into the right way of saluation, by the steppes of true and vnfayned religion.

Therfoꝛe I and my fellowes, as your gestes and kins-men, accoꝛding to equitie doe pꝛocure and wish the same vnto you. A man and his life consisteth in thꝛee things as yee shal vnderstande, that is body, soule, and goodes: as foꝛ your goodes and ritches, whiche is the least that wee desire, foꝛ yee know well that we haue taken nothing foꝛ-cible from you, but onely those things whiche yee haue frely and liberally giuen vs. Likewise we haue not hurt, misused oꝛ molested your persons, wiues oꝛ chyldꝛen, noꝛ yet do meane any such thing, your soules health onely is the thing we seeke, foꝛ your saluation, and that we nowe pꝛetende to shewe, and to giue vnto you perfite notice of the true and euerlasting God. There is none of naturall iudgement can denie, but that there is one God, but yet thꝛough ignoꝛaunce and deceyte of the Diuell, will also thinke that there are many Goddes, and not arette vnto the true God. But I doe say and most assuredly certifie you, that there is no other true God, but onely he whome we Chꝛistians doe serue, adoꝛe, and woꝛshippe, the which is one eternall, without beginnyng and without ende, the

the onely creator & gouernour of things created: he alone
made the heauens, the Sunne, the Mone, and Starres,
the whiche his creatures ye doe worship: he (I say) founded and made the Sea, and the sundry and maruelous fishes therein: he planted and made the lande with all the
monstrous beastes therein, foules likewise in the ayre,
plantes, Hearbes, Stones and suche like. Al the whiche
creatures ye as blinde and ignorant do hold for Goddes

Our almighty God after he had finished and made al
the former workes with his own blessed hands, made one
man & one woman, and being so formed and wrought, he
put a soule and breath into each body, and then deliuered
the worlde vnto them, shewyng them Paradise and glory. So that of that manne and woman, we all mortall
menne proceded in generation, and in this sorte are
the handy worke of God, kinsmen and brethren. Nowe
if we will come vnto God our father, it is nedefull and
necessary that we be good, vertuous, pitifull, innocent and
vnder obedience, the whiche yee can not be if you worshippe statues, images, idols, and vse bloudy sacrifice of
mans fleshe. Is there any of you that woulde willingly
be slayne? no truely: why then doe you slea other so cruelly, and where you can put no soules, why doe you take
them from thence? there is none of you, nor your false
Gods, that can make soules, nor can forge mens bodies
of fleshe and bone, for if yee coulde, there is none of you
woulde be without children, accordyng to your owne ap-
petite and desire, in fashion, beautie and workemanship.
But where our God of heauen dothe make al creatures,
he vseth therein his owne discretion, and giueth chyldren to whome hee pleaseth: and therefore is he GOD
alone, and for these causes shoulde yee haue, esteeme, and
worshippe him for suche a mightie God, desiryng of him
by prayers to giue rayne and temperature, that the earth

Ff.   may

may bʒyng foʒth Coʒne, Fruite, Hearbes, Flethe, Foule, and all other neceſſaries foʒ the ſuſtentation of lyfe. All theſe thyngs the harde ſtones giueth not vnto you, no noʒ yet your dʒy woodden images & colde mettall, neyther yet the ſmall ſeedes wherewith your ſeruaunts and ſlaues, with theyʒ filthy handes doe make theſe images and foule ſtatues, the whiche yee doe woʒſhippe. O what

fonde people and madde religious perſons, who woʒſhip theyʒ owne woʒkemanſhippe, doe ye thynke that they are Gods that rotte and moloʒe away, and haue no lyfe, and can neyther helpe noʒ kill? Therefoʒe I ſay vnto you, that nowe and hereafter there is no cauſe that yee ſhoulde haue any moe idolles, noʒ yet any moe ſlaugh- ters foʒ ſacrifice, no noʒ yet to make any moe pʒayers oʒ ſupplications vnto them, beyng bothe Blinde, Deafe, and Dumme.

Will yee knowe who is God, and where he is? liſte vp your eyes vnto Heauen, and then ſhall you vnder- ſtande that aboue is a Godhead oʒ Deitie that moueth the heauens, and gouerneth the courſe of the Sunne, ru- leth the Lande and repleniſheth the Sea, who pʒouideth foʒ Man and Beaſt bothe Coʒne and Water. This God whome yee nowe imagine in your hartes, him (I ſay) ſerue and woʒſhippe, not with death of menne oʒ bloud- dy ſacrifice abominable, but with deuotion and humble pʒayer as we Chʒiſtians doe. And conſider well, that to teach and inſtruct you theſe things, was the cauſe of our commyng hither.

With this exhoʒtation, *Cortes* aplaked the yʒe of the Pʒieſtes and Citizens: theyʒ idols beyng thʒowen downe, *Mutezuma* tooke oʒder that no moe ſhoulde be ſette vp, commaundyng to ſweepe and make cleane the Chappels of the ſtinking bloud that was in thē, foʒbidding ſacrifice of mans fleſh. *Mutezuma* and his officers made a ſolēpne
vowe

vowe and pꝛomiſe to permitte no moꝛe ſlaughter of men, and to ſet vp a Croſſe foꝛ remembꝛance of the death and paſſion of Jeſu Chꝛiſte boꝛne of the virgin Marie. The whiche their pꝛomiſe was well fulfilled, foꝛ after that day the Spanyardes coulde neuer heare, noꝛ finde of any moe ſacrifice: But yet there abode in their hartes a moꝛtall rancoꝛ, the whiche coulde not long be diſſimuled.

Truely in this woꝛthy facte *Cortes* gotte moꝛe honour than though he had ouercomen them in battayle.

The burning of the Lorde Qual-
popoca and other Gentlemen.

After twentie dayes that *Mutezuma* had bene pꝛyſoner, returned the meſſengers who had gone with the ſeale foꝛ *Qualpopoca*, and bꝛought him, his Sonne, and other fiftene pꝛincipall perſons, with them, the whiche by inquirie made, were culpable and partakers in the counſell and death of the nine Spaniardes. *Qualpopoca* entred into *Mexico* accompanied like a greate Loꝛde as he was, beyng boꝛne vpon his ſeruaunts ſhoulders in rich furniture. As ſone as he had ſaluted *Mutezuma*, he & his Sonne were deliuered vnto *Cortes*, with the other fiftene Gentlemen. *Cortes* placed them aſunder, and commaunded them to be put in Irons, and theyr examinations taken, they confeſſed that they had ſlayne thoſe Spaniardes in battayle.

Cortes demaunded of *Qualpopoca* if he were ſubiect to *Mutezuma*, why (quoth he) is there any other Pꝛince to whome I might be in ſubiection? giuing almoſt to vnderſtand that he was a Loꝛde abſolute. *Cortes* anſwered, that a farre greater Pꝛince was the King of Spayne, whoſe ſubiects vnder colour of friendſhip and ſalfeconduct he had flayne. But (quoth he) nowe shalte thou make payment thereof. And beyng agayne moze straighter examined, they confessed that they had slaine two Spaniards by the aduice and inducement of the greate pzince *Mute-zuma*, and the residue were slayne in the warres, and had assaulted their houses, and entred their countrey, wherefoze they helde it lawfull to kill them.

Through the confession pzonounced by their owne mouthes, sentence was giuen against them, and they condemned to be burned, whiche sentence was openly executed in the market place in sight of all the people, without any mutine oz slaunder, and with great silence, terrour & feare of the newe maner of iustice which they sawe there executed vpon so noble a man, in the chiefe seate and kyngdome of *Mutezuma*, beyng gestes and straungers.

The caufe of the burnyng of
Qualpopoca.

At the time that *Cortes* departed from *Vera Crux*, he left in commission to *Pedro Hircio*, to pzocure to inhabite in that place which is called *Almeria*, & not to permit *Francifco de Garray* to soiourne there, foz so much as once he was dziuen frō that coast. Now *Hircio* to fulfill his commission, sente to requyze those *Indians* with peace and friēdship, and to yeeld themselues foz vassals of the Emperour. *Qualpopoca* Lozde of *Nahutlan*, which is now called as afozesaid *Almeria*, sent to aduertise *Pedro Hircio*, that he coulo not come to yeelde his obedience, foz the enimies that were in the way: but if it would please him to sende some of his men, foz the securitie of the way, he would willyngly come vnto him. *Hircio* hearing this answere, sent foure of his men, giuing

credite

credite to his message, and for the desire he hadde to inhabite there.

When the foure *spanyardes* came into the prouince of *Nahutlan*, there mette with them many armed men, who slew two of them, and made thereof a great triumph: the other two escaped sore wounded, and returned with that newes to the Towne of *Vera Crux*. *Pedro Hircio* beleeuing that *Qualpopoca* had done that iniurie, armed out agaynst hym fiftie *spanyardes*, and ten thousand *Indians* of *Zempoallan*, with two horses, and two peeces of Ordinance.

Qualpopoca hearing this newes, came with a mightie power to driue them out of his Countrey, and in that encounter, seauen *spanyardes* were slayne, and many *Zempoallanezes*, but at the ende he was ouercome, his Countrey spoyled, and Towne sacked, and many of his army slaine and taken captiues. The prisoners declared, that by the commaundement of the greate Lorde *Mutezuma*, all this vprore was attempted by *Qualpopoca*: it mighte well be, for at the houre of death they confessed the same. But some affirme, they sayde so, but to excuse themselues, and to lay the fault to the *Mexicans*. *Hircio* wrote these newes to *Cortez* beeyng in *Chololla*, and through these letters *Cortez* apprehended *Mutezuma* (as is afore declared.)

Hovv Cortez put a payre of giues on *Mutezuma* his legges.

Efore the execution of *Qualpopoca* and hys fellowes, *Cortes* declared vnto *Mutezuma*, that *Qualpopoca* and his company had confessed, that by hys aduice and commaundemente, the nine *spanyardes* were slayne, wherein he had done very euill, they being his friendes and guestes: but (quoth he) if it were not in respect of the

loue I beare vnto you, this matter fhoulde not in this
fort be fhut vp, and then knocked a payre of giues on his
legges, faying, he that killeth ought to be killed, accorbing
to the lawes of God. Thefe things did *Cortes*, bycaufe
he fhoulde occuppe himfelfe in his owne griefe and for
row, and to let other mens paffe.

   Mutezuma waxed pale wt countenäce of death, through
the great feare that he was in, feeyng himfelfe in Irons,
a new and ftrange thing for fuche a great King, excufing
himfelfe that he was innocent of the facte. And as fone
as the execution of burning was done, *Cortez* commaun
ded to put away the Irons that *Mutezuma* ware, offering
him libertie, and willing him to goe vnto his owne pal
lace, who reioyced much to fee himfelfe out of the Irons,
and gaue *Cortes* moft hartie thankes, and refufed to goe
home to his owne pallace, furmifing that the offer was
but wordes, or elfe fearing leaft his fubiects woulde kyll
him, feeing him out of the *Spanyardes* power, for permit
ting himfelfe to be taken prifoner, and fo to be kept. Hee
fayd alfo, that if he went from them, his fubiects woulde
rebell, and compell him to kill the *Spanyardes.*

   Truly the poore fimple foule was of fmall hearte and
courage, to fuffer himfelfe to be taken prifoner, and after
his imprifonment woulde neuer procure libertie, *Cortes*
offering it vnto him, and many of his noble men defiring
him. And remayning in that order, there was none in
Mexico durft offende any *Spanyard* for feare of difpleafing
him, for *Qualpopoca* came 70. leagues with only warning
him that the great Lorde had fent for him, fhewing hym
the figure of his feale: yea and al the peeres of his realme
that dwelte fartheft off, were ready to obey hys com
maundementes.

                                                     HOW

Hovv Cortez sent to seeke for Mines
of golde into diuers places.

Ortez had a greate desire to knovv hovve farre the Empire of *Mutezuma* dyd extende, and what friendship was betwixte him and other Kings and Princes *Comarcans*, and also to gather togither a good summe of gold, to send to *Spayne* to the Emperoure, for his custome or fifte parte, with full relation of the Countrey people, and things happened vntill that day. Wherefore he prayed *Mutezuma* to shew him where the mynes were, from whence he and his subiectes had the golde and plate. *Mutezuma* graunted to his request, and incontinent appoynted eyght *Indians*, of the which four were Goldsmythes, who had knowledge and vnderstanding of Mynes, and the other foure were guydes for the iourney. He commaunded them that by two and two they shoulde goe into foure prouinces, that is to say *Zucolla*, *Malinaltepec*, *Tenich*, and *Tutepec*, with other eyghte *Spanyardes* whiche *Cortez* appoynted, to haue knowledge of the riuers and mynes of gold, and to bring a moster of the same. The eyght *Spanyardes* departed on their iourney, with the other eyghte *Indians*, with tokens from *Mutezuma*. *Zucolla* is 80. leagues from *Mexico*, and the Lord therof is subiect to *Mutezuma*, who shewed vnto the *Spanyardes* three riuers with golde, and gaue of each riuer a moster thereof, although it were but little, for with want of knowledge they knew not wel the maner how to get it out of the riuer. These messengers in their iourney to and fro, passed through three prouinces full of people and habitatió, with good buildings & frutefull ground, and the people of the one of them called *Tlamacolapan*, are of good reason and iudgemente, and better apparelled than the *Mexicans*.

Malinal-

Malinaltepec is 70. leagues from *Mexico*, from whence also they brought mosters of golde, the which is had out of a great riuer, by the naturals of that Countrey.

Tenich standeth vp towarde the head of the same riuer of *Malinaltepec*, who are people of another language, and would not permitte our men to haue relation of the thing that they saught. The Lorde of that place is called *Coatelicamatl*, who is not subiecte to *Mutezuma*, nor yet is his friende, thinking that his men hadde bin espyes : but when he was enformed who they were, he gaue the *Spanyardes* licence to be resolued of their affayres, but straitly commaunded, that the *Indians* of *Mexico* should not presume to come into his dominion. When the *Mexicans* hearde these newes, they required the *Spanyardes* not to credite that *Cazike*, saying, that he was an euill and a cruell man, and would surely kill them. Our men were somewhat amazed, fearing to talke with *Coatelicamatl*, although they hadde his licence, seyng the people of the countrey armed with Launces of fiue and twenty foote lōg : but yet at lēgth leauing cowardise aside, they proceded forwards. *Coatelicamatl* receyued thē curteously, and shewed them sire or seauen riuers with golde, out of the which graynes of golde were taken in his presence, who gaue the same moster vnto them, and sente also his Embassadors to *Cortez*, offering his lande and person vnto him, with certayne mantels, and Iewels of golde.

Cortez more reioyced of the Embassage, than of the gold and presents, knowing thereby that *Mutezuma* hys enimies desired his friendchippe : but *Mutezuma* and hys counsell liked not the matter, for although *Coatelicamatl* is no great Lord, yet his people are good souldyers, and his countrey full of wildernesse, of Rockes and Mountaynes. The other that wente to *Tutepec*, which standeth néere the sea coast, and twelue leagues frō *Malinaltepec*,

returned

returned likewife with moffer of golde of two Riuers, and broughtnewes that the Countrey was fit to buylde vppon, with hope to reape muche golde, finding once an arte to get it out of the riuer.

Cortez hearing thefe news, prayed *Mutezuma* to build a houfe there in the name of the Emperoure *Charles,* who incontinente fente thither workemen and labourers, whyche within two monethes hadde built a greate houfe, and other three little houfes round aboute it, with a ponde of water full of fifhe, and fiue hundred Duckes, and a thoufand fiue hundred Turkie cockes and hennes, and muche houfholde ftuffe, fo that the gifte was worth twentie thoufand Caftlins of golde. He gaue vnto hym alfo twenty bufhels of the grayne called *Centli,* readye fowen, and two thoufand ftockes of trées called *Cacauatl,* whiche bringeth forthe the fruite *Cacao,* that ferueth for money and meate. *Cortes* began this hufbandrye, but yet made not an ende thereof, with the comming of *Pamfilo de Naruaz,* and the vprore in *Mexico,* whiche fhortly followed. He alfo befoughte *Mutezuma* to certifie him if there were any fure porte or harbor on the Sea coaft, where the Spanifh nauie mought ride in fafetie: he aunfwered that he knew of none, but that he woulde fende to make enquirie thereof. And forthwith he commaunded all that coaft to be painted in a cloath made of cotten woll, with all the riuers, bayes, créekes and capes that were within his dominion. In all the fame portrapture did not appeare anye porte, fkale, or fure roade, fauyng a gulfe that falleth out of the Mountaynes, which place is now called the harbor of *Saint Martine,* and *Saint Anthonie* in the prouince of *Coazacoalco.* The Spanyards thought the fame to be a ftraight or paffage into the South fea, to paffe vnto the *Maluccos* and fpicerie, but they were deceiued although they beléeued the thing that they defired.

Gg. *Cortes*

Cortes for this purpose sent tenne Spanyardes, all good marriners and Pylots, in companye of the *Indians* that *Mutezuma* sent on that voyage at his owne cost.

They departed, and came to *Chalohicoeca*, where first they came aland, the which place is now called *S. Iohn de Vlhua.*

They wente 70. leagues along the coast, without finding any Riuer, although they mette with many brookes of shallowe water, not fytte for a roade for Shyppes.

They aported at *Coazacoalco*, the Lorde whereof was enimie to *Mutezuma*, hys name was *Tuchintlec*, who friendly receyued the Spanyardes, for he hadde intelligence of them, at their lying at *Potonchan*. He gaue vnto them boates, to sounde and seeke the Riuer, where they found sixe fadome in deapth, and wente vppe that Riuer twelue leagues, wher they descryed many great townes, and it seemed a fruitefull soyle. This *Cazike Tuchnitlee*, sente vnto *Cortes* with the Spanyards certayne gold, precious stones, and cloth of cotten, with apparrell made of skynnes, and tygers, requesting his friendship, and to admitte him tributarie to the Emperour, paying yeerely a certayne portion of his riches, with suche condition, that the *Indians* of *Culhua* should not enter into his iurisdictiō.

Cortes muche reioysed with these messages, and was glad of the finding of the faire riuer, for the Marriners hadde enformed him, that from the riuer of *Grijalua* vnto *Panuco*, was no riuer to be found, but I beleue they were deceyued. *Cortes* returned backe agayne some of those messengers, with a present of Spanish ware for *Tuchnitlec*, and to be better enformed of all his meaning, with a speciall charge to knowe the cōmoditie of that porte and Countrey, who went, and in shorte time returned wel satisfyed of their demaund: wherevpon *Cortes* sente thyther *Iohn Velasques de Leon*, for Captayne of a hundred and fifty Spanyardes,

Spanyardes, with commiſſion to build a fozt.

The impriſonment of Cacama, King
of Tezcuco.

He weake courage and ſtomake of *Mutezuma*, cauſed his ſubiectes not onely to murmure, but alſo to ſeeke meanes of rebellion, eſpecially his nephew *Cacamizin*, Lozde of *Tezcuco*, who was a ſtoute pong man and an honozable, and one ẏ receiued greate griefe of his Uncles impzſonment: and ſeeing that ẏ matter ſeemed long, he beſought his Uncle to pzocure his libertie, and to ſhew himſelfe a Lozde, and not a ſlaue: but ſeeing at length that he could not accepte and follow his councell, he began to ſtirre in the matter, thzeatning the death and deſtruction of the Spanyardes. Some ſaid, that *Cacama* did begin that matter, to reuenge the iniurie and diſhonoz done vnto his Uncle. Others ſaide, that his meaning was to make himſelfe Kyng of *Mexico*. Others held opinion, that his pzetence was only to make an ende of ẏ Spanyards. But let it be foz what ſoeuer purpoſe. Once he gathered a great army, which he could not want, although *Mutezuma* was pzſoner, eſpecially againſt ẏ Spanyards. He publiſhed that he would redæme his Uncle out of Captiuitie, and expulſe the Straungers, oz elſe kill and eate them.

This was a terrible newes foz the Chzſtians, but yet foz all thoſe bzagges *Cortes* diſmayde not, rather hæ determined fozthwith to pzepare himſelfe foz the warres, and to beſiege him in his owne houſe and Towne, ſaming that *Mutezuma* diſturbed him, ſaying that *Tezcuco* was a place very ſtrong, and ſcituated in water, and that *Cacama* was a man of bolde and ſtoute courage,

and

and had at commaundemente the *Indians* of *Culhua*, and was also Lorde of *Culhuacan* and *Otumpa*, whiche were sortes of great strength, thinking to bring the matter to a better passe another way : so that *Cortez* ruled himselfe by the counsell of *Mutezuma*, and sent vnto *Cacama*, praying him to haue in remembrance the friendshippe that hadde bin betwixt them two, from the time that he came and broughte hym into *Mexico*, and that alwayes peace was better than warre, and especially for a noble man of vassals, for the begynnyng of warres was pleasant to hym that knewe not what warres meante : and in so doyng, he shoulde do both pleasure and seruice to the Kyng of *Spayne*.

Cacama aunswered, that he had no friendship with him that woulde take away hys honor and kingdome, and that the warres whych he pretended, was profitable for his vassals, and in defence of their Countrey and Religion, yea and before he determined peace, he meante to reuenge hys Uncles wrongs and his goddes.

Cacama was vvise.

Also (quoth he) what haue I to doe wyth the Kyng of *Spayne*, who is a man that I know not, no nor yet would gladly heare of hym.

Cortez turned agayne to admonishe and require hym diuers tymes to leaue off his determination, and wylled *Mutezuma* to commaunde hym to accepte hys offer.

Wherevpon *Mutezuma* sente vnto hym, desiryng him to come vnto *Mexico*, to take some order in those controuersies and discordes betwixte hym and the Spanyardes.

Cacama aunswered very sharply vnto his Uncles request, saying, if you had bloud in your eye, or the hearte of a Prince, you woulde not permit your selfe to bee prisoner, and captiue of foure poore straungers, who
with

with their fayꝛe ſpeache and flatterpng talke haue be-
witched pou,and bſurped pour kingdome, no noꝛ pet, ſuffer the Goddes of *Culhua* to be thꝛowen downe and ſpop-
led,pea and the *Mexican* religion and holp places, biola-
ted and troden with theeues feete and decepuers:likewiſe
the honour,gloꝛp,and fame of pour pꝛedeceſſoꝛs blotted
and abaſed,thꝛough pour faput ſtomacke and cowardiʒe.
But notwithſtanding,accoꝛdpng to pour requeſt,and to
repapꝛe our religiõ,to reſtoꝛe the Goddes to their Temples,to pꝛeſerue the kingdome,and to pꝛocure libertie foꝛ
pou and the Cittie, J will obap pour commaundement :
But how:not with mp handes in mp boſome, but lpke a
warrier, to kill thoſe Spaniardes who haue ſo affrented
the nation of *Culhua*. Dur men ſtode in great perill, as
well of the loſing of *Mexico* as of their owne liues ,if this
warre and mutinie had not ſœne bene qualified:foꝛ whp:
Cacama was baliant,ſtoute, and a good ſouldier, pea and
well furniſhed of men of warre: alſo the Citiʒens of *Me-*
xico,were deſirous of the ſame, foꝛ to redeeme *Mutezuma*
their pꝛince,and to kill the Spaniardes, oꝛ elſe to erpulſe
them out of the Cittie.

But poꝛe *Mutezema* remedied the matter, knowpng
oꝛ foꝛeſeing,that warres would not pꝛeuaple,pea and beleued,that at the ende all ſhoulce fall bpon his backe. He
dealt with certapne Captapnes e Gentlemen that dwelt
in *Tezeuco* with *Cacama*,to appꝛehend him,and bꝛpng him
pꝛpſoner,cõſidering that he was their king and pet aliue.
But whether it were, that thoſe Captapnes had ſerued
Mutezuma in the warres, oꝛ whether it were foꝛ giftes e
rewardes, thep appꝛehended *Cacama* being in counſell a-
mong them, treatpng of his warres pꝛetended, and embarked him in a boate armed foꝛ the purpoſe, and ſo
bꝛought him to *Mexico* without anp further ſlander oꝛ
ſtrpfe, and when he was comen to *Mexico*, thep put him

on a riche seate, as the Kings of *Tezcuco* were wonte to sitte vpon, beyng the greatest Prince in all that lande next vnto *Mutezuma*: and in this sorte brought him before his vncle, who would not looke vpon him, but commaunded him to be deliuered vnto *Cortes*, who incontinent clapped a payre of giues on his legges, and a payre of manacles on his handes, and put hym into sure Guarde and custodie.

Cacama pryſoner.

After that *Cacama* was in this order pryſoner, with the consent of *Mutezuma* was elected Lorde and Prince of *Tezcuco* and *Culhuacan*, *Cucuzca*, *Cacama* his yonger brother, who was abidyng in *Mexico* with his vncle, and fled from his brother: *Mutezuma* did entitle him with the ceremonies accustomed vnto Princes newly elected and chosen. So that forthwith he was obeyed in *Tezcuco* by *Mutezuma* his commaundement, for he was there better beloued than *Cacama*, who was somewhat of a croked nature. In this sorte was remedied all the former perill, but if there had bene many *Cacamas*, it would haue fallen out otherwise.

Here *Cortes* made kings, and comaunded with as great auctoritie as though he had obtayned already the whole Empire of *Mexico*: and certainely sithens his first entry into that countrey, he had an assured hope to win *Mexico*, and to be Lorde ouer the whole state of *Mutezuma*.

The Oration that Mutezuma made
vnto his Noble men, yeelding himselfe to the
King of Castile.

 Fter the imprisonment of *Cacama*, *Mutezuma* proclaymed a Parliament, vnto the which came all the Seniors *Comarcans*, and beyng all together, he made the Oration followyng vnto them.

My kinſmen,frienðes anð ſeruants, yée ðo well know
that eightene yeares I haue bene your kyng, as my fathers and Grandfathers were, and alwaies I haue bene
vnto you a louing Prince, and yée vnto me good and obe-
dient ſubiectes, and ſo I hope you will remayne all the
dayes of my life. Ye ought to haue in remembrance,that
eyther ye haue heard of your fathers,or elſe our abeuines
haue inſtructed you,that we are not naturalles of this
countrey, nor yet our kingdome is durable, bycauſe our
forefathers came from a farre countrey, and theyr king
and captayne who brought them hither,returned againe
to his naturall countrey, ſaying that he woulde ſende
ſuche as ſhoulde rule and gouerne vs, if by chaunce hée
himſelfe returned not.Beléeue ye aſſuredly,that the king
whiche wée haue looked for ſo many yeares, is he that
hath nowe ſente theſe Spaniardes, whiche yée here ſée.
Who dothe certifie,that wée are their kinſmen, and that
they haue had notice of vs a long tyme : lette vs therefore gyue thankes vnto the Goddes,that nowe they are
comen in our dayes, beyng a thing that we ſo muche deſired.

A fonde beliefe.

Yée ſhall nowe doe me ſeruice and pleaſure, that yée
yéelde your ſelues vnto this Captayne for vaſſals of the
Emperoure King of Spayne our ſoueraygne, I my
ſelf haue already yéelded me for his ſeruitour and friend,
praying you that from hence forwardes ye obey him as
ye haue obeyed mée. And that yée yéelde and pay vnto
him the tributes,cuſtomes and ſeruice that ye were wont
to pay vnto me, and in ſo doyng, ye can doe me no greater pleaſure.Hys harte then woulde not ſuffer hym to
ſpeake any more, with the ſobbes, ſighes, and teares,
that fell from hys eyes. All his ſubiectes there preſente
fell into a crie, weepyng and mournyng, that for a good
ſpace they had no power to ſpeake:they gaue ſhrykes,and
ſighings,

Poore Muſ-tezuma.

sighings, vtteryng with their mouthes many dolefull, and sorowfull speaches, yea that it pitied our owne men at the hartes. But in conclusion, they answered that they would obey his commaundement. Then Mutezuma and the Burgesses of Parliament in order yelded themselues for vassals of the king of Castile, promising loyaltie. This acte was set downe by the Notarie, and with witnesses auctorized. Then the Indians departed home to their houses with sorowfull hartes, God knoweth, as you may imagine. It was a straunge thing to see Mutezuma weepe with so many Noble men and Gentlemen, yea and with what griefe they became subiects to an vnknowe Prince, but they coulde not otherwise doe, seyng that Mutezuma did commaunde the same.

Also they had a certaine Prognostication and forwarning by their Priestes of the comming from the east parties a straunge people, white of colour and bearded men, who should winne and rule that countrey. Likewise there was a secrete talke amóg them, that in Mutezuma should ende and finishe, not alone the lynage of Culhua, but also the Empyre and kingdome : therefore some were of opinion, not to name him Mutezuma whiche signifieth, agrieued with missfortune. They say also that Mutezuma himself had many times answere of the Oracle of the Gods, that in him shoulde finishe the Mexican Emperours, and that no childe of his shoulde succeede in his kyngdome, and' that he should lose his seate in the eyght peare of his raigne: & for these causes he woulde neuer procure warre to withstande the Spaniardes, beleuyng that they should be his successours. Yet on the other side he thought his opinion would take no place, for that he had raygned seuentene yeares : But this should seeme to come from the prouidence of God, whiche giueth kingdomes and taketh them away.

A true prophecie.

Cortes

Cortes gaue vnto *Mutezuma* moste hartie thankes on the behalfe of the Emperour, and for himself, and comforted him, who was very sad, promysing also that alwayes he should be kyng and Lorde, commaunde as heretofore he had done, and better, yea and also he should be chiefe ruler of all the other landes and countreys, that he shoulde gette and bryng to the seruice of the Emperour.

The Golde and Iewels that Mutezuma gaue vnto Cortes for tribute.

Fter certaine dayes that *Mutezuma* and his counsell had yealden their obedience, *Cortes* sayde vnto him, how that the Emperour was at great costes & charges in his warres, wherfore it should be necessary that his newe vassals shoulde begin to serue in some thing, and to pay their tribute, willyng him to sende throughout his dominion to see what coulde be gathered of Gold, and that he himselfe should beginne firste to pay tribute to the example of others. *Mutezuma* answered that he was contented so to do, willyng that some of his men shoulde goe vnto the house of foule for the same. There went many, and there sawe golde in planches like brickebattes, Iewels, and peeces wrought in a hall, and two chambers which were opened vnto the. The Spaniardes wondering at the sight, would not touch any thing, without giuing firste aduertisement to *Cortes*, who incontinent went thither, and caused it all to be carried to his lodgyng: besides this treasure *Mutezuma* gaue vnto him rich clothes of cotten and feathers maruelously wouen in figures & colours, it seemed without comparison, for the Spaniardes had neuer seene the like: he gaue vnto him more, twelue shooting tronkes, wherewith he himself was wont to passetime:some of them were paynted with birdes, beasts, floures & trées very persite, a worke surely much to be commended:and some of them were engraué very curiously, with their mouldes and pellets of golde.

He sente also his seruants by two and two, and fiue and fiue, ech company with one Spaniarde, to the Lords of other prouinces, fourescore, and a hundred leagues fró *Mexico*, to gather in golde for the accustomed tributes, and newe seruice to the Emperour. Euery Lorde and Seignior payde the quantitie appointed & tared by *Mutezuma*, in golde, plate, iewels, stones and pearles.

The messengers returned, although they had taried somewhat long on their iourney, of whom *Cortes* receyued all that they brought, and caused it to be molten, out of the whiche was had in fine golde.1600000. Castlins, of the value of seuen shillings and sixe pence the péce, and rather more, and also fiue hundred markes of plate, after sixe Ducates the marke.

This treasure was deuided among the Souldiers, but not all : euery man was payde accordyng to his office. The horsemen had twise as muche as the footemen. Also *Cortes* was payde out of the stocke the money promised him in *Vera Crux.*

There came to the kings parte.32000. Castlins and a hundred markes of plate, the whiche was wrought there in platters, saucers, cuppes, ewers and other péces, accordyng to the *Indian* fashion, to be sent to the Emperour. Besides this, the present that *Cortes* layde aside, and také out of the stocke to send to ƴ Emperour, was worth.100000. Ducates, in pearles, precious stones, golde, and feathers, feathers and siluer, and many other iewels, as the gallant tronkes, whiche beside their value were straunge to behold, wrought with the brauery aforesayde. This present appoynted, was not sent, for that and al the rest was

after

afterwarde loſſe at the troubles in *Mexico*, as hereaftet ſhall moze playnly appeare.

Hovv Mutezuma required Cortez
to departe from Mexico.

Ortes ſeyng himſelfe riche and mightie, he occupied hymſelfe in thzée things, the one was to ſende vnto *Santo Domingo* and other Ilandes, newes of his pzocéedings and pzoſperitie, and alſo money to pzouide menne, hozſes and armour, foz his owne company were to fewe foz ſo greate a countrey. The other was, to take fully and wholly the ſtate of *Mutezuma*, hauing him pzíſoner, and alſo at his commaundement *Tlaxcallan*, *Coatelicamath*, and *Tuchintlec*, knowyng alſo that the *Indians* of *Panuco*, *Tecoantepec*, and *Mechuacan*, were moztall enimies to the *Mexicans*, who woulde ayde and aſſiſt him hauing néede of their helpe, his thirde pzetence was, to pzocure all the *Indians* to be Chziſtened, the which purpoſe he tcœke fírſt in hand, as a thing moſt nedefull. On the other ſide, *Mutezuma* repented himſelfe, hauyng newes that *Pamfilo de Naruaiz* was arriued, who came as enimy to *Cortes*, yea and after all this he was at length dziuen out of *Mexico*. Theſe notable things ſhalbe reherſed in their ozder. But now *Mutezuma* came, and deſíred *Cortes* to departe out of his countrey, aduiſíng hym that otherwiſe bothe he and his menne were in perill of killyng, ſaying alſo, that thzée eſpeciall cauſes moued him to this requeſte: the one was, the dayly ſute of his ſubiectes, who enpoztuned him to come out of captiuitie, and to murder the Spanyardes, ſaying, that it was a great ſhame foz them to ſuffer theyz Pzince to bée in pzyſon in the power of ſo fewe ſtraungers, whom they might vſe as a fœtebal: hauing diſhonozed thé and robbed them of their goodes, gatheryng and heaping vp their gold for themselues, & for their king, who as seemed by their doings, was but a poore fellowe, and if hee would not accept their offer and sute, that then of theyr owne auctoritie they would take the thyng in hande, for so much as he refusing to be theyr king they woulde also refuse to be his vassals, giuyng warnyng and aduice that he should looke for no better rewarde at the Spaniardes handes, than *Qualpopoca* and *Cacama* his Nevewe had receiued, although they shoulde flatter him neuer so muche.

An other cause was that the Diuell had appeared vnto him, and willed him to kill those Christians, or dryue them out of the lande, threatnyng him that if he did not so, that then he woulde goe from him and neuer talke any more with him, for (quoth he) with their gospels, baptisme and deuotion, they doe muche displease me. *Mutezuma* answered him, that there was no reason to kill thē being his friendes and honest men, but he would entreate them to departe, (vnto this) the Diuell answered that hee should do so, and therein he would receyue great pleasure, for eyther he woulde goe his way and leaue him, or else that Christian fellowes should departe, for they sow here (quoth he) a Christian fayth ȳ which is much against our Religiō, and can not dwell both togither. Another cause was, that *Mutezuma* was not well pleased with the imprysonment of *Cacama*, who once he loued exceedyng wel: so in fine, secretely hee repented him of all that was past in the Spanyardes fauour, and chiefly by the persuasion of the Diuell, who sayde that he coulde not doe vnto him a more acceptable seruice, and of greater pleasure to the Goddes, than to expell the Spaniardes and abolishe the name of Christians, and in so doyng, the seate of kings should not finish in the linage of *Culhua*, but rather be enlarged, & his childrē should raigne after him, wishing him
not

not to beleue in prophesies, sithence the eight yeare was past, and was nowe in the eyghtenth yeare of his raigne. For these causes, or possible for other whiche we knowe not off, *Mutezuma* prepared an army of a hundred thousand men so secretely, that *Cortes* knew not thereof, to the effecte, that if the Spanyardes woulde not departe, being once more required, that then he meant not to leaue one of them aliue. With this determination, he came forth one day into the yard or courte, and had long conference and consultation with his Gentlemen aboute this matter. This done, he sente for *Cortes*, who liked not this newes, saying to him selfe, I pray God this message be to good purpose, and taking twelue of his men whych were readyest at hand, went to know wherefore hee had sente for him. *Mutezuma* arose from the place where hee sate, and toke *Cortez* by the hande, commaunding a stoole to be brought for him, and so sate them downe both togither, and beganne his talke as followeth. Sir, I beseeche you to departe from this Citie and Countrey, for my Gods are sore offended with me, bycause I doe, and haue permitted you here so long: demaunde of me what you please, and it shall be giuen you, bycause I loue you well: and thinke you not, that I giue you this warning in iest, but rather in good earnest, therefore it is conuenient, that you depart. It seemed strange vnto *Cortez* this talke. Also he saw by the countenance of *Mutezuma*, that some thing was a working, and before the interpreter of *Mutezuma* had made an end of his talke, *Cortes* willed one of his men to goe forthwith, and to aduise all his fellowes, saying, ye the waight of their liues was in question. Then our men called to remembrance what was tolde them in *Tlaxcallon*, considering that it was needeful of courage and help from God to bring them out of that daunger. Whe *Mutezuma* had ended his tale, I haue (quoth *Cortes*) vnderstood

Yb.iij.   your

your meaning, and doe thanke you for the same: also I
would know when it is your pleasure that we should depart, and it shal be done. Euen when it please you (quoth
Mutezuma) take the time that you thinke meete, and a-
gainste that time will I prepare a hundred waighte of
gold for you, and fiftie pound waight to each of your mē.

Cortes sayde, you knowe, that when I came into thys
Countrey, I commaunded all my Shippes to be sonke,
so that nowe I haue neede of time conueniente to builde
vessels to carrie vs into oure Countrey: wherefore my
requeſt is, that you commaund some of your Carpēters
to be called, to cutte downe timber for the purpose, for I
haue men that can make the vessels. And this done, wee
will departe, so that you giue vs the golde whiche you
haue promiſed, and certifie you the same to youre Gods
and vassals.

Mutezuma recepued great pleaſure at this aunſwere,
and sayd, your requeſt shall be fulfilled: and incontinente
he sent for many Carpenters. Likewiſe *Cortes* prepared
certayne of his Marriners for Shipwrightes. All the
which workemen went vnto great woodes of Pinetrees,
and there cut downe the timber neceſſarye for the purpose. *Mutezuma* being a simple man, gaue credite to all
Cortez his talke: *Cortes* likewiſe aduertiſed his men of his
proceedings, and sayd vnto them, *Mutezuma* would haue
vs departe out of his Countrey, bycauſe his vassals and
the Diuell hathe entiſed him therevnto: wherefore it is
needefull that we build shipping, and therefore I praye
you goe with theſe *Indians*, and procure to cut downe the
beſt timber fit for oure purpoſe, and in the meane ſeaſon
God will prouide for vs, whoſe affayres we haue nowe
in hand, of remedie and ſuccour in ſuche ſort that we loſe
not this frutefull countrey. It is alſo neceſſary, that whē
you come vnto the woode, that you make all the delay
possible,

poſſible, giuing a ſhew that you are buſſe occuppeb, and with great deſire to make an enbe, that thoſe *Indians* may ſuſpect nothing of oure p2etence. Departe in Gods name, and abuiſe me alwayes what both paſſe in your affaires.

The feare that our men ſtoode in to
be ſacrifiſed.

Ight dayes after their departure toward the woodes, arriueb fiftéene ſaile of ſhips at the coaſt of *Chalchicoeca.* The *Indians* of that coaſt abuiſed *Mutezuma* therof, who was not a little afraibe with the newes, & called *Cortes* vnto him, who feared aſmuch ſome vp2o2e there, and when they ſhewed *Cortez* ỹ *Mutezuma* was come fo2th into the parbe, he ſuſpected that if *Mutezuma* pleaſed, they ſhoulbe be al! deſtroyed. Wherefo2e he ſaid vnto his men, maiſters and friends, *Mutezuma* hath ſent me, conſibering what paſſed this other day, I hold it fo2 no good token. I nowe goe to knowe his wyll: wherefo2e, whatſoeuer happen, be you alwayes vigilant and ready, commenbing your ſelues to God. Remember alſo whome ye are, and who are theſe Infibels, abho2red of God, and frienbs vnto the Diuel, without weapon, and experience in warre: if we chance to fight, the handes of each of vs ſhal ſhew by déebe with ſwo2d, the vallo2 and courage of our heartes: yea, and although we all bie, yet ſhall we remaine with victo2y, fo2 that we haue fulfilled the thing we toke in hand, and the ſeruice which we owe vnto God as faithfull Ch2iſtiās, with our buctie as true ſubiects to our p2ince. They all anſwered, ſaying, we wil do all our poſſibilitie while life laſteth, withoute feare of perill o2 baunger, fo2 we leſſe eſtéeme beathe than hono2. With this aunſwere *Cortes* wente to *Mutezuma*, who ſayde vnto him, *Senior* Captayne, you ſhall vnberſtanbe
that

that now you haue Shippes wherein you may departe, therefore now at your pleasure make you ready.

Cortez answered, not knowing of that shipping, saying, Mightie Sir, when my Shippes are finished I will depart, nay (quoth *Mutezuma*) I meane not those Shyppes, for there are ariued eleuen other Shippes at the coast néere vnto *Zempoallan*, and shortlye I shall be certifyed, whether the people that are come in them, are come a shore, and then shall we know what people, and how many they are in number. Blessed is Iesu Christe (quoth *Cortez*) vnto whome I giue most hartie thankes for his great mercies shewed vnto me, and to the Gentlemen of my company. One of *Cortes* his men went to shewe the glad tidings to their fellowes, who then receyued double strength, praysing God, and embraced one another wyth great pleasure and ioy. And *Cortes* with *Mutezuma* béeing in communication togither, came another poast, who broughte newes of foureschore Horsemen that were landed, with eyght hundred footemen, and twelue péces of

At the time of néede prouideth God. Ordinance, and shewed painted in a cloth the whole relation both of men, horses, shippes, and ordinance.

Mutezuma hearing the newes that this poast hadde broughte, arose from his seate, and toke *Cortes* in hys armes, saying, now do I more loue you, than I haue done héeretofore, and will this day dyne with you. *Cortes* gaue him thankes for the one and the other, and in this sorte wente hande in hand to *Cortes* his Chamber, who willed his Spanyardes not to make any extraordinary ioy, or alteration, but that they shoulde képe all togither with vigilant watche, and to giue hartie thankes vnto God for the comfortable newes. *Mutezuma* and *Cortes* dyned togither with greate content and pleasure, the one thynking to abide and to enioy the kings state and Countrey, the other thinking that then they woulde auoyd the land.

But

But notwithstanding all these ymaginations, a certaine *Indian* Captaine importuned *Mutezuma* secretely to kill all *Cortes* his menne, being but few in number, and then should he be the readier to dispatch the others that were newly come, and not to permitte them to ioyne one with another: yea and againe, when the newe come menne shoulde knowe of the deathe of their countreymen, they would not presume to abide in the lande.

With this counsell *Mutezuma* called many his friends and chiefe estates to counsell, propounding the case and iudgement of the Captaine, whych béyng among them throughly hearde, there were many of sundrye opinions, but the conclusion was, to permitte the other Spanyards to come, saying, the more enimies, the more gaine, and if we kill but those whiche are héere, then the others wyll returne to their shippes, and so shall we not make the solemne sacrifice of them to the Gods, according to our desire. *Mutezuma* was occupyed in this counsell with fiue hundred noblemen and Gentlemen dayly, and according to determination, they commaunded to cherish and serue *Cortes* and his company more than ordinary, saying their ioy was at an ende.

A drunken reckoning.

Hovv Iames Velasques sent Pamfilo de Narvaiz against Cortes.

Ames Velasques béyng sore agréeued, with desire of reuenge against *Cortes*, not only for his expences at the time of preparation of *Cortes* his fléete, whiche was but small, but of méere hatred of the present honor & prosperitie of *Cortes*. Whereupon he inuented greate causes and quarrels against him, saying and alleaging, that *Cortez* hadde not giuen

Ii.   accompt

accompt of his pzocedings vnto him, beyng Gouernoure of *Cuba*, and *Cortez* his Deputie, but rather without his consent and knowledge, had sente to *Spayne* to the
King, aduise of his discouery, as who would say, that was
treason, oz an euill facte: but chiefly his fury was, knowing how *Cortes* had sent an honozable pzesent, with the
Kings parte oz poztion of treasure vnto *Spayne*, yea and
whole relation of the discouery, with *Francisco de Monteio*,
and *Alounso Fernandez Portocarrero*, the whiche pzocedings *Iames Velasques* meant to disturbe, foz that he hadde
layde in ambushe a coupell of caruels, to haue taken *Cortes* hys pzesente, and messengers, the whiche his pzetence
and purpose toke no place, so that with the pzosperous
newes of *Cortes*, his furie and madnesse the moze encreased, ymagining still his destruction.

And being occupyed in these fonde ymaginations, it
happened that his Chaplin, one *Benito Martine*, bzoughte
letters from the Emperoure vnto him, with title and letters pattentes, of Generall and chiefe Gouernour of all
that then was discouered, inhabited, and conquered in
the land and coast of *Yucatan*. With this newes, *Velasques*
began to triumph, not only so much foz the honoz, as also
to dziue *Cortez* from *Mexico*. Whereupon, he incontinent
pzepared this Flete oz Nauie of eleuen Shyppes, and
seauen Uergantines, with nine hundzed men, and foure-
scoze Hozses, and appoynted one *Pamfilo de Naruaez* foz
Captayne Generall, and his Deputie in the regiment of
the Countrey: and foz his moze quicker dispatch, he himselfe wente with him thzoughout that Ilande, till they
came to *Guaniguanico*, whiche is the Westermost harboz
of the Ilande, and being there *Naruaez* ready to departe
foz *Mexico*, and *Velasques* to returne to *Cuba*, came the li-
senciat *Lucas Vasques de Aillon*, a chiefe Iudge of *Santo
Domingo*, in name of the whole Chancery, to require *Velasques*

lasques vpon great penalties, that he should not permitte
or suffer *Pamfile de Naruaez* to proceede on that voyage
agaynst *Cortes*, whiche woulde bee cause of Murther, ciuil warres, and other mischiefes among the Spanyards,
yea and that *Mexico* should be in daunger of losing, wyth
all the rest that was conquered, and in quiet to the Kings
vse, saying vnto him moreouer, that if there were anye
discorde betwéene them for goodes, or poyntes of honor,
that then it did apperteyne to the Emperoure to iudge,
and determine the cause, and not that he himselfe should
be iudge in his owne cause, vsing force against the other
partie, praying them for the seruice of God and the
King, that if they would goe to conquere, that then they
shoulde séeke other Countreys, hauing so good an armye
and fléete, and Countreys ynough to séeke. This diligéce,
request and authoritie of the Licenciate *Aillon*, to *Velas-*
ques and *Naruaez* preuayled not: he séyng their obstinacie and little regarde to him being a chiefe Iudge, deter- A noble
mined to goe with *Naruaez* in his Shippe, to lette and di- Iudge.
sturbe the great hurte that might follow, thinking there
in the newe *Spayne* to perswade *Naruaez*, better than in
the presence of *Velasques*, yea and also if néede should bée,
to be a meane of quietnesse betwixt them.

    Pamfilo de Naruaez tooke shipping in *Guaniguanico*, and
sailed till he came néere vnto *Vera Crux* with al his fléete,
and hauing intelligence that there were a hundred and
fiftie Spanyards of *Cortes* his band, he sente vnto them a
Priest, with one *Iohn Ruiz de Gueuara*, and *Alonso de Ver-*
gara, to require them to recevue him for their Captayne
and gouernoure. But the newe Citizens would giue no
eare to their talke, but rather apprehended them, & sente
them prisoners to *Mexico* to *Cortez*, to aduertise hym of
their embassage, wherevpon *Naruaez* vnshipped his men,
horses, armor, & artillery, & wét to thé directly to *Zépoalla*.

The _Indian Comarcans_ being as well friends to _Cortez_, as vaſſals to _Mutezuma_, gaue vnto him golde, mantels, and vittayles, thinking that they had bin _Cortez_ his men.

The ſubſtance of a letter that Correz

wrote vnto _Naruaez_.

Eſoʒe _Cortes_ knew the effect of the cōming of this new fléete, his head was ſoʒe troubled, foʒ, on the one ſide he was glad of the comming of his owne nation, on the other ſide he liked not ſo great an armye. Likewiſe he ymagined, that if they came to ſuccour him, he helde the Countrey foʒ conquered: alſo if that they were come againſte him, he iudged the Countrey to bée loſt. He iudged alſo, that if they were come from _Spayne_, that then they hadde bʒought to him the thing loked foʒ, but if they were come from _Cuba_, he feared ciuil warres. He alſo thought, that from _Spayne_ could not come ſo many folke in ſo ſhoʒte ſpace. Finally, he démed, that his olde enemie _Iames Velaſques_ was come perſonally, but when he knew the whole truth, then was he muche moʒe penſiue, thinking that the thʒead of his pʒoſperitie was cut aſunder, yea and that they would be meane to ſtoppe the gappes of the whole diſcouery, both of the ſecretes of the land, mines and treaſure, as alſo, in the knowledge of the friends oʒ enimies of _Mutezuma_. It ſhoulde be alſo a let to inhabite the places which he had begunne, yea and alſo to Chʒiſten the _Indians_, whiche was the pʒincipall thing that he pʒetended, yea & a let oʒ ſtop of many other things begun in ẏ ſeruice of God & the pʒince, fearing alſo by flying from one inconuenience, to fall into many, and alſo if he ſhould permit _Pamphilo de Naruaez_ to come vnto _Mexico_, it ſhoulde be a meane of hys perdition:

it

If likewise he should encounter him, he feared some rebellion in the Citie, and the setting at libertie of *Mutezuma*, putting in perill his owne honour, life, and trauayle: and to auoyde all these daungers and inconueniences, he determined remedy. First, he dispatched two men, the one vnto *Iohn Velasques de Leon*, who was gone to inhabite at *Coazacoalco*, willyng him at the sight of his letter to repaire vnto *Mexico*, giuing him aduise of the comming of *Naruaez* and of the great neede that he stode in, of him & his company. The other messenger he sent to *Vera Crux*, to bryng full relation of the arriuall of *Naruaez*, and what was his pretence.

The letter sent to *Iohn Velasques*, came no sooner to his hande, but forthwith he obeyed and fulfilled the same, contrary to the expectation of *Naruaez*, for he was his brother in law, and kinsman vnto *Iames Velasques*. *Cortes* seing his constancie, had him euer after that tyme in great estimation.

From the *Vera Crux* came twentie of the townes men with certificat what *Naruaez* had published, and brought with them a priest, with *Alonso Gueuara* and *Iohn ruiz de Vergara*, who had comen to *Vera Crux* to amotiue the towne, vnder colour that they had brought the commissiõ from the king. *Cortes* on the otherside, sent vnto *Naruaez* seignior *Bartholome de Olmedo*, with other two Spaniards, to offer vnto him his friendship, & otherwise to require & commaunde him on the behalfe of the kyng & of his owne, as chiefe iustice of the land, and in the name of the rulers and Aldermen of the towne of *Vera Crux*, who were then in *Mexico*, that he shoulde enter peaceably, without making any alteration vntill his auctoritie and commissiõ were seene and allowed, and to make no slaunder or vproze to the hinderāce of the king his maisters procedings.

But al this diligence and letters of *Cortes* and the other

Ii.iij. rulers

rulers preuailed not,he seing this,set at libertie the priest that was brought prisoner,and sente him vnto *Naruaez*, with certaine riche collers of gold,and other iewels with a letter,wherein he wrote, that he was more gladder of his comming in that fléete than any other, for the friend-ship and olde acquaintaunce that had bene betwixt them, desiring him that they mought talke and côferre togither, alone,for to take order to prohibite wars, sedition,bloud-shedde and disquietnesse among them,beyng of one natiô and brethren, requestyng him to shew his cômission from the king vnto him, or vnto the counsell of *Vera Crux*, and he would willingly obey it as reason did require:and if he had not brought any such commission,yet he would make some honest agrement with him. *Pamfilo de Naruaez* seing himselfe strong and mightie, did little regarde *Cortes* his letters, offers, nor requestes, and chiefly bycause *Iames Velasques* was sore displeased with *Cortes*.

The talke of Naruaez to the Indians,
and his answere to Cortes.

Amphilo de *Naruaez* declared to the *Indiâs* that they were deceyued with their opiniô in *Cortes*, for that he alone was Captayne generall and chiefe Lorde, and that *Cortes* was but a naughty man, and so were all they of his company which are now in *Mexico*,who were all but his boyes,and that his present commyng was to cut of *Cortes* his head, and to chasten the others, likewyse he meant to dryue them all out of the countrey, & then to depart himselfe,and to leaue them in full libertie.

A foule bragge.

¶The *Indians* gaue credite to his talke seyng so many bearded men and horses, and thereupon began to attende and serue him, leauyng their olde friendes in *Vera Crux*.

Also

Alſo *Naruaez* began to flatter *Mutezuma*, and ſente him
worde that *Cortes* aboade in that countrey againſt the will
of his Prince, & that he was a couetous rebell, who rob⸗
bed his countrey, and that he pretended to kill *Mutezuma*,
and to make himſelf king. Alſo that his comming was to
ſet him at libertie, and to reſtore vnto him all that thoſe
wicked fellowes had taken from him. And bicauſe that o⸗
thers ſhould take example of their factes, he would com⸗
maunde them all to be ſlaine, willing him to take no care,
for in ſhort ſpace they would ſée ech other. And that when
he had ſet him at libertie with reſtitution of his goodes, he
would incontinent departe his countrey. Theſe treaties
were ſo foule & abhominable, with the iniurious wordes
which *Pamfilo de Naruaez* ſpake openly againſt *Cortes* and
his men, yea they ſéemed odious vnto all his owne hoſte &
armp, and ſome of his own mé checked him for the ſame,
eſpecially *Barnardino de Santa Clara*, who ſeyng the coun⸗
trey ſo peaceable and ſo well pleaſed with *Cortes*, he could
not let but reprehende *Naruaez* in his wordes. Alſo the li⸗
cenciat *Aillon* required him diuers times to ceaſe frō his
ſlanderous talke, vpon paine of death & loſſe of his goodes,
& alſo not to procéede towarde *Mexico*, for the great hurte
that might enſue, with ſlander among the *Indians*, diſquiet⸗
neſſe among the Spaniardes, and offence to the Empe⸗
rour his Maieſtie. *Pamfilo de Naruaez* being moued with
his talke layde hand vpon *Aillon*, being a chiefe iudge for
the King, and apprehended alſo his Secretary & an other
officer, and forthwith ſhipped them, and ſente thé to *Iames
Velaſques* gouernour of *Cuba*. But when *Aillon* ſaw him⸗
ſelfe at ſea, and fré from *Naruaez*, he began to threaten ỹ
Mariners, cōmanding thé not to preſume to carrie him tɔ
Cuba tɔ *Velaſquez* his power, but onely tɔ *Santo Domingo*,
where he was one of ỹ kings coūſell in chancery: the Ma⸗
riners fearing the Kings iuſtice, obeyed his cōmandemét

And

and when he was aported at *Santo Domingo*, he wholly enformed the Counsell there, of *Naruaez* and his wicked dealyng, whose testimonie and information did much blemishe the credite of *Velasques*, & exalt the trauels of *Cortes*.

A cruell
proclama-
sion.

After that *Naruaez* had shipped away *Aillon*, he proclaymed warre with fire and swozde agaynst *Cortes*, and promised certayne markes of Golde to him that shoulde apprehende oz kill him, oz *Pedro de Aluarado*, and *Gonsalo de Sandoual*, with other principall persons of his company.

A madde
reckenyng.

Also he made diuision of his goodes among his men befoze they came to possesse it. Surely these three poyntes were of a man without wisedome oz discretion.

Many of *Naruaez* his company did amotiue themselues, through the commaundement of the Licenciat *Aillon*, and through the fame and liberalitie of *Cortes*. Wherevpon incontinent one *Pedro de Villalobos* a Poztingal, and sire oz seuen moze fledde vnto *Cortes*, yea and others wzote vnto him, offeryng themselues to his seruice, if by chaunce they should encounter.

A good ca-
ptayne and
a wise.

Cortes recepued the letters, but kept in silence from his company the firmes of those whiche had wzitten to hym. Some doe thinke that *Cortes* had subozned them with letters, fayze pzomises, yea and a hozse loade of chaynes and planches of golde, which he sente secretely to *Naruaez* his campe with a seruaunt of his, publishing likewise, that he had an army of twoo hundzeth Spaniardes in *Zempoallan*, where he had none at all: these policies mought well be, foz he was pzudent, carefull and quicke in his businesse, and *Pamfilo de Naruaez* was slouthfull and carelesse.

Naruaez made answere to *Cortes* his letter by seignioz *Bartholome de Olmedo*, the substaunce of his message was, that foorthwith he shoulde repayze to the place where he was abiding, and there he should see the Emperours commission & ozder, wherein was auctozitie giuen to hym to

take

take and kéepe that countrey for *Iames Velasques*, yea and that already he had made a towne of men onely, with all officers therebnto appertayning.

After this letter and message sent, he dispatched likewise one *Barnaldino de Quesada*, and *Alonso de Mata*, to requyre *Cortes* to depart and leaue the countrey bpon paine of death, and to notifie bnto him these actes by order of law. *Cortes* layde hande bpon *Alonso de Mata*, bicause he named himselfe the kings Notary, and shewed no title or authoritie for the same.

The talke that Cortez had vvith *his owne Souldiers.*

Ortes perceyuing the small fruyte that his letters (presentes) and messengers, obtayned at the handes of *Naruaez*, and that in no case, he woulde shewe his commission whiche came from the kyng, he determined to goe bnto him, and according to the olde Prouerbe, Face to face doth get respect, and likewise if it were possible, to agrée bpon some good order and quietnesse: whereupon he sent *Rodrigo Aluarez* his surueyor, with *Iohn Velasques*, and *Iohn del Rio*, to treate with *Naruaez* of many matters, whereof thrée things were the principalest. The first was, that they two might méete alone, or else so many, for so many, and that *Naruaez* shoulde permit *Cortes* to abyde in *Mexico*, and he withall his company shoulde cóquere *Panuco* or other kingdomes, also that *Cortes* woulde pay the charges, and haue consideration to gratifie his souldiers, or else that *Naruaez* shoulde abide in *Mexico*, and deliuer bnto *Cortes* 400. of his men, to the intent that with them, and his owne men he myght procéde to séeke other countreys to conquere. Laste of all, he required to sée the

Kk. kings

kings commiſſion,foz that he would obey the ſame. Naruaez liked none of theſe offers, only he accepted that they
ſhould méete togither with ech of them ten Gentlemé foz
ſecuritie,bound with ſolemne othe,and firmed this agré-
ment with their names. But it toke no effect,foz *Rodrigo*
Aluarez aduiſed *Cortes* that *Naruaez* had made a ſnare
to apprehend him, oz to kill him at their méeting. *Cortes*
vnderſtode the matter,oz elſe he had ſome other intelligence by ſome that loued him wel.And this foꝛmer agrement taking no place, *Cortes* determined to goe vnto him.

But befoꝛe his departing,he declared vnto his cõpany,
ſaying,I truſt ye haue in remembꝛãce what ⁊ how much
I haue done foꝛ you,ſince ẙ beginning of this enterpꝛiſe,
yea ⁊ alſo how louingly ⁊ friendly ye̍ haue dealt foꝛ me:
Ye̍e ſhall now vnderſtand that *Iames Velaſques*,in ſte̍ede of
thankes giuing vs,hath ſent to murder vs, *Pamſilo de Nar-*
uaez,who is a ſtubboꝛne ⁊ an vnreaſonable man,one readie to execute our good deſertes done in the ſeruice of God
⁊ our Pꝛince,with an euill reward. And the cauſe is only,
foꝛ doyng our duetie in the ſending of the kings parte ⁊
poꝛtiõ to his Roiall perſon ⁊ not vnto him.Alſo this *Nar-*
uaez hath already confiſcated our goodes, and giuen them
to other men,and our bodies condemned to the Gallows,
yea and our fame and honour plaide at tables,with great
iniurious ⁊ ſlanderous woꝛdes pꝛoclaymed agaynſt vs,
which things truly are not of a Chꝛiſtian, no noꝛ yet we
with Gods helpe will let the matter ſo to ſlippe: yea and
though we ought to leaue the reuengment vnto God, yet
we will not ſuffer them to eniop our trauayles ⁊ paynes,
who are now comen white fingered to ſpoile the bloud of
their neighbours, yea ⁊ like madde men to ſtriue againſt
their owne nation, ſowing ſlander among thoſe *Indians*
which ſerued vs as our frie̍ds,yea ⁊ pꝛocuring moꝛe cruel
warres,than the ciuill warre betwene *Mario* ⁊ *Sila*, oꝛ of
Ceſar

Cesar & *Pompeio*, who turned vpsidowne the Romaine Empire. Wherfore I do determine to méete him by ý way, & not to suffer him to come vnto *Mexico*, for it is better to say, God saue you, than they to come & say who is there? yea & though they are many, a good hart doth breake euil fortune, as it hath appered by vs, who haue passed thorow the pikes since our cóming hither: moreouer, I doubte not but that many of *Naruaez* his cópany will come vnto vs. Therfore my déere friends doe I giue you aduise of my pretence, to the entent ý thofe which wil go with me, may them prepare théfelues, & thofe that will not, let them remaine to kéepe *Mexico* & *Mutezuma*, whiche is as much in effect. At the end of his talke he promifed great rewards if ý with victory he returned. His mé anfwered al wo one voyce, ý they were al at his cómandemét, & ready to fulfil his wil, yet fome feared the pride & blindneffe of *Pamfilo de Naruaez*: on the other fide the *Indians* began to be lufty, to fée diffention among the Spanyardes, & that the *Indians* of the coaft were ioyned in league with the new come mé.

The requefts of Cortez to Mutezuma.

Fter al his talk & anfwer of his fouldiers, he wét to vifite & to comune wo *Mutezuma* for to departe on his iourney, wo fomewhat ý leffer care, & alfo to proue the minde & wil of *Mutezuma*, vnto whome he vttered his mind as foloweth. Sir, you know ý loue ý I haue, & defire to ferue you, & chiefly the truft againe, that you will haue to my cópanions whé I am gone fró this citie. Therfore I pray you, that it may pleafe you to remaine here in this lodgyng, & to haue regard vnto thefe ftrangers, which I leaue with you: alfo I cómend vnto you, the gold & iewels whiche is in their cuftodie, and gyuen vnto vs of your owne liberalitie. For I doe now goe to fignifie vnto thofe

Oh vvſić Cortes.

Kk.ij, which

which of late are comen in the new fléete, how your highneſſe doth commaunde that I departe from this land, and
that they doe not agrauate oꝛ moleſt your ſubiectes, noꝛ
yet pꝛeſume to enter into your countrey, but that they remayne on your coaſt, vntill we be ready to departe with
them, accoꝛding to your will and pleaſure. And if in the
meane ſeaſon, any of your ſubiects be ſo vnaduiſed, as to
moleſt my men, whiche now remayne in your power and
Guarde, that then it may pleaſe you to be their ſhielde,
ſuccour, and onely defence. *Mutezuma* pꝛomiſed to fulfill
his requeſt, wiſhing him moꝛeouer, that if any in his iourney ſhoulde offende him, then immediatly to aduiſe him,
and that he would ſende his men of warre to chaſtē thē,
yea and alſo (if it pleaſed him,) he woulde giue vnto hym
guydes to ſalfe conduct him thꝛough his owne dominion
to the Sea coaſt, who ſhould pꝛouide him of all neceſſaries by the way. *Cortes* kiſſed his handes foꝛ his curteſie,
with moſte hartie thankes foꝛ the ſame, and gaue vnto him certayne Spaniſhe apparell, and other glaſen
Iewels, and alſo other like treaſure to his Noble men,
which ſtode by at all the talke. But in effect he tolde him
not what he pꝛetended to doe, noꝛ yet the newes of *Pamfilo de Naruaez* his pꝛocedings was not come to his eare,
oꝛ elſe, it may be that *Mutezuma* diſſimuled the matter
with inwarde pleaſure, that one Chꝛiſtian ſhould kill the
other, thinkyng thereby to haue moſt ſure his libertie, and
the Goddes pleaſed.

The impriſonment of Pamfilo
de *Naruaez*.

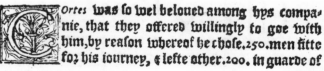Ortes was ſo wel beloued among hys compa-
nie, that they offered willingly to goe with
him, by reaſon whereof he choſe .250. men fitte
foꝛ his iourney, & lefte other .200. in guarde of
Mute-

Mutezuma and the Citie, with *Pedro de Aluarado* for their Captayne. He lefte also with them the artillerie and foure Foystes readye made, to haue the lake in subiection, beseeching them onely to haue speciall regard that *Mutezuma* fled not from them to *Naruaez*, and not to permitte him to goe out of their fort or strong house.

With those fewe Spanyards *Cortes* tooke his iourney with no moze but eyght oz nine Hoꝛſemen, and certayne *Indians* for his ſeruice, and carriage.

Paſſing through *Chololla* and *Tlaxcallan*, he was honorably receyued and lodged, and aboute fiftéene leagues from *Zempoallan* where *Naruaez* was abiding, he mette with two Pꝛieſtes, and his old eſpeciall friend *Andres de Duero*, who had lente him money for the ſetting forthe of that voyage. Theſe thꝛée perſons came to require him to obey the Generall lately come as Lieutenant to the Gouernour *Velaſques*, and to deliuer vnto him the Countrey, with all the fortes oz Caſtels therein, aduiſing him, that if he would not accompliſh the ſame, that then he woulde pꝛocéde againſt him, euen as an enemie and Rebell, to the execution of death. Likewiſe, if he would fulfill the requeſt made vnto him, that then he ſhoulde haue libertie, and conueniente ſhipping to depart, both for him, and as many as would goe with him. *Cortes* aunſwered, that hée would rather ſuffer deathe, than to leaue the Countrey whiche he had conquered and pacifyed with his handes and induſtrie, without anye commaundemente from the Emperoure: and (quoth he) if againſte all equitie and iuſtice, he will contend with me in warre, I will defend me as well as I may, and if I haue the victoꝛy (as I truſt in God and the righte that I haue on my ſide,) I ſhall not ſtand in néede of ſhipping, and if I be ſlaine, muche leſſe. Therefoꝛe I doe require him to ſhew vnto me his commiſſion and authoꝛitie had from the Emperour, for vntil

I

A ſtoute man.

I doe both ſée and reade the ſame, I will accepte no a-
gréemente: and if(quoth he)that he refuſe the ſame, that
then I dare warne,admoniſh,and require him to returne
to *Cuba*,the place from whence he came,and if he wil not
obey my precept, I will then apprehende him, and ſende
him priſoner in prons to the Emperoure: and with thys
aunſwere diſpatched the thrée meſſengers, ſending alſo a
notarie of his owne, to commaund him to take his ſhipping, and to departe without making any altercation in
the Countrey,or ẏ enſuing of further murders and ſtrife,
and if not, that vppon Whitſonday, whiche was within
thrée dayes following, he meante to be with him at ſupper. *Pamfilo de Naruaez* made a mockery and ieſt at
his commaundemente, and tooke Priſoner the Notarie
whiche came ſ m *Cortes* with that order, holding *Cortes*
for madde, who made ſo manye bragges with ſo ſmall a
company. And before *Iohn Velaſques de Leon,* and *Iohn de
Rio, Cortes* his friendes,he muſtered his men, who were
in number foureſcore Hargabuſhers, a hundred and twé-
tie Croſſebowes,ſire hundred men, with other weapon,
and foureſcore Horſemen, ſaying,how will *Cortes* defend

An vncer-
tayne rec-
koning. himſelfe againſte vs, nay at length he will know his dutie: he promiſed money to him that ſhoulde eyther kyll,
or take *Cortes* priſoner.   And the ſame offer made *Cortes*
againſt *Pamfilo,* who made a rounde of his ſootemen,and
ſkirmiſhed with his Horſemen,ſhooting off his artillerie,
to put in feare the pore *Indians.*

Naruaez ſignifyed againe vnto *Mutezuma* with the
meſſengers who carried all the triumph and muſter
pointed, all his former dealings, but hearing that *Cortes*
was néere at hande, he ſente out hys lyght Horſemen to
dyſcrie his Campe.

All *Naruaez* his Horſes were readye ſadled and bride-
led, and his men armed. *Cortes* entred ſo cloſe and ſecret,
                                                     that

that no man almost hearde him, and the firste wordes hee
spake, hauyng all hys men within with him, was, shut
the gates, and strike, downe with them. There were at
that time many shining wormes, whiche with their glistering seemed matches of Hargabushe, so that if one
péece at that time had bin discharged, they woulde haue
bin in a great feare.

Narvaez béeing about to put on his priuie coate, came
one vnto him, saying : Sir, *Cortes* is nére your lodgyng,
let him come in (quoth he) for he commeth to talke with
me. *Narvaez* had his men in foure Towers of his lodging, and he himselfe was in the one, with a hundred
Spanyardes, and at his dore thirtéene péeces of Ordinance ready charged. *Cortes* commanded his chiefe Sheriffe *Gōsalo de Sādoual*, with fortie or fiftie of his fellowes,
to goe vp into *Narvaez* his Chamber, and he himselfe
with other twentie men abode at the dore to defende and
kéepe that none might enter thereat, vntill he had finished
his businesse. The residue of his men besieged the other
Towers, so that they might not succoure one another.

Narvaez hearing the noyse, woulde nédes fighte, although he was required to stay his handes, and comming out at his Chamber dore, they strake out one of his
eyes with a pike, and then they layde hande vpon hym,
dragging and drawyng him downe the stayres by the
héeles, and when he sawe hymselfe broughte before *Cor-*
tes, he sayde, oh *Senior Cortes*, thanke your great fortune,
in hauyng my person prisoner : who aunswered hym a-
gaine, oh *Narvaez*, the hauing of thy body prisoner, is the
least thing that I haue done, sithence I came into thys
lande. *Cortes* commaunded forthwith to lay him in prōs,
and to carrie him to the riche towne of *Vera Crux*, where
he abode prisoner certayne yeares.

This combat endured but a while, for within one houre

*A darke
night for
Narvaez.*

Pamfilo

Pamfilo de Naruaez and the chiefest of his company were taken prisoners, and their weapons & armour taken from all the rest. There were slayne of *Naruaez* his men sixtéene, and of *Cortes* his side were killed only two persons with a péece of Ordinance. They had no leysure to giue fire to their Ordinance, with the great diligence and hast of *Cortes*, sauing vnto one péece that killed the two men. The tutche holes were stopped with ware, through the great raine that had fallen. By this meane those that were ouercome, did take occasion to ymagine that *Cortes* had suborned the maister gunner, and others.

Cortes vsed great sobrietie and discretion, for he would not permitte anye of the prisoners to be reuiled or misused with any iniurious wordes, no nor yet *Naruaez*, who hadde spoken so much euill of him, although many of hys men desired reuengement. *Pedro de Maluenda* seruaunt to *Iames Velasques*, who was chiefe Stewarde to *Naruaez*, fledde to the Shippes with all the stuffe that he coulde gette, without any lette of *Cortes*. Héere may you sée what difference and aduantage is betwixt man and man, what did eache of these Captiues say, thinke, and doe, seldome time dothe happen that so fewe of one nation dothe ouercome so many of the same nation, especially the greater number béyng fresh, lustie, and in a strong holde.

The Rebellion of Mexico against
Cortes.

 Fter that *Cortes* had obteyned victorye against *Naruaez*, he knew very well the most part of his company, vnto whome he spake curteously, praying them to forget the things past, and so would hée also. And also likewise, that it mighte
pleafe

pleale them to goe with him to *Mexico*, whiche was the
richest Citie of all that *India*. He also restored to euerye
man his armour and weapons, whiche were taken from
them in their ouerthrowe. Hée also left very few of them
prisoners with *Naruaez*. The Horsemen toke the fielde
with stomacke to fight, but after they had hearde of hys
offer, they submitted themselues. In conclusion, all those
that were come, hoping of spoyle, were glad to accepte
his offer, and to goe with him with faithfull promise
truly to serue him.

He renued his power in *Vera Crux*, and brought thyther the nauie of *Naruaez*. He also dispatched two hundred Spanyardes to the riuer of *Garay*, and sent also *Iohn
Velasques de Leon* with other two hundred men. To inhabite of *Coazacoalco*. He dispatched also a Spanyarde
by post to *Mexico*, with newes of the victory, and hée
himselfe followed towarde *Mexico*, with the great care
that he had of those whome he had lefte there in guard of
Mutezuma and the Citie.

The Post that wente on this iourney, in steade of
thankes, was sore wounded by the *Indian* Rebelles, but
although he was so hurte, yet he returned to *Cortes*, wyth
newes that *Mexico* was reuolted, and that they had burned the foure Foystes, also assieged the Spanish house,
and throwen downe a wall, and myned another, yea and
set fire vpon the munition, taken away their vittayles,
and had broughte them to suche extremitie, to be eyther
slayne, or remayne prisoners, sauing that *Mutezuma* commaunded to ceasse the combate, yea and for all that they
woulde not leaue their armoure, nor departe from the
siege, only they somewhat amayned their furie for theyr
princes sake.

These newes were sorrowfull to *Cortes*, for thereby
his pleasure was turned into care, the rather to make

half to succoure his friendes and fellowes, for if he hadde delayed hys comming but a small whyle, he had founde them eyther slayne, oz else their bodyes ready to sacrifice : but his greatest comfozte was, that *Mutezuma* remayned styll pzisoner. He mustered his men in *Tlaxcallan*, and founde of his Spanishe nation a thousand fotemen, and neere a hundzed Hozsemen. He pzocceded fozwardes towarde *Tezcuco*, where he founde none of the Gentlemen of his acquaintance, noz yet he there was recepued, as in time past he had bin, but rather he found a great alteration in the Coutrey, and also many townes without people, oz else rebelled. In *Tezcuco* met with him a *Spanyarde*, whome *Aluarad*, had sente to desire him to come vnto them, and to certifie hym of all the pzemisses, saying mozeouer, that with his comming their furye woulde be pacifyed.

With this messenger came another from *Mutezuma*, who declared vnto *Cortes*, that hys Lozde was innocent of all that was done, pzaying hym, that if he had conceiued any euill opinion agaynste hym, to putte away the same agayne, and that it mighte please hym to goe directly to hys own house, where hee abode hys comming, wyth the Spanishe guarde that he hadde lefte with him, who were aliue and in good healthe as he hadde lefte them.

With thys message, *Cortes* and hys companye reposed all that nyghte, and the nexte daye, beeyng Midsommer Daye, he entred into *Mexico* at dynner tyme, with hys hundzed Hozsemen, and the thousande fotemen, with a greate companye of theyz friendes of *Tlaxcallan*, *Huexocinco*, and *Chololla*, but he saw but few folke in the streetes, and small entertaynement, with manye bzidges bzoken, and other euill tokens.

He came to hys lodgyng, and all those of his companye

nye whyche coulde not well bée lodged there, hée sente
them to the greate Temple, *Mutezuma* came foꝛth into
the parde to receyue hym, full heauie and foꝛowfull, as
it féemed, of that offence whiche his fubiectes had done,
ercufing hymfelfe : and then euery one entred into hys
loogyng and Chamber : but the ioy and pleafure of *Pedro de Aluarado* was incomparable , faluting the one
the other, with demaundes and queftions howe they fa-
red, yea and how much the one company declared of pꝛo-
fperitie and pleafure, the other againe replyed as muche
of foꝛow and trouble.

The caufes of the Rebellion.

Cortes pꝛocured to knowe the pꝛincipall
caufe of the infurrection of the *Mexican
Indians* , and hauing a generall daye of
hearyng, the charge béeyng layde againſt
them, fome fayd, that it was thꝛough the
letters and perfuafion of *Narvaez* : Others aunfwered,
their defire and meaning was, to expell the ſtraungers,
accoꝛding to agrémente made, foꝛ in theyꝛ ſkirmiſhes
they cryed nothing but gette you hence, get you hence:
Other fayde, that they pꝛetended the libertie of *Mutezuma*, foꝛ in theyꝛ Combates they woulde fape, lette goe
oure God and Kyng, if you liſt not to bée ſlayne. O-
thers fayde, that they were Théeues, and hadde robbed
theyꝛ golde and plate from them, whyche was in baleme
moꝛe than feauen hundꝛed thoufande duckettes: Others
cryed, héere ſhall you leaue the golde that you haue
taken from vs. Others fayde, that they coulde not a-
byde the fyghte of the *Tlaxcaltecas* , and other theyꝛ
moꝛtall enimies. Manye beléeued that the muttaye
was foꝛ thꝛowyng downe theyꝛ Goddes and Idolles.

Ll.ij.   Eache

each of thefe caufes were fufficient to rebell, how muche moze altogither.

But the chiefeſt and moſt pzincipall caufe was, that after the departure of *Cortes* towarde *Naruaez,* happened a folemne holiday, whiche the *Mexicans* were wont to celebzate, and deſiring to obferue the fame, as they were wont to do, they came and befoughte Captayne *Aluarado* to graunt them licence, & not to ymagine that they were ioyned togither to kill the Spanyardes. *Aluarado* gaue them licence, with fuch conditions, that in their Sacrifice ſhoulde no mans bloude be fpilte, noz yet to weare anye weapon.

At this feaſt, fixe hundzed Gentlemen and pzincipall perſons ioyned togither in the greate temple : fome doe faye, that they were moze than a thoufande perſons of greate eſtate, but that nighte they made a maruellous great noyfe, with coznets, ſhels, clouen bones, wherewith they made a ſtraunge muficke : they celebzated the feaſt, their naked bodyes couered with tele, made and wzought with pzecious ſtones, collers, girdels, bzacelettes, and many other iewels of golde, filuer, and aliofar, with gallant tuffes of feathers on their heads. They daunced a daunce called *Mazenalizeli,* which is to fay, deferte wyth payne, and fo they call *Mazenali* a hufbandman. Thys daunce is like *Netorilizeli,* which is another daunce. The manner is, that they lay mattes in the Temple parde, and with the founde of their Dzummes, called *Atabals,* they daunce a round, hande in hande, fome finging, and others anfwere, which fongs were in ŷ honoz and pzayfe of the God oz Sainde, whofe feaſt it is, hoping foz thys feruice to haue rayne, cozne, healthe, victozy, peace chyldzen, oz anye other thing that they maye wiſhe foz, oz defire.

These

Thefe *Indian* Gentlemen being occupied in their daunting and ceremonies, it foztuned that *Pedro de Aluarado*
went to the Temple of *Vitzilopuchtli* to beholde their doings, and whether his goyng was of his owne accozde, oz
by the confent of his cópany I am not certaine, although
fome fay that he was aduifed howe the mutinie was
there confpired, as after did follow: others holde opinion,
that their onely goyng to the Temple was to beholde the
maruaplous and ftraunge daunce. And then feyng them
fo richely attyzed, they coueted their Golde and Iewels
whiche they were, and befieged the Temple with tenne
Spaniardes at each doze, & the Captayne entred in, with
fiftie men, and without any Chziftian refpect flewe and
murdered them al, and tooke from them all their treafure.
Although this facte feemed odious vnto *Cortes*, yet he diffi-
muled the mater, foz feare leaft he fhoulde hurte his owne
pzoceedings, as time did then require knowyng not, what
neede he might haue of them, but efpecially to auoyde contention among his company.

A coue-
tous defire
and a vice.

The threatenings of the Mexicans
agaynft the Spaniardes.

H̶e caufe of this rebellion, beyng well
knowen, *Cortes* demaunded how they e-
nimies fought, mary (quoth they) after
they had taken weapon agaynft vs foz
the fpace of ten dayes arew, they neuer
feafed with great fury to affaulte and có-
bat our houfe, and we with feare leaft *Mutezuma* fhoulde
efcape and flee vnto *Narvaez*, durft not goe out of dozes
to fight in the ftreate, but onely to defende the houfe with
efpeciall care of *Mutezuma*, accozdyng to your charge giuen vnto vs. Alfo we being but few and the *Indians* many,

who

who ſtill refreſhed their men, they did not onely werye vs, but also put vs in great feare and ſloane out of courage, yea and if at the greateſt brunt, *Mutezuma* perſonally had not aſcended to the toppe of our wal, commaunding them if euer they meant to ſee him aliue, to ſtay and ceaſe from their enterpryce.

At the ſight of *Mutezuma* they were all amaʒed, and incontinent ceaſed the combat and aſſault. They ſayde alſo that with the newes of the victory had agaynſt *Pamſilo de Narua͠ez*, *Mutezuma* requyred his men to leaue off from theyr pretence: notwithſtandyng, the *Indians* calling to remembraunce, that *Cortes* was comming with a greater company, at whoſe returne they ſhould haue the more to doe, began afreſhe to aſſaulte the houſe, whereuppon ſome doe thinke, that it was agaynſt the will of *Mutezuma*. But it followed, that one day the Spaniardes ſtanding in greate perill, charged their greateſt péece of ordinaunce, and gyuing fire, the péece diſcharged not: the *Indians* ſeyng the ſame, began a freſhe with a marueylous terrible noyſe, vſing ſtaues, Bowes, lances, ⁊ ſtones that came as thicke as Hayle, ſaying, nowe will wée redéeme our King, ſette our houſes at libertie, and reuenge our iniuries. But in the middeſt of theyr fury the péece wente of, without any more prymyng or touche, with a greate and fearefull thunderyng, the péece beyng great and ful of hayle ſhotte, with the mayne pellotte, made a ſtraunge ſpoyle among them, and with feare they retyred. But yet they beganne to ſay, well, well, ſhortely ſhall your fleſhe be boyled, although wée meane not to eate it, for truely it is very carrayne and good for nothing. But yet we will beſtowe the ſame vpon the Eagles, Lions, Tigres and Snakes, who ſhal be the graues for your filthy carcaſes.

But if forthwith ye let not *Mutezuma* departe, and reſtore

ſtoꝛe him to his libertie, yꝭ ſhall quickly haue your rewarde,foꝛ your pꝛeſumption & pꝛide, who durſt be ſo bold;
as to lay hande on *Mutezuma* being our God and Loꝛde
that giueth vs our dayly foode. And yet yꝭ with your filthy thꝭues handes pꝛeſumed to touch him,oh why dothe
not the earth open & ſwallow you which taketh other mẽs
goodes? But marke the end,foꝛ our Gods whoſe religion
you did pꝛofane, will rewarde you accoꝛding to your deſerte: & if they do not ſhoꝛtly execute their wꝛath, then let
vs alone, foꝛ we will out of hande make an ende of you.
And as foꝛ thoſe thꝭues and villaines of *Tlaxcallan* your
ſlaues,ſhall not depart pꝛayſing their gaynes, who nowe
pꝛeſume to take their maiſters wiues,ye and to demaund
tribute of them, vnto whome they themſelues are tribu-
toꝛs. Theſe & ſuch like were the woꝛdes of the *Mexicans*.
But our men, although they were in a maruelous feare,
yet they repꝛehended their folly as touchyng *Mutezuma*,
ſaying that *Mutezuma* was no God,but a moꝛtall mã as
they were,and no better,and that their Gods were vayne
idols,and their religion moſt falſe and abhominable, and
that only our God was holy , iuſte, true,and infinite,

The great extremitie and daunger that
our men were put in by the Mexicans.

IN hearyng the foꝛmer talke in defenſe of
the houſe,and pꝛouiding of things necef-
ſary, the night paſſed away . And in the
moꝛnyng to pꝛoue the *Mexicans* intent,
Cortes commaunded the market to be vſed
as in time paſt. *Aluarado* wiſhed *Cortes* to
ſhew ymſelf toward him as agrieued & not well pleaſed,
makyng as though he would appꝛehend & coꝛrect him foꝛ
the things paſſed, thinking that *Mutezuma* and his men
would

would haue entreated for him. *Cortes* paſſed not for that talke, ſaying that they were infidels, diueliſh and wicked people, with whome ſuche complementes ſhoulde not bee vſed.

But he commaunded a certaine principal Gentleman of *Mexico*, who ſtode there preſente, that out of hande he ſhould commaunde the market to be furniſhed as in time paſt. This *Indian* vnderſtåding that *Cortes* had ſpoken euil of them, made as though he went to fulfill his commandement: but he wente to proclayme libertie, publiſhyng the heynous and iniurious wordes whiche he had harde, ſo that in ſhorte ſpace the matter beganne to waxe heate, for ſome went and brake downe the bridges, others went to call all the Citizens, who ioyned themſelues togither, and beſieged the Spaniardes houſe, with ſuche ſtraunge noyſe that one coulde not heare another: the ſtones flewe lyke hayle, Dartes and arrowes filled the Spanyardes yarde, which troubled them much. *Cortes* ſeing this broyle, he with certaine of his men went out at one dore, and another Captayne at another, with eache of them two hundred men. They fought with the *Indians*, who ſlewe foure Spaniardes, and wounded many moe, and of them were ſlayne very fewe with their ſuccor and defence at hande. If our men fought with them in the ſtreates, then would they ſtoppe their paſſage at the bridges: if they aſſaulted their houſes, then they were beaten with ſtones from the toppe of their houſes whiche were ſlatte ruffed, and at their retire they perſecuted them terribly.

They ſette fire vpon the Spaniardes houſe in ſundry places, but chiefly in one place they coulde not ſlake the fire a great whyle, vntill they threwe downe certayne chambers and walles, whereas they had entered at pleaſure, had it not bene for the Artillerie, Croſſebowes and handgunnes, whiche were there in defence of that place.

This

This combat endured all that day vntill night, yea and in the night also they had their handes full: our men had litle leasure to sleepe, but rather spente the night in mendyng the walles and dores, and curing the wounded men who were moe than foure score, & likewise to set their men in oder & readinesse for the fight of the next day following.

It was no sooner day, but the *Indians* beganne theyr assault afresh, with more courage and furie than the day before, so that our men were fayne to trust to their artillery, the whiche the *Indians* feared not a whitte: for if a shotte carried ten, fiftene or twentie *Indians* at a clappe, they would close againe, as though one man had not bene missyng. *Cortes* came out with other fiue hundreth men, and gate some bridges, burned some houses, and slew many that defended them. But the *Indians* were so many in number, that no hurte appeared, yea and our men were so fewe in comparison of them, that although they fought al the day, yet had they much a doe to defend themselues, how much more to offende. That day neuer a Spaniarde was slayne outright, but thre score of them were wounded and hurte, wherby they had inough to do to cure them for that night, and to procure remedy and defence against the hurtes whiche they receyued from the house toppes. They inuented Engines of timber made vpon wheeles, and foure square, couered on the toppe, and with arte to passe through the streates: there were placed on eache of them twentie men with Pikes, Hargabush, Crossebowes and one double Base. Behinde the Engines wente men with shouels and Mattockes, to throwe downe houses, bulwarkes, and to rule and gouerne the Engines.

A strange inuention.

The death of Mutezuma.

All the while that the Engines were a making, our men came not out to fight, beyng occupied in the worke, but onely to defende their lodgyng. The enimies thinkyng that they were all sore hurte and wounded, beganne their warres agayne, reuilyng them with many iniurious wordes, threatnyng them, that if they woulde not deliuer *Mutezuma*, that they woulde giue them the moste cruellest death that euer man suffered, and came with great force to haue entred the house.

Cortes desired *Mutezuma* to goe vp into the sotie, which is the toppe of the flatte roufe of the house, and to commaunde his subiects to ceasse from their heate and furie. At *Cortes* his request he wente vp, and leaned ouer the wall to talke with them, who beginnyng to speake vnto them, they threw so many stones out of the streate, houses and windowes, that one happened to hitte *Mutezuma* on the temples of his head, with whiche blowe he fell downe to the ground: this was his ende, euen at the handes of his owne subiectes and vassalles agaynst theyr willes: for the truth is that a Spaniarde helde a Target ouer his head, wherby they knew him not, nor yet would beléeue that he was there, for all the signes and tokens whiche were made vnto them. *Cortes* forthwith published the hurte and daunger of life of *Mutezuma*: some gaue credite to his tale, and othersome woulde not, but rather sought very stoutly. Thrée dayes *Mutezuma* remayned in extréeme payne, and at the ende departed his life.

And bicause it shoulde appeare that his death was of the stripe that they had giuen, and not by any hurte reteputed at their handes, he caused two gentlemé of *Mexico*, who were prysoners, to carry him out vpon their backes,

who

who certified the Citizens of the certentie of his death,
that at that presente time were giuyng battery to the
house. But yet for all this they woulde not leaue off the
combat, nor yet the warres, as some of our men thought
they woulde, but rather proceeded on their purpose, with
greater courage and desire of reuenge. And when they retyred, they made a pitpfull lamentation, with preparation
to bury their king in *Chapultepec*. On this sorte died *Mu-*
tezuma, who was holden for a God among the *Indians.*
Some say that hée desired to be Baptised at the Shrone-
tide before his death, and they prolonged the matter, thinking at Easter followyng to haue christened him with
honour and triumph. But as it happened, it had bene better to haue done it at that time according to his request.
But with the comming of *Pamfilo de Naruaez* the thyng
was also delayed, and after hée was wounded it was
likewyse forgotten, with the troubles that they were in.
It was credibly enformed, that *Mutezuma* was neuer
consentyng to the death of any Spaniarde, nor yet in con-
spiracie agaynst *Cortes*, but rather loued him entierly : yet
some are of an other opinion, and bothe giue good reasons
to approue their arguments, but the truth could not wel
be knowen, for at that tyme our men vnderstode not the
language, and agayne *Mutezuma* after his death, left
none to open that secrete.

The *Indians* affirme that he was of the greatest bloud
of all his linage, and the greatest kyng in estate, that e-
uer was in *Mexico*. It is also to be noted, that when the
kingdomes do most florish, then are they niest to a chãge,
or else to change their Lorde, as doth appeare in this history of *Mutezuma*. Our men lost more by ý death of *Mu-*
tezuma than the natural *Indians*, if we côsider the murder
and destruction that incontinent did follow. *Mutezuma*
was a man very moderate in his diet, and not so vicious

as

as other *Indias*, although he had many wiues. He was al∣so liberal and frée harted: he was estéemed fo2 a very wise man, in my iudgement he was eyther wise in lettyng things passe after that so2te, o2 else a very foole, that did not vnderstande their doings: he was as deuoute as war∣lyke, fo2 he had bene p2esente in many battayles: it is re∣po2ted that he wanne and had victo2y in nine battayles, & also other nine times victo2ie man fo2 man in the fielde, he reygned seuentene yeares and certaine moneths.

The combat betvveene the Spa-
niardes and the Indians.

Fter the death of *Mutezuma*, *Cortes* sente vnto his Neuewes, and to the other no∣blemen who maintepned the warres, de∣siryng thé to come and speake with him, and they came, vnto whome *Cortes* spake from the wall where *Mutezuma* was slayne, saying, that it were méete that they should cease from warre, and to chose another king, and also to burie the dead, and that he woulde come to his buriall as his friende : likewise he signified vnto them, that fo2 the loue he bare vnto *Mutezuma* who had intreated fo2 them, he had stayed from the finall spoyle of the cittie, & co2rection of them fo2 their rebellion and obstinacie. But now that he had not vnto whome to haue respect, he woulde bothe burne their houses, and chasten them, if that they submit∣ted not themselues to his friendship.

They answered, that they woulde noyther leaue the warres, no2 yet estéeme his friédship, vntill they saw thé∣selues in their libertie, and their w2ongs wholly reuen∣ged, yea and that without his counsell they coulde elect the King vnto whom of right ý kingdome did apertaine.

And

And ſithens the Gods hath taken our welbeloued *Mutezuma*, we will giue his body a Sepulchre, as vnto ſuch a King doth apperteyne: yea and if he would goe and beare his friend *Mutezuma* company to the Gods, that then he ſhould come forth, and they would quickly diſpatch him: and as for the reſidue, they would haue rather warre thā peace, yea and that they were not menne that did yéelde with wordes. Alſo ſeeing their King was dead, for whoſe reſpecte they ceaſſed to burne their houſes, roſt their bodyes, and eate their fleſhe, but nowe (quoth they) if ye depart not, we will not dally long time with you.

Cortez finding them ſtoute and ſtubborne, liked not the bargaine. Againe, he knewe well that their meaning was, that if they hadde departed from the Citie, to haue ſpoyled and murthered them by the way. And ſeeing that their liues, rule and gouernement conſiſted in ſtrength of hand and good courage, he came forth in a morning with the thrée engines, foure péeces of Ordinance, and fiue hūdred Spanyards, and thrée thouſand *Tlaxcaltecas*, to fighte with the enimies, and to burne and ſpoyle their houſes. They broughte the engines néere vnto certaine greate houſes whiche ſtode néere vnto a bridge, caſting theyr ſcaling ladders on the walles, and ſo gote vp to the toppe where manye people were, and there combated awhile, but ſhortly turned to their forte againe, without doing any greate hurte, with one Spanyarde ſlayne, and manye wounded, and alſo the engines broken and ſpoyled, yea the multitude of *Indians* were ſo thicke, and flewe vppon the Ordinance in ſuche ſorte, that they had no leyſure to diſcharge them. The ſtones came alſo ſo thicke from the houſe toppes, that the engines were ſone at an ende. And the Citizens hauing houſed them againe in the forte and lodging, began to amende the hurt done in their houſes, and to recouer the ſtréetes that were loſt: alſo ỹ great

Temple,

Temple, in the Tower whereof, fiue hundred principall
men hadde fortifyed themselues wyth vittayles, stones,
and long Launces, piked with yron and flint stone verye
sharp, but truly they did most hurt with stones. This
Tower was high and strong, as I haue before declared,
and stode neere vnto the Spanyardes forte, whiche from
that tower receiued muche hurt. Although *Cortes* was
somewhat sadde and heauie, yet he ceassed not like a god
Captayne to comfort and encourage his menne, and alwayes was the firste man at any brunt or assay, and hys
heart coulde not permitte him to remaine penned vp in
that sort, wherefore he toke three hundred Spanyardes,
and went to assiege the high tower. Three or foure dayes
he ceassed not that enterprise, but coulde not come to the
toppe, being so high a thing, and manye persons in defence of the same, well prouided, with fitte munition for
the purpose, so that our men came dayly tumbling downe
the stayres, flying to their house with broken pates, so
that our Spanyardes dysmayed more and more, and many murmured at the matter : you may well iudge howe
Cortes his heart was afflighted, for the *Indians* encreased
still in courage, hauing the better hand, and dayly victory
from the high Tower. But nowe *Cortes* determined to
leaue his house, and not to returne thereunto agayne,
vntill he had wonne the Tower. He bounde his Target
to his arme whiche had bin hurt before, and beseged the
Tower againe with many of his men , *Tlaxcaltecas* and
other friends, and many times, although they were beaten downe, arose agayne, succoring one another, tyll at
length they gote to the toppe, and there foughte with the
Indians, till some of them lept out of the Tower, and stod
hanging vpon the listes of the wall, which were three in
number, the one higher than the other, and a fote broad.
Some fell downe to the ground, who besides their falles,
were

A valiant
man;

were reteyued vpon the swordes poynt, and in this sorte
they left none aliue. Three houres they fought on the top
of the Tower, bycause y multitude of *Indians* wer great.
In conclusion, the whole fiue hundred men there dyed
very valiantly, and if their weapon and knowledge had
bin equall, the victory had bin doubtfull, *Cortes* set fire on
all the Chappels, and other three Chappels, where infinite Idols were, yet those sely *Indians* lost no poynte of
courage with the losse of their Temple and Gods, which
touched them at the hearte, but rather began with more
furie to assault the Spanish house.

Hovv the Mexicans refused the offer
of peace made by Cortez.

Cortez considering the great multitude of *Indians* his enimies, and also the greate courage,
with desire of reuengement : and waying also
how his men were weake and wéeryed with
fight, yet (I may say) with great desire to goe frō thence,
if that the Citizens would haue suffered them : he began
againe to require them with peace, and to desire them of
truce, saying vnto them also, that they should consider,
how that many of their side were slayne, and yet they
coulde kill none of them. They béeing more hard harted
than before, answered that they vtterly refused his offer,
saying, that they neuer woulde haue peace with those
who had slaine their men and burned their Gods : yea
(quoth they) and although some of vs are killed, yet wée
also do both kill and hurt, for ye are mortall men, and not
immortall, as we are : beholde ye also the number of vs,
vpon *Zoties*, in windowes and stréetes : assure youre
selues there are thrée tymes as manye within the houses. So wée shall sooner make an ende of you by kyllyng one and one, than you shall doe of vs by
killing

killing a thousande by thousande, or ten thousand by ten
thousand : for ending all these whome you see, there wyll
come so many more, and after them so manye more: but
if ye were once killed, there woulde come no more Spanyardes,yea and when oure weapons can not throughly
destroy you, that then we will serue you to deathe with
hunger and famine, yea and though nowe you would depart,it is too late, bycause ý bridges are throwen downe,
and the calseys broken, and succoure by water you haue
none.   In this communications the daye was spente,
and night at hand, their heads occupyed, and heartes full
heauie,for hunger alone hadde bin ynough to finish theyr
dayes,without any further warre. That nighte, the one
halfe of the number of Spanyardes armed themselues,
and late in the euening came forthe into the Citie. The
Indiās nowe being not accustomed to fight at such houres,
the Spanyardes burned aboue three hundred houses in
one streete, and in some of them found many Citizens, of
whome they left not one aliue. They burned and spoyled
three *Zoties* neere vnto their owne lodging, whiche hadde
greatly annoyed them before. The residue of the Spanyardes whiche abode at home, amended the engins, and
repaired their houses. As this iourney hapned well
vnto them, early in the morning they proceeded out a-
gaine, and wente to the bridge where their engins hadde
bin broken, and although they founde there greate resistance, yet the matter imported their liues. They foughte
with noble courage, and gote manye towers, houses and
Zoties. They wanne also four of the eyght bridges which
were in the Citie, leauing gard in those places whyche
were wonne, returning to their Campe with manye
woundes, being both weery and full of care and sorrow.
    The next daye they came forth againe, and wanne the
other foure bridges, and dammed them vp with earth, in
                                                    such

such sorte, that the Horsemen that way followed the enimies to the firme lande. Cortez being occupyed in damming vp the ditches, and making plaine way of the bridges, there came certayne messengers vnto him, saying, that néere at hand, abode many noblemen and Captaines to treate of peace, requiring hym to come vnto them, praying him to bring *Tlamacazque* his prisoner, who was one of the principallest of the Diuels Cleargie there, to heare the treatie of the matter.

Cortes wente, and carried the Priest with him, whome he appoynted to require them to ceasse from contention, and to remoue their siege, but he came not backe wyth aunswere. All thys was a fayned fetche, to sée the state of the Christian Campe, or else to recouer their religious *Tlamacazque. Cortes* séeyng theyr decepte, wente hys way to dinner, and was no sooner sette at hys meate, but certayne *Tlaxcaltecas* came running in with an open crye, saying, that theyr enimies hadde recouered agayne the bridges, and wente armed vp and downe the stréetes, and hadde also slayne the most of the Spanyardes that were lefte in garde of the bridges. Incontinente *Cortes* wente out with the Horsememne, who were readyest at that tyme, and made way through the troupe of enimies, following them euen vnto the firme lande, but at theyr returne, the footemen that were hurt and wéeried in kéeping of the stréete, coulde not susteyne the force and furie of the infinite number of *Indians*, whyche came vpon them, yea with muche adoe they coulde escape home to their forte. The multitude was not so greate of *Indians* in the stréete, but also by water in *Canoes*, so that stones flewe on both sydes, and galled oure men cruelly. *Cortes* was hurte in one of hys knées very sore, whereuppon it was blowen abroade through the Citie, that *Cortes* was slayne, whiche newes dyd greately discourage our men, and much animate the *Indians*. But yet *Cortes* for all hys payne and hurt, ceassed not to embolden & encourage bys Souldyers, who set afreshe vpon the enimies. At the farthest bridge fel two Horses, which troubled muche oure men that followed. *Cortes* made suche way among the *Indians*, that the Horsemen hadde reasonable passage, and keeyng ye hindmost man himselfe, he was in great peril of taking. It was a maruell to see what a spring hee gaue with hys Horse, and thereby escaped, but in conclusion, with stones they were forced to returne to their hold, beyng very late.

As soone as he had ended his supper, he sente some of his men to gard the streete and bridges, and to defend the same againste the enemie. They were somewhat ioyfull of their proceedings and good successe whiche they hadde the same day.

Hovve Cortez fledde from *Mexico.*

BUt *Cortes* waying the substance of the matter, sawe in effecte that his syde wente to wracke, wherefore he requested hys menne to departe from thence, who were not a little ioyfull to heare their Captayne pronounce that saying, for few or none of them escaped vnhurt and wounded. They feared death, but yet wanted not stomacke and hearte to dye. The *Indians* were so many, that if the Chrystians shoulde but onlye haue cutte their throtes without resistance, yet they had bin too few for that purpose.

They were also in suche necessitie of bread, that pinched them sore. Their pouder and shotte was spente, and almost all other prouision. Their house was welnigh
beaten

beaten downe about their cares. All these caufes were
fufficient to leaue Mexico, and to feeke to faue their liues:
yet on the other fide, they iudged it an euill cafe, to turne
their backes to their enimies, for (quoth they) the very
ftones rifeth vp againft hym that flyeth. They feared a-
gayne the paffage of the arches where the bridges hadde
bin, fo that now they were full befette with forrow, care,
and mifery: but in fyne, they all agreed to departe that
nights, for many dayes before, one of their companye
called Botello, who prefumed to haue good fkyll in the Arte
of Nigromacie, did declare vnto them, that if they would
depart from Mexico at a certayne houre appoynted, that
then they fhuld efcape, or elfe not: but whether they gaue
credite to his fayings or no, they fully determined to departe that night, and like vnto politike and good Souldyers, they prepared a bridge of tymber to carrie wyth
them, to paffe ouer the arches where bridges hadde bin.
This is moft certayne, they were all priuie and agreede
to the departure, and not as fome report, that Cortes fledde
away, leauing aboue two hundred Spanyardes in the
houfe, who knewe nothyng of hys departure, and were
afterwardes all flayne, facrififed, and eaten in Mexico,
for out of the Citie he coulde not haue departed fo fecretely, but it fhoulde haue come to their eares: howe
muche more out of one houfe, where they were all togither.

Cortes called Iohn de Guzman hys Chamberlayne, commaunding him to open the hall where the treafure was,
and called all the officers and others, to fee the diftribu-
tion of the fame. Firft the kings portion was deducted,
and he gaue a Horfe of his owne, and men to carrie it:
and for the remainder, he willed euery man to take what
he lifted, for he gaue it frankely vnto them. The fouldiers
which had come with Naruaez, & now ferued Cortes, were

Revvarde
of a coue-
tous mind.

somewhat hungry of treasure, so that they tooke as much golde and other riches, as they myghte possible carrie, but it cost them dere, for at their going out of the Citie, with the waight of their heauie burthens, they coulde neyther fighte, nor yet make hast on their way, vppon whiche occasion, the *Indians* caught many of them, and drewe them by the héeles to the slaughterhouse of Sacrifice, where they were slayne and eaten: yet those that escaped, had eache of them some profyte, for that pray was well worth seauen hundred thousand Duckettes: but béeyng things wrought in greate péeces, they were troublesome to carrie, so that he whiche carried least, escaped best. Yet some doe thinke, that there remayned in that house a great parte of the treasure, but it was not so, for after our men had taken what they would, then came in the *Tlaxcaltecas*, and made spoyle of all the rest.

Cortes gaue charge to certayne of his menne, to garde with much respecte, a sonne and two daughters of *Mutezuma*, *Cacama*, and his brother, and manye other greate Gentlemen his prisoners.

He also appoynted other fortie mé to carrie the bridge of timber, and other *Indians* to carrie the Ordinance, and a little grayne of *Centli* that remayned.

The vantgarde he committed to *Gonsalo de Sandoual*, and *Antonio de Quiniones*: and the reregarde he committed to *Pedro de Aluarado*, and he hymselfe remayned with a hundred men, to vse his discretion. In this order, and with good deliberation, at midnight he departed from *Mexico* in a darke myst, and so quietely, that none of the *Indians* knewe thereof, commendyng themselues vnto GOD, beséechyng hym in theyr prayers, to delyuer them from that presente daunger, and tooke the way of *Tlacopan*, béeyng the same way that he came into the Citie.

                                                      The

The firste arche whereof the bridge was throwen downe, they passed with the timber bridge whiche they carried with them at ease.

In this meane time the watche and espies which warned in the hiest temples, had descried their flight, and began to sounde their instruments of warre with a marueilous crie, saying, they flie, they flie: And sodenly with this noyse, they hauing no armour to put on, nor other impedimet, ioyned an infinite company of them togither, and followed with greate celeritie, yea and with suche a heauy and terrible noyse, that all the lake pronounced the Eccho, saying, let the cursed and wicked be slayne, who hath done vnto vs such great hurte.

But when *Cortes* came to plante his bridge vpon the second arche of the Cittie, there mette him a greate company of *Indians* to defende the same, yet with much adoe he planted his bridge and passed therbvpon with fiue horsemen and a hundred Spaniardes, and with them procæded through the Calsey to the mayne lande passing many perilous places, wherein swamme both man and horse, for the bridge of timber was broken: this done, he lefte his foote menne on the firme lande, vnder the gouernement of *Iohn Xaramillo*, and returned backe with the fiue horsemen for to succour and helpe the residue of his company whiche were behinde. But when he came vnto them, he found some fighting with great courage, but many slaine. He lost also his golde and fardage, his ordinance and prisoners, yea in fine he founde a maruellous change and alteracion of the estate he lefte them in, wherevpon lyke a good Captayne he shewed his wisdome and valour, helpyng and recouerpng as many of his men, as he myght, and brought them into safetie. He lefte also Captayne *Aluarado* to succour the resse.

But *Aluarado* with all his power and strength coulde

not refiste the fury of the enimies, wherefore with the
Lance in his hande he beganne to flie, feyng the greate
flaughter of his company, fo that hée was forced to paffe
ouer the dead carkafes, yea and vpon fome that were not
throughly dead, who made a lamentable, pytifull, and
dolefull mone. And commyng to the next arche, whofe
brydge was broken downe, of neceffitie he tooke hys
Lance, and therewith leaped fuche a fpace, that the *Indians* were amafed to fée, for none of his fellowes could doe
the like, although they approued the enterprife, and were
drowned for their labour.

When *Cortes* fawe this forrowfull fight, he fate hym
downe, not to take any reft for his wearineffe, but only to
bewayle the dead men, yea and alfo them that were aliue
and in greate daunger, and alfo to ponder the vnftedfaft-
neffe of cruell fortune in the perdition of fo many his
friends, fuch great treafure and lordfhippe, fo greate a Citie and kingdome, but alfo to bewayle the forrowfull
eftate that he himfelfe ftode in, feyng the motte of his
men wounded & hurte, and knowyng not whyther to goe,
for that he was not certayne of the helpe and friendfhip
of *Tlaxcaltecas.* Yea and what harde hart, woulde not haue
relented to behold the dead bodies, who a litle before had
entred that fame way, with fuche magnificall triumphe,
pompe and pleafure. But yet hauing care of thofe whom
he had lefte on the firme lande, he made hafte to *Tlacopan.*

This forrowfull night, which was the tenth of July in
*An.*1520. were flaine aboute.450. Spantardes, 4000. *Indian* friends, and.46. horfe, yea & (as I iudge) all the prifo-
ners which were in his company. If this mifhap had fortuned in the day time, poffible fo many and fo great a nû-
ber had not perifhed. But where it fortuned by night, the
noyfe of the wounded was forrowful, & of the victors horrible and feareful. The *Indians* cried victory, calling vpon
their

their diuelish and filthy Goddes with ioy & pleasure, our
men being ouercome, cursed their vnfortunate lot, yea the
hower, and he that brought them thither, others cried vnto God for succour, others sayd helpe, help, for I stande in
daunger of drowning. I know not certenly whether moe
perished in the water or the lande, hopping to saue themselues by swimming and leapyng ouer the sluces and broken places, for they say, that a Spaniarde was no sooner
in the water, but an *Indian* was vppon his backe. They
haue great dexteritie & skill in swimming, so that catch-
ing any Spaniarde in the water, they would take him by
the one arme, and carrie him whither they pleased, yea &
would vnpanch him in the water. If these *Indians* had not
occupied themselues in taking the spoyle of those that
were fallen and slaine, certenly one Christian had not escaped that day: but in fine, the greatest number of Spaniardes that were killed, were those that went moste laden
with golde plate and other iewels, & those whiche escaped,
were they that carried least burdens, & the first that with
noble courage made way to passe through the troupe of
Indians.

Nowe wee may safely say, that the couetous desire
of golde, wherof they had plenty, was cause of their death,
and they may answere that they died riche. After that
those, whiche had escaped, were passe the calsey, the *Indi-*
ans stayed and followed them no further, eyther for that
they contented themselues with that whiche they had
done, or else they durst not fight in open fieldes: But principally it is thought, that they abode to mourne and la-
ment for the death of *Mutezuma* his chyldren, not knowing till then their sorrowfull ende. But nowe seyng the
thyng present before their eyes, they wrang theyr hands,
and made a pitifull dole and crie, and the rather, bycause
they themselues had slayne them against their willes.

The

The battayle of Otumpan, a notable victory.

He Inhabitants of *Tlacopan*, knewe not how our men came spoyled, hurte, and ouerthrowen, and againe our men stoode in a maze, and knew not what to doe nor whither to goe. *Cortes* came vnto them, & conforted them & placed them in order before him, requyring them to make hast, vntill they might come into the broade field, before such tyme as the men of *Tlacopan* should heare of the newes passed, & so to arme themselues and to ioyne with fourtie thousande *Mexicans*, who after the mournyng for their friends, came marchyng after them. He placed in the vantgard the *Indians* his frieds, and passed through certayne tilled grounde, and continually fought as they went, vntill they came to a high hill, where was a tower and a Temple, whiche is called our Lady churche at this day.

The *Indians* slewe some of the Spaniardes whiche came in the reregard, and many of their *Indian* friends, before they could get vp to the toppe of the hill. They loste muche of the golde, that had remayned, and with greate hazarde escaped through the multitude of *Indians* with life, their horses whiche remayned aliue, were foure and twentie, who were tyred both with trauell and hunger, & the Spaniardes their maisters, with the residue coulde scarsely stirre hande or foote with wearinesse of fightyng, and penurie of hunger, for al that day and night they ceassed not from fight, eating nothing at all.

In this Temple were reasonable lodgings, where they fortified themselues as well as they myght, and dranke one to an other, but theyr supper was very sleder. After their simple feast was ended, they went and beheld

A very iourney.

gn

an infinite number of *Indians*, whiche had beset them, almost rounde about, makyng a maruellous shoute and crie, knowyng that they were without viƈuals, whiche onely is a warre woꝛſer than to fight with the enimie. They made many fires with the wꝏde of ſacrifice, rounde about the tower and Temple, ⁊ with this pollicie, at midnight departed ſecretely. It happened that they had *Tlax calteca* to be their guide, who knew well the way, aſſuring to bꝛing them into the iuriſdiƈion of *Tlaxcallan :* with this guide they began to iourney. *Cortes* placed his wounded men and fardage in the middeſt of his company, the ſouldiers that were whole and in health, he deuided into the vantgarde ⁊ reregarde: he could not paſſe ſo ſecretly, but ⅌ they were eſpied by the *Indian* ſcoute, whiche was neare at hand, who gaue aduiſe therof incõtinent. Fiue hoꝛſemẽ which went befoꝛe to diſcouer, fell among certayne cõpanies of *Indians*, which attended their cõming to robbe the, ⁊ ſeing the hoꝛſemen, they ſuſpeƈed that the whole army was at hand, wherbpon they fled, but yet ſeing them few in number ſtade and ioyned with the other *Mexicans* that followed ⁊ purſued our men thꝛee leagues vntil they came to a hill where was another temple with a gꝏd tower ⁊ lodgyng, where they lodged that night without ſupper. They departed in the moꝛnyng from thence, and wente thꝛough a cragged ⁊ naughty way, to a great towne the enhabitantes whereof were fledde foꝛ feare, ſo that they abode there two daies to reſt thẽſelues, to cure their mẽ, ⁊ hoꝛſes: alſo they ſomewhat eaſed their hũgery ſtomakes and carried frõ thence pꝛouiſion, although not muche, foꝛ they had none to carrie it. And being departed frõ thence, many enimies purſued them ⁊ perſecuted them very ſoꝛe. Likewiſe ⅌ guide erred out of his way, ⁊ at lẽgth came to a little village of few houſes, where they repoſed ⅌ night. In the moꝛning they pꝛoceeded vpon their way, and the

A payneful man.

Cortes
vvounded
vvith a
flyng.

enimies still pursuyng and troubled them sore all the day.

Cortes was wounded with the stripe of a sling, and therewith was in greate daunger of life, for his head so rancbled, that of necessitie they were forced to take out certaine péeces of his skull, wherupon he was driuen to séeke a solitarie place in the wildernesse to cure him, and in goyng thitherwardes, the enimies wounded fiue Spaniardes and foure horses, whereof one died, and that was eaten among them for a sumptuous supper, and yet not sufficient for them all, for there was none of them whiche were not vexed with hunger. I speake not of their woundes and wearinesse, things sufficient to haue made an ende of lyfe. But certainely the Spanishe nation can abide more hunger than any other, and especially these with *Cortes* dyd shewe the proofe. The nexte day in the Oh noble
Cortez. mornyng departing from a litle Uillage, and fearyng the multitude of enimies, *Cortes* commaunded eche horseman to take a sicke manne behinde him, and those that were somewhat stronger, to holde by the horse tayles and stirroppes : he likewise made cruches for other some to ease them, and woulde not leaue one of his men behinde him to be a pray and supper for the *Indian* enimies. This aduise was very profitable as things fell out, yea also there were some of them that carried vpon their backe their fellowes, & thereby were saued. They had not iourneyed a full league into a playne fielde, when there mette them an infinite number of *Indians* who compassed them round aboute, and assaulted our men in such sorte, that they verily beléeued that day to ende generally their liues, for there were many *Indians* that durst wrastell with our men, man to man, yea and layd some of them in the dust, and drewe them by the héeles, whether it were with the great courage whiche they had, or whether it were with the trauayle, hunger and hurtes of our men I know not,
but

but great pittie it was to sée, how they were drawen by the *Indian* enimies, and what grieuous mone they made.

Cortes that wente with bigient care comfortyng his men, as muche as was possible to doe, and well perusing the great daunger that they were in, commendyng him selfe to God, sette spurres to his horse and made way thorow the greatest troupe of *Indians*, and came vnto the captayne generall who bare the Royall standart of *Mexico*, and passed him through with his Lance, whereof he incontinent died. But when the *Indians* sawe the standart fallen, they threw their auncient on the grounde and fled, scattering them here and there like men amazed, knowing not whither to fly, for such is their custome in warre, that when they sée the generall slayne, they forthwith leaue the fielde. Then our wery soules began to recouer hart and strength, and the horsemen followed the to their great anoyance and slaughter. It was credibly reported, that there were that day in fielde. 2000 00. *Indians*. And the fielde where this battayle was fought is called *Otumpan*: there was neuer a more notable facte done in *India*, nor greater victorie since the first discouery of the same. And as manye Spaniardes as sawe *Hernando Cortes* fighte that day, did holde opinion, that neuer one man did more greater feates in armes, and that he only was the meane in his owne person to saue and deliuer them all.

Oh valiant Cortez.

200000. Indians.

The entertaynement vvhiche the
Spaniardes had in Tlaxcallan.

After this victory obtayned, *Cortes* with his company went to lodge in a house planted alone, in a playne grounde, from whence appeared the Mountaynes of *Tlaxcallan*, whereof our menne muche reioyced: yet

Do.ij.   on

on the other side they ſtode in doubt whether they ſhould finde them their friendes in ſuch a daungerous ſeaſon, foʒ bycauſe the vnfoʒtunate man that ſlieth, findeth nothing in his fauour, foʒ all thing that he pʒetendeth, happeneth cleane contrary. That night *Cortes* himſelfe was ſcoute, not bycauſe he was moʒe whole than his fellowes, but like a good Captayne, he deuided the trauayle & paynes equally, euen as their hurte and damage was come.

Being day, they iourneyed in plaine and ſtraight way, directly to the Mountaynes and Pʒouince of *Tlaxcallan*, they paſſed by a ſwéete foutaine of water, where they wel refreſhed themſelues, and after they came to *Huazilipan*, a towne of *Tlaxcallan*, of. 4000. houſholdes, where they were louingly receiued & abundantly pʒouided foʒ thʒée dayes, whiche they abode there refreſhing & curing their weary bodies. Some of the townes men would giue thē nothing without payment, but the moſte parte did vſe them very gently : Unto this Towne came *Maxixca*, *Xicotencatlh*, *Axotecalth*, and many other pʒincipall perſons of *Tlaxcal-*
50000. mē. *lan*, and *Huexozinco* with. 50000. men of warre, who were going to *Mexico* to ſuccour the Spaniardes, knowyng of their troubles, but not of their hurte and ſpoyle, yet ſome holde opinion that they hauyng certayne knowledge of all theyʒ miſhappes and flight from *Mexico*, came only to comfoʒte them, and in the name of all theyʒ communaltie and ſtate, to offer them their Towne., in concluſion, they ſéemed ſoʒrowfull foʒ their miſfoʒtunes, and againe ioyfull to ſée them there : Yea ſome of them with
Faythfull friendes. anguiſhe of harte wepte, and ſayde, wée did aduiſe and warne yée, that the *Mexicans* were Traytours and wickedperſons, and yet yée woulde not beléeue vs : wée doe pyttie and bewayle your troubles, but if it pleaſe you, ſette vs goe thither to reuenge your iniuries, and the death of your Chʒiſtians, and our Citizens: and if now ye
will

will not, that then it may please you to goe with vs home to our houses, for to recreate youre persons, and to cure your woundes.

Cortes did cordially reioyce, to heare and finde such succour and friendship, in such good men of warre, whereof he stoode in doubt as he came thitherward. He gaue them most hartie thankes for their louing offer, curtesie, and good will. He gaue vnto them of such Iewels as remayned, and sayd vnto them, the time will come, that I shall desire your helpe against the *Mexicans*, but now presently it is nædefull, to cure my sicke and wounded men.

The noble men that were there present, besought him to giue them leaue to skirmish with the *Indians* of *Culhua*, for as yet many of them wandered there aboute. *Cortes* graunted their request, and sente with them some of hys men, which were lustie, and in good health, who procæded forth all togither, and in that iourney slewe many *Indian* enimies, so that after this time, the enimies appeared no more. Then with triumph, pleasure, and victory, they departed toward the Citie, and oure men followed. It is credibly reported, that twenty thousande men and women met them by the way with sundry kindes of meates: I do belæue that the most of them came to sæ them, for the great loue whiche they bare vnto them, and likewise to enquire of their friends which had gone with them to *Mexico*, of whome few returned. In *Tlaxcallan* they were honorably receyued, and well vsed. *Maxixca* gaue hys house to *Cortes*, and the residue of hys company were hosted at Gentlemens houses, who cherished them excædingly, whereby they forgate the paynes, sorrowes, and trauels past, for in fifténe dayes before, they lay on the bare ground.

Certaynely the Spanyardes were much indebted to the *Tlaxcaltecas*, for their loyaltie and faithfull friendship,

Oo.iij.   especially

especially vnto that good and vertuous Gentleman *Maxixca*, who threwe *Xicotencatl* downe the stayres and steppes of the chiefe Temple, for giuing his counsell to kyll the Spanyardes , meaning to reconcile hymselfe with the *Mexicans.*

He also made two Orations, the one to the men, and the other to the women, in the greate fauoure and prayse of the Spanyardes,putting them in remembrance,howe that they hadde not eaten salt, nor worne cloth of cotten woll in many yeares before,vntil now that their friends were come : and to this day these *Indians* doe muche presume of their fidelitie, and likewise of the resistance and battayle they made with *Cortes* in *Teoacazinco*, so that now when they celebrate any great feast, or receyue any Christian biseking , there commeth of them out into the field sixtie or seauentie thousande men, to skirmishe and fight in the same order as they did with *Cortes:*

The protestation and request
of the Souldyers to Cortes.

When *Cortes* departed firste from *Tlaxcallon* towardes *Mexico* to visit *Mutezuma*, hée lefte there twentie thousande Castlins of golde and moe, besides the Kings portion which was sent with *Monteio* and *Portocarrero*. He lefte there also manye other things if néede should haue happened in *Mexico* of money, or other things to prouide his men in *Vera Crux*, and this he lefte there 'also, to proue the fidelitie of his friendes in *Tlaxcallon.* And after he had obteyned the victory againste *Naruaez*, he wrote vnto the Captayne that he shoulde sende for the same, for reason required that in all things they should haue their partes.

The

The Captaine of *Vera Crux* sente fiftie Spanyardes and fiue Horsemen for the same, who at their returne, were slayne and taken prisoners with all that treasure, by ẙ men of *Culhua* who had rebelled through the comming of *Pamfilo de Naruaez*, robbing and spoyling sundrye dayes. But when *Cortez* vnderstode this newes, his ioy was turned to sorrowe, not onely for the golde and treasure so muche, as for the losse of his menne, fearyng also some other warre or vprore to haue bin in the riche Towne of *Vera Crux*, wherevpon hée sente a messenger thyther, who returned in shorte time, certifying that all the inhabitantes there were in good health, and also all the *Comarcans* quiet, and without any token of alteration. This newes and answere pleased *Cortes* and all his company, whiche desired to goe thither, but he woulde not permitte them, wherefore they began to murmure and to exclayme, saying, what thinketh *Cortes*, what meaneth he to doe with vs? why, will he kéepe vs héere to dye an euill death? what haue we offended him, that he will not let vs goe? we are alreadye full of wearinesse, our bodyes are yet ful of fresh woundes, we haue spente our bloude, and are nowe withoute strength and apparell: wée sée oure selues in a straunge Countrey, and full of miserye, enuironed with enimies, yea and without hope to come to that hygh place from whence we fell, yea then mighte wée hée accompted for worse than madde men, to come into the perils from whence wée escaped: wée meane not nowe to ende oure lyues so desperately, as he would haue vs, for wyth the insatiable thirste of honoure and glorye, hée estéemeth not hys life, neyther oures. He doth not lykewyse consider, that he wanteth menne, horses, artillerie, and armoure, things so necessarye for the warres, yea he also wanteth victuall, whyche is a thyng moste principall: what shall wée saye,

Exclamation.

but

but that,he erreth, and is deceyued, in giuing credite to
these *Tlaxcaltecas*, who are, like vnto the other nations
of *India*, which are light, changeable, and louers of newe
things,yea and rather, in effecte of troth,they better loue
the *Culhuacans*, than the Spanishe nation, yea and although they nowe dissemble, yet when they shall sée a
greate army of *Mexicans* come vpon them, they will then
deliuer vs aliue, to be eaten, and sacrificed, for it is an
olde rule, that friendship dothe not long endure betwixte
them that are of sundry religion,apparell,and spéech.

After all these complayntes and murmurations amóg
themselues, they made a protestation and request, in
forme as it were in the name of the King and all the
company, praying him incontinent to departe fró thence,
and to goe with them to the Towne of *Vera Crux*, before
the enimies mighte disturbe their way and passage, and
then they to remayne both bought and solde, and shutte
vp as it were in a prison: also they declared, that in *Vera
Crux* they should haue better oportunitie to make themselues strong, if that he meante to returne agayne vpon
Mexico, or else to take shipping,if so it shoulde séeme conuenient.

Cortes hearing this request, and determination of hys
Souldyers, was at his wits ende, ymagining that theyr
pretence was, onely to procure him to goe from thence,
and afterwardes to rule him at their pleasures, and béeing a thing cleane contray to his pretended purpose, hée
aunswered them as followeth.

                                                    The

The Oration made by Corteż in an-
ſwere to his Souldyers demaunde.

Y maiſters, I would do and fulfill youre
requeſt, if it were a thing méete and conueniente foz you, foz there is not one a-
lone of you, how much moze all in generall, foz whome I ſhoulde not willingly
aduenture my goodes and life, if he ſhuld
néede the ſame: foz why? your déedes haue bin ſuch, that I
ſtand bound neuer to fozget thé, oz elſe to ſhewe my ſelfe
an ingratefull man. And thinke you not good friendes, although I do not fulfill the thing whiche you ſo earneſtly
deſire, that therefoze I eſtéeme not youre authozitie: but
in not graunting to the ſame, I do exalt and eſtéeme you
in greater reputation: foz why? in oure departing nowe
from hence, oure honoz is blotted and ſtayned foz euer-
moze, and in abiding héere, we ſhall like valiant menne
pzeſerue the ſame. What nation is there, that had rule,
dominon, and Empire in this wozld, that hath not bin o-
uercome at ſome time? What famous Captayne returned home to his houſe, foz the loſſe of one battayle? none
truly, foz he that dothe not perſeuer, ſhall neuer triumph
with Lady Victozy: he that retyzeth, ſheweth that he flyeth, and remayneth a mockingſtocke foz all men: but hée
that ſheweth nobly his face, dothe vtter the courage of
his heart, yea and is both feared, and alſo beloued.

If we now ſhould depart from hence, theſe our friéds
would accept and iudge vs foz cowardes, and refuſe per-
petually our friendſhip. Likewiſe oure enimies woulde
iudge the ſame, and neuer héereafter ſtande in feare of
vs, which ſhoulde be a greate ſhame vnto oure eſtimatiõ.
Is there any amõg vs, that would not holde himſelfe

affrented,

affrented, if it ſhoulde be ſapde, that he turned his backe and fledde, how much moze would it be a diſhonoz foz vs all to haue the ſame repozt?

I doe muche maruell at the greateneſſe of your inuin̄cible heartes in battell: you were wont to be deſirous of warres, and nowe that ſuche iuſt and laudable warre doth offer it ſelfe, you doe feare and refuſe the ſame: ſure it is a thing cleane contrary to oure nature. What is hē that will pzate of harnes, and neuer ware none? It was neuer yet ſéene in all this *India* and new wozld, that any of our nation retired with feare. And woulde you nowe that it ſhould be ſaid, that *Cortes* and his company fledde, being in ſecuritie, and without perill oz daunger? I bē ſéech God not to permitte any ſuche thing. The warres doe muche conſiſt in fame: why then? what better thyng twould you deſire, than to be hére in *Tlaxcallan* in deſpite of all youre enimies, yea pzoclayming open warres a̅ gainſte them, and they not dare to annoy vs? Therefoze you map well conſider, that hére you are moze ſure than if you were from hence, ſo that hére in *Tlaxcallan* you are honozed with ſecuritie and ſtrength, and beſides this, you haue al things neceſſary foz phiſick and medicine to cure youre woundes and obteyne your health: yea, and I am bolde to ſape, that if you were in youre owne naturall Coūtrey, you ſhould not haue the like, noz yet be ſo much made off.

I do nowe meane to ſend foz our men that are in *Coa̅zacoalco* and *Almeria*, and ſo we ſhall haue a reaſonable army: yea and although they come not, wée are ſufficient, foz we were fewer in number when firſt we entred into thys Countrey, hauyng no friendes: and likewiſe you knowe well, it is not the number that doth ſighte, but the couragious hearte and minde. I haue ſéene one of you diſcomfyte a whole army, as *Ionathas* did, yea and many

among

among you haue had victory againſt a thouſand, yea ten
thouſand *Indians*, as King *Dauid* had againſte the *Phi-
liſtines*. I looke dayly for Horſes from the Ilandes, and
other armoure and artillerie we ſhall haue from *Vera
Crux*. And as for vittayles, take you no care, for I wyll
prouide you abundantly, for they are thinges that alwayes followe the Conqueroures : and as for theſe
Citizens of *Tlaxcallan*, I binde my ſelfe that you ſhall
finde them truſtie, loyall, and perpetuall friendes, for ſo
they haue promiſed me vppon their ſolemne othes, yea,
and if they had meante otherwiſe, what better oportunitie of time could they haue wiſhed, thã theſe latter dayes,
where as we lay ſicke in their owne beddes and houſes,
yea ſome of vs lame, wounded, and in manner rotten,
and they like louing friendes haue not only holpen you,
but alſo ſerued you with diligence of ſeruantes, for they
woulde rather chooſe to be your ſlaues, than ſubiectes to
the *Mexicans* : theyr hatred is ſucke to them, and their
loue ſo great to you. And bycauſe you ſhall ſée the troth,
I will now proue them and you, againſte theſe of *Tepeacac*, who ſlewe of late dayes tvvelue Spanyardes. And if
this iourney happen euill, then will I followe youre requeſt, and if it pleaſe God that it happen well, then wyll
I entreate and pray you to follow my counſell.

The Souldyers hearing this comfortable ſpéeche, began to lay aſſde their deſire to goe from thence to *Vera
Crux*. They anſwered generally, that they woulde obey
his commaundemente, it ſhoulde ſéeme with the promiſe
made, touching the ſucceſſe of the victory in *Tepeacac*,
and lightly ſeldome it happeneth, that a Spanyard ſaith
no, when he is required to goe on warfare, for it is holden for a diſhonor and ſhame.

The vvarres of Tepeacac.

Ortez found himselfe at hearts ease with this
answere, for it was a thing ŷ had much troubled him: & vndoubtedly if he had followed his
fellowes demand, he shoulde neuer haue recouered *Mexico* agayne, & they likewise had bin slayne in the
way towards *Vera Crux*, for they hadde manye perillous
places to passe. Eache one of them waxed whole of his
wounds, sauing some which dyed for wāt of loking to in
time, leauing their wounds filthy & vnbound, as Surgiōs
doe affirme, with also their great trauell & weakenesse.
And likewise other some remayned lame and halt, which
was no small griefe and losse: but the most parte recouered healthe, as I haue declared. After twenty dayes
fully past, whiche they had abode in *Tlaxcallan*, *Cortes* determined to make warre with the *Indians* of *Tepeacac*,
which is a great Towne, and not farre from thence, for
they hadde slayne twelue Spanyards, whiche came from
Vera Crux towardes *Mexico*. Likewise they were of the
league of *Culhua*, and therfore were holpen by the *Mexicans*, and did many times great hurt to the inhabitantes
of *Tlaxcallan*, as *Xicotencatl* did testifye. *Cortes* desired hys
louing friende *Maxixca*, and diuers other Gentlemen, to
goe with him, who forthwith entred into counsell wyth
the states and comunaltie of the Citie, and there determined with generall consente to gyue vnto him fortie
thousand fighting men, besides many *Tamemoz*, who are
foote carriers, to beare the baggage, victuall, and other
things. With this number of *Tlaxcaltecas*, his owne men
and horses, he wente to *Tepeacac*, requiring them in satis-
faction of the death of ŷ twelue Christiās, that they shuld
now yeelde themselues to the obedience of the Emperor,
and that heereafter neuer moze to receiue any *Mexican*

into

into theyr towne oz houſes, neyther yet any of the prouince of *Culhua.*

The *Tepeacacs* anſwered, that they had ſlaine the Spaniardes foz good and iuſte cauſe, whiche was, that being tyme of warre they preſumed to paſſe thzough their countrey by fozce, without their will and licence. And alſo that the *Mexicans* and *Culhuacans* were their friendes and Lozdes, whom alwayes they would friendly entertayne within their towne and houſes, refuſing vtterly their offer and requeſt, pzoteſting to giue no obedience to whom they knew not, wiſhyng them therefoze, to returne incontinent to *Tlaxcallan,* excepte they had deſire to ende their werie dayes.

Cortes inuited them diuers times with peace, and ſeing it pzeuailed not, he begã his warres in earneſt. Their enimies lykewiſe with the fauour of the *Culhuacans* were bzaue and luſtie, and began to ſtoppe and defend their pzetended entraunce. And they beyng many in number, with diuers valiant men among them, began to ſkirmiſhe ſundzy times, but at the end, they were ouerthzowen, and many ſlayne, without killing any Spaniarde, although many *Tlaxcaltecas* were killed that day.

The Lozdes and pzincipall perſons of *Tepeacac* ſeyng theyr ouerthzow, and that their ſtrength coulde not pzeuaple, yéelded themſelues vnto *Cortes* foz vaſſalles of the Emperour, with condition to baniſh foz euer their allied friendes of *Culhua.* And that he ſhould puniſhe and cozrect at his will and pleaſure, all thoſe whiche were occaſion of the death of the twelue Spaniardes. Foz which cauſes and obſtinacie, at the firſte *Cortes* iudged by his ſentence, that all the townes whiche had bene pziuie to the murder, ſhould foz euer remaine captiues and ſlaues: others affirme that he ouercame them without any condition, and cozrected them foz their diſobedience, being Sodomites,

idola-

idolaters and eaters of mans flesh, and chiefly for exāple
of all others. And in conclusion, they were condemned for
flaues, and within twenty daies that these warres lasted,
he pacified all that prouince,which is very great: he drane
from thēce the *Culhuacans:* he threw downe the idols, and
the chiefest persons obeyed him. And for more assuraunce
he builte there a towne,naming it *Segura de la Frontera:* he
appoynted all officers for the purpose, being a towne fituated in the high way from *Vera Crux* to *Mexico,* where=
by the Christians and straungers mighte passe without
daunger. In these warres serued lyke faithfull friendes
the *Indians* of *Tlaxcallan, Huexocinco* and *Cholalla,* promp=
sing the lyke seruice and succour agaynst *Mexico,* yea and
rather better than worse. With this victory the Spa=
niardes recouered great fame, for they were thought to
haue bene slayne.

The great auctoritie that Cortez
had among the Indians.

Fter all these things were finished, *Cortes*
cōmaunded & gaue licence to al the *Indian*
friēds, to returne home vnto their houses,
except his assured friends of *Tlaxcallan,* whō
he kept in his company for the warres of
Mexico: he nowe dispatched a poste to *Vera
Crux,* commaundyng that foure of the shippes which *Naruaez* had brought,should be sent with al spéede to ŷ Iland
of *Santo Domingo,* for men, horses, armour, pouder & other
munition,also for wollen cloth, linnen, shooes, and many
other things: and wrote his letters for the same to the licenciat *Rodrigo de Figueroa,* and to the whole magistrates
of Chancery, certifying them of all their proceedings in
that countrey, beséechyng them of helpe and succour, and
that

that fozthwith to be sent by the messenger.

This done, he sente twentie hozsemen, twoo hundzed Spaniardes, and many *Indians* vnto *Zacatami* and *Xalaxinco*, whiche were townes subiect to the *Mexicans*, and placed in the high way to *Vera Crux*, who had slayne certaine Spaniardes passyng that way. This company wente thither, with their accustomed pzotestations, whiche pzeuayled not, wherevpon followed fire and spoyle: many Gentlemen and other pzincipall persons came to yéelde themselues to *Cortes*, moze foz feare than foz good will, craupng pardon foz theyz offence, pzomising also not to offende agayne, noz yet at any tyme to take armour agaynst the Spaniardes. *Cortes* pardoned them, & then hys armie returned, with determination to kéepe his Chzistmasse in *Tlaxcallan*, whiche was within twelue dayes followyng. He left a Captaine with thzée scoze Spaniards in the newe towne of *Segura*, to kéepe that passage, and also to put in feare the *Comarcans* that dwelled thereabout: he sente befoze him his whole armie, and he himself went with twentie hozsemen from thence to *Coliman* to lodge there that night, being a cittie of his allied friendes, and there to ozdaine and make by hys auctozitie, bothe Noble men and Captaynes in lue of them whiche died with the disease of small pockes. He aboade there thzée dayes, in the whiche the newe Lozdes were ozdeyned, who afterwardes remayned his especiall friendes. The nexte day hée came to *Tlaxcallan*, beyng fiue leagues distant from thence, where he was triumphantly receyued. And truely at that time he made a iourney most woozthie of renowne and glozy.

At this seafon his dére friende *Maxixca* was departed this transitozie lyfe, foz whome he mourned clothed in blacke, after the Spanishe fashion: he lefte behinde him certaine sonnes, of whom the eldest was.xij.yéeres of age,
whome

whome *Cortes* named and appoynted for Lorde of his fathers estate,and the commons did certifie it to appertaine vnto him . This was no small glory for *Cortes* to giue estates,and also to take them away at his pleasure, yea and that those *Indians* should haue him in suche feare and respect,that none durste doe any thyng in acceptyng the inheritaunce of their fathers without his good will and licence.

Now *Cortes* procured that every man shoulde make his harneys,weapons and prouision readie and in good order: he made also great haste in building Uergantines,for his timber was already cutte and seasoned : he sente vnto *Vera Crux* for saples, tacle, nayles, roapes and other necessarie things, whereof there was store remaynyng of the furniture of the shippes that were sunke.And hauyng wante of pitche,for inthat countrey the *Indians* knewe not what it meant,he commaunded certayne of his Mariners to make the same in the highe Mountaynes where was store of Pine trées,and not farre from the cittie.

The Vergantines that Cortez commaunded to be built,and the Spaniardes which he had ioyned togither to besiege Mexico.

He fame of prosperitie whiche *Cortes* enioyed,was wonderfully blowen abroade with the newes of the imprisonment of *Mutezuma*,and the victory against *Pamfilo de Naruaez*, wherevppon there came many Spaniardes by twenty and twentie in a company from *Cuba*, *Santo Domingo*,and other Jslandes. Although that iourney coste some their liues, for in the way they were murdered by those of *Tepeacac* and *Xalacinco*,as is before declared,yet notwithstanding there
came

came many to *Tlaxcallan*, whereby his hoste was verye
encreased, beseechyng him to make haste towarde the
warres.

It was not possible for *Cortes* to haue espies in *Mexico*,
for the *Tlaxcaltecas* were knowen by their lippes, eares,
and other tokens, and also they had in *Mexico* garde and
great enquirie for that purpose, by reason wherof he could
not certainely knowe what passed in those parties, accordyng as he desired, for to haue prouided himself of things
needefull: yet a Captayne whiche was taken pryson̄er in
Huacacholla, certified that *Cuetlauac* Lorde of *Iztacpalapan*,
Nephewe to *Mutezuma*, was elected Emperour after his
Uncles death, who was a wise and valiant man, and hee
it was that had dryuen *Cortes* out of *Mexico*, who now had
fortified *Mexico* with many bulworkes and caues, and
with many and sundry sortes of weapon, but chiefly very long Lances, yea and planted them in the grounde to
resiste and molest the horsemen. He proclaymed pardon
and free libertie, without paying any tribute for the space
of one whole yeere, yea and further as long as the warres
should laste, he promysed also great rewardes to all them
that shoulde kill any Christian, or expulse them from that
countrey. This was a policie whereby he gatte muche
credite among his vassals, yea and gaue them greate courage to play the valiant men. All this newes was founde
to be true, sauing onely *Cuetlauac* was dead. And that
Quahutimoccin, Nephew also, as some doe say, of *Mutezuma*,
raygned at that tyme, who was a valiant man and a good
warrier, as hereafter shalbe declared, who sente his messengers through out his Empyre, proclaymyng as great
rewardes as *Cuetlauac* had done before, declaring vnto
them that it was more reason to serue him than straungers, and also to defende they olde auncient Religion,
and not to credite suche Christians as woulde make

Dq. them

themselues Lordes of other mens goodes, yea and make them slaues and captiues as they had done in other places. *Quahutimoc* encouraged muche his subiectes, and kindled with his talke their wrath agaynst the Spaniardes: yet there were some prouinces that gaue no eare to his information, but rather leaned to our side, or else medled with neyther side. *Cortes* seyng the effect of the matter, determined forthwith to beginne the warres: he mustered his men on Sainct Steuens day, and founde fourtie horsemen, and fiue hundreth & fourtie fotemen, wherof foure score were Hargabushiers, and crossebow men, niene peces of ordinaunce, and little powder: his horsemen he diuided into foure squares, and his fotemen into nine: he named & appointed captaynes, and other officers for the host, vnto whom in general he spake as followeth.

The exhortation of Cortez to
his Souldiers.

MY louyng brethren, I gyue moste hartie thankes vnto Iesu Christ, to see you now whole of your woundes and free from diseases: likewise I muche reioyce to see you in god order trimly armed, yea and with suche desire to sette agayne vpon *Mexico*, to reuenge the death of our fellowes, and to winne that greate Citie, the whiche I truste in God shalbe brought to passe in shorte time, hauing the friendship of *Flaxcallan* and other prouinces, who haue as great desire to see the ouerthrowe of the *Mexicans*, as we our selues, for therein they gette both honour, libertie & safegarde of life. Also it is to be considered, that if the victory should not be ours, they pore soules should be destroyed and remaine in perpetuall captiuitie. Also the *Culhuacans* do abhorre them worse than vs, for
                                                              recey‐

receyuing vs into their houses and countrey: therefore sure I am that they will sticke vnto vs vnfaynedly. I muste needes confesse their vnfayned friendship, for presente workes doe testifie the same. They will not onely be a meane to bryng others their neyghbours to our seruice, but also haue now in readinesse 100000. me of warre, to sende with vs, besides a great nuber of Tamimez, or carriers to carrie at our prouition. We also, are now the same which alwaies heretofore ye haue bene, for I as witnesse beyng your captayne, haue had the victory of many battayles fighting with a, 100. yea 200000. enimies: we got also by strength of arme many strog cities, yea & brought in subiection many prouinces, not beyng so many in number as we are nowe, for when we came firste into this countrey we were not so many as now presently we are. Agayne in *Mexico* they feare our coming: it should also be a blot vnto our honour that *Quahutimoc* should inherite ý kingdome that cost our fried *Mutezuma* his life. Likewise I esteeme al that we haue done is nothing, if we winne not *Mexico*, our victories shoulde also be sorowfull if we reuenge not the death of our deere fellowes. The chiefe and principall cause of our coming into this countrey, was to set forth the faith of Iesu Christ, & therwithal doth folow honour & profite which seldome times do dwell togither. In those fewe dayes that we were in *Mexico*, we put downe the idols, we caused sacrifice and eatyng of mans flesche to bee layde asīde, and also in those dayes wee beganne to conuerte some to the fayth. It is not therefore nowe reason to leaue of so laudable an enterpryse, so well begonne. Lette vs now goe whither holy fayth doth call vs, and where the sinnes of our enimies deserueth so great a punishment, and if pe well remember, the Citizens of that citie were not cōtent to murder such an infinite number of men, women & childrē before the idols,

Qq.ij.   in

in their filthy sacrifice, for honour of their Diuelithe
Goddes, but also to eate their fleshe, a thyng inhumayne,
and much abhorred of God, and al good men doth procure,
and especially, Christians, to defende and punishe suche
odious customes.

Besides all this, they committe that horrible sinne for
the whiche the fiue cities with *Sodom* were burned by fire
from heauen: Why then what greater occasion should
any man wishe for in earth, than to abolish such wickednesse, and to plant among these bloudy tirants the fayth
of Iesu Christ, publishing his holy gospel: Therfore now,
with ioyfull hartes lette vs proceede to serue God, honour
our nation, to enlarge our Princes dominions, and to en-
riche our selues with the goodly pray of *Mexico*, to morrow God willyng we will beginne the same.

All his men answeared with cheerefull countenaunce,
that they were ready to departe when it pleased him, promising their faithful seruice vnto him. It should seeme the
rather with the desire of that pleasure and greate treasure whiche they had eyght monethes enioyed before.

Cortes commaunded to proclayme throughout his army, certaine ordinaunces of warre for the good gouernement of his hoste, whiche he had written among others:
and were these that followeth:

That none should blaspheme the holy name of Iesus.

That no Souldier should fight with his fellowe.

That none shoulde play at any game, his horse nor armour.

That none should force any woman.

That none should robbe or take any *Indian* captiue without his speciall licence and counsellers.

That none should wrõg or iniurie any *Indian* their friends:
he also tared vpon worke and apparell, for cause of the
excessiue prices that they were there solde for.

The

The exhortation made by Cortez to
the Indians of Tlaxcallan.

The nexte daye following, *Cortes* called before him all the Lordes, Captaynes, and principall persons of *Tlaxcallan, Huexocinco, Chololla, Chalco,* and of other townes, who were there presente at that time, saying as followeth. My Lordes and friendes, you know the iourney which I haue nowe in hande, to morrowe God willing I will departe to the warre and siege of *Mexico,* and enter into the land of youre enimies and mine: And the thing that now I do require, and also pray, is, that you remayne faithfull and constant in your promise made, as hitherunto you haue done, and so I trust you will continue. And bycause I can not bring so soone my purpose to passe according to youre desire and mine, without the *Vergantines* which are now a making, and to be placed in the lake of *Mexico,* therefore I praye you to fauoure these workemen which I leaue héere, with suche loue and friendship, as héeretofore you haue done, and to giue them all things necessary for their prouission, and I do faithfully promise to take away the yoke of bondage, which the inhabitantes of *Culhua* haue layde vpon you, and also will obteyne of the Emperoure great libertie and priuiledges for you.

All the *Indians* shewed countenance of obedience, and the chiefest Gentlemen aunswered in few wordes, saying, we will not onely fulfyll youre requeft, but also when your véssels are finished, we will bring them to *Mexico,* and we all in generall will goe with you, and truly serue you in your warres.

Q.g.ii.   How

Hovv Cortez tooke Tezcuco.

ortez departed from *Tlaxcallan* wyth hys
souldyers the good oyde, whyche was a
godly sight to beholde: for at that time he
had eyghtie thousande men in his hoste, and
the most of them armed after their man-
ner, whiche made a gallant shewe: but *Cortes* for diuers causes woulde not haue them all with him, vntill the *Vergantines* were finished, and *Mexico* beseged, fearing wante of
vittayle for so greate an armye: yet notwithstanding hée
tooke twentie thousand of them, besides the Carriers, and
that night came to *Tezmeluca*, whiche standeth fire leagues
from *Tlaxcallan*, and is a village apperteyning to *Gua-
xocinco*, where he was by the principall of the Towne wel
receyued. The next day he iourneyed foure leagues, into
the territorie of *Mexico*, and there was lodged on the side
of a hill, where many had perished with colde, had it not
bin for the store of woode whiche they found there. In the
morning he ascended vpwards on this hill, and sente hys
scoute of foure footemen and foure horsemen to discouer,
who found the way stopped with great trées newly cutte
downe, and placed crossewise in the way: but they thynking that yet forwards it was not so procéeded forthe as
wellas they might, till at length the let with great hugie
trées was such, that they coulde passe no further, and with
this newes were forced to returne, certifying *Cortes* that
the Horsemenne coulde not passe that way in any wise.
Cortes demaunded of them, whether they hadde séene any
people, they aunswered no, whereuppon he procéeded forwarde with all the Horsemen, and a thousande footemen,
commaundyng all the residue of hys armye to followe
hym wyth as muche spéede as myghte bée, so that wyth
that

that companye whyche he carried with him, he made
waye, takyng away the trées that were cutte downe to
disturbe his passage: and in this order, in short time passed his hoost, without any hurt or daunger, but with great
payne and trauell, for certaynely if the enimies had bin
there to defende that passage, oure menne hadde not passed, for it was a very euill way, and the enimies also
thoughte the same to be sure with the trées whiche were
crossed the way, whereuppon they were carelesse of that
place, and attended their comming in playne grounde:
for from *Tlaxcallan* to *Mexico* are thrée wayes, of the
whiche *Cortes* chose the worst, ymagining the thing that
afterwards fell out, or else some hadde aduised him howe
that way was cléere from the enimies. And béing past
this crooked passage, they slipped the lake of *Mexico*, and
gaue vnto God most hartie thankes for the same, and
there made a solemne vowe and promise, not to returne,
vntill they had wonne *Mexico*, or lost their liues. They
aboode there and rested themselues, till all the whole armye were come togither, to descende downe into the
playne, for nowe they myghte descrye the fires and
beacons of theyr enimies in sundrye places, and all
those whyche hadde attended theyr comming by the
other two wayes, were now gathered togyther, thynkyng to sette vppon them benmixte certayne bridges,
where a greate companye aboade, expecting theyr comming: but *Cortes* sente twenty horsemen, who made
way among them, and then followed the whole armye, who slewe manye of them, wythoute receyuyng anye hurte. And in thys order they came to *Qua-
huitpec*, whiche is of the iurisdiction of *Tezcuco*,
where they aboade that nyghte, and in that place
founde togyther manye, nor woman, but not farre
off was pytched the Campe of the *Indians* of *Culhua*,
which

which myght be nere a hundzed thousand men of warre, who were sent by the Seniozs of *Mexico*, and *Tezcuco*, to encounter oure armye, in consideration whereof, *Cortes* kept good watch with tenne Hozsemen, and all his Souldyers were warned to be in readynesse at a call, if nede should happen.

The next day in the mozning he departed from thence towarde *Tezcuco*, whiche standeth thzee leagues distante, and procéeding on their iourney, foure pzincipal persons, inhabitantes of *Tezcuco*, mette with them, bearing a rod of golde, with a little flagge, in token of peace, saying, that *Coacuacoyozin* their Lozd had sent them to desire him not to make any spoyle in his Countrey, and likewise to offer his friendship, pzaying also, that it might please him with his whole army to take his lodging in the Towne of *Tezcuco*, where he shoulde be well receyued. *Cortes* reioyced with this message, although he suspected, that it was a fayned matter, but one of them he knewe very well, whome he saluted, saying : My comming is not to offend any, but rather to do you good. I will also receyue and hold your Lozd foz a friende, with condition, that hée doe make vnto me restitution of the treasure whyche hé tooke from fiue and foztie Spanyardes, and thzée hundzed *Tlaxcaltecas*, all the which were by his commaundemente also slayne of late dayes. They aunswered that *Mutezuma* caused them to be murthered, who had likewise taken the spoyle, and that the Citizens of *Tezcuco* were not culpable in that fact, and with this aunswere they returned.

Cortes went fozward on his way, and came to *Quahutichan* and *Huaxuta*, which are suburbes of *Tezcuco*, where he and all his host were plenteously pzouided of al things necessary, and thzew downe the Idolles. This done, hé entred into the Citte, where his lodging was pzepared in a great house, sufficient foz him and all the Spanyardes,
                                                    with

with many other the *Indian* friends. And bycaufe that at his firſt entry, he fawe neyther women nor childꝛen, hee fufpected fome treafon, and foꝛthwith pꝛoclaymed, vpon payne of death, that none of his men ſhould go out. The Spaniards began to triumph in their lodgings and chãbers, placing euery thing in good oꝛder. In the euening they went vp into the *Zoties* and galleries, to beholde the Citie, which is as bigge as *Mexico*, and there they fawe the greate number of Citizens that fledde from thence with their ſtuffe, fome towardes the mountaines, and others to the water fide to take boate, a thing ſtraunge, to fée the great haſt and ſtirre to pꝛouide foꝛ themfelues, at the leaſt ther were twentie thoufand litle boates (called *Conoas*) occupyed, in carying houſhold ſtuffe and paſſengers. *Cortes* would fayne haue remedied it, but that night was fo nygh at hand, that he coulde not. He would gladly alfo haue appꝛehended the Loꝛd, but he was one of the firſt that fledde vnto *Mexico*. *Cortes* caufed many of the Citizens, to be called befoꝛe him, and hauing in hys company a yong gentleman of a noble houfe in that coũtrey, who was alfo laſt chꝛiſtened, & had to name *Hernãdo*, *Cortes* being his godfather, who loued him well, fayde vnto the citizens, that this new Chꝛiſtian loꝛd, *Don Hernãdo*, was fonne vnto *Nezaualpincintli* their louing Loꝛd, wherfoꝛe he required them to make him their king, conſidering that *Coacnacoyocin*, was fled vnto the enimies, laying alfo befoꝛe them his wicked fact in killing of *Cacuza* his own bꝛother, only to put him from his inheritance & kingdome, thꝛough the enticemente of *Quahutimoccin*, a moꝛtal enimie to the Spaniards. In this foꝛt was *Don Hernando* elected king, and the fame therof being blowen abꝛoade, manye citizens repayꝛed home againe to viſite their newe Pꝛince, fo that in ſhoꝛt fpace the citie was as wel repleniſhed with people, as it was befoꝛe, and being

Kr.   alfo

also well vsed at the Spaniardes handes, they serued them dilygentlye in all thyngs that they were commaunded. And *Don Hernando* aboade euer after a faithfull friende vnto the Spaniardes, and in short tyme learned the Spanishe tongue : and soone after came the inhabitants of *Quahutichan,* *Huaxuta* and *Auntenco,* to submytte themselues, crauing pardon, if in any thyng they had offended. *Cortez* pardoned them, and gaue them licence to departe home vnto their houses.

Quahutimoc, *Coacnacoso* and other magistrates of *Culhua* sente to rayle vppon those townes, for yeldyng themselues to the Christians, but they layde hold vpon the messengers, and brought them vnto *Cortes*, of whome he enformed himselfe of the state of *Mexico,* and sent them backe againe, requiring their Lordes of peace and friendshippe : but it preuayled not, for they were fully armed for the warre.

A good correction.

At this instante certaine friendes of *Iames Velasques* went vp and downe the Campe, procuring secretly a mutenie among the souldiers, to haue them to returne to *Cuba*, and vtterly to destroy *Cortes* his proceedings. This thing was not so secretly wrought, but that *Cortes* had knowledge, wherevppon he apprehended the doers thereof, and by their confessions the matter did plainely appeare, whervpon he condemned to death one *Antonio de Villafania,* who was natural of *Samora,* and forthwith executed the sentence, wherwith the punishment and Mutinie was ended, and ceassed.

The

The Spaniardes vvhich vvere
sacrificed in Tez-
cuco.

Ayly increaſed *Cortes* in ſtrength and
reputation, and many townes as wel
of the partes of *Culhua* as others
came vnto his friendſhip and obedience. VVithin two dayes that *Don Hernando* was made king, came certayne
gentlemen of *Huaxuta* and *Quahutic-
chan*, to certify vnto him, how al the power of the *Mexicans* was comming towardes them, and to knowe if it
were his pleaſure, that they ſhould carry their wiues,
children, and other goods into the Mountaines, or els to
bring them where he was, their feare was ſo great.
Cortes made vnto thē this anſwere, ſaying: be ye of good
courage, and feare ye not. Alſo I pray you to cōmaunde
your wiues & families to make no alteratiō, but rather
quietly to abide in your houſes. And cōcerning the enimies, I am glad of their comming, for ye ſhal ſee how I
will deale with them. But the enimies wente not to
Huaxuta, as it was thought: neuertheleſſe *Cortes* hauing
intelligence where they were, wente out to encounter
them, with two pieces of Ordinaunce, twelue horſemen
and two hundred Spaniardes, with many *Indians* of
Tlaxcalla. He fought with the enemie, and ſlew but few,
for they fledd to the water. He burnt certaine townes
where the *Mexicans* were wonte to ſuccour themſelues.
Thē next day came the chiefeſt men of thoſe townes to
craue pardon, and to beſeech him not to deſtroy thē, promiſing neuer to harbour nor ſuccour, any of *Culhua*.

The *Mexicans* hearing what these townes men pretended, with greate pre made a foule correction among them, as dyd appeare by many of them, which came vnto *Cortes* with broken heads, desiring reuengement.

The inhabitaunts of *Chalco* sent also vnto him for succour, declaring that the *Mexicans* made greate spoyle among them. But *Cortes* being ready to send for his Uergantines, could not relieue them all, and especially wyth Spaniardes: wherefore he remitted them to the helpe of the *Tlaxcaltecas*, and vnto the of *Huexocinco*, *Chololla*, *Huacacholla* and other friends, promising that shortly he would come himselfe. But this answere pleased him not, yet for the present nade they required his letters to be written vnto those townes. And being in this communication, there came messengers from *Tlaxcallan*, with news, that the Uergantines were ready, and to knowe if he stoode in nade of any succour, for of late, (quoth they) we haue sane many beacons, and fiers, which are greater tokens of warre, than heretofore hath bene sane.

There came at that time, a Spaniard also from *Vera Crux*, with certaine newes, that there had arriued a ship, whiche had brought thirtie Souldiers besides the mariners of the shippe, with eight horses, great store of pouder, shotte, crossebowes, and Harquebushes. The plesent newes reioyced much our men, wherevpon *Cortes* sente forthwith to *Tlaxcallan* for the Uergantines, *Gonzalo de Sandoual*, with two hundered Spaniards, and fiftane horsemen, and commaunded that in their way they shold burne and destroy the towne where the fourty fiue spaniardes, and thrae hundered *Tlaxcaltecas* were slayn, with fiue horses moe, when *Mexico* was last besieged: and ye village is in ye iurisdiction of *Tezcuco*, and bordereth vpon the territorie of *Tlaxcallan*, yea, and for that purpose hae would gladly haue corrected and punished the dwellers of of *Tezcuco*, but time then permitted not ẏ same, although they had deserued moze punishment than the others. Foz why? in their town they were sacrifised and eaten, yea the walles painted with their blood, shewing mozeouer perfit tokens, how it was spaniards blood. They pluckt off also the hozses skinnes & tanned thē in the heare, and afterwards hung them vppe, with the hozseshoes in their great temple, & next vnto them, the spaniards garmētes, foz a perpetual memozy.

Sandoual went vnto that place with determinate entēt to follow his cōmission, & also befoze he came to ẏ place, he found wzittē in a house w̄ a cole, these wozds: here in this house was a pzisoner ẏ vnfoztunate *Iohn Iust*, who was a gentleman, and one of the fiue hozsemen that wer taken. But the people of that towne, being many, fledde when they saw the Spaniardes appzoch neare vnto thē. But *Sandoual* followed them, and slewe many of them: he toke also pzisoners, manye women and childzen, who pelded themselues vnto his mercie, and their bodies foz slaues. He seeing so little resistance, and beholding the pitiful mone of the wiues foz their husbandes, and the childzen foz their fathers, had compassiō on them, and wold not destroye their towne, but rather caused the dwellers to come again, and pardoned them, with othe, that hereafter they shoulde serue them truely, and be vnto them loyal friends. In this sozte was the death of the Chzistians reuenged, yet *Sandoual* asked them howe they slewe so manye Chzistians without resistaunce, marye (quoth they) we made an ambush in an euil and narrow way, ascending vp a hill, and there as they went vppe by one and one we spoyled them, foz there, neyther hozses noz other weapon could defend oz help thē, so ẏ we toke them pzisoners and sente them to *Tezcuco*, where, as is befoze declared, they were sacrificed in the reuengement

of

of the impʒisonment of *Calame*.

Hovv the Vergantines vvere brough ͭ frō
Tlaxcall to Tezcuco.

Owe when the enemies which murde-red the Spaniardes , were reduced and chastened , *Sandoual* pʒocǽded foʒwarde towarde *Tlaxcallan* , and at the boʒder of that pʒouince , he mette with the Uergā-tines whiche were bʒoughte in pieces, as tables, plan-ches, and naples, with all other furniture, the whyche eight thousand men caryed vpon their backes.

There came also foʒ their safecondui te twentie thousande men of warre, and a thousande *Tamemez*, who were the carriers of victuals , and seruantes. Thē the Spanishe Carpenters sayde vnto *Sandoual* , that foʒ as muche as they were nowe come into the countrey of enimies, it might please him to haue regarde therbnto, foʒ daungers that myght happen: he allowed wel theyʒ iudgement.

Nowe *Chichimecaterl*, being a pʒincipal man and a ba-liant also, was cap aine of a thousande men, & desired to haue the bantguard with the Tymber, and hauing had the same charge hitherbnto, it should be an affront foʒ him, to be put from it, and gaue manye reasons in hys behalfe . But notwithstanding his request, he was en-treated to take the reregarde. And that *Tutipil* and *Teu-tecotl* captaines, bery pʒincipal gentlemen, should haue the bantgard, with ten thousand men . In the myddest were placed the *Tamemez* , and those that carryed the foyst, with all the apparell of the Uergantines. Befoʒe those two captaynes, went a hundered Spaniardes, and eight

eight hozſemen,and behind and laſt came *Sandoual* with all the reſidue,and ſeuen hozſemen. But now although *Chichimecatetl* was offended, touching his firſte charge, now much moze bycauſe the Spaniardes were not in his company, ſaying(quoth he) ye take me not foz vali= ant, oz elſe not faithful.That matter being pacified,and euery thing in good ozder, they toke theyz way towarde *Tezcuco*, with a marueplous noyſe,crying, Chziſtians, Chzistians,*Tlaxcallan*,*Tlaxcallan*,and Spayne.

On the fourth day they entred into *Tezcuco*, in verye good ozder, with the ſounde of dzummes, ſnaple=ſhelles, and other like inſtrumentes of Muſicke, and againſte their entry into the Citie,they put on al their bzauerye of clothes,and buſhes of feathers, whiche truely was a gallant ſight : they were ſire houres,in entryng into the towne,keping their array.

Cortez came fozth to recepue them, and gaue greate thankes vnto the gentlemen,and all the company, and pzouided them of good lodgings and entertayne= ment.

Of the Docke or trench vvhich
was made to launch, the Vergan-
tines.

Anye pzouinces of *India*, came to ſub= mitte and offer their ſeruice vnto *Cor= tes*, ſome foz feare of deſtruction, and o= thers foz the hatred whyche they bare to the *Mexicans* : So that nowe *Cortes* was ſtrong both with Spaniardes and *Indians*.Alſo the Spaniſhe Captaine of *Segura*,ſent a letter to *Cortez*, the which letter he had recepued of another

another spaniard, the effect therof was as foloweth. Noble gentlemen, diuerse times I haue written vnto you,
but as yet I neuer receiued answere, nor yet nowe doe I
I thynke otherwise, notwithstanding yee shall vnderstande, that the Culhuacans haue done much hurte in thys
countrey, but we remayne with victorie. This prouince
desireth to sée and knowe Captaine Cortez, for to render
themselues vnto him, and nowe they stande in neede of
our nation, wherfore it may please you to sende vnto vs
thirtie Spaniardes.

Cortez aunswered the letter in suche sort, that he then
presently coulde not sende the thing desired, for that he
was readye to the siege of Mexico: notwythstanding hée
gaue them great thankes, with hope shortlye to sée the.
He that writte the former letter, was one of the Spaniardes that Cortez hadde sente to the prouince of Chi-
nanta, a yeare passe, to enquire of the secretes of that
place, and to séeke for golde and other commodities.
And if it so happened, that the Lorde of that place
made that Spaniarde a Captayne, agaynste the Culhuacans theyr enemyes, for Mutezuma made them
warre béeyng farre from Mexico, bycause they had en-
terapned the Spaniardes. But through the industrie of
that Christian, the Lorde aboade alwayes with victorye, and hauing vnderstanding that some of hys nation
were in Tepeacac, he wrote so often as the letter de-
clareth, but none of them came to their handes, but only this last letter: our men reioyced muche to heare that
the Spaniardes were aliue, and also the Lorde of Chi-
nanta to be their friende: likewise they marueyled much
howe they had escaped, for at the time that they fledde
from Mexico, all other Spaniardes that were abidyng
in the Mynes and other Lordshippes, were slaine by the
Indians.

Cortes

Cortes made his preparation for the siege of *Mexico* with all hast, and furnished hym with scalling ladders, and other necessaryes, fitte for such a purpose. His *Vergantines* being nayled, and throughly ended, he made a sluise or trench of halfe a league of length, twelue foote broad & more, and two fadome in depth. This worke was fiftie dayes a doyng, although there were foure hundred thousand mē dayly working, truly a famous worke and woorthy of memory.

The *Vergantines* were calked with Towe and cotten wooll, and for want of tallow and oyle, they were (as some reporte,) driuen to take mans greafe, not that they slewe men for that effect, but of those which were slayne in the warres. The *Indians* who were cruell and bloudy butchers, vsing sacrifice, would in this fort open the dead bodye, and take out the greafe. The *Vergantines* being launched, *Cortes* mustered his men, and founde nine hundred Spanyardes, of the which were 86. Horsemen, and a hundred and eyghtéene with Crossebowes and Hargabushes, and all the residue had sundry weapons, as swords, daggars, Targets, Launces, and Halbertes. Also they had for armour, corslets, coates of mayle, and Jackes. They had moreouer thrée great péeces of cast yron, fiftéene small péeces of brasse, and tenne hundred waighte of powder, with store of shotte. All that ye haue hearde, was the prouission that *Cortes* had for the siege of *Mexico*, the strongest and greatest Citie in all *India* and newe world. In eache *Vergantine* he placed a péece of brasse. He proclaymed agayne all the institutions and ordinances of the warre, praying and commaunding that they might be well and faithfully obserued, and said, Brethrē and my fellowes, now do you sée our vessels readye, yea and also you do remember howe troublesome a thyng it hathe bin to bring them hither with the coste and sweate

Sf. of

of our friendes, and one of the chiefeſt hopes that I haue
ſhoztly to winne *Mexico*, are theſe veſſels, foz with them
we will burne all their *Canoes*, oz elſe we will ſo locke
them vp, that they ſhall not help them, whereby we wyll
annoy our enimie as muche that way, as our army ſhall
do by land. I haue alſo a hundzed thouſand men of warre
my friends to beſéege this Citie, who are (as you know)
ÿ valianteſt men in all theſe parties. You haue alſo your
vittailes pzouided abundantly, and that which now im=
pozteth, is, that you play the menne, as héeretofoze you
haue done, and moſt humbly to pzay vnto God foz victo=
rie, foz that this warre is his.

The order of the hoſt and army of
Cortes for to beſeege Mexico.

He nexte day following, *Cortes* ſente vnto the
pzouinces of *Tlaxcallan*, *Huexocinco*, *Chololla*,
Chal, and other Townes, warning thé within
tenne dayes to come vnto *Tezcuco*, with theyz
armoure, weapon, and other neceſſaries, foz the ſéege of
Mexico. He certifyed them alſo, how the *Vergantines* were
ready with all other furniture accozdingly, and the Spa=
nyardes were very deſirous to loſe no time, wherefoze
they meante not to delay their pzetence, farther than the
day appoynted.

The *Indians* hearing this newes, and bycauſe they
would not come to late to the beginning of the aſſaulte,
came incontinente, and entred into *Tezcuco* in god ozder
of warre, aboue ſixtie thouſand men, gallantly trimmed
after their vſe and cuſtome, *Cortes* friendly welcommed
them, and pzouided them lodgings accozdingly.

On Whitſonday, all the Spanyardes came into the
fielde, whereas *Cortes* made thzée chiefe Captaynes, a=
mong

mong whome he deuided his whole army. Unto *Pedro de Aluarado* the first Captayne, he appoynted thirtie horse-men, and a hundred and seauentie footemen of the Spa-nyardes, two péeces of ordinance, and thirtie thousande *Indians*, commaunding him to campe in *Tlacopan*. Unto *Cristoual de Olid* the seconde Captayne, he gaue thrée and thirtie Horsemen, and a hundred and eyghtéene footemen of the Spanish nation, two péeces of ordinance, and thir-tie thousand *Indians*, and appoynted him to pitch his camp in *Culhuacan*. To *Gonsalo de Sandoual* who was the thyrde Captayne, he gaue thrée and twenty Horsemen, and 16c. footemen, two péeces of Ordinance, and 40000. *Indians*, with commission to chose a place to pitch his Campe.

In euery *Vergantine* he planted a péece of ordinace, sire hargabushes, or crossebowes, and 23. Spaniards, mé most fittest for that purpose. He appointed also Captaynes for eache, and himselfe for general, whereof some of the chie-fest of his companye began to murmure that wente by lande, thinking that they had bin in greater daunger, wherefore they required him to goe with the mayne bat-tell, and not by water. *Cortes* little estéemed their words, for although it is more daunger in the water than in the land, yet it did more importe to haue greater care in the warres by water, than on the land, bycause his men had bin in the one, and not in the other.

On the tenth of May *Aluarado*, and *Cristoual de Olid* departed, and went that night to a Towne called *Acol-man*, where was betwéene them greate discorde touchyng their lodgings, yea and if *Cortes* had not sente to take vp the matter, much mischiefe had ensued. The nexte daye they lodged in *Xolitepec*, whych was not inhabited. The thyrde daye they came vnto *Tlacopan*, whyche was al-so as all the Townes of the lake, wythout people, there they were lodged in the Lordes house of the Towne.

Sl.y.   The

The *Tlaxcaltecas* began to viewe *Mexico* by the caſſey, and ſoughte with their enimies, vntill the nighte made them to ceaſſe.

On the thirtéenth of May, *Criſtoual de Olid* came to *Chapultepec*, and brake the conduites of ſwéete water, whereupon *Mexico* was deſtitute of the ſame, being the conduit that did prouide all the Citie. *Pedro de Aluarado* wyth his company procured to amende all the broken places of the caſſey, that the horſemen might haue frée paſſage, and hauing muche to do in theſe affaires, he ſpente thrée dayes, and fighting with many enimies, ſome of his men were hurt, and many *Indian* friendes ſlayn. *Aluarado* abode in *Tlacopan* with his armye, and *Criſtoual de Olid* retired to *Culhuacan* with his men, accordeing to the inſtruction recepued from *Cortes*, and fortifyed themſelues in the Lordes houſes of the Towne, and euery daye skyrmiſhed with the enimies, and ſome went to the Townes néere at hande, and brought *Centli*, fruite, and other prouiſion. In this buſſineſſe they occupyed théſelues a whole wéeke.

The Battaile and victory of the Vergantines againſt the Canoas.

He newe Kyng *Quahutimoc* hauing intelligence how *Cortes* hadde launched hys *Vergantines* and ſo mightie a power to beſéege *Mexico*, entred into counſell wyth the chiefeſt péeres of hys Realme. Some were of opinion, and dyd prouoke hym to the warres, conſidering theyr greate multitude of people, and fortitude of the Citie.

Others were of opinion, who tendred muche the common weale, that no *Spanyarde* that ſhoulde happen to
be

be taken pzploner ſhoulde be ſacrificed, but rather to be
pzeſerued foz concluſion of peace if néede ſhoulde ſo re⸗
quyze. And finally ſome ſayde,that they ſhould demaunde
of their Goddes what was beſt to doe.

The Bing that inclined himſelfe moze to peace than to
warre,ſayde that he woulde remitte the matter to the
iudgement of the idolles,and that he would abuiſe them
what anſwere ſhould-be made vnto him,but: in harte he
deſired to come to ſome boneſt ozder and agréement with
Cortes,fearing the thyng that after did enſue. But ſeyng
his Counſell and ſubiectes ſo determined to warre, he cō⸗
maunded foure Spaniardes whiche he had pzyſoners in
a cage,to be ſacrificed vnto the Goddes of warre,with a
great number moze of *Indians*.

He ſpake to the Diuell in the image of *Vitzilopuchtli*, A Diuelish ſentence.
who anſwered him that he ſhoulde not feare the Spani⸗
ardes being but fewe, noz yet thoſe whiche were conten
to helpe them,foz that they ſhoulde not long abide in the
ſiege, commaunding him to goe fozth and to encounter
them without feare,foz he would helpe them and kill his
enimies. With this anſwere of the diuel, *Quahutimoc* com⸗
maunded fozth with to bzeake downe the bzidges,watche
the Cittie, make bulwarkes, and to arme fiue thouſande
boates,and ſayde vnto the Spaniardes, that the Goddes
woulde be pleaſed with the ſacrifice of their bodies, the
Snakes filled with their bloud, and the Tigres relieued
with their fleſh, they ſayde alſo to the *Indians* of *Tlaxcallan*,
ah yé Cuckold knaues,ſlaues and traytozs to your gods
and kyng,will you not repent the wickedneſſe whiche yé
haue committed agaynſt your maiſters, therefoze ſhall
you nowe die an euill death, foz either you ſhall die with
hunger, oz elſe vpon the knife:and then wil we eate your
fleſhe , and make thereof ſolemne a banket as the like
hath heretofoze neuer bene ſéene,and in token therof hold

take

take thefe armes and legges whiche we throwe vnto you of your owne men, which we haue now facrificed for the obtayning of victory. And, after thefe warres we will goe vnto your countrey and fpoyle your Towne, & leaue no memory of your bloud or generation. The *Tlaxical-tecas* laughed at their madde talke, and fayd, that it fhould be better for them to yælde and fubmitte themfelues to *Cortes* his mercy, and if not, yet it were more honorable to fight than to bragge, willyng them to come out into the field. And bad them affuredly beléue, that the ende of all their knauery was at hande: it was a world to heare and fée the bragges and crakes on both fides. *Cortes* hearyng of all thefe matters, fent *Sandoual* to take *Iztacpalapan,* and he enbarked himfelfe to méete him at that place.

Sandoual combated the towne on the one fide, and the townes menue and people with feare fledde vnto *Mexico,* on the otherfide by water: he burned the towne. *Cortes* came at y time to a ftrõg rocke lyke a tower, fituated in the water, where many men of *Culhua* were, who feyng them approche with their Uergantines, fette theyr bea-cons on fire, and threwe downe vpon them ftones and fhotte of theyr arrowes. *Cortes* wente afhore with a hun-dreth and fiftie menne, and combatted the forte, till at length he wanne the battlement, whiche was the *Indians* befte defence, and with muche adoe hée came to the toppe, and there fought vntill he had not lefte one aliue, fauyng women and chyldren. It was a fayre victorie, although fiue and twentie Spanyardes were hurte and wounded, yet the forte was ftrong, and the ouerthrowe a great dif-couragyng of the enimie.

At this inftant were fo many beacons and other fires made rounde aboute the lake and vpon the hilles, that all féemed a lighte fire. And alfo the *Mexicans* hearyng that the Uergantynes were commyng, they came out in their

boates,

boates, with fiue hundreth Gentlemen whiche came to
ſee ſuche newe kinde of veſſelles, and to proue what they
were, beyng a thyng of ſo greate a fame. *Cortes* embarked himſelfe with the ſpoyle of the forte, and commaunded his men to abide all togither for the better reſiſtance,
and bycauſe the enimies ſhoulde thynke that they feared,
wherevpon they mighte without any good order gyue the
onſette vpon the Chriſtians, and ſo to fall ſuddenly into
the ſnare. But it followed, that when they came within
ſhotte of the Spaniardes ordinaunce: they ſtayed abydyng more company, but in ſhorte ſpace there came ſo
many *Canoas*, that it ſeemed a wonder to beholde: They
made ſuche a terrible noyſe with theyr voyces, drummes,
Snayle ſhelles, and other like inſtruments of warre, that
they could not beare one an other, with ſuch great crakes
and bragges, as they had done in time paſſe.

And beyng bothe parties in a readineſſe to fight, there
happened ſuche a poupewinde to the Vergantines which
came from the ſhore, that it ſeemed meruellous. *Cortes* the
prayſing God, commaunded al his Captaines to gyue the
onſet altogithers, & not to ceaſſe vntill the enimies ſhould
be dryuen to retire into *Mexico*, for that it was the pleaſure of God to ſende vnto them that proſperous winde in
token of victory. This talke ended, they beganne to ſette
vpon the enimy, who ſeyng the Vergantines come with
ſuch lucky winde, yea & ſuch a ſight as the like vnto them
had not bene ſeene, they began to flie with ſuche greate
haſte, that they ſpoyled, brake, and ſunke many of them,
and ſuche as ſtode to defende themſelues were ſlayne,
ſo that this battayle was ſoone ended. They purſued
them two leagues, vntill they had locked them vp
in the water ſtreates of *Mexico*, and toke many Lordes
and Gentlemen priſoners. And the key of al theſe warres
cōſiſted in this victory, for our men remayned for Lordes of
the

the whole lake, and the enimie with great feare and losse: they had not bene so soone spoyled, but that there were so many of them, who disturbed one an other. But when *Aluarado,* and *Cristoual de Olid* saw the fortunate successe of *Cortes* by water, they entered the calsey with their army, and tooke certaine bridges and bulwarkes, and draue the *Indians* from them, with all their force and strength. But with the helpe of the Uergantines which came vnto them, the *Indians* were driuen to runne a whole league vpon the calsey, and where they founde the calsey broken, they procured to leape ouer, and so fel into the middest.

Cortes proceeded forwards, and finding no *Canoas,* he landed vpon the calsey that commeth from *Iztacpalapan,* with thirtie men, and combatted two towers of idoles whiche were walled with wall of lyme and stone: it was the same place where *Mutezuma* receyued *Cortes.* He wan those towers in shorte time, although they were defended with all possibilitie: he vnshipped three peeces of ordináce to scoure the calsey, which was full of enimies: at the first shotte he did great hurte among thé, and beyng the night at hande, they seased on bothe sides for that day. And although *Cortes* had determined otherwise with his Captaynes, yet he aboade there that night, and sente to the campe of *Gonsalo de Sandoual* for powder and fiftie mé, with halfe the company of *Indians* of *Culhuacan.*

Hovv Cortez besieged Mexico.

He night of *Cortes* his abiding there, was perillous, for he had not aboue a hundreth men in his cópany, and aboute midnight set vpó him many *Mexicans* both by water and lande, although they accustomed not to fight in the night, but the Uergantines

tines made them sone to retire.

In the mozning came vnto Cortes from Criftoual de Olid, right hozsemen, and foure score footemen. The Mexicans combated the towers, where Cortes was lodged, who incontinent came forth & draue them along the calsey, vntill he had wonne an other bzidge and a bulwarke, and made a great spoyle among them, with the ozdinaunce & hozse men, pursuyng them to the vtmoste houses of the Cittie: and bycause many of the Canoas whiche were on the other side of the calsey galled Cortes and his menne, he bzake downe so muche of the calsey, that he mighte well passe some of his Uergantines to the otherside, the which with few encounters shutte vp the Canoas on that side, within the succour of Mexico: and in this wise he remayned Lozd ouer bothe the lakes.

The next day Sandoual departed from Iztacpalapan toward Culhuacan, and in his way he tooke and spoyled a little Cittie that standeth in the lake, bycause they came out to resitt him. Cortes sente vnto him two Uergantines to passe his men where the calsey was bzoken. Sandoual left his company with Criftoual de Olid, and wet to Cortes with tenne hozsemen, and when he came he found him in fight with the enimies, and he alightyng from his hozse, an Indian perseo him thzough the foote with a dart. Many Spaniardes were hurte that day, but theyz griefe was well reuenged, foz from that day forwarde the Indians courage was muche abated. With the paynes, labour and vicozy already obtayned, Cortes might now at ease pitche his campe at his owne pleasure where he woulde, and also pzouide his army of victuals: sire dayes he ceassed not skirmishyng, and the Uergantines likewise founde out channels that they mighte goe rounde aboute the Cittie, yea and wente spoylyng and burning many houses within the Suburbes.

Ct.　　　　Mexico

Mexico was beſieged in foure places, although at the firſt they determined but thꝛée. Cortes was placed betwixt the twoo towers of the calſey: Pedro de Aluarado in Tlacopan: Criſtoual de Olid in Culhuacan: Gonſalo de Sandoual in Xaltoca: foꝛ they had aduiſe that the ſame way they would ſlée out of the Cittie, ſeyng themſelues in any daunger. It would not haue grieued Cortes to haue lefte a paſſage foꝛ the enimy, but only bycauſe they ſhould not pꝛofite themſelues vpon the lande, and pꝛouide the Cittie that way of armour & victuall, yea, he alſo thought to pꝛeuaile againſt his enimies better vpon the lande than vpon the water. And againe accoꝛding to the olde pꝛouerbe, When thine enimy flieth make him a bꝛidge of ſiluer.

The firſt ſkirmishe vvithin the
cittie of Mexico.

Ortes pꝛetended to enter the Cittie, and to gette what he could, & alſo to ſée what ſtomacke the enimy had: he ſent to aduiſe his captaines, that eche of them ſhould do the like, requiring them to ſende vnto him ſome of their hoꝛſemen and footemē. He gaue ſpeciall commaundement to Criſtoual de Olid to haue regard to the kéeping of his calſey, and to foꝛſée that the inhabitants of Xochmilco, Culhuacan, Iztacpalapan, Vitzilopuchtli, Mexicalcinco, Cuetlauac, & other cities thereaboutes come not that way behinde them and vnwares. He commaunded that the Uergantines ſhould goe along the calſey on bothe the ſides, if any néede ſhoulde happen. Cortes early in the moꝛning came out of his campe with. 200. Spaniardes and. 80000. Indian friends: they had gone but a ſmall ſpace, when they met with their enimies well armed, keping the gappe where the calſey was bꝛoké, which bꝛoken place mought be a ſpeares length, and as much in depth.

depth.They fought with them, who for a great space defended themselues behinde a bulwarke, but in fine he
wanne the passage, and followed them vnto the entrance
of the citie, where was a Tower, and at the foote thereof
a bridge drawen, where a good streame of water passed.
This place was very strong to combat, yea and fearefull
to behold the passage where the draw bridge was. They
ceased not shotyng of arrowes and hurlyng of stones, so
that our men coulde not come neare, vntill the Mergantines came, and by meanes of them they wanne that fort
with lesser paynes than they imagined : for without the
Mergantines it had not bene possible to haue entred the
Cittie.

The enimies being now fled from that holde, our men
alanded there, with the Indian friendes, who incontinent
dammed vp the broken place with stones and earth. The
Spaniardes of the vantgarde, tooke another bulwarke,
which was planted in the largest and fayrest streate of
the Citie, and pursued the enemy to another draw bridge,
which remayned, but with one poste or beame, vppon the
which many of the Indians passed ouer, and then toke y
beame awaye and abode to defende the place : but when
our men approched & sawe how the matter went, *Cortez*
commaunded two pieces of Ordinaunce to be broughte,
with the whiche, and with their Harquebushes, they did
great hurt among the *Mexicans*, who began to fainte, and
lose their courage, the which being vnderstode, certayne
Spaniards swā ouer where the draw bridge was, wt their
weapons in their mouthes. But when the enimy sawe
them passe ouer, they began, as well from that place as
from the house toppes, zoties and bulwarke, whiche they
had defended for the space of two houres, to flie. *Cortes*
and his whole army beyng passed ouer, he commaunded
to damme vp that broken place of the draw brydge,

with earth, rubbishe and stones, and proceeding foorwarde
they came to an other bridge whiche had no bulwarke,
but was neare one of the chiefest places of the cittie, and
there placed a péece of ordinaunce wherewith they dyd
great hurte, and seyng them now past all the bridges, they
determined to enter into the harte of the Citie. When
the *Mexicans* perceyued their determination, they beganne
to prouide euery one for himselfe, for some fledde one way
and some another, but the moste wente to the great temple of Idols. The Spaniardes and theyr friends pursued
after them, and among the throng gotte into the Temple,
where they slewe many, and at length they wente vp into
the high tower, and there threwe downe the idols, among
whome they made a great spoyle.

Quahutimoc beganne to reprehende his men for their
cowardie and flight, who gathered themselues togither,
and consdering theyr ouersight, and that there were no
horses, began a freshe to sette vppon the Spanyardes, and
with foorce and strength draue them out of all the circuite
of the Temple, and made them trusse to their féete. But
when *Cortes* sawe his menne come flying, he caused them
to returne and to shewe face vnto the enimy, declaryng
vnto them how shamefull a thyng it was to flie: But seing the strength and multitude of their enimies, they had
no other remedie but onely to retire to the greate market
place, yea & from thence also they were expelled, and lost a
péece of their ordinaunce. But beyng nowe in this extremitie, there came thrée horsemen who played the valiant men and made way through the troupe of enimies,
who at the sight of the horses began to flie, and our men
to follow with suche harte and courage, that in short time
they wan the great temple agayne: then came other fiue
horsemen who ioyned with the other thrée, and lay in ambushe, where they slew. 30. *Mexicans.* The day being now
farre

farre ſpent, and the nighte at hande, *Cortes* commaunded
his army to retire, and they obeying his commandemēt,
hadde not ſo ſone turned their backes, but an inſinite
number of enimies were at their héeles, who if it hadde
not bin for the Horſemen, had ſlayne many Spanyardes,
for they came vpon them like rauening dogges without
any feare, yet with the ſuccoure of the Horſemen, the e-
nimie was putte agayne to flighte, and our men burned
many houſes, to auoyde at their next comming the daunger of ſtones whiche were throwen from their toppes,
The other Captaynes, who were *Sandoual* and *Aluarado*, fought valiantly on the other ſide of the Citie.

The great hurt and dammage in the
houſes of *Mexico* with fire.

 N this meane while, *Don Hernando* of
Tezcuco, wente throughout his Lordſhip,
to allure his vaſſall to the ſeruice and
friendſhip of *Cortes*, accordzing to his former promiſe: and whether it were ſeyng
the Spanyards proſperitie in the ſiege of
Mexico, or otherwiſe, he broughte almoſt the whole prouince of *Culhuacan*, whiche is vnder the gouernemente of
Tezcuco, with ſixe or ſeauen of his owne bréthzen, for
more he could not, although he had more than a hundred
bréthzen, as héereafter ſhall be declared. One of them
named *Iztlixuchilb* béyng a valiant yong man, of the
age of foure and twenty yeares, he appoynted generall
Captayne ouer fiftie thouſande men of warre, well armed and trimmed according to their faſhion, *Cortez* dyd
friendly receyue and welcome them, giuing them greate
thankes for their ayde and good willes. Of theſe new-
come men, he tooke into his owne hoſt thirtie thouſande,

and deuided the resedue equally among the other Capitaynes.

This was a sorrowfull newes to the *Mexicans*, to heare of the succoure which *Don Hernando* badde sente to serue *Cortes*, and with-holden the same from them, yea and also among them were come kinsmen, brethren, and fathers to many of them which were in *Mexico* in the seruice of *Quahutimoc*.

Two dayes after that these menne were come, there came also men of *Xochmilco*, and certayne husbandmen of the Mountaines, who spake the *Oromitlh* speech, beseeching *Cortes* to pardon their long tarrying, offering also both men and vittayles for the seege. *Cortes* was pleased wyth their comming and gentle offer, for they being his friends, he was assured of them of *Culhuacan*, and sayd vnto them, within these three daies (God willing) I wil combate the Citie, therefore againste that time I praye you prepare your selues accordingly, and therein shall I knowe whether you are my friendes or no: and with this aunswere they departed, promising to fulfill his requeste, as they did in deede. This done, he sente three *Vergatines* to *Sandoual*, and other three to *Aluarado*, for to disturbe anye succoure that mighte come from the land to the Citie, and likewise to defende and ayde the Spanyardes at all times, when they would land vpon the calsey, to combate the Citie, for he well vnderstwde howe profitable those vessels would be neere vnto the bridges.

The Captaines of the *Vergantines* ceased not night and day to runne the coast and Townes of the lake, where they toke manye boates from the enimies, laden with men and victuall, and permitted none to come into the Citie, nor yet any to come out.

The daye appointed to the enimies for the combate, *Cortes* made his prayers vnto God, & then enformed each

Captayne

Captayne what he should do, and came forth with twē-
tie horsemen, thrée hundred Spanyardes, and a great
number of *Indians*, with their péces of Ordinance, and
where in thrée or foure dayes before they had not skirmished, time serued the *Mexicans* at will to open al those
places which were dammed vp before, and also to builde
better bulwarkes thā those which were throwen downe,
attending with that horrible noyse accustomed. But whē
they sawe the *Vergantines* on eache side, theyr ioy was
turned into sorrowe, and beganne to fainte, the whiche
oure men vnderstood well, and therewith alanded themselues vpon the calsey, and wanne the bulwarke and the
bridge. Our army procéedyng forward, set vppon the e-
nimies, vntill they came to another bridge, the whyche
was likewise wonne in shorte time, and this pursued
from bridge to bridge, alwayes fighting, vntill they had
driuen them from the Calsey and strétes.

Cortes for his part lost no time, for he with tenne thousande *Indians* laboured to damme vp againe the sluses
and broken places of the bridges, making the way plaine
both for Horsemen and footemen: it was so much to doe,
that all those ten thousand *Indians* were occupyed therein from the morning vntill the euening.

The other Spanyards and *Indian* friends skirmished
continually, and slew many of their enimies. Likewyse
the Horsemen so scoured the strétes, that the enimies
were forced to locke them vp in their houses & Temples.
It was a notable thing to sée how our *Indians* played the
menne that daye againste the Citizens: sometimes they
would chalenge them the fielde: other times they would
conuite them to supper, and shewe vnto them legges,
armes, and other péces of mās flesh, saying behold your
owne flesh which shal serue for our supper and brekefast,
and to morrow we wil come for more, therefore flye not,

pot

you are valiant fellowes, yet it were better for you to
dye fighting than with hunger. And after all this speéch,
euery one of them called vppon the name of his owne
Towne with a loude voyce, setting fire vppon their houses. The *Mexicans* were replenished with sorrow, to seé
themselues so afflicted with Spanyardes, but yet theyr
sorrowe was the greater, to heare their owne vassals so
raile againste them, saying and crying at their owne
dores, victory, victory, *Tlaxcallan, Chalcho, Tezcuco, Xochmilco*, and other Townes: the eating of their fleshe greéued them not, for they did the like.

Cortes seéing the *Mexicans* so stoute and hard harted,
with full determination eyther to defend themselues or
else to dye, therevpon he bethought himselfe vppon two
things, the one was, that he shoulde not obteyne the treasure whiche he had seéne in the time of *Muteʒuma*: the o-
ther was, that they gaue him occasion totally to destroy
the Citie. Both these things greéued him much, but especially the destructió of the citie. He ymagined with himselfe what he mighte doe, to bring them to acknowledge
their error, and the hurt that mighte fall vpon them, and
for these considerations he pluckt downe their Towers,
and brake their idolles. He burned also the greate house
wherein he was lodged before, and the house of foule
which was neére at hád. There was not one Spanyard
who had seéne that magnificall building before, but lamented sore the sight: but to agreéue the Citiʒens, it was
commaunded to be burned. There was neuer *Mexican*,
that thought any humaine force, how much lesse so fewe
Spanyards, shoulde haue entred into *Mexico* in despite of
them all, and to sette fire vpon their principallest edifices
within the Citie. While this house was a burning, *Cortes* gathered his men, and retired to his Campe. The
Mexicans woulde fayne haue remedyed the fire, but it was

to

to late, and ſæing our men retire, they followed wyth their noyſe accuſtomed, and ſlue ſome of our men, who were laden with the ſpoyle, and came behinde the reſte. The boreſmen relieued our men, and cauſed the enimy to retire, in ſuch wiſe, that befoze night al our men were in ſafetie and the enimies in their houſes, the one ſozte full of ſozowe, and the others wearied with fighte and trauel. The ſlaughter was great that day, but the burning, and ſpoyle of houſes was greater, foz beſides thoſe which we haue ſpoken of, the Uergantines did the like where they wente, and the other Captaines alſo were not idle where they were appointed.

Things that happened to Pedro de *Aluarado through his bolde attempt.*

Edro de *Aluarado*, would paſſe his army to ŷ market place of *Tlalulco*, foz he toke much payn & ſtode in perill in ſuſteyning ŷ bzidges which he had gotten, hauing hys foztte almoſt a league frō thence. And again, he being a man of a haughtie ſtomacke, thinking as wel to get honoz as his general, and likewiſe being pzocured by his company, who ſayde, that it were a ſhame foz them if *Cortez* ſhould winne that market place, being moze nearer vnto them, than vnto him: whervpon he determined to winne thoſe bzidges which as yet wer vnwonne, and to place himſelfe in the market place. He pzocæded with all his army vntill they came to another bzoke bzidge, which was ſirtie paces of length, and two

Ab. fadom

fadome depe, the whiche with the helpe of the Wergantines, he wan in short space, and gaue order to certaine of his men to damme it vppe substancially, and he himselfe pursued his enimies, with fiftie Spaniardes. But when the Citizens sawe so few in number, and al sootemen, (for the horses coulde not passe the sluce so soone,) they came vpon them so sodainely fiercely, that they made our men to turne their backes, and trust to their legges, yea and our men fel into the water, they knewe not which way. They slew many of our *Indias*, and four Spaniards, who forthwith they sacrifised, and eate their sleshe in the open sight of al the army.

Aluarado saw his owne folly, in not beleauing *Cortes*, who had always forewarned him, not to procede soreward, vntil he had made the way sure behinde him: but *Aluarndo* his counsellers payde their counsel with like *Cortes* sorrowed for the same, for the like had happened vnto him, if he had giuen credite to their counsel. But as a prudent captain, he considered the matter better, for euery house was then an Ilande, the calsey broken in many places, and the zoties or house toppes beset with stones, for these, and suche like places vsed *Quahutimoc.Cortes* went to see where *Aluarado* had pitched hys campe, and also to rebuke him for that which was past, and to aduise him what he shold do: But when he came and found him so farre within the libertie of the Citie, and the daungerous places which hadde passed, he dyd highly comend his valiaunt and good seruice: he also communed with him of manye things concerning the siege, and then returned to his owne campe.

The

The tryumph and facrifice vvhich the
Mexicans made for their victorie.

Ortez delayed the time to pitche his campe in the market place of *Mexico*, although daily his menn entrede and fkirmifhed with in the Citie, for the caufes before alleaged, and likewife to fée if *Quahutimoc* would yæld himfelf. And alfo the entrie could not be but very daungerous, for the great multitude of enimies that filled vp the ftreates.

Al his company Spaniardes ioyntly, with the kings Treafurer, féeing the determination of *Cortes*, and the hurt already receyued, befought and alfo required him to paffe his campe vnto the market place: who aunfwered them, that they had fpoken like valiaunt men, but as yet(quoth he) it is not time conuenient, & we oughte to confider better of the matter: for why? the enimies are fully determined to ende their liues in defence of that place. But his men replyed fo muche, that hee was compelled to graunte to theyr requeffe, and proclaymed the entraunce for the nexte daye following. Hee wrote alfo in his letters to *Gonfalo de Sandoual*, & to *Pedro de Aluarado*, the inftructions of the things that they fhoulde doe, whiche was in effect, to *Sandoual*, that hee fhoulde remoue hys campe wyth all hys fardage, as thoughe he woulde retire and flye, and that vppon the calfey he fhoulde haue tenne horfemen in ambufhe, behinde certaine houfes to the intent that when the Citizens fhould efpie thé flie, and would purfue after, thé to paffe betwixt them and home with the faid horfemen, &

Bb.ij. after

after the hurt done among them, in this ſozt, that then he
with al his army ſhoulde come where *Pedro de Aluarado*
aboade, with other tenne hozſemen, a hundered fœtemen,
and the Nauye of Uergantines, and leauing with hym
his men, ſhould then take thzée of the Uergantines, and
to pzocure to winne that bzoken bzidge, where *Aluarado* of late receiued the foyle: and if he fortuned to wynne
that place, that then he ſhould damme it vp, and make it
ſure, befoze he paſſed anye further : and the like ozder he
gaue vnto him foz al other bzoken places that he ſhould
paſſe.

Unto *Aluarado* he gaue commiſſion, that he ſhoulde
paſſe as farre into the Citie as he myght poſſible, requyring him alſo to ſend vnto him eightie Spaniardes. Hé
alſo appointed the other ſeauen Uergantines, to paſſe
into both ẏ lakes, with thzée thouſand *Canoas*. He deuided
likewiſe all his army into thzée companies, bycauſe they
had thze ways to enter into the citie. By the one of theſe
wayes oz ſtreates, entred the Treaſurer and Auditoz,
with ſeauentye Spaniardes, twentie thouſande *Indians*,
eight hozſemen, twelue labourers with pickeares and
Shouels, and many other ydle felowes, to cary earth and
ſtones, and to fill vp the bzoken places, and to make the
way plaine.

The ſeconde ſtreate he commended to *George de Aluarado* and *Andres de Tapia*, with eightie Spaniardes,
tenne thouſande *Indians*, two pieces of Ozdinaunce, and
eight hozſemen. *Cortes* himſelfe toke the thirde way, wyth
a great number of friendes, and a hundzed Spaniardes
fœtemen, of the whiche were twentye fiue with Croſſebowes and Harquebuſhes, and comaunded his hozſemé
which were eight in number, to abide there behinde, and
not to folow after, vntil he ſhold ſende foz them. In thys
ozder, and al at one inſtant, they entred the Citie, ſhewing

ing the harts of baltaunt men,greatly annoying the enemy,and wan many bridges , but when they came neare
vnto ẙ towne house called *Tianquiztli*,there gathered togither such a number of the *Indian* friendes , who before
theyr eyes scaled, entred, and robbed their houses, that
they thought assuredly,that ẙ same day the citie had bin
wonne.*Cortez* commaunded that they should procede no
further, saying, that they had done sufficientlye for that
day,for also he feared afterclappes.He likewise demanded whether all the broken bridges were made sure, in
the whych(quoth he)cōsisteth the peril and victorie. But
those that went with the Treasurer, following victorie
and spoyle,had left a bridge not well dammed vp,but very hollowe and false , the whiche was of twelue paces
broad,and two fadom in depth. When *Cortez* was aduertised hereof,he went thither to remedy the same, but he
was no sooner come, when he sawe his men fleeing, and
leaping into the water, with feare of the cruel enimies,
which followed,who leapt after them into the water, to
kill them There came also along the calsey manye *Indian* boates of enimies,who toke many of ẙ *Indian* friends
and Spaniards aliue.Then *Cortes* and other fifteene persons,which were with him, serued for no other purpose
but to helpe out of the water those that were fallen,some
came wounded,and others halfe drowned, and without
armour:yea and the multitude of enimies so beset *Cortes*,
and his fifteene companions,who wer helping their mē,
and so occupyed in the same, that they had no regarde to
their owne peril. Wherupon certaine *Mexicans* layd hād
vpō *Cortes*,who truly they had carried away if it had not
bin for one *Francisco de Olea* his seruāt,who cut off at one
blowe the armes of them that had hold of him,and he by
the enemies was immediately slain , so that he died to
saue his maisters life, Then came *Antonio de Quinionez*

A kinde
harted cap-
taine.

captaine of the guard, who caught *Cortes* by the arme, ¢
by force pluckt him out of the throng of enimies, wyth
whom valiantly he fought. But thē wtth the same that
Cortez was prisoner, came many spaniards, among whō
was one horseman, who made some rowme, but in shorte
space they thrust him through the throte with a launce,
and made him to retire. The fight ceassed a little, ¢ *Cortes* had a horse brought vnto him, on the which he light-
lye amounted, and gathering his men togither, came
to the streate of *Tlacopan*, whiche was large and faire.
There died Guzman his Chamberlayne, giuing a
horse vnto his maister, whose death was much lamented among them all, for he was a man valiant, honeste,
¢ welbeloued. There fel also into the water two horses,
the one was saued, but the other was killed by the *Indians*. As the Treasurer and his company were Combatting a bulwarke, the enimies threw out of a window
thrē Spaniards heads vnto them, saying, thē like they
would do with their heads, if they went not from thence
the sooner. They sēeing this sight, and likewise cōsidered
the great hurte and spoyle made among them, began to
retire by little and little.

The *Mexican* Priestes went vp into the Towres of
Tlatelulco, and made their fiers in chafing dishes, and
put therevnto the swēete gūme of *Copalli* in token of victorie, and forthwith stripped fiftie Spaniards captiues
as naked as they were borne, and with their fine rasors
opened them in the breastes, and pluckt out their hartes
for an offering to the Idols, and sprinckled their blond
in the ayre. Our men seing before their eies the doleful
sight, would fain haue gone to reuēge the cruel custome.
But as time then required they had ynough to doe, to
put themselues in sauetie through the great troupe of
Indians which came vpon them, who now feared neither
horse

hoꝛſe noꝛ ſwoꝛd. This day as ye haue heard, were foꝛtie
Spaniards ſacrificed , and *Cortes* wounded in one of hys
legges, and thirtie moe of his men : they loſte a piece of
Oꝛdinance, and foure hoꝛſes. Alſo that day was ſlayne a-
boue two thouſand *Indian* friends, and many *Canoas* loſt
and the Bergantines in great daunger, and the captain
and maiſter of one of them were wounded. Whereof the
captaine died within eight dayes, the ſame day wer alſo
ſlaine foure of *Aluarado* his men, that daye was an vn-
foꝛtunate oꝛ diſmal day, and the nyght heauy, ſoꝛrowfull
and repleniſhed with lamentable griefe among the ſpa-
niardes and their friendes. On the other ſide, the *Mexicās*
tryumphed with ioy, and made great boneſiers, blewe
their hoꝛnes, ſtroke vp their dꝛummes, daunced, banqueted, and dꝛanke themſelues dꝛunk: they alſo opened their
ſtreats and bꝛidges, as they were befoꝛe, and placed their
ſcout and watch about the Citie. And as ſoone as it was
day, the king *Quchutimoc*, ſent two Chꝛiſtians heads, and
two hoꝛſe heads into al the comarcanes there aboute, to
ſignifye their victoꝛie and to require them to foꝛſake the
Chꝛiſtians friendſhip, pꝛomiſing in ſhoꝛt ſpace to make
the like ende of all thoſe that remayned , and deliuer the
countrey from warre, theſe things encouraged ſome pꝛouinces to take armour againſte *Cortes* being his allied
friendes, as *Malinalco* and *Cuixco*. This newes was ſoone
blowen abꝛoade into many pꝛouinces, whereuppon our
men feared rebellion among their new friends, yea and
mutinie in their owne campe , but it pleaſed god that it
fel out otherwiſe. The next day *Cortes* came out againe
to fight, to ſhewe face to the enimies, but he turned again
from the firſt bꝛidge, without doing any great act.

ſhe

The determination of Cortez to de-
ſtroy the citie of *Mexico.*

Hichimecatl, **a noble man**
of *Tlaxcallan,* (who hadde
brought the Timber of ẙ
Uergantines, frō whence
it was wrought, and was
placed in the companye
of *Aluarado* at the beginning of the ſiege of *Mexico,*) ſæing that the Spa-
niards fought not as they
wer wont to do, he alone
with ẙ men of his owne countrey, went forth to cōbate
the Citie, being a thing which twoſore he had not attēp-
ted, gaue aſſault againſt thoſe which defended a certain
bꝛidge, and with great noyſe cryed and named his City
and lynage, and in ſhoꝛt ſpace wanne the bꝛidge, where
he left foure hundered archers, and followed after the
enimie, who of induſtrie fledde, thinking to take
him at his returne, and at length the enemy returned
vppon him, where they made a fayꝛe ſkirmiſhe, foꝛ the
fight was equall. There were many hurt and ſlaine on
both ſides, ſo that with the dead carcaſſes they ſupped
at will. But they thoughte to ouerthꝛowe him at the
bꝛidge, not knowing of ẙ foure hundered archers which
were there to attend *Chichimecatls* comming, by meanes
of whome, he paſſed at pleaſure, to the greate grieſe
of the *Mexicans,* yea and remayned not a little amazed to ſæ the valoꝛ and bolde attempte of the *Tlaxcaltecas.*

                                        The

The Spanyards likewise highly commended the fact, for where oure men combated not as they were wont to do,the *Mexicās* ymagined that the cause was cowardize, infirmitie, or want of vittayles : wherevpon one daye at the sunne rising, they set vpon *Aluarado* his Camp, whiche being espyed by the watch, they began to crye,arme, arme,who came forth as well fotemen as horsemen,and put them to flight,at whiche retire many of the *Mexicans* were drowned,and others sore hurt and wounded. Then said the *Mexicans*, that they desired to talke with *Cortez*, who came vnto a drawe brydge to knowe what they would haue,vnto whome sometime they sayd,that peace was their requeſt, and other times they demanded truce, but finally required that the Spanyards should departe from that Countrey. All this policie was but to fele what ſtrength and courage our menne had, and to haue truce for a certayne time; for to prouide them of such neceſſaries as they wanted,for their determinate purpoſe was, to dye in the defence of their countrey and religion. *Cortes* aunſwered, that truce was not conueniente for eyther partie, but peace was laudable at al times,the whiche for his parte, although he hadde beſeged the Citie, should not be denyed: therfore he willed them to wey his plentifull eſtate of vittayles, and their owne nede and neceſſitie of the ſame. They being in this communication with their interpreters, appeared Guauntien a man on the toppe of the Bulwarke,who in the ſighte of them all, pluckt bread out of his ſatchell pece by pece, and began to eate,giuing them to vnderſtand, that they had no nede of vittayles, and ſo made an ende of their talke.

The ſiege of this Citie ſemed a long tame to *Cortez*, for in nere fiftie dayes that he had begun the ſame, yet could not he bring his deſire to paſſe, yea and much mar-

       Xx.   uelled,

uelled that the enimies coulde endure so long a season
with dayly skirmithing, and also how they refused peace
and concord, knowing how many thousands of them had
bin slayne, and ended their miserable liues with hunger.

Yet once agayne he sente this last message vnto them,
that if they woulde not yéelde themselues, then he ha‐
uing them enuironed by land and water, woulde slea thē
all, and not permitte anye kinde of victuall to come vnto
them, so that theyr extremitie shoulde be so greate, that
they should eate one another : their aunswere was, that
firste the Spanyardes shoulde tast of the same cuppe, so
that threatning increased their courages, and occupyed
themselues in carrying stones to the market place, and
many other strǽtes, to stoppe the way against the Hor‐
ses and their maisters.

Cortes, although it grǽued him to destroy totally so
beautifull a Citie, yet he determined to bring all the hou‐
ses of the strǽtes that he should winne to be equall with
the ground, and to stoppe with them the Chanels of wa‐
ter. He cōmuned the matter with his Captaynes, who
liked well of his intente, although it was a troublesome
thing.   He also aduertised the Gentlemen *Indians* hys
friends of his determination, who highly commended his
deuice.

Cortes séeyng the towardnesse of all his armye, he cal‐
led and prepared all his labourers, with their pikeaxes
and shouels, so that in these affaires, and in setting hys
men in good order, he spent foure dayes, and then he begā
to cōbate the strǽte, which goeth directly to the market
place, then faynedly the Cittizēs desired peace. Cortes stay‐
ed, and asked for their King : they aunswered, that they
had sentfor him, wherevpon *Cortes* taried an houre, and
then they began to reuile him, and to throwe stones, and
shot at him, The Spanyardes séeing this, gaue the onset,

                                                            and

and wanne a forte, and came into the chiefe place of the
Citie. They cleansed the stretes of the stones whiche
they had laide to disturbe their passage, and stopped so vp
the water strete in that place, in suche wise, that neuer
after it was opened againe, and threw downe all the houses, making the entrance into the Citie an open playne
high way, and then retired to their camp. Also sire dayes
arowe they did the like, without receyuing any hurt, sauing the last day two horses were hurt.

The nexte day *Cortes* laide an ambush with fiftie hors-
men, and sent before him the Uergantines, but hée himselfe with thirtie horsemen, abode in certaine great houses in the Market place. They foughte that day in many
places of the Citie, and at the retire, one shot of a handgun, whiche was the token that those whiche lay in ambushe should come forth. The enimies folowed our men,
that séemed to flée with maruellous greate courage. But
they were not so soone passed the snare, when *Cortes* came
forth with his thirtie horsemen, saying, vpon them, vpon
them: By this onely meane were slaine aboue fiue hundred *Mexicans*, besides the prisoners.

Our *Indian* friends had a good supper that nyght with
mans flesh, whiche as yet they would not be perswaded
to leaue. Certaine Spaniards went vppe into a Tower
of Idols, and there opened a sepulchre, where they found
fiue hundred Castlins in golde : With this ouerthrowe
the *Mexicans* remayned in suche feare, that all their
threatnings and triumphes were turned into mourning:
and euer after whê they saw our men retire, they would
not folow them, fearing the like danger, so that this was
a meane, the sooner to win *Mexico*.

Xr.ij.   The

The hunger and infirmitie vvhich the
Mexicans suffered with greate courage.

Wo poore soules who were vexed wyth hunger, came in the nighte season out of the citie vnto *Cortes* his Camp, who certifyed, how the Citizens were in greate necessitie, and so manye dead with hunger and sicknesse, that there were heapes of dead bodyes in the houses, only to kéepe close their extreame miserie: and said also, that in the night season manye came out to fishe betwéene the houses with feare of the *Vergantines,* and others came out to séeke for woode, hearbes, and rootes to eate.

Cortes hearing these newes, determined to knowe the troth thereof, so that the nexte night he commaunded the *Vergantines* to goe round about the Citie, and he himselfe with fiftéene Horsemen, a hundred footemen, and manye *Indian* friends, placed themselues betwixte certaine houses, with order to his espyes, to aduertise him what they shoulde sée. It was no sooner day, but manye poore folke came out to séeke for foode, and when *Cortes* had intelligence thereof, he made a greate slaughter among them, whereas at that time of vnarmed men, women, and chyldren, were slayne to the number of eyght hundred: and the *Vergantines* on their side made another spoyle. The pitiful noise being heard into the Citie, the Citizens were astonyed, and knew not what to doe, fearing the like ambushe that they had séene and fealt the day before, & also wondered, that at such an houre not accustomed, y Spanyardes were so nigh. The next day following, béeing S. Iames his euen, *Cortes* entred againe into the Citie, accordyng as he had done before, and wanne the stréete of *Tlacopan,* where he burned the riche and faire houses of

A cruell fact of Cortez.

of king *Quabutimoc*, whiche were motted round aboute: so
that nowe of foure partes of the citie, thꝛee partes were
wonne, and the Spaniardes might safely passe from *Cor-*
tes his campe, to the campe of *Aluarado*, by reason that all
the houses were burned, and beaten downe playne with
the grounde.

But yet the poꝛe *Mexicans* would say to the *Indians* of
Tlaxcallan, goe to, go to, make hast, burne and destroy these
houses, foꝛ time will come that yꝛ shall buylde them a-
gaine at your owne coste. Foꝛ if we haue victoꝛy then
shall ye buylde them foꝛ vs, and if we be ouercome then
shall yꝛ buylde them foꝛ these straungers. A true pro-
phesie.

Within foure dayes after, *Cortes* entred the citie a-
gaine, and also *Aluarado* on his side, who to shewe hys
haultie stomacke, laboured all that was possible to gette
two towers of the temple of *Tlatelulco*, the whiche at the
length he wan, although he loste thꝛee hoꝛses in the cōbat.

The next day followyng, the hoꝛsemen walked vp and
downe in the greate market place at pleasure, the poꝛe
Mexicans beholding that soꝛowful sight frō their houses.
And as the Spaniardes wente walking in the cittie, they
founde heapes of dead bodies in the houses, streates, and
in the water: they found also the barke of trees and rootes An ex-
treme pe-
nurie.
gnawen by the hungry creatures, and the men so leane
and yellow, that it was a pitifull sighte to beholde. *Cortes*
yet agayne required them to yeelde, and they although
they were so leane of body were strong in harte, and answered that he should not speake of any friendshippe, noꝛ
yet hope of their spoyle, foꝛ when no foꝛtune would fauour them, then they woulde eyther burne their treasure, oꝛ thꝛowe it into the lake, where they should neuer
pꝛofite therby, and that they would fight while one alone
shoulde remayne aliue. At *Cortes* his next entry into the
citie, he founde the streates full of women, childꝛen, olde

folke, and many miserable sicke persons whiche were pe-
rishyng for want of foode.

Cortes commaunded that none of his army should doe
any hurte vnto such miserable creatures. The principall
folke who were whole and sounde, they stode in their soties or house toppes, without weapon, and clothed in mã-
tels. It was thought that they kepte a certaine holy day,
peace was againe offered, but they answered with dissi-
mulation. The next day followyng Cortes required Aluarado on his side to combat a streat of ,1000. houses that
was not yet won, and that he would doe the like on the o-
thersyde: for a little space the Citizens defended theselues,
but their defence endured not, but were driuen to flie, being not able to resiste the force of theyr contraries. So
that the Spanishe army wan also that streate, and slewe
12000. Cittizens, the murder was so great bicause the Indian friends would shewe no mercie or compassion vpon
them, although they were required to the cõtrary. So that
now the Mexicans hauing lost this streate also, the houses
that were not beatẽ downe could scarcely hold the people
y̆ were aliue, the streates also being so full of dead car-
casses and sicke bodies, that our men coulde not passe but
must needes treade vpon them. Cortes desirous to sée what
remayned of the cittie to win, went vp into a high tower,
and hauyng well vewed the Cittie, he iudged that of eight
parts one remained yet to win. And y̆ next day following
he assaulted the same, with speciall cõmaundement giuen
to his army, not to kil any but only such as should resist:

The sorrowful Citizens bewayling their vnfortunate
fate & destinie, besought the Spaniards to make an ende,
and to kill them all out of hande. Then certayne of the
horsemen called Cortes in great hast, who went vnto them
incontinent, hopping of some agrement of peace: and standing at the brymme of the water neare vnto a drawe
bridge,

bꝛidge,the *Mexicans* ſayde, oh captayne *Cortes*,conſideryng that thou art the childe of the Sunne,why doeſt thou not entreate the Sunne thy father,to make an ende of vs: oh thou Sunne that canſt goe rounde about the woꝛlde in a day and a night,we pꝛay thée make an end of vs,and take vs out of this miſerable lyfe,foꝛ we deſire death to go and reſt with our God *Quetcauatlh* who tarieth foꝛ vs. After theſe ſpeaches they made a lamentable/crie,callyng vpon their Goddes with loude voyces.*Cortes* anſwered what he thought good, but yet could not perſwade them to yéelde, truely it was a pitefull ſight to beholde. _{A ſorovv-full tale.}

The impriſonment of Quahutemoc.

ortes ſeing the great extremitie that theſe pooꝛe wꝛetched people were in, thinkyng nowe that they woulde yéelde vnto him, therevppon hée ſpake to an vncle of *Don Hernando de Tezcuco,* who was taken pꝛiſoner thꝛée dayes befoꝛe,whom he deſireꝺ to go to the king & treate of peace: this Gentleman refuſes the meſſage, knowyng the determinate will of *Quahutimoc,* but thꝛough muche entreatie he graunted to his requeſt. So the next day followyng *Cortes* entred into the Cittie,& ſent that Gentleman & certaine Spaniardes befoꝛe him. The *Indian* guarde of that ſtreate receyued him with the honour which vnto ſuch a noble man did appertayne. He pꝛocéeded foꝛward toward the king,& being comſe where he was,he declared vnto him his embaſſage. When *Quahutimoc* had hearde his tale, he was ſo moued with pꝛe & choller,that foꝛthwith he commaūded him to be ſacrificed,and gaue the Spaniardes foꝛ theyꝛ anſwere blowes with ſtones, ſtaues and arrowes, ſaying alſo that they deſired death and no peace, and fought ſo ſtout- ly that day, that they ſlewe many of our menne, and one hoꝛſe. Lykewiſe on their ſide many were ſlayne. _{An euil re-vvarde,}

The

The nexte day *Cortes* entred the cittie agayne, but he fought not, hoping then that they woulde submitte themselues, but yet the Citizens had no such thought. He came néere vnto a certayne bulwarke on horsebacke, and spake vnto certaine Gentlemen with whome he was acquaynted, saying that now within a shorte space he could make an ende of their finall destruction, but yet of meare compassion he wished it not, for the loue whiche he bare vnto them, so that they would in time réder themselues: wherfore (quoth he) entreate yée the king to doe the same, and in so doyng ye shalbe well vsed, and haue victuals sufficient. The Gétlemen hearing these wordes, fell on weping, and answered, that now they knew well their errour, and felte their losse and destruction, notwithstáding they were bounde to obey their king and Goddes. But yet (quoth they) abide a while, and we will certifie *Quahutimoc* what you haue sayde, and in shorte space they went and returned againe, saying that the next day without fayle their Lord woulde come and talke with him in the markette place. With this answere *Cortes* returned to his campe, and thought at their méeting to concluce an honorable peace. So against the next day he caused a Canapie and chayre of estate to be sette in the markette place, accordyng to the *Mexican* vse, and also a dinner to be prepared. Thé day followyng came *Cortes* at the houre appoynted, with many of his men armed, but the king came not: neuerthelesse he sente fiue noble men to treate of the matter, excusing the kyng, saying he was not well at ease. *Cortes* welcomed those Gentlemen, and was gladde of their cóming, hoping thereby to concluce and make some good ende. And when they had dined and well refreshed their hungry bodies, *Cortes* gaue them victuals, and desíred them to returne agayne to the King, and to declare vnto him that without his presence the conclusion coulde not be

certaine.

certayne. They wente and returned againe within two
houres, and brought vnto Cortes certaine mantels made of
cotten woll, very good & well wrought, with anſwere that
the king would not come in any wiſe, both foz ſhame and
feare. And the next day theſe meſſengers came agayn, ſaying that the king would come to the place appointed. But
yet he came not, although Cortes attended his commiyng
moze than foure houres: who ſeing the mockerie, he foꝛthwith ſente Sandoual with his Uergantines one way, and
he himſelf went an other, combatting the houſes & foꝛtes
that yet remayned, where he founde ſmall reſiſtaunce, ſo
that he might doe what he pleaſed. There was that day
ſlayne and taken pꝛyſoners aboue. 40060. perſons, & then
he retired to his campe. The lamentable crie and mourning of the women and childꝛen woulde haue made a ſto-
ny hart relent, the ſtench alſo of the dead bodies was wõ-
derfull noyſome. That night Cortes purpoſed to make an
end the next day of the warres, and Quahutimoc pꝛetended
to flie, and foꝛ that purpoſe had enbarked hymſelfe in a
Canoa of twẽtie oꝛes. When the day appeared Cortes, with
his men, and foure peeces of oꝛdinance, came to the coꝛner
where thoſe that yet remayned were ſhut vp, as cattell in
a pounde. He gaue oꝛder to Sandoual and Aluarado what
they ſhold do, which was, to be ready with their Uergã-
tines, and to watche the comyng out of the Canoas whiche
were bidden betwixte certayne houſes, and eſpecially to
haue regard vnto the kings perſon, and not to hurte hym,
but to take him aliue. He commaunded the reſidue of hys
men to foꝛce the Mexican boates to goe out, and he himſelfe wente vp into a tower, inquiryng foꝛ the king, and
there founde Xihuacon, gouernour and Captayne generall of the Cittie, who woulde in nowiſe yeelde himſelfe.
Then came out of the Cittie a greate multitude of olde
folkes, men, women and childꝛē to take boate. The thꝛong
Pp. was

was so great with hast to enter the *Canoa*, that many by
that means were drowned in the lake. *Cortes* required his
mē not to kil those miserable creatures: But yet he could
not stay the *Indians* his friends, who slewe and sacrificed
aboue fiftene thousand. After this, there was a great rumour among the cōmon people, that the king would flie,
making a piteous mone and saying that they sorowfull
creatures knew not whither to goe: But yet procuryng
to goe into the *Canoas*, whiche were so full that there was
no roume for thē, by reason thereof many were drowned.

The men of warre stode in the house toppes and roties
beholding their perdition. All the nobilitie of *Mexico*
were enbarked with the kyng. Then *Cortes* gaue signe
with the shotte of a handgunne, that his captaines should
be in a readinesse, so that in shorte space they wanne fully
and wholy the great Cittie of *Mexico*. The Uergantines
likewise brake in among the fleete of boates, without any
resistaunce, and euery one sought where he might beste
succour himselfe, the Royall Standarte was beaten
downe. *Garcia Holguin*, who was captayne of a Uergantine, had espied a great *Canoa* of .xx. ores deepe laden with
men. And one of his prysoners sayde vnto him, that the
king wente in that greate *Canoa*. *Holguin* beyng gladde of
the newes, gaue chase to that *Canoa* and ouertoke him.
In his foreship he had three crossebowe men. And when
Quahutimoc who stode on the puppe of the *Canoa* ready to
fighte, sawe those bowes ready bente, and many drawen
swordes, he yeelded himselfe, declaryng that he was the
king. *Garcia Holguin* being a gladde man of his prysoner,
toke and carried him vnto *Cortes* who receiued him reue-
rently. When *Quahutimoc* came neare vnto him, he layde
his hande vpon *Cortes* his dagger, saying, I haue done all
my possibility to defende me and mine, accordyng to my
duetie, hoping not to haue come to this estate and place
                                                           where

where now I ſtande: And conſidering that you may doe with me what you pleaſe, I beſeeche you to kill me, and that is my only requeſt. *Cortes* comforted him with faire wordes, giuyng him hope of life and ſeniory, and toke him vp into a zotie, requiring him to commaund his ſubiectes to yælde and render themſelues: he obeyed his requeſt. At that time there was about thre ſcore and tenne thouſande perſons, who in ſeing their Prince, threwe downe their weapons, and ſubmitted themſelues.

The taking of Mexico.

IN the order before declared, wanne *Hernando Cortes* the famous cittie of *Mexico*, on tueſday being the xiij. of Auguſt, *An.1521.* in remembraunce wherof, and of the great victory, euery yære on that day they make a ſumptuous feaſt & ſolemne proceſſion, wherin is carried the ſtandart royall, with the whiche the cittie was won. The ſiege endured thre moneths, & had therein. 200000. *Indians*, 900. Spaniardes. 80. horſes. 17. pæces of ordinaunce, 13. Vergantines, 6000. *Canoas*. In this ſiege were ſlayne fiftie Spaniardes & ſixe horſes, & no great number of the *Indians* their friends. There was ſlaine on the cótrary ſide a hundred thouſand, and ſome affirme many moe: but I ſpeake not of them that died with hunger and peſtilence.

At the defence of the citie were al the nobilitie, by reaſon wherof many were ſlayne. The multitude of people was great, who eate litle, dranke ſalte water, and ſlepte among the dead bodies, where was a horrible ſtenche: for theſe cauſes the diſeaſe of peſtilence fell among them, and thereof died an infinite number. Wherevpon is to be conſidered, their ſtedfaſte determination, for although they were afflicted with ſuch hunger, that they were dryuen to eate boughes, ryndes of trées, and to drinke ſalte

water,

water, yet woulde they not yéelde themselues. But at the
laste they woulde haue submitted them, and then their
kyng Quahutimoc woulde not, bycause at the begynnyng
they refused his will and counsell, and also with their generall deaths, should appeare no cowardise, for they kept
the dead bodies in theyr houses to kéepe that secrete from
theyr enimies. Here also is to bée noted, that although
the Mexicans eate mans fleshe, yet they eate none of their
owne Cittie or friendes, as some doe thynke: for if they
had, there woulde not so many haue died with hunger.
The Mexican women were highly commended, not onely
bycause they aboade with their husbandes and Fathers,
but also for the greate paynes they toke with the sicke
and wounded persons, yea and also they laboured in makyng slings, cuttyng stones fitte for the same, and throw-
yng stones from the soties, for therein they dyd as muche
hurte as their men. The Cittie was yéelded to the spoyle,
and the Spanyardes toke the Golde, Plate and Feathers, the Indian friendes had all the rest of cloth and other
stuffe.

Cortes commaunded greate bonfiers to be made in token of victory, and also to mortifie the horrible stenche
of the dead bodies, whome he lykewise commaunded to
be buried, and some of the prysoners menne and women
he caused to be marked in the face, for the Kings slaues,
and pardoned all the residue. He commaunded the Uergantines to bée brought ashore, and appoynted one Villa
fuerte, with 80 men to guarde thé, fearyng least the Mexicans shold set fire or otherwise destroy them. In this businesse he occupied himself foure dayes, & then remoued his
campe to Culhuacan, where he rendred hartie thanks to all
the Gentlemen his friendes, promysing to gratifie their
good and faythfull seruice, desiryng them to departe
home to theyr houses, considering the warre was at an end,
wherevpon

wherevpon they departed almoſt all in generall, both rich and iocond with the ſpoyle of *Mexico*, and alſo to remayne in the fauour and grace of *Cortes*,

Maruellous ſignes and tokens of the
deſtruction of *Mexico*.

Ot long before *Hernando Cortes* came vnto the newe *Spayne*, did many nightes after the midnightꝭ appeare in the aire, and in the ſame port and place where *Cortes* entred into that land, great lightning of fire, whiche amounted vpward, and ſuddaynely vaded away. The *Mexicans* at that time ſaw flames of fire toward the orient, where now *Vera Crux* ſtandeth, with a great and thicke ſmoke, that ſéemed to touche the heauen and earthe: thys ſight was fearefull vnto them.

They alſo ſaw the figures of armed men fighte in the aire one with another, a new and ſtrange ſight for them, and a thing that filled their heads with ymaginations: for when there was a prophecie ſpoken of among them, how that white men with beardes ſhould come and rule their kingdome in the time of *Mutezuma*. The Lordes of *Mexico* and *Tlacopan* were much amazed, ſaying, that the ſword whiche *Mutezuma* hadde, was the armes of thoſe folke, whoſe figures they had ſéene in the ayre, with their apparell and attire. *Mutezuma* had muche adoe to pacifie them, ſaying that the weapon and apparell was of hys forefathers, and bycauſe they ſhould ſée the troth thereof, he gaue them the ſworde, and willed them to breake it if they coulde, and they prouing to breake the ſame and could not, they maruelled thereat, and alſo were reſolued of their opinions.

It ſhould ſéeme, that a little before theſe things happened,

pened, some of *Mutezuma* his subiectes founde a cheſt of apparell and a ſworde in it on the ſea coaſt, which came floting out of ſome ſhippe that had wracked there about, and broughte it to their prince. Others affirme, that the cauſe of alteration among the noble men, was, when they ſaw the ſword and apparell that *Cortes* had ſent vnto *Mutezuma* by *Teudilli*, ſeeing it a thing ſo like the attire of the figures whiche they had ſeene in the ayre, but howſoeuer it was, they beleeued with theſe new tokens, that their kingdome ſhoulde haue an ende, when they ſaw thoſe ſtraungers come into their Countrey.

The ſame yeare that *Cortes* came into *Mexico*, appeared a viſion vnto a certaine *Malli*, which is to ſay, a ſlaue taken in the warres to be ſacrificed, who at the time of his deathe and Sacrifice, bewayled his ſorrowfull ende, calling vppon the God of Heauen, who at that inſtante ſawe in ſpirite a viſion, and heard a voyce, bidding hym not to feare that death, for the God whome he had called vpon, would haue mercy vpon hym, willing hym alſo to ſay vnto the prieſtes and miniſters of the Idols, that their wicked ſacrifice and bloudſheding was neere at an ende, and that there was a people at hand, that ſhould take away all that wicked and abhominable religion.

This *Malli* was ſacrificed in the middeſt of the market place of *Tlatelulco*, where at this daye is the place of execution.

They remembred, and noted well the wordes of the *Malli*, and the viſion whiche they called a breath from heauen.

The earth alſo brake open, out of the whiche iſſued a maruellous greate ſtreame of water, with many greate fiſhes, which they iudged and held for a ſtrange pronoſtication.

The *Mexicans* did reporte, that when on a time *Mutezuma*

zuma came triumphantly with victozy of *Xochmuxco*, said
vnto the Lozde of *Culhuacan*: Now (quoth he) *Mexico* is
strong and inuincible, foz I haue in subiecti..n *Xochmuxco*,
and other pzouinces, so that now I am without feare of
any enemie. The Lozd of *Culhuacan* aunswered, saying,
trust not good lucke too muche, foz one fozce fozceth another, with the whiche aunswere, *Mutezuma* was not a
little offended. But when *Cortes* hadde taken them both
pzisoners, then he called to remembzance the fozmer
talke, and held that saying foz a pzophesie.

The building vp agayne of
Mexico.

Ortes pzetended to reedifie againe the Citie of *Mexico*, not onely foz the scituation
and maiestie, but also foz the name & great
fame thereof, and also to builde vp that
which he hadde beaten downe, by reason
whereof he trauelled to make this Citie greater, better,
and to be moze replenished with people. He named and
appoynted Judges, Aldermen, Attourneys, Towneclearke, Notaries, Skauengers, and Seriants, with all
other officers, necessarie foz the common weale of a Citie. He deuided the Citie among the Conquerozs, hauing first taken out places foz Churches, market places,
townehouse, and other necessarie plottes to builde houses, pzofitable foz the common weale. He also separated
the dwellings of the *Spanyards* from the *Indias*, so that the
water passeth and maketh deuision betwixt them. Hee
pzocured many *Indians* to come to the building of the Citie, foz auoiding charges, although therein he had somewhat to do, by reason that many kinsmen of *Quahutimoc*
were not as yet come vnder obedience.

He

He made Lozde of *Tezcuco*, *Don Carolus Iztlixuchitl*, by the consent of the Citie, in place of *Don Hernando* his bzother, who was deceassed, and commaunded many of hys vassals to labour in the wozkes, bycause they were Carpenters, masons, and builders of houses. He pzomised also to them that were naturals of the Citie of *Mexico*, plottes to build vpon, inheritance, freedome, and other liberties, and the like vnto all those that woulde come and inhabite there, whiche was a meane to allure many thither. He sette also at libertie *Xihuaco* the generall Captayne, and made him chiefe ouer the *Indians* in the Citie, vnto whome he gaue a whole stræte. He gaue likewyse another stræte to *Don Pedro Mutezuma*, who was sonne to *Mutezuma* the King. All this was done, to winne the fauoure of the people. He made other Gentlemen Seniozs of little Ilands and stræetes to builde vpon, and to inhabite, and in this ozder the whole scituation was reparted, and the wozke began with great ioy and diligence: but when the fame was blowen abzoade, that *Mexico* should be built againe, it was a wonder to sæ the people that resozted thither, hearing of libertie & freedome, the number was so greate, that in a whole league compasse was nothing but people both men and women. They laboured soze, and eate little, by reason whereof, many sickned, and pestilence followed, whereof dyed an infinite number. Their paines was great, foz they bare on theyz backes, and dzew after them stones, earth, timber, lyme, bzicke, and all other things necessary in this sozt, and by little and little, *Mexico* was built againe with a hundzed thousande houses, moze stronger and better than the olde building was. The Spanyardes also built their houses after the Spanish fashion. *Cortes* built his house vpon the platte where *Mutezuma* his house stode, whiche renteth now yéerely foure thousand duckates a yeare. *Pamfilo de Naruaez*

Naruaez accused him for the same, saying, that he hadde
spoyled the woodes and mountaynes, and spente seauen
thousand beames of Ceder trées in the worke of his own
house. The number séemeth more héere than there, for
where all the Mountaynes are replenished with Ceder
trées,it is a small matter.   There are Gardines in *Tezcuco*, that haue a thousand Ceder trées for walles and circuite, yea and there are Ceder trées of a hundred & twéty
foote long,and twelue foote in compasse from ende to end.
They built faire dockes couered ouer with arches for þ
Uergantines, whereas(for a perpetuall memorie)all the
thirtéene Uergantines do remayne vntil this day. They
dammed vp the stréetes of water, where now faire houses stand, so that *Mexico* is not as it was wont to be, yea
and since the peace of 1524.the lake decreaseth,and sometime casteth out a vapour of stench, but otherwise it is
a wholesome and temperate dwelling, by reason of the
Mountaynes that standeth round about it, and well prouided through the fertilitie of the Countrey, and commoditie of the lake, so that now is *Mexico* one of the greatest Cities in the world, and the most noble in all *India*,
as well in armes as policie.   There are at the least two
thousande Citizens, that haue each of them his horse in
his stable, with riche furniture for them. There is also
great contractation, and all sortes of occupations. Also
a money house, where money is dayly coyned: a large
schole, whiche the Uizeroy *Don Antonio de Mendosa* caused to be made. There is a greate difference betwixte
an inhabitant of *Mexico*,and a Conqueror,for a Conqueror is a name of honor, and hathe landes and rentes,and
the inhabitante or onely dweller payeth rente for hys
house. When this Citie was a buildong,& not through-
lye furnished, *Cortes* came from *Culhuacan* to dwell there.
The fame of *Cortes*,and maiestie of *Mexico*, was blowen

abroade into farre prouinces, by meanes whereof, it is now so replenished, as I haue before declared, yea & hath so many *Spanyards*, who haue conquered aboue 400. leagues of land, being all gouerned by the princely seate of *Mexico*.

Hovv the Emperour sent to take accompt *of Cortes of his gouernement in the newe Spayne.*

IN these dayes *Cortes* was the man of the greatest name of all the Spanish nation, although many had defamed him, and especially *Pamfilo de Naruaez*, who was in the Court of Spaine accusing him. And where, of long time the Counsell of *India* had receyued no letters from him, they suspected, yea and beléeued, whatsoeuer euil was spoken of him. Whereupon they prouided the Admirall *Don Diego Colon*, for Gouernour of *Mexico*, who at that time went to lawe wyth the king, pretending the said office and many others, with condition to carrie at his owne coast a thousand men to apprehend *Cortes*. They prouided also for Gouernour of *Panuco*, one *Nonio de Gusman*, and *Simon de Alcaçaua* portingall, for gouernour of *Honduras*. To kindle more thys mischiefe, and to set this businesse forward, one *Iohn de Ribera*, the Attourney of *Cortes*, was a fitte and an earnest instrument against his maister, and the cause was, for falling out with *Martin Cortes*, father vnto *Hernando Cortes*, about foure thousand Duckates which *Cortes* had sent by him to his father, which money the said *Ribera* his Attourney kept to his owne vse, and therefore raised many slaunders against his maister, yea and credite was giuen to his tales, but on a night he had a morsell of bacon gyuen him vppon a skaffolde, wherewith he was choked in the

the chiefe time of his businesse. These newe officers, and
their prouisions, were not so secretely obteyned, but the
matter was as secretely talked in the Courte, whiche at
that time was abiding in the Citie of *Toledo*, and the pro
cedings seeme not iust vnto the friends of *Cortes*. The
Commendador *Pedro de Piña* opened the matter to the Li
cenciat *Nonez*, and vnto father *Melgarejo*, whereuppon
they reclaymed of the Counsels determination, bese
ching them to stay for a season, to se what newes should
come from *Mexico*. Also the Duke of *Beiar* tendred the
cause of *Hernando Cortez*, for that *Cortez* by promise of
faith and troth, was assured in marriage to his brothers
daughter, named the Lady *Iane de Zuniga*, who aplaked
the Emperoure his anger, and the saide Duke became
suretie to aunswere in all causes for him.

The matter standing in this estate, there arriued in
Spayne Diego de Zoto, with a whole Coluerin made of sil
uer, and 70000. castlins in golde, the newes whereof was
blowen ouer all *Spaine*. And to say the troth, this presente
was ý cause, that *Cortes* was not put out of his office, but
a Iudge of residence was sent thither to take an accompt
of him. Now a wise and a learned man was sought for
that purpose, yea suche a one as could rule the matter, for
some souldiers are oftentimes vnmanerly: wherupon they
thought the Licenciat, *Lewes pance de Leon* a fitte man, who
had bin Lieutenante to *Don Martin de Cordoua*, Earle of
Alcaudete, & chiefe gouernour of the citie of *Tolledo*. This
Licenciate with power sufficient, was sent vnto the new
spaine, who carried in his company as assistant, the bat-
cheler *Marcos de Agaillon*, who hadde ruled in time past,
in a worshipfull office of Iustice in the Ilande of *Santo
Domingo*.

With prosperous weather they departed from
Spayne, and in shorte tyme arriued at *Vera Cruz*,
Cortes

Cortez hauing newes of their arriuall by foote poftes within two dayes. And vppon Midfomer day came letters to *Cortes* from the Licenciate *Ponce*, with another letter from the Emperour, wherby he vnderftood ye caufe of their comming. He returned backe incontinēt an aunfwere, and defired to know which way he would come to *Mexico*, eyther by ye way inhabited, oz elfe the other way which is néerer. The Licenciate replyed, that he woulde foz a while abide in *Vera Crux*, to refrefh himfelfe, béeping feaficke, and a man ye had not héeretofoze at any time paffed the feas, thinking that *Cortes* meante to haue done iuftice on certain offenders, yea ⁊ alfo to haue takē hym by the way: wherefoze he fufpected, that *Cortes* had fent, bycaufe he woulde knowe whiche way he meant to come, wherevpon he fecretely tooke poft hozfe, with certaine Gentlemē, and other religious perfons that came in hys company, ⁊ paffed thzough the Townes, although it was the farther way, and made fuche hafte, that in fiue dayes he came to *Iztacpallapan*, refufing the entertaynement and pzouifion of meate and lodging that *Cortes* had pzepared by his Gentlemē, that wēt both the wayes to méete him.

In *Iztacpallapā* they recepued him with great feaft and maieftie, but after dinner, the Licenciate fell a bomiting, and the moft of hys companye, and after the bomite, they fell into a flire. They thoughte that certayne hearbes was the caufe thereof, whiche were in a diffe of curdes. The Licenciate was fomewhat gréedie of the curdes, and tooke the diffe, and offered it to father *Thomas Ortiz*, no (quoth the Stelwarde) hys reuerence fhall haue another diffe, no (quoth father *Ortiz*) I will none of thefe, noz yet of anye other, of whythe wozdes there were afterwardes Uerfes made, fufpecting fomething of the curdes: but truely there was no hurte, oz anye euill thyng putte in them, (as héreafter
fhall

halbe declared)for the Comendador, Proano, who was then chiefe Sheriffe, did eate of all those dishes, yea in the same dishe that the Licenciat eate of, who neyther vomited nor yet recepued any hurte or alteration. But I thinke, that they comyng hoate, wery and hungry, did eate to muche, and dranke also colde water, whereby their stomackes reuolted, and thereof followed the fluxe with vomite. On the behalfe of Cortes there was presented to the Licenciat a riche present, but he refused it.

Cortes with al the flower of Gentlemen in Mexico, came to receyue him, and giuyng him the right hand, they went togyther vntill they came to Sainct Frances abbay, where after their praiers made, Cortes demaunded to see the kings prouisions, who answered, that the nexte day he woulde shew them vnto him: then they accompanied him to his house, where he was well lodged.

The nexte day followyng, all the magistrates of the Cittie mette the Licentiat in the cathedrall Church, and by acte, before the notary, he presented his auctoritie from the Emperour. He toke the Mares of Justice from the Judges and Sargeants, and incontinent restored them agayne, and saide with gentle speach, this rodde of the Senior gouernour, I will haue for my selfe. Cortes with all the other Magistrates kissed the Emperours letters, and put them vpon the crowne of their heads, in toke of great obedience, saying, that they woulde obserue and obey all that was therein contayned, as the commaundement of their king and Lorde, reqnyring the same to be set downe by acte and testimony.

After these things done, they proclaymed the residence and account of iustice, of Hernando Cortes, to the intent that all persons who coulde accuse him of any vnrightful dealyng, shoulde come and make their complaint, and to haue remedy for the same. There shoulde you then see the stirre and talke among them, euery officer fearyng his owne cause, with defire to fée the ende of their bufinelle.

The death of the Licenciat
Luys Ponce.

He Licenciat comming one day from *Saint Frances* abbay from feruice, fell into an extréeme burnyng feuer, and lay him downe in his bedde, where he remayned the fpace of thrée dayes, as a man out of his wittes, and the feuer ftil encreafing, fo that on the feuenth day he yéelded vp the ghoft. In the time of his fickenelle he receyued the communion, and made his lafte will & teftament. He left for fubftitute in his office, the bacheler *Marcus de Aguillar.* Cortes made as greate forrow for his death, as if he had bene his owne father, his funeralles were celebrated with great pompe.

The enimies of *Cortes* publifhed, that he died of poyfon. But the Licenciat *Pero Lopez,* and Doctor *Hoieda,* who were his Phifitions, fwore that he died of a burnyng feuer, and fhewed a further confequence, that the euenyng before he deceafed, he defired them to play the measures vpon a lute, and as he lay in his bedde, fhewed with ftirryng his féete the compalles and pointes of the daunce. It was a thing which diuers perfons faw, and forthwith he loft his fpeach, and that night towarde the dawning of the day he yéelded vp his fpirite. I thinke that fewe men do die dauncing, as this Lawier did. The number of a hundred perfons came out of Spayne with the Licenciat, whereof the mofte parte died by fea and on the lande. It was fufpected to be a peftilence, for one of them infected another. There were in his company many Gentlemen & ech of them had an office. There was a Frier who was

A madde daunce.

a very flaunterous fellow, & repozted that *Cortes* had poy-
foned the Licenciat, and alſo that the Licenciat had an ex-
preſſe ozder from the Emperour to cut of *Cortes* his head,
as ſone as he had taken the Mare of Juſtice from him.
The ſubtle Frier, had thought to haue gotten money of
the one, and thankes of the other, and at the ende had nothyng.

Hovv Cortez came into *Spayne.*

Here one *Alonſo de Eſtrada* gouerned the
ſtate of *Mexico*, as ſubſtitute of *Marcus de
Aguillar*, accozdyng to the Emperours
commaundement, *Cortes* conſidered with
himſelfe that it was not poſſible for him
to haue agayne his office, except he wente
perſonally to the Emperours court, where he had many
aduerſaries and fewe friendes, ſo that he was afflicted on
euery ſide: yet he in fine determined to goe into Spayne,
as well for buſineſſe of impoztaunce of his owne, as alſo
matters touchyng the Emperour and his new kingdoms
whereof I will reherſe particularly ſome.

As touchyng his owne cauſes, firſt he beyng a man of
god yeeres, went to marry, hoping to haue childzen, vnto
whom he might leaue the profite of his labour and payne:
alſo to appeare befoze the King his maiſter face to face,
and to enfozme his Maieſtie what Landes and Kyng-
domes he had wonne and bzought vnto his royall
crowne. To ſignifie lykewiſe vnto hym, of the diſſention among the Spanyardes hys ſubiectes in *Mexico*,
and to anſwere for himſelfe, to any falſe repoztes whiche
had bene made agaynſt hym: And finally, to recevue
a condigne rewarde for hys wozthie and faythfull ſeruice. *Cortes* beyng in theſe imaginations, there was
bzought

bzought a letter vnto him, from the reuerend father *Garcia de Loaisa* ghoſtly father vnto the Emperour, and afterwarde was ozdeyned Cardinall, in the whiche letter he conuited him earneſtly to come vnto Spayne, to the entent that the Emperours Maieſtie mighte bothe ſée and know him, aſſuring him of his friendſhippe. After the recepte of this letter, he made al the haſt poſſible to departe vpon his iourney, ceaſing from his vopage whiche he had in hande, foz to inhabite the riuer *De las Palmas*. Befoze his departure he diſpatched two hundzed Spaniardes, & thzée ſcoze and ten hozſemen, with many *Mexicans* foz the countrey of *Chichimea*, to inhabite there, finding the lande riche of ſiluer mines, as it was repozted, giuyng vnto thoſe men expzeſſe ozder, that if the people of that pzouince did not entertayne them with friendſhip, that then they ſhould accept thē as enimies, and fozthwith to make warre, and to take them foz ſlaues, foz that they are a barbarous people. He wzote his letter to *Vera Crux*, to pzepare with all ſpéde two good ſhippes, and foz that purpoſe he ſent *Pero ruiz de Eſquiuel*, who was a Gentleman of Siuill : But he wente not on the iourney, foz a moneth after, they founde him buried in a little Iland of the lake, with one hande out of the graue, whiche was eaten with dogges and foule : he was buried in his dublet and his hoſe : he had one onely wounde in his fozehead : And a *Negro*, his ſlaue, who wente in his company, was neuer hearde of, noz yet the *Canao* and *Indians* that wente with him, ſo that the truth of his death was neuer knowen.

   Cortes made an Inuentary of his moueable goodes, whiche was balued at two hundzed thouſande Caſtlins of golde : he left foz gouernour of his owne eſtate, the Licenciat *Altamirano* his kinſman, with other two friends : he furniſhed two ſhippes, and pzoclaymed frée paſſage and victuals vnto all thoſe that would goe in his company.

he

he shipped for his owne account a thousand fiue hundred markes of siluer, twentie thousand Castlins in good gold, and ten thousand Castlins of base golde. He tooke in his company *Gonsalo de Sandoual*, *Andres de Tapia*, and other of the chiefest of the conquerours. He brought with him a Sonne of *Mutezuma*, & another Sonne of *Maxixca*, who was become a Christian, & named *Don Lorenso*, with many other *Indian* Gentlemen of *Mexico*, *Tlaxcallan*, and other cities: eight players with a cudgell, twelue tenis players, with certaine men & women of that countrey, who were white of colour, and other dwarfes & deformed persons. He brought also wilde beasts, as Tigres, & other strange beastes called *Aiotochtli*, and one *Tlaquaci*. Moreouer he brought a great number of mantels made of feathers & Conny heare, Targets, bushes or tuffes of galant feathers, and looking glasses of stone. In fine, he came lyke a great Lorde, & arriued in Spayne, in the ende of the yéere 1528. the Courte being then in *Tolledo*. The newes of his arriuall was blowen through out all Spayne, and euery one desirous to sée him.

The honour vvhiche the Emperour
shewed vnto Hernando Cortes, with rewarde.

He Emperour receyued *Cortes* magnifically, and to giue him the greater honour, he went & visited him at hys owne lodging.

The Emperour beyng in a readinesse to passe into Italy, to be there crowned with the Emperiall crowne, *Cortes* went in his maiesties company vnto the Citie of *Saragoza*, whereas his Maiestie calling to remembrance his worthy seruice, & valour of his person, made him *Marques del valle de Huaxacac*, according

cordyng to his defire, on the.vj. of July, *An.* 1528, and
Captayne generall of the newe Spayne, with all the prouinces and coaſt of the south sea, chiefe diſcouerer and inhabiter of the same coaſte and Ilandes, with the twelfth
parte of all that after that tyme ſhould be diſcouered, for
a ſure inheritaunce to him and his diſcendentes: he offered
vnto him also the habite of the order of Knighthœde of
Saint Iames, the whiche offer *Cortes* refuſed, bycauſe
there was no rent gyuen with the habite, but he beſought
his Maieſtie to graunt vnto him the gouernmēt of *Mexico*, the whiche requeſt the Emperour denied, bycauſe that
no Conquerour ſhoulde thinke that the office of gouernment and iuſtice is due vnto hym, for the like demaunde
was deſired of the kyng *Don Fernando*, by *Criſtoual Colon*
who firſte diſcouered the *India*, and also the great Captaine *Gonſalo Hernandoz de Cordoua*, who conquered *Naples*. *Cortes* deſerued muche, and also the Emperour gaue
him much, to honour him as a moſt bountifull and gratefull King, who neuer taketh away that whiche once he
giueth. He likewiſe gaue vnto *Cortez* all the kyngdome of
Michuacan, but hœ had rather haue had diuers other
townes whiche he demaunded, many other great fauours
and rewardes he receyued at the Emperours handes, but
the principall are thoſe before declared.

The Mariage of Cortez.

Hen it was knowen in Spayne, that the
lady *Catherin Xuares*, wife vnto *Cortes*, was
deceaſſed in *India*, by interceſſours he was
aſſured vnto the Duke of *Beiar*, his brothers daughter, who was named the Lady
Iane of *Zuniga*: hyr fathers name was *Don
Carolus de Arrellano*, Earle of *Aguilar*. This Lady was

a

a bewtifull Dame, and hyr brethrene noble perſonages,
who were highly in fauour with the Emperour. And
Cortes to matche with ſo honorable an houſe and lynage
he iudged himſelfe fortunate and well maried.

Among many Jewelles whiche _Cortes_ broughte with
him, were fiue moſte riche and fine Emeraldes, whiche **The riche**
were valued at a hundreth thouſande Duckets: the one **Emeraldes.**
was wrought lyke vnto a Roſe, an other like a Cornet,
an other lyke a fiſhe with the eyes of golde, whiche was
a maruellous péece of worke, beyng wrought among _In-_
dians: an other péece was wrought lyke vnto a bell, with
a great and a riche pearle for the clapper, garniſhed with
golde, ingrauen about with letters, whiche ſayde, Bleſſed
is he that created thée. The fifth was made lyke a cuppe
with the foote of gold, and had foure little chaynes of gold,
that were ioyned all at the top togither, in a great pearle,
and the brimme of this cuppe was of gold, with this verſe
ingrauen rounde aboute, _Inter natos mulierum non ſurrexit_
maior. For this onely péece the Merchantes of _Geneua_ did
offer fourtie thouſand Ducates, for to ſel the ſame again
to the great Turke. But at that tyme _Cortes_ woulde not
giue it for any money, although afterwarde he loſt them
all in the warres of _Argel_, beyng there with the Emperour. It was told _Cortes_ that the Empreſſe deſired to haue
thoſe péeces, meaning to demaunde them of him, and that
the Emperour ſhoulde pay for the ſame, for whiche cauſe
he ſent them to the Lady his newe wife, with many other
Jewelles before he came at the Courte, and there, when
he was enquired for them, he anſwered, and excuſed himſelfe, for then certaynely he gaue ſuche Jewels vnto his
Eſpouſe, that the lyke neuer Lady had in Spayne. And
after he was maried to the Lady _Iane_ of _Zuniga_, he departed with hyr to the newe Spayne, with title of _Marques_.

Aaa.ij.

Hovv

Hovv the Chancery vvas first placed
in Mexico, and certayne Diuelishe pretences
wrought against Cortes.

Efore *Cortes* his cōming into Spayne, *Pamfilo de Naruaez* his old enimy wēt vp & down in the Court, procuring the conquest of the riuer *De Palmas* & *Florida*, where at the laste he died, and alwayes when he saw time conuenient he made cōplaints against *Cortes*, yea and to the Emperours owne hand he deliuered a scrole of many articles, amōg the which was one, wherein he affirmed that *Cortes* had as many barres of gold and siluer, as in *Biscay* were barres of yron, and offered to proue the same: but although it was not true, yet it was suspicious. He also earnestly procured that he shold be punished, saying that he had plucked out one of his eyes, & killed with poyson the Licenciat *Luys ponce de Leon*, & *Francisco Garay*. Through his many and importunate petitiōs, it was determined to send to *Mexico*, *Don Pedro de la Cueua*, who was bothe fierce and seuere, and Lorde stewarde of the Emperour his house, and afterwarde made general of the ordinance, and chiefe Comendador of the order and knighthood of *Alcantara*, who findyng the accusation true, should cut off *Cortes* his head.

But as God woulde, in the meane season came the testimoniall from the Doctor *Hoieda*, and the Licenciat *Pero Lopez*, Phisitions, who had cured the persons that were reported to haue bene poysoned, wherupon that commißion ceased. And when *Cortes* came into Spayne, *Don Pedro de la Cueua* would many times laugh and iest with him, saying, From farre places long lies.

The Emperour and his councell of *India* prouided a Courte

Courte of Chancery in *Mexico*, as chiefe place, where as all controuerfies and matters of righte throughout the new *Spayne* mighte there be determined, and alfo to correct the mutinies, and partes taking among the Spanyardes: likewife to take refidence and accompte of *Cortes*, and to be fatiffyed both of his feruice and offences. Moreouer that they fhould vifite the officers, and royall Treaforie there. *Munio de Gufman* was appoynted prefident and gouernoure, with other foure Licenciates for Judges to accompany him. He departed toward *Mexico* Anno 1529. and at his comming, he began to vnderftande in his regimente and office, with the Licenciate *Iohn Ortiz*, for the other three Iudges died by the way. *Cortes* being nowe abfente, and vppon his iourney toward *Spayne*, this newe Iudge made a terrible refidence and condemnation againfte him, and commaunded all his goodes to be folde by out-thrappe, for a greate deale leffe than hys goodes were worth, and in his abfence they calles him by Proclamation: but if he hadde bin there prefent, his life had bin in daunger, although face to face fome refpect is had, and it is an ordinarie rule that the Iudge fheweth rigoure againft him that is abfent. This hatred was not onely againft *Cortes*, but alfo againfte his friendes, for hee apprehended *Pedro de Aluarado*, who was newly come from *Spayne*, bycaufe he fpake in the fauour of *Cortez*, laying to his charge the rebellion of *Mexico*, when *Naruaez* was there. He alfo apprehended *Alonfo de Eftrada*, & manye others, doing manifeft wrongs vnto them.

In fhorte fpace the Emperour had more complayntes againft, *Nunio de Gufman*, and the other Iudge, than had bin heeretofore againfte any other, wherevpon he was put out of office in the yeare 1530. His wrongful dealing in iuftice was not onely proued in *Mexico*, but alfo in the Court of *Spayne*, with many perfons that were come

from

Aaa.iij.

Before thé Iudges came, Cortex vvas gone to Spayne.

from thence, so that the nexte president and Iudges that
went thither, did pronounce *Nunio de Gusman* and his fellowe for partiall Iudges, and enimies vnto *Cortes*, and
condemned him to pay all his goodes whiche were euill
solde. But whē *Nunio de Gusman* vnderstoode that he was
put out of office, he then was afraide, and tooke his iourney against the *Teuchichimecas*, seeking after the Towne
of *Culhuacan*, from whence the *Mexicans* descended. He caried in his company fiue hundred Spanyardes, whereof
the most were horsemen, and many of them went as prisoners, and against their willes.

In *Mechuacan* he tooke prisoner the King *Caconcin*, who
was a great friende vnto *Cortes*, a seruitor vnto the Spanyards, and vassal to the Emperour, and as the fame goeth, he tooke from him tenne thousande markes of plate,
and much golde, and afterward burned him, and many o-
ther Gentlemen, and principal persons of that kingdome,
bycause they shoulde not complayne, saying, that a dead
dogge biteth not. He tooke from thence sixe thousand *Indians* for the seruice of his army, and with them conquered *Xalixco*, whiche is nowe called the new *Gallizia*. He a-
bode there, vntill the Vizeroy *Don Antonio de Mondoza*,
and Chancery of *Mexico*, caused him to be apprehended,
who sent him prisoner into Spayne, to giue accompte of
his office. If *Nunio de Gusman* had bin so good a gouernour
and Iudge, as he was in bloud a Gentleman, he had then
enioyed the best plot of all the West *India*, but he behaued himselfe euill, both with the *Indians* and *Spanyards*.

The same yeare that he came from *Mexico*, went thyther for president *Sebastian Ramirez*, who was a Bishop,
and had in time past bin presidente in *Santo Domingo*, and
the Licenciates *Iohn de Salmeron*, *Gasco Quiroga*, *Francisco
Ceynos*, and *Alonso Maldonado*, for Iudges to accompany
him.

These

*A good
Sentence.*

*Abhomi-
nable fact.*

These Judges gouerned well the land, and caused the Citie of *Angels* to be inhabited which the *Indians* called *Cuetlaxcoapan*, that is to say a Snake in water. The reason was, bycause they haue two fountaynes, the one of euill water, and the other of good. This Citie standeth twentie leagues from *Mexico*, in the high way to *Vera Crux.* The Bishop set the *Indians* at libertie, and therefore many Spanyards departed from thence, who hadde inhabited there before, and wente to seeke their liuing at *Xalixco, Hunduras, Quahutemallan*, and other places where warre was.

The returne of Cortez to Mexico.

 T this season arriued *Cortes* at the riche Towne of *Vera Crux*, and when his comming was published, how he came wyth title of Marquez, and had broughte hys wife with him, an infinite number of *Indians* came to visite him, and almost all the Spanyards of *Mexico*, so that in few dayes there came a thousand persons of his owne nation, who made theyr complaintes vnto him, how they were vndone, and that the Iudges which had bin there, had destroyed both him and them, and asked his iudgement whether that nowe they might kill both them and theirs. *Cortes* hearing their odious request, reprehended them, and also gaue them hope shortly to releeue their necessitie with new discoueries, and in this order fearing some mutinie, he held them in pleasure and pastime.

When the president hearde howe *Cortes* was visited of the Spanyardes, they commaunded forthwith euery one of them shoulde immediatly returne to *Mexico*, or else, where their dwelling places were vpō paine of death, yea and they were aboute to apprehende *Cortes* for a stirrer
of

of vproze, and to sende him backe againe prisoner into Spayne. But when he saw howe soone these Iudges were moued, he commaunded to proclayme himselfe openly in Vera Crux Captayne Generall of all the dominions of the new Spayne, and there caused the Emperours letters pattentes to be redde, whiche thing being knowen to the Mexican Iudges, it caused them to wring their noses. After this diligence ended, he departed toward Mexico wyth a great company of Spanyards and Indians, among whom were a good company of horsemen: but when he came to Tezcuco, the President sent to commaund him not to enter into Mexico, vpon payne of losse of his goodes, and hys body to be at the Kings pleasure.

He obeyed the commaundemente with greate wysedome, being a thing conuenient to the seruice of the Emperour, and profite of the land, which he had wonne wyth great toyle and laboure: but yet he abode in Tezcuco with a greater maiestie and court, than the President in Mexico, and wrote vnto him, that he should consider his good will and whole intent, and not to giue occasion to the Indians to rebell, and for the Spanyards he might assure hymselfe.

The Indians vnderstäding ý discord betwixt the President and Cortes, slew as many Spanyards as they coulde get at aduantage, so that in fewe dayes there wanted aboue two hundred of the Spanish nation, being slayne as well in Townes, as in the high wayes, yea and also they had communed among themselues to rebell in deede. But when the Bishop and the Iudges heard this newes, they began to feare the matter, and considering that they had no better remedy, nor other sure defence, but only ý name valor, person, and authoritie of Cortes, they sente to desire him to come vnto Mexico, wherevpon he obserued theyr commaundement and request, & wente toward the Citie,
well

well accompanyed with men of warre, so that he shewed himselfe in estate a generall captaine. All the Citizens came out to receiue him and the lady Marques his wife: his entrie into the cittie was a day of great pleasure a mong them. Then the president and iudges entred into counsell for to remedie the greate hurt whiche had bene done by the *Indians*. Cortes toke the matter in hand, and apprehended many Indians, of whom some he burned, others wer torne with dogges, he did such correction, that in shorte time al the countrey was quiet, and the highe wayes without daunger, a thing worthy of great thanks.

The letters that the Indians vsed in *Mexico*.

Here hath not bin found letters at any time in the Weast *India*, onely in the newe Spain were vsed certain figures which serued for letters, with the which they kepte in memorie, and preserued their antiquities. The figures ý the *Mexicans* vsed for letters are great, by reason whereof they occupy gret volumes: they ingraue them in stone or timber, and paint them vpon walles, and also vpon a paper made of cotten wool, and leaues of the tree *Metl*. Their bokes are great and folded vp like vnto our broade clothes, and written vpon both sides. There are some bokes rolled vp like a piece of flannel. They pronouce not. b. g. e. f. Therfore they vse much. p. e. l. r. This is the Mexicall speéch, and *Nahual*, which is the best, playnest, and moste eloquent, in al Newe Spayne. There are some in *Mexico* that do vnderstand ech other, by whistling, whiche is ordinarily vsed among louers, & theeues, a speéche truely to wonder at, & none of our men could come to the knowledge therof.

The order hovy to recken.

Ce	One
Ome	Two
Ei	Thȝée
Naui	Foure
Macuil	Fiue
Chicoace	Sire
Chicome	Seauen
Chicuei	Eight
Chiconaui	Nine
Matlac	Tenne
Matlactlioce	Eleuen
Matlactliome	Twelue
Matlactlomei	Thirtéene
Matlactlinaui	Fourtéene
Matlactlinacui	Fiftéene
Matlactlichicoace	Sirtéene
Matlactlichicome	Seuentéene
Matlactlichicuei	Eightéene
Matlactlichiconaui	Ninetéene
Cempoalli	Twentie

Euery number is simple, vntil you come to sire, and then they count, sire and one, sire and two, sire and thȝée. Ten is a number by himselfe, then you must counte ten and one, tenne and two, tenne and thȝée, tenne and foure, tenne and fiue.

Then you count, ten fiue and one, tenne fiue and two, ten fiue and thȝée. Twenty goeth by himselfe, and al the greater numbers.

                                   The

The Mexican yeare.

The *Mexicans* yeare is thre hundered sirtie dayes, for they haue in their yere eightæne monethes, and euery moneth contayneth twentie dayes. They haue other fiue odde dayes, whiche goeth by themselues, in the which they vsed to celebrate greate feastes of cruell and bloudy sacrifice, with much deuotion. And reconing after this sort, they could not chose but erre, for they could not make equal the punctuall course of the Sunne. Yea the Christian yere is not perfit, although we haue learned Astronomers. But yet these simple *Indians* wente neare the marke.

The names of the moneths.

Tlacaxipenaliztli.
Tozcuztli.
Huei Tozeuztli.
Toxcalt.
Ecalcoalizeli.
Tocuilhuicintli.
Hueitecuilhuitl
Miccailhuicigtli.
Veymiccailhuisl.
Vchpanizeli.
Pachtli.
Huei Pachtli.
Quecholli.
Panquecalizeli.
Hatemuzeli.
Titiilh.
Izcalli.
Coavislenac.

The names of dayes.

Cipaātli	A Spade
Hecatl	Ayre or Winde
Calli	A House
Cuez Pali	A Lizart
Couale	A Snake
Mizquiātli	Death
Macatl	A wilde Hart
Tochtli	A Cōny
Atl	Water
Izcuyntli	A Dogge
Ocumatli	An Ape
Malinalli	A Brome
Acatlh	A Cane
Ocelotl	A Tigre
Coautli	An Egle
Cozcaquahutl	A Bussard
Olin	A Temple
Tepatlh	A Knife
Quiauitl	Rayne
Xuchitl	A Rose

Although these twentie names serue for the whole
yere, and are but the dayes of euery meneth, yet therfore euery moneth beginneth not with *Cipaātli*, which is
the first name, but as they followe in order, and the fiue
odde dayes is the cause thereof. And also bycause theyr
weeke is of thirtéene dayes, which changeth the names,
as by example, *Cecipaātli* can go no further thā vnto *Mat-
laālomeiacatl*, which is thirtéene, and then beginneth an
other wéeke: and we do not say *Matlaāllinaui Ocelotl*, whiche is the fourtéenth day, but we say *Ceocelotl* whiche is
one, and then recken the other fixe names, vnto twenty.

And

And when al the twentie dayes are ended, begin againe to recken from the firſt name of the twentie, but not frõ one, but from viij. And bicauſe ye may better vnderſtand the matter, here is the example.

Cecipaﬅli.

Omehecatl.

Ei Calli.

Naui Cuezpali.

Macuilcouatl

Chicoacen Mizquinth.

Chicome Macatl.

Chicuei Tochtli.

Chiconauiatl.

Matlaciz Cuintli.

Mailaﬅlioce Ocumatli.

Matlaﬅliome Malinalli

Matlaﬅlomei Acatlb.

The next wéeke following doth begin his dayes from one. And that one is the fouretéenth name of the moneth and of the dayes, and ſaith.

Ceotelotl.	Macuil Tecpatl.
Ometoauth.	Chicoacen Quiauitl.
Eicozcaquahutli.	Chicome Xuchitl.
Naui Olui.	Chicoei Cipaﬅli.

In this ſecond wéeke, *Cipaﬅli* came to fal on the eighte day, being in the firſt wéeke the firſt day.

Cemacatl.

Ometochtli.

Eiatl.

Nauiizcuintli.

Macuil Ocõmatli.

And

And so proceede on to the thirde wéeke, in the which this name *Cipactli* entreth not, but *Macatl*, which was the seuenth day in the first wéeke, & had no place in ỹ second, and is the first in the third. This reconing is no darker, than ours, which we haue in a.b.c.d.e.f.g. For they also change with time, and runne in such sort, that. a. whiche was the firste letter of this moneth, commeth to be the fift daye of the nexte moneth, and the thirde moneth he counteth to be the third day, and so orderly doth the other sixe letters.

The accounting of yeares.

These *Mexicans* had another order to recken theyr yeares, which exceded not aboue foure in number, as one, two, thrée, foure, wherewith they accounte a hundred, fiue hundred, a thousand, and as many moe as they lust. Those foure figures or names are, *Tochtli, Acatlh, Tecpatlh, Calli,* and do signifye, a Conny, a Caue, a Knife, and a House, saying.

Ce Tochtli	One yeare
Ome Acatlh	Two yeares
Ei Tecpatlh	Thrée yeares
Naui Calli	Foure yeares
Macuil Tochtli	Fiue yeares
Cicoacen Acatlh	Sixe yeares
Cicome Tecpatlh	Seauen yeares
Chicuei Calh	Eight yeares
Chiconaui Tochtli	Nine yeares
Matlactli Acatlh	Tenne yeares
Matlactlioce Tecpatlh	Eleuen yeares
Matlactliome Calli	Twelue yeares
Matlactliomei Tochtli	Thirtéene yeares

So that the reconing paſſeth not aboue thirtéene, whiche is one wéeke of the yeare, and endeth where he began.

Another Weeke.

Ce Acatlh	One yeare
Ome Tlepatlh	Two yeares
Ei Calli	Thzée yeares
Naui Tochtli	Foure yeares
Macuil Acatlh	Fiue yeares
Chicoacen Tecpatlh	Sire yeares
Cinicome Calls.	Seuen yeares
Chicuei Tochtli	Eight yeares
Chiconaui Acatlh	Nine yeares
Matlactli Tecpatlh	Tenne yeares
Matlactlioce Calli	Eleuen yeares
Matlactliome Tochtli	Twelue yeares
Matlactliomei Acatlh	Thirtéene yeares

The third vyeeke of yeares.

Ce Tecpatlh	One yeare
Ome Calli	Two yeres
Ei Tochtli	Thzée yeres
Naui Acatlh	Foure yeres
Macuil Tecpatlh	Fiue yeres
Chicoacan Calli	Sire yeares
Chicome Tochtli	Seauen yeares
Chicuei Acatlh	Eight yeares
Chiconaui Tecpatlh	Nine yeares
Matlactli Calli	Tenne yeares
Matlactliome Tochtli	Eleuen yeares

Twelue

Matlacsliome Acatlh	Twelue yeares
Matlacsliomei Tecpatlh	Thirtéene yeares

The fourth Weeke.

Ce Calli	One yeare
Ome Tochtli	Two yeares
Ei Acatlh	Thrée yeares
Naui Tecpatlh	Foure yeares
Macuil Calli	Fiue yeares
Chicoacen Tochtli	Sire yeares
Chicome Acatlh	Seauen yeares
Chicuei Tecpatlh	Eight yeares
Chiconaui Calli	Nine yeares
Matlacsli Tochtli	Tenne yeares
Matlacslioce Acatlh	Eleuen yeares
Matlacsliome Tecpatlh	Twelue yeares
Matlacsliomei Calli	Thirtéene yeares

Ech of these wéekes, which our men cal Indition, doth conteyne thirtéene yeares, so that all the foure wéekes make two and fiftie yeares, which is a perfit number in the reconing, and is called the yeare of grace, for from fiftie two yeres, to fiftie two yeares, they vsed to make solemne feastes, with strange Ceremonies, as hereafter shall be declared. And when fiftie two yeares are ended, then they beginne againe, by the same order before declared, vntil they come to as many moe, beginning at *Ce Tochtli,* and so forwarde. But alwayes they begin at the Conny figure. So that in the forme of reconing they kepe & haue in memorye, things of 8 50. yeares, and by this Cronicle they know in what yere euerye thing hapned, and how long euery king raygned : howe many children they had, and all things else that importeth to the estate of the gouernement of the lande.

The

The Indians beleeued that fiue ages

were paſt, which they called Sunnes.

He *Indians* of *Culhua* did beléeue that the Gods had made ẏ woʒld, but they knew not how, yet they beléeued that since the creation of the woʒld four Sunnes were paſt, and that the fift and laſt is ẏ Sunne that now giueth light to the woʒld.

They helde opinion that the firſte Sunne periſhed by water, and at the same time all liuing creatures periſhed likewise.

The second Sunne (say they) fell from the heaués, with whose fall all liuing creatures were ſlayne, and then (said they) were manye Giantes in that Countrey, and certayne monſtrous bones, which our men found in opening of graues, by pʒopoʒtion whereof, some ſhoulde séeme to be men of twenty ſpannes high.

The third Sunne was consumed by fire, whiche burned day and night, so that then all liuing creatures were burned.

The fourth Sunne finiſhed by tempeſt of ayʒe oʒ winde, which blew downe houses, trées, yea and ẏ mountaynes and Rockes were blowé asunder, but the lignage of mankinde periſhed not, sauing that they were conuerted into Apes. And touching the fift Sunne, which now raigneth, they know not how it ſhall consume. But they say that when the fourth Sunne periſhed, all the woʒlde fell into darkeneſſe, and so remained foʒ the space of fiue and twenty yeares continually, and at the fifteenth yeare of that fearefull darkeneſſe, the Gods did foʒme one man and a woman, who bʒought foʒth childʒen, and at the end of the other tenne yeares, appeared the Sunne whiche was newly boʒne vppon the figure of the *Conny* day, and

Ccc.   there-

therfoze they begin their account of yéeres at ẙ day,⁊ reckoning from the yeare of oure Lozde 1552. their age oz
Sunne is 858. so that it appeareth that they haue vsed
many yeares their wziting in figures: and they had not
onely this vse from *Cetocheli*, whiche is the beginning of
their yeare, moneth, and day of their fifth Sunne,but also they hadde the same ozder and vse in the other foure
Sunnes which were past:but they let many things slippe
out of memozie,saying, that with the newe Sunne, all a-
ther things should be likewise new. They held also opinion,that thzée dayes after this last Sunne appeared, all
the Gods did dye, and that in pzocesse of time the Gods
whiche nowe they haue,and wozshippe,were bozne. And
thzough these false opinions, our Diuines did sone conuert them to the knowledge of the true lawes of God.

The nation of the Indians called
Chichimecas.

IN the lande nowe called newe *Spayne*,are dyuers and sundzy generations of people: but
they holde opinion,that the stocke of most antiquitie, is the people nowe called *Chichimecas*, whiche pzocéded out of the house of *A-
culhuacan*,which standeth beyond *Xalixco*,about the yeare
of our Lozde,720. Many of this Generation did inhabite
aboute the lake of *Tenuchtitlan*, but their name ended by
mixture in marriage with other people. At that time
they hadde no King, noz yet did builde eyther house oz
Towne. Their only dwellings was in caues in ẙ Moū-
taynes.They went naked, they sowed no kind of graine,
noz vsed bzead of any sozte. They did mainteyne themselues with rotes, hearbes,and siluester fruites:and béeing a people cunning in shoting with the bowe,they kylled

led deare, hares, connyes, and other beaftes and foule, which they eate alfo, not fodden or roffed, but rawe, and dryed in the Sunne. They eate alfo Snakes, Lizardes, and other filthye beaftes, yea and at this day there are fome of this generation that vfe the fame dyet. But although they liued fuche a beftiall life, & being a people fo barbarous, yet in their diuelifh religion they were verye deuout. They worfhipped the Sunne, vnto whome they vfed to offer Snakes, Lizards, & fuch other beafts. They likewife offered vnto their God all kinde of foule, from the degrée of an Eagle, to a little Butterflie. They vfed not facrifice of manflaughter, nor had any Idolles, no not fo muche as of the Sunne, whome they helde for the fole and only God. They married but with one woman, & in no degrée of kinred. They were a ftoute and a warlike people, by reafon whereof, they were Lordes of the land.

The Coronation of the Kings of Mexico.

Lthough one brother was heire to another among the *Mexicans,* and after their deceaffe, did inherite the Sonne of the eldeft brother, yet they tooke no poffeffion of the ftate nor name of King vntil they were annoynted and Crowned openlye.

As fone as any King of *Mexico* deceaffed, and his funerals ended, then were called to Parliamente the Lorde of *Tezcuco,* and the Lorde of *Tlacopan,* who were the chiefeft eftates, and then in order all other noble men, who owed any feruice to the Mexican Empire. And béyng come togither, if any doubt of the inheritáce of ẏ crowne happened, then the matter was decided with al haft: then the newe King being knowen, he was ftripped ftarke naked, except a cloth to couer his priuie partes, and in thys forte was carried among them, to the greate Temple

af

of *Vitzilopuchtli* with greate silence, and without any ioy
oz pleasure: Two Gentlemen of the Citie whose office
it was, ledde him vppe the staires of the Temple by the
armes, and befoze him wente the Pzinces of *Tezcuco* and
Tlacopan, who that day did weare their robes of Cozona-
tion, wherevpon was paynted their armes and title. Uery
rye fewe of the Laytie wente vp into the Chappels, but
only those that were appoynted to attire the newe king,
and to serue in other Ceremonies, foz all the residue
stode vpon the steppes and belowe, to beholde the Cozo-
nation. These Magistrates being aboue in the Chappell, came with great humilitie and reuerence, knælyng
downe vpõ their knæs befoze the Idoll of *Vitzilopuchtli*,
and touched the earth with one finger and then kissed the
same. Then came the high pzieste clothed in his pontifi-
call vestmentes, with many others in his company, who
did weare surplices: and withoute speaking any wozde,
they paynted oz couloured the Kings person, with ynke
made foz the purpose, as blacke as any cole. After thys
Ceremonye done, they blessed the annoynted Kyng, and
spzinckled him foure times with a certayne holly water,
that was made at the time of consecration of the God,
made of dowe oz paste, with a spzinckle made of boughes
of Cane leaues, Ceder, ⁊ willow leaues. Then they put
vpon his head, a cloth painted with the bones and skulles
of dead men, and next they clothed him with a black garment, and vpon ỹ another blewe, and both were paynted
with ỹ figures of dead mens skulles ⁊ bones. Then they
put about his necke certaine laces, whereat did hang the
armes of ỹ Crowne. And behind his backe they did hang
certain little bottels ful of powders, by vertue wherof he
was deliuered from pestilence and diseases, accozding to
their opiniõ: yea ⁊ therby witches, noz witchcrafts could
not hurt him, noz yet euill menne deceyue him. In fyne,

*The oynt-
ment.*

with

with those relickes he was sure from all perill and daunger. Upon his lefte arme they bounde a litle bagge of incenfe, and then brought vnto him a chaffyng dilhe of imbers made of the barke of an Oke trée. Then the king a-
rose, and with his owne hande threw of the fame incenfe
into the chaffing dilhe, and with great renerence brought
the fame to the God *Vitzilopuchtli*, and after he had fmo-
ked him therewith, he fatte him downe, then came the
high Priest and toke his othe to mainteyne the religion
of the Goddes, to kéepe alfo all the lawes and cuftomes of
his predeceffours, to mayntepne iuftice, and not to agra-
uiate any of his vaffals or fubiects, and that he fhould be
valiant in the warres, that he fhoulde caufe the Sunne to
giue his light, the clowdes to yéelde rayne, the riuers to
runne, and the earth to bring foorth all kinde of grayne,
fruytes, and other néedefull hearbes and trées. Thefe and
many other impoffible things the newe kyng did fweare
to performe: and then he gaue thankes to the high priest,
and commended himfelf to the Goddes and to the lookers
on, and they who brought him vp in the fame order, ca-
rieth him downe agayne. Then all the people cried, the
Goddes preferue the newe kyng, and that he may raigne
many yéeres in health with al his people. But then fome
began to daunce, other to play on their inftrumēts, fhewing outwardly their inwarde ioyes of harte. And before
the king came to the foote of the fteppes, all the noble men
came to yéelde their obedience, and in token of louing and
faythfull fubiectes they prefented vnto him feathers,
ftrings of fnayle fhelles, collours, and other Iewelles of
golde and filuer, alfo mantels paynted with death, & bare
him company vnto a great hal within the compaffe of the
temple, and there lefte him. The king fitteth downe vnder his cloth of eftate, called *Tlacatecco*, and in foure daies
departeth not out of the circuyte of the temple, the whic'

he spendes in prayers, sacrifice and penaunce, he eates then but once a day, and euery day he bathes himselfe, and agayne in the night in a great ponde of water, and then lettes himselfe bloud in his eares, and senseth therewith the God of Water, called *Tlaloc*: he likewise senseth the other idols, vnto whome he offereth bread, flowers, Papers and little Canes died in the bloudde of his owne tongue, nose, handes, and other partes of his body. After the foure dayes expired, then come all the Noble men to beare him company to his palayce with great triumphe and pleasure of all the Cittie, but after his consecration fewe or none dare looke him in the face.

And now with the declaryng of the actes and Ceremonies that the *Mexican* Kings are crowned, I shall not néede to rehearse of other kyngs, for generally they all do vse the same order, sauyng that other Princes goe not vp to the toppe of the Temple, but abide at the foote of the steppes to be crowned, and after theyr Coronation they come to *Mexico* for their confirmation, and then at theyr returne to their countrey, they made many drunké feasts and banquets.

The opinion of the Mexicans
concerning the Soule.

He *Mexicans* did beléue that the Soule was immortal, and that they receyued eyther ioy or payne accordyng to theyr desertes & liuyng in this worlde, vnto which opinion all their religion did attayne, and chiefly appeare at their burials. They helde for an assured faith, that there were nine places appointed for soules, & the chiefest place of glory to be neare vnto the Sunne, where the soules of those whiche were
god

good men flaine in the warres, & thofe which were facrififed were placed, and that all other fortes of euill perfons
their foules abode on the earth, & were deuided after this
forte, children that were dead borne went to one place,
thofe which died of age or other difeafe went to another,
thofe which died of fodden death to another, thofe whiche
died of woundes or contagious difeafes went to an other
place, thofe which were drowned went to another, thofe
which were put to death for offence by order of iuftice, as
for robbery and adultery to another: Thofe which flewe
their fathers, mothers, wiues or childre, to another place
by themfelues, alfo thofe who flew their mayfters or any
religious perfon went to another place. The common
forte of people were buried, but Lordes and rich men had
their bodies burned & their afhes buried. In their fhreudes
they had a greate difference, for many dead bodies were
buried better apparelled than when they were on liue.
Women were fhrewded after another forte. And he that
fuffered death for adulterie was fhrewded like vnto the
God of leachery, called *Tlazoulteutl*, he that was drowned
like vnto the God of water named *Tlacoc*, and he that died
with drunkenneffe was fhrewded like vnto the God of
wyne called *Ometochtli*. But the Souldier had an honorable fhrewde like vnto the attyre of *Vitzilopuchtli*, and the
lyke order in all other fortes of deathes.

The buriall of Kings in
Mexico.

Hen any kyng of *Mexico* happened to
fall ficke, they vfed forth-with to put a
vifor vppon the face of *Tezcatlipuca*, or
Vitzilopuchtli, or fome other Idoll,
whiche Vifor was not taken awaye,
vntill

vntill they fawe whether the kyng did amend, oz elfe die:
But if he chaunfed to die, then wozde was fent throughout all his dominions to bewaile his death, and alfo other
poftes were fent to call the Noble menne that were his
nigheft kinfmen, and to warne them within foure dayes
to come vnto his buriall.

The dead body was layde vpon a fayze matte, & was
watched foure nightes, with great lamentation and mournyng: then the body was washed, and a locke of heare
cut from the crowne of his head, whiche was pzeferued
as a great relicke, faying that therein remayned the remembzance of his foule. This done, a fine Emerald was
put into his mouth, and his body fhzewded in feuentene
riche mantles, of colours, both riche and coftly wzought.
Vpon the vpper mantle was fette the deuife oz armes of
Vitzilopuchtli oz *Tezcalipuca*, oz of fome other idoll, in
whome the kyng had greate confidence in his lyfe tyme,
and in his temple fhould the body be buried. Vpó his face
they put a bifoz, paynted with foule and Diuelifh ge-
ftures, befette with many iewelles, pzecious ftones, and
pearles. Then they killed his flaue, whofe office was to
light the Lampes and make fire vnto the Goddes of his
pallayce. Thefe things done, they carried the dead body
vnto the Temple: fome followed him with dolefull tune,
others fong the death of the kyng by note, foz fo was the
cuftome.

The Noble men and Gentlemen of his houfholde carried Targets, Arrowes, Mafes, and Enfignes to thzowe
into the fire where the body fhould be buried in the Temple. The high Pzieft and all the Clergie recepued him at
the Temple gate, with a fozrowfull fong, and after he
had fayde certayne wozdes, the body was thzowen into a
great fire made foz the purpofe, with all the iewels that
he had aboute him, and all the other things whiche was
bzought

b²ought to honour the burial: also a dogge newly ſtrang-
led with an arrowe, whiche was to guyde him his way.
In the meane whyle that the king and dogge were
burying, the Pꝛieſts ſacrificed two hundꝛed perſons, hol-
beit in this Ceremonie there was no oꝛdinary rate, foꝛ
ſometymes they ſacrificed many moe: they were opened
with a raſour of flinte in the bꝛeaſtes, and their partes
taken out and thꝛowen into the fire where the kings body was. Theſe miſerable perſons beyng ſacrificed, and
their bodies thꝛowen into a hole, they beleeued aſſuredly
that thoſe ſhoulde ſerue foꝛ his ſlaues in another woꝛlde:
ſome of them were dwarſſes, monſtrous and defoꝛmed
perſons, with ſome women. They placed about the dead
body of the king befoꝛe his buriall, Roſes, flowꝛes and
ſundꝛy diſhes of meate and dꝛinke, and no creature durſte
touche the ſame, but onely ÿ Pꝛieſts, foꝛ it ſeemed to be an
offeryng.

The nexte day followyng, all the aſhes were gathered
togither, and the teeth with the Emerald that was in his
mouth, the whiche things were put into a cheſt, paynted
on the inſide with hoꝛrible figures of diuels, and the locke
of heare whiche was cut from his crowne, and another
locke of heare which was pꝛeſerued from the tyme of his
birth. Then the cheſt was lockte, and an image of wood
made and clothed like vnto the kings perſon, which was
ſet on the toppe of the cheſt. The obſequies endured foure
dayes, in the whiche the wiues and daughters of the king
offered great offerings at the place where his body was
buried, and befoꝛe the cheſt and his image.

On the fourth day after the buriall, fiftene ſlaues
were ſacrificed foꝛ his ſoule, and on the twentith day o-
ther fiue perſons were alſo ſacrificed, likewiſe on the ſixte
thꝛee, and foureſcoꝛe, whiche was lyke vnto the yeeres
minde.

Ddd.   The

The order of buriall of the Kings
of Michuacan.

He kingdome of *Michuacan* is almoste as great as the Empire of *Mexico*, and when any king of that countrey happened to be visited with sicknesse, and brought to suche extremitie, that hope of life were past, according to the opinion of Phisitions, then would he name and appoint whiche of his Sonnes shoulde inherite the estate, and beyng knowen, the new king or heyre, incontinent sent for all the gouernours, Captaines, and valiant souldiers, who had any office or charge to come vnto the buriall of his Father, and he that came not, from thenceforth was helde for a Traytour and so punished. When the death of the olde King was certayne, then came al degrées of Estates and brought presents to the newe king, for the approbation of his kyngdome, but if the King were not throughly dead, but at the poynt of death, then the gates were shut in, and none permitted to enter, and when hys lyfe was departed, then beganne a generall crie and mournyng, and they were permitted to come where their dead kyng lay, and to touche him with their handes: this beyng done the carkasse was washed with swéete waters, and then a fine shyrte put vpon him, and a payre of shoes made of a Déere skinne put on his féete, and aboute his ancles were tied certayne belles of golde, about his wrestes of his handes were put Manyllias of Turkies, and other bracelets of golde, lykewise aboute his necke they hong other collers of precious stones and golde, and rings in his eares, with a greate Turkise in his neather lippe. Then his body was layde vpon a large beare, whereon was placed a good bedde vnder him: on his one side lay a bowe with a quyuer of arrowes, and on

his

his other side lay an image made of fine mantels of his
owne stature o? bignesse with a greate tuffe of fine feathers,shoes vpon his feete,with b?acelets and a coller of
gold. Whyle this wo?ke was a doyng, others were bu-
sied in washyng the men and women whiche shoulde be
slayne fo? to accompany him into Hell:these w?etched folke
that should be slaine were banqueted & filled with d?inke,
bycause they shoulde receyue their death with lesse paine.
The newe kyng did appoint those who shoulde die fo? to
serue the king his father, but yet many of them had rather bene without his seruice,notwithstanding some simple soules esteemed that odious death fo? a thyng of im-
mo?tall glo?y. First seuen Gentlewomen of noble pa-
rentage were appoynted to die, the one to haue the office
of keper of his iewels which he was wont to were, another fo? the office of cup bearer, another to giue him water with a basen and ewer, another to giue him alwayes
the b?inall, another to be his Cooke, and another to serue
fo? landres. They slewe also many women slaues, and
free maydens fo? to attende vpon the Gentlewomen,and
mo?eouer one of euery occupation within the citie. When
all these that were appoynted to die were washed & they?
bellies full with meate & d?inke, then they paynted their
faces yellow, and put garlandes of sweete floures vpon
each of their heads. Then they went in o?der of p?ocessio
befo?e the beare whereon the dead king was caried, some
wente playing on instruments made of snayle shelles, o-
thers played vpon bones and shelles of seaturtils, others
went whistlyng and the most part weping:the Sonnes of
the dead kyng & other noble men carried vp? their shoulders the beare where y cor?se lay, & p?oceded with an easie
pace towarde the Temple of the God *Curicaueri*: his kinsmen went round about the bere,singyng a so?owful song.
The officers and houshold seruants of the Court w other

Magistrates and rulers of iustice bare the Standartes and diuers other armes.

About midnight they departed in the order aforesayde out of the kings palayce with great light of fire brandes and with a heauy noyse of trumpets and drummes. The Citizens which dwelt where the corse passed, attended to make cleane the streate. And when they were come to the temple, they wente foure tymes rounde about a great fire made of the woodde of Pine trée, whiche was prepared to burne the dead body: then the beare was layd vpon the fire, and in the meane while that the body was burnyng, they mawled with a clubbe those whiche had the garlandes, and afterwarde buried them by foure and foure, as they were apparelled behind the Temple.

The nexte day in the mornyng, the asshes, bones and Iewels was gathered and layde vpon a riche mantle, the whiche was carried to the temple gate, where the priestes attended to blesse those Diuelishe relickes, whereof they made a dowe or paste, and thereof an image whiche was appareled lyke a man, with a visor on his face, and all other sortes of Iewels that the dead king was wonte to weare, so that it séemed a gallant idoll. At the fote of the temple stayres, they opened a graue ready made, whiche was square, large, & two fadome déepe, it was also hanged with new mattes rounde about, and a fayre bed therein, in the whiche a religious man placed the idoll made of asshes, with his eyes towarde the cast parte, and honge rounde aboute the walles Targets of golde and siluer, with bow and arrowes, & many gallant tuffes of feathers with earthen vessels, as pottes, disshes & platters, so that the graue was filled vp with houshold stuffe, shelts couered with leather, apparell, iewels, meate, drinke, and armour. This done, the graue was shut vp & made sure with beames, bordes, and flored with earth on the toppe.

All

All thofe Gentlemen which had ferued o2 touched any thing in the buriall, wafhed them felues, and wente to dinner in the Courte, o2 parde of the Kings houfe, without any table, and hauing dined, they wiped their hands vp on certayne lockes of Cotton wol, hanging downe their heads, and not fpeaking any wo2d, except it were to afke fo2 d2inke. This Ceremonie endured fiue dayes, and in all that time no fire was permitted to be kindled in the Citie, except in the Kings houfe and Temples, no2 yet a ny co2ne was ground, o2 market kept, no2 none durft goe out of their houfes, fhewing all the fo2row that might be poffible fo2 the death of they2 King.

The order of Matrimony among

the Indians.

N *Tlaxcallan* and many other Cities, was vfed as a p2incipall Ceremonie and to ken of marriage, that the B2idegrome and his B2ide, againft the day of marri age, had their heads polled, whiche was to fignifie, that from that day fo2ward, al childifhe o2ders fhould be laide afide, and from that tyme new heare myght grow, to declare another kind of lyfe. The chiefeft knotte of marriage vfed in *Michuacan* was, that the B2ide doe loke directly vppon hir fpoufe, fo2 o therwife the Matrimony was not perfite no2 anaylable.

In *Mixteoapan* which is a greate p2ouince, they vfe to carrie the B2idgrome to be married vpon their backes, which is to be vnderftode, that he goeth againft his wil. But yet they take hands, in token that the one fhall helpe the other, and then they knitte both their mantels togy ther with a great knotte, fignifying that they ought con tinually, while life lafteth, to dwell togither.

Ddd.iij.

The

The *Indians* called *Macatecas*, consume not their Matrimony in twenty dayes after their marriage, but abide in fasting and prayer all that while, sacrificing their bodyes, and annoynting the mouthes of the Idolles wyth their owne proper bloud.

In *Panuco* the husbandes buy their wiues for a bowe, two arrowes, and a nette, and afterwarde the father in lawe speaketh not one worde to his sonne in lawe for the space of a whole yeare. And when the husbande hapneth to haue any child, he lyeth not any more with his wife in two yeares after, for feare leaſt ſhe might be with childe againe before the former childe were out of daunger, although ſome doe ſucke vntyll twelue yeares of age, and for this conſideration they haue many wiues. Likewiſe there is an order among them, that no woman may touch or dreſſe any thing being with theyr menſtruall ordinarie.

Diuorcement was not permitted without a iuſt cauſe and authoritie of Iuſtice, among thoſe who were openly married, but the other ſort might be as eaſily forſaken as taken.

In *Mechuacan* was not permitted any diuorcemente, excepte the partie made a ſolemne othe, that they loked not the one on the other ſtedfaſtly and directly at the time of their marriage. But in *Mexico* they muſt proue how the wife is barraine, foule, & of a naughty cōdition: but if they put away their wiues without order and commaundemente of the Iudge, then the heare of the offenders head is burned in the market place, as a ſhame or puniſhment of a man without reaſon or witte.

The payne of adultery was death, as well for the mā as the woman: but if the adulterer were a Gentleman, his head was decked with feathers after that he was hāged, and his body burned, and for this offence was no
pardon,

pardon, eyther for man or woman, but for the auoyding of adultery they do permitte other common women, but no ordinary ſtewes.

Of the Iudges and order of Iuſtice.

Ꞓ Mexico were twelue Iudges, who were all noble men, graue, and well learned in the Mexican lawes. Theſe men liued only by the rentes that properly apperteyne to the maintenance of Iuſtice, and in anye cauſe iudged by thē, it was lawfull for the parties to appeale vnto other twelue Iudges, who were of the princes bloud, and alwayes abode in the Court, and were mainteyned at the Kings owne coſt and charge. The inferior Iudges came ordinarily once euery moneth to cōſult with the higher. And in euery foureſcore dayes came the Iudges of euery prouince within the Mexican Empire, to conſult with the Iudges of Mexico, but all doubtfull cauſes were reſerued to the King, onely to paſſe by his order and determination. The Painters ſerued for notaries, to paint al the caſes which were to be reſolued, but no ſute paſſed aboue foureſcore dayes without finall ende and determination. There were in that citie twelue Sergeants, whoſe office was to arreſt, and to cal parties before the Iudges. Their garments were painted mantels, wherby they were knowen a farre off. The priſons were vnder ground, moyſt and darke, the cauſe whereof, was to put the people in feare to offend. If anye witneſſe were called to take an oth, the order was, that he ſhoulde touche the grounde with one of his fingers, and then to touch his tong with the ſame, whiche ſignifyed that he had ſworne and promiſed to ſpeake the troth wyth hys tōg, taking witnes therof, of ẏ earth which did mainteine him. But ſome do interprete the oth, ẏ if the partie ſware

not

not true, that then he mighte come to such extremitie, as to eate earthe. Sometime they name and call vppon the God of the crime, whose cause the matter touched.

The Iudge that taketh bribes or giftes, is forthwith put out of his office, whiche was accounted a most vyle and shamefull reproch. The *Indians* did affirme, that *Nécaualpincintli* did hang a Iudge in *Tezcuco*, for giuing an vniust sentence, he himselfe knowing the contrary. The murther is executed without exception.

The woman with child that wilfully casseth hir creature, suffereth deathe for the same, bycause many women did voluntary vse that fact, knowing their children could not inherite. The punishment of adultery was death.

The Théefe for the first offence was made a slaue, and hanged for the second. The traytor to the King and comon weale, was put to death with extreame torméts.

The woman taken in mans apparel dyed for the same, and likewise the man taken in womans attire. Euerye one that challéged another to fight except in the warres, was cōdemned to die. In *Tezcuco* the sinne of *Zodomy* was punished with death, & that law was instituted by *Necaualpincintli*, & *Necaualcoio*, who were Iudges, which abhorred y filthy sinne, & therfore they deserued great praise, for in other prouinces y abbominable sin was not punished, although they haue in those places comon stewes, as in *Panuco*.

The order of cruell Sacrifice
vsed among the Indians.

T the ende of euery twenty dayes, is celebrated a festiuall feast called *Tonalli*, which falleth continually the last daye of euerye moneth, but the chiefest feast in the yeare, when most men are sacrificed & eaten, is at the

the ende of euerye fiftye two yeares . But the *Tlax-caltecas* and other common weales, do celebzate this feaſt euery fourth yeare.

The laſt day of the firſt moneth is called *Tlacaxipe-nalizeli*, on the which day were ſlaine a hundzed ſlaues, which were taken in the warres, and after the ſacrifiſe, their fleſh was eaten in this ozder. Al the Citizens, ga-thered themſelues togither in the high Temple, and thē the Miniſters oz Pzieſtes came and vſed certaine cere-monies, the which being ended, they toke thoſe whyche were to be ſacrifiſed, by one and one, and layd them vpon their backes vpon a large ſtone, and then the ſlaue be-ing on liue, they opened him in the bzeaſt, with a knife made of flinte ſtone, and toke out his hart, whiche they thzew immediately at the fote of the Aulter, as an offe-ring, and anoynted with the freſh bloude, the face of the God *Vitzilopuchtli*, oz any other Idol. This done, they pluckt of the ſkinnes of a certaine number of them, the which ſkinnes ſo many auntient perſons put incontinēt vppon their naked bodies, al freſh & bloudy, as they wer fleane from the deade carcaſſes. And being open in the backe part and ſhoulders, they vſed to lace them, in ſuch ſozte that they came fitte vppon the bodies of thoſe that ware them, and being in this ozder attired, they came to daunce among many others. In *Mexico* the king him ſelfe did put on one of theſe ſkinnes, being of a pzinci-pall captiue, and daunced among the other diſguiſed perſons, to exalte and honoz the feaſt, and an infinite number followed him to behold his terrible geſture, al-though ſome hold opinion that they followed him to cō-template his greate deuotion . After the ſacrifiſe en-ded, the owner of the ſlaues did carry their bodies home to their houſes, to make of their fleſhe a ſolemne feaſte to all their friendes, leauing their heades and hartes to the Priests, as their dutie and offering. And the skinnes were filled with cotten wool, or strawe, to be hong in the temple, and kings pallayce, for a memorie.

The slaues when they went to their sacrifice, were apparelled in the habite or deuise of the Idol vnto whom ech of them did commende himselfe : and moreouer they Decked them with feathers, garlands and floures. Many of these sort of people, do go to the slaughter with ioyfull countenannce, dauncing, demaunding almes through the Citie for their sacrifice, all the whiche almes is due vnto the priestes. When the gréene corne was a foote aboue the ground, they vsed to go vnto a certain hil whiche was appointed for such deuotion, and there sacrificed two childrén, a boy, and a girle of thrée yeares of age, to the honor of *Tlaloc* god of water, beséeching him therefore deuoutlye, to haue alwayes a care to prouide them water: these childrén were frée borne, and therfore theyr hartes were not taken out of their bodies, but after that their throtes were cut, their bodies were wrapped in a new mantel, and then buried in a graue of stone.

The feasse of *Tozoztli* was, when the fields of *Maiz* were growen two foote high, then a certaine summe of merchandise was gathered among the dwellers in the towne, wherewith were bought foure little slaues betwixt the age of fiue and seuen, and they were likewise sacrificed to the god *Tlaloc*, for continuall shoures of rayne. And those dead bodies were shut vp in a caue appointed for the same purpose. The beginning of this sacrifice of foure childrén was, at the time when in foure yeres space it rayned not, in the whiche season ý springs were dryed vp, and al gréene things perished: wherfore they were forced to leaue the countrey, and went to inhabite at *Nicaragua*. In the moneth and feast of *Hueitozotli*, when the corne fields of *Maiz* waxed ripe, then euery

uery one in generall gathered his handful of *Maiz*, and
brought it vnto the temple for an offering, with a certaine drinke called *Atuli*, whiche is made of the ſame
Maiz. They brought alſo the ſweete gum *Copalli* to ſenſe
the gods whichdo cauſe the corne to growe: and all that
night they ceaſſed not daunting without drunkenneſſe.
At the beginning of ſummer they celebrate an other
feaſt called *Tlaxuchimcaco*, with all kinde of Roſes and
ſweete floures that might be gotten, and thereof they v-
ſed to make garlands to ſet vpon the Idols heades, and
ſo ſpente all that day in dauncing. And to celebrate the
feaſt called *Tecuilhuitli*, al the gentlemen, and principall
perſons of ech prouince, do come vnto the Citie, on the
euening of the feaſt, and then they apparell a woman
with the attire of the Gods of ſalt, who daunced among
a great company of hir neighboures. But on the nexte
day ſhe was ſacrificed with all the Ceremonies and ſo-
lempnitie accuſtomed, and al that day was ſpent in grei
deuotion, burning of incenſe in the fire pannes of the
temple.

The merchants who had a temple by themſelues dedicated to the god of gaines, made their feaſt vppon the
day called *Miccailhuitl*, wherein they ſlewe many ſlaues
in ſacrifice, which they had bought, and banqueted that
feaſt with mans fleſh, dauncing al the day. The feaſt of
Vchpuniztli they ſacrificed a woman, and afterward hyr
bodye was ſlayne, and hir ſkinne put vppon an *Indians*
backe, who daunced two days a row with al the townſ-
men, which were apparelled in their beſt attire to celebrate ŷ feaſte. The day of *Hatamutzili* ŷ feaſt is kept in
Mexico, where they enter into ŷ lake w a great nūber of
Canoas, & there they drown a boy & a girle in a litle boke,
which they cauſe to be ſonke, in ſuch ſorte, that neuer
after that boat appeareth again: and they hold opinion ŷ

thoſe

those children were in company with the Goddes of the lake. So that, that daye was spente in feasting in the temples,and annoynting the Idols cheekes, with gum called *vlli*. There were some Images that had their faces two ynches thicke with that gum,

The order of certaine religious
women,

O the backe side of euerye greate Temple, in euerye Cittie was made a greate Hall or lodgyng, standing alone, where as manye women did eate, drincke, lodge, & leade their liues.And although suche houses had no orders, they aboad there sure ynough. These women which lay in the houses of the Goddes, were of sundry intentions. But none of them came to abide there al their life time,although among them wer some olde women. Some entered into those religious houses being sicke and disseased, hoping there to recouer theyr health:others came thither through pure neede, and necessitie,to be there relieued:other some came thither to be good and vertuous:and some entered into the religion, hoping that the Goddes woulde giue vnto them riches, and long life. But generallye their comming thyther was,to haue good husbandes , and manye chyldren:eche of them bowed the time that shee woulde or ment to abide in that order,andafter that time expired they marryed.

The first thing that they did comming into the religion,was to polle their heads,to be knowen frō others.
Their

Their offices were to spinne cotton wool and feathers, and to weaue cloth, for to apparel the Goddes and themselues, to swepe the yarde and lodgings of the temple (for the stayres and high chappels, the ministers themselues did make cleane) they vsed also to let them bloud in certaine partes of the body, to offer to the Diuellish Idols. On euery festiual day they went on procession with the priestes, but it was not lawful for them to presume to go vppe the stayres of the temple, nor yet to sing. They liued on almes, for their kinsefolke being rich, did mayntaine them with almes as a charitable seruice done vnto the Goddes: their foode was boyled flesh, and hote bread, to the intent that they should offer therof to the Goddes, that they might tast of the smoke of that vidual: they vsed to eate in communitie, and lay altogither, in one dormitorye, as a flocke of sheepe : they lay alwayes in theyr clothes, for honestie sake, and also to be the sooner ready in the morning to serue the Gods, & to go to their worke. And yet I know not why they shold put off their clothes, for they went almost naked. On the holy dayes they vsed to daunce before the Gods, and shethat either talked or laughed with any religious or secular person, was reprehended for the same. And if any of them committed whoredome, then both the man & the woman were slain, yea they beleeued that all suche offenders fleshe woulde rotte and consume away, and especially those which had lost their Uirginity in the time of their religion. So that with feare of punishmente and infamie, they were good women al the while that they aboade there.

Eee.iij.   Hovv

Hoyv the Diuell appeared to
the Indians.

He Diuell did many times talke wyth the prieftes, and with other rulers and perticular perfons, but not with al forts of men . And vnto him to whom the Diuel had appeared, was offered & prefented great giftes. The wicked spirit appeared vnto thē in a thoufand shapes, and fashions, & finally he was conuerfant and familiar among them very often. And the fooles thought it a greate wonder, that Gods would be fo familiar with mortal men. Pea they not knowing that they were Diuels, and hearing of them many things befoze the had hapned, gaue great credite and beliefe to their illufions and deceites. And bycaufe he commaunded them, they facrificed fuche an infinite number of creatures. Likewife he, vnto whom he had apeared, carried about him painted, the likeneffe wherin he shewed himfelf the firft time. And they painted his image vpon their dozes, benches, and euery coz-ner of the houfe. And as he appeared in fundzy figures & shapes, euen fo they painted him, of infinite fashions, yea and fome foule, grieflye, & feareful to beholde, but yet vnto them, it femed a thing delectable. So this igno-rant people giuing credite to ý condēned spirite, were growen euen to ý higheft hil of crueltie, vnder the cou-lour of deuont & religious perfons, yea they had fuche a cuftome, that befoze they would eat oz dzink, they wold take thereof a little quantitie, & offer it vnto the fun and to the earth. And if they gathered cozne, fruite, oz rofes, they would take a leafe befoze they would fmel it, & of-fer the fame. And he that did not obferue thefe & fuch o-ther ceremonies, was iudged one ý had not god in his

hart

bart, yea ƺ (as they ſay) a man out of the gods fauour.

The Viceroys of Mexico.

He greatneſſe of the newe Spayne, the Maieſtie of *Mexico*, and the qualitie of the conquerets, required a man of noble bloude to gouerne, whereupon the Emperour ſente thither *Don Antonio de Mendoſa*, brother vnto the Marques *de Moniar*, foꝛ viceroy, at whoſe a-riual there returned from thence *Sebaſtian Camires*, who had gouerned that countrey with great diſcretion and woꝛthy commendation. In recompéce wherof the Emperour made him pꝛeſident of the chancery of *Valladolid*, and biſhop of *Culuca*. *Don Antonio de Mendoſa* was appointed viceroy in the yeare. 1534. who carried with him many artificers verye experte in their ſciences, likewiſe thꝛough his interceſſion, a money houſe was erected in *Mexico*: he alſo cauſed ſilke to be made and wꝛought in that countrey, and planted many Mulbery trées foꝛ the ſame, although the *Indians* little care foꝛ ſuche things thꝛough their ſlouthfulneſſe and gret liberty. This viceroy *Don Antonio*, called all the Biſhoppes, cleargy, and learned men togither, to conſult vpó eccleſiaſtical matters, which tended to the doctrine of the *Indians*. At that inſtant was decréed, that the *Indians* ſhoulde be inſtructed only in the latin tong, which they learned verye wel and alſo the Spaniſhe tong. They learne the Muſicke with gꝺ wil, eſpecially the flaute: their voyces are not gꝺ foꝛ the pꝛicke ſong. At that ſeaſon was alſo decréed, that no *Indian* ſhould take oꝛder of Pꝛieſthꝺ.

The

The viceroy *Don Antonio* built certaine townes with Romaine pillers, in honor of the Emperour, and caufed his name to be grauen in Marble. He also began the Kay or wharfe in the porte of *Medellin*, a coftly and neceffarie worke: he alfo reduced the *Chichimecas* to ciuel liuing: he fpente muche money in the entraunce of *Sibola*, without any profit, and alfo thereby remayned an enemy to *Cortes*. He likewife difcouered much land on the fouth coaft neare *Xalixco*: he fente alfo fhippes to *Molluca*, for fpices, which were loft: he behaued himfelf very prudently in the rebellion time of the *Indians* of *Piru*.

The Emperour commaunded him afterwarde to goe vnto the *Piru* for viceroy, confidering the licenciat *Gafca*, who gouerned there, was returned into Spain, and likewife hauing vnderftood his good gouernement in the newe Spaine, although fome complaintes were made of hym. It grieued *Don Antonio de Mendofa*, to departe from the newe Spaine, where he founde himfelfe wel beloued among the *Indians*, who had cured him of fundry diffeafes with bathes of Hearbes, where before he was ftarke lame, and alfo poffeffed of lands, Cattel, and other riche things, whiche he was loth to leaue. Likewife he defired not to haue to deale with other newe men, whofe conditions he knewe not, although he knewe that the *Piruleros* were ftubborne and vnruely felowes. But of neceffitie he was compelled to take that iourney by lande from *Mexico* to *Panama*, which ftandeth fiue hundred leagues diftant, in the yeare a 1551. And that yere came *Don Luys de Valafco* for viceroie to *Mexico*, who was a Gentleman wife and difcrete in his gouernement. The office of viceroy in the newe Spaine, is a charge of great honor and profite.

The

The conuersion of the Indians.

Ḣ how greately are thofe *Indians* bound to pꝛayſe God, who being ſeruants of Satan, and loſt Shǽpe, yet it pleaſed the gꝺneſſe of the Almighty to haue compaſſion of thē, who hath giuen them light to come out of darkeneſſe, and bꝛought them to the knowledge of theyꝛ cruell and abbominable life, and hath nowe giuen vnto them the holy Ghoſt in baptiſme: oh moſt happie *Cortes*, thy paynes was well employed, oh valiant Conquerozs, your names ſhall liue foꝛ euer. I am now bolde to ſaye, that all that lande which is conquered in the new *Spaine*, the people thereof are generally conuerted vnto the faith of Ieſus Chꝛyſte: oh what a greate felicitie is it vnto thoſe bleſſed Kyngs who were the beginners there= of.

Some doe ſaye, that in the newe Spayne onely are conuerted Chꝛiſtians ſire Millions. Others hold opini= on of eyghte Millions. And otherſome doe aſſuredly af= firme, that aboue tenne Millions are Chꝛiſtened. But in concluſion, I am aſſured, that within the limittes of four hundꝛed leagues, there are none vnchꝛiſtened.

The conuerſion began with the Conqueſt, but wyth the diligence in pꝛoſecuting the warres, little gꝺ was done, vntyll the peare 1524. and then the matter wente foꝛwarde effectuallye, by reaſon that certayne learned menne wente thyther foꝛ the ſame pur= poſe.

At the begynnyng it was a troubleſome thyng to teach them, foꝛ wante of vnderſtandyng the one of the o= ther, wherefoꝛe they pꝛocured to teache the chyldꝛen of Gentlemen whiche were moſt apteſt, the Spaniſhe tong,

Fſſ.   and

and they likewiſe learned the *Mexican* ſpéeche, in the whiche language they dayly preached. It was at the firſte a paynefull thing to make them leaue thoſe Idols in whome they hadde euer beléeued, yea and the Diuell gaue them cruell warres in ſpirite, and manye times, in appearing in diuers formes vnto them, threatning, that if they dyd call vpon the name of Ieſus Chriſt, it ſhould not rayne, and that all their delight and pleaſure ſhoulde be taken from them, prouoking them ſtill to Rebellion againſt the Chriſtians, but his wicked counſell woulde not preuaple.

Through greate puniſhmente they haue left off the horrible ſinne of Sodomy, although it was a great griefe to put away their number of wiues.

There are nowe in the newe Spayne eyght Byſhoprikes, whereof one is an Archbiſhoprike.

The death of Hernando
Cortes.

Here was a greate contention betwéene *Hernando Cortes*, and *Don Antonio de Mendoſa*, the Vizeroy, as concerning the prouince of *ſibola*, for each of them pretended a title vnto the ſame through the Emperoures gift, the one by meanes of his office of Vizeroy, and the other by his office of Captayne Generall, vpon the whyche matter they grewe into ſuch hatred, that perfyte friendſhippe coulde neuer after take place betwéene them, although at the beginning they were familiar and louing friendes: but malice grewe to ſuche extremitie, that eache of them wrote vndecently agaynſte other, to the Emperoure theyr maiſter, the

the whyche theyr doyngs blemished both theyr credites.

Cortes wente to lawe with the Licenciat *Villa Lobos* the Kings Attourney, aboute certayne of his vassals, and also the Uizeroy assisted agaynste him as muche as hée myghte. Upon consideration whereof, he was enforced to come into Spayne in Anno 1540. and broughte *Don Martin* his sonne and heyre, béyng a childe of eyghte yeares of age, and hys sonne *Don Luys*, to serue the Prince : he came very riche, but not so riche as the fyrste time. He entred into great friendship with the Cardinal *Loaysa*, and the Secretarie *Cobos*, but it preuayled not, for the Emperoure was gone into Flanders about matters of Gant.

In the yeare 1541. the Emperoure personally wente to the siege of Argell with a mightie armye, and *Cortez* with his two sonnes went also thither to serue him with a good companye of men and Horses, but it pleased God to raise vp suche a tempest, wherewith the most parte of the fléete perished. *Cortes* then being in the Galley of *Don Henrike Enrikes*, called the *Esperanca*, and fearing to lose his rich emraldes and other Jewels at the time that the Galley was driuen by violence of weather vpon the shore, he then bound about him the sayde fyue rich emraldes, estéemed in a hundred thousande Duckates, yet notwithstanding through the throng of people, and hast to escape out of oese and mire, the Jewels fell from him, who could neuer heare more of them, so that the present warres cost hym more than any other, except the Emperoures maiestie, although *Andrea de Oria* lost eleuen Galleys.

But the losse of treasure gréeued hym not so much, as the excluding hym out of the Counsell of the warres, where as other yong Gentlemen of lesse knowledge

and

and abilitie were accepted, which was a cause of greate murmuryng among the hoſt. And where in the counſell of warre it was determined to leaue the ſiege and to depart, it grieued manye, whereupon *Cortes* made an open offer, that he alone with the Spaniſhe nation would preſume to take *Argell*, hauyng but the one halfe of the *Tudeſcos* and *Italians*, if it woulde pleaſe the Emperoure to graunte vnto hym the enterpriſe. The Souldyers on the lande dyd hyghly commende hys courage, but the Sea menne woulde giue no eare vnto him, ſo that it is thoughte that the offer came not to the Emperoures knowledge. *Cortes* wente vp and downe in the Courte a long ſeaſon, being ſore afflicted in a certaine ſute aboutes hys vaſſals, and alſo the proceſſe and allegations of *Nunio de Guzman*, layde vnto hys charge in hys reſidence. The whole proceſſe was ſiene in the counſell of *Indias*, but iudgemente was neuer pronounced, whyche was a greate hartes eaſe for *Cortes*. And then hiee departed from the Courte towarde Siuill, with determinate wyll to paſſe vnto the newe Spayne, and to ende his lyfe in *Mexico*, and alſo to recepue the Lady Mary, *Cortes* hys daughter, who was come from *India*, and promiſed in marriage vnto *Don Aluar Perez Oſorio*, with a hundred thouſande Duckates in dowry, and hyr apparell, but the marriage toke no effecte, through the faulte of *Don Aluar* and hys father.

He then fell ſicke of a flire and indiſgeſtion, whiche endured long, ſo that on hys iourney towarde the Citie of Siuill, he departed thys tranſitory lyfe, in a little Uillage called *Caſtilleia de La Cueſta*, whyche ſtandeth a myle from the Citie of Siuill, on the ſeconde of December Anno 1547. bieyng thrieeſcore and thrie yeares of age:

His body was depoſited wᵗ ̷y dukes of *Medina Sidonia*.

He

He left a Sonne and thée Daughters begotten of the Lady *Iane de Zuniga* his wife, his Sonne was called *Don Martin Cortes*, who did inherite his fathers eſtate, and was married vnto the Lady *Ana de Arellano*, his couſine, daughter to the Countie *De Aguilar*, by order of his father.

The doughters vnto *Cortes* were named as foloweth, the lady *Donea Maria*, *Donea Catalina*, and *Donea Iuana* who was the youngeſt. He had another Sonne by an *Indian* woman, and he was called *Don Martin Cortez*. He had alſo another baſe ſonne by a Spaniſh woman, who was named *Don Luys Cortez*, and thée daughters by thrée ſeuerall *Indian* women.

Cortez buylt an hoſpitall in *Mexico*, and gaue order for a Colledge to be alſo erected there. He builte alſo a Temple in *Coioacan*, where he willed in his Teſtament that his bones ſhoulde be buried at the charges of his Sonne and heyre. He ſituated foure thouſand Ducates of rent, whiche yéeldeth yéerely his houſes in *Mexico* for the purpoſe aforeſayd, of the which foure thouſande Ducates, two thouſand ſhould be to mayntteyne the Studients in the Colledge.

(∵)

FINIS.

A Table expressyng the Chapiters vvhiche are conteyned in this Historie.

Hovv

The Table.

The

The Table.

FINIS.

DATE DUE

DEMCO 38-297